Research Methods and Statistics

To my daughter. Dedicated teacher, gifted therapist, and cherished friend.

— *Janie*

To my mother, for all of her support while writing this book and over the years.

— *Shauna*

SAGE was founded in 1965 by Sara Miller McCune to support the dissemination of usable knowledge by publishing innovative and high-quality research and teaching content. Today, we publish over 900 journals, including those of more than 400 learned societies, more than 800 new books per year, and a growing range of library products including archives, data, case studies, reports, and video. SAGE remains majority-owned by our founder, and after Sara's lifetime will become owned by a charitable trust that secures our continued independence.

Los Angeles | London | New Delhi | Singapore | Washington DC | Melbourne

Research Methods and Statistics

An Integrated Approach

Janie H. Wilson
Georgia Southern University

Shauna W. Joye
Georgia Southern University

Los Angeles | London | New Delhi
Singapore | Washington DC | Melbourne

FOR INFORMATION:

SAGE Publications, Inc.
2455 Teller Road
Thousand Oaks, California 91320
E-mail: order@sagepub.com

SAGE Publications Ltd.
1 Oliver's Yard
55 City Road
London EC1Y 1SP
United Kingdom

SAGE Publications India Pvt. Ltd.
B 1/I 1 Mohan Cooperative Industrial Area
Mathura Road, New Delhi 110 044
India

SAGE Publications Asia-Pacific Pte. Ltd.
3 Church Street
#10-04 Samsung Hub
Singapore 049483

Acquisitions Editor: Reid Hester
Editorial Assistant: Alex Helmintoller
eLearning Editor: Morgan Shannon
Production Editor: Kelly DeRosa
Copy Editor: Cate Huisman
Typesetter: C&M Digitals (P) Ltd.
Proofreader: Sarah J. Duffy
Indexer: Shauna W. Joye
Cover Designer: Michael Dubowe
Marketing Manager: Katherine Hepburn
Interior Illustrations: Sarah Yeh

Printed in the United States of America

Library of Congress Cataloging-in-Publication Data

Names: Wilson, Janie H., author. | Joye, Shauna W., author.

Title: Research methods and statistics : an integrated approach / Janie H. Wilson, Georgia Southern University, Shauna W.Joye, Georgia Southern University.

Description: 1 Edition. | Thousand Oaks : SAGE Publications, 2017.

Identifiers: LCCN 2016022276 | ISBN 978-1-4833-9214-1 (pbk.)

Subjects: LCSH: Psychology—Research—Methodology. | Psychometrics.

Classification: LCC BF76.5 .W557 2016 | DDC 150.72/1—dc23
LC record available at https://lccn.loc.gov/2016022276

This book is printed on acid-free paper.

16 17 18 19 20 10 9 8 7 6 5 4 3 2 1

Brief Contents

Detailed Contents

Section I Foundations of Design and Analysis

Section IV   Grouped Designs With Independent Samples

Section VI
Advanced Design

Appendices

Preface

What do you want to know? In psychology, we enjoy the freedom of asking research questions and finding answers. We even share our results at conferences, in journals, and with the general public. After all, ultimately we want to give psychology away to the world.

But first . . .

You must learn how to ask questions and find answers, always in a highly ethical way. Research questions and answers require a marriage between methods and statistics. You cannot design a study and hope for a flash of insight on analysis later. In this textbook, we show you how to choose an appropriate statistic while constructing a method. Preparing for analysis before data collection offers you peace of mind that the data will be able to address your research question.

Throughout the text, we focus on methods and statistics that students generally encounter. As an undergraduate student, you should learn several common designs used to address research questions, and you should know a few key statistics. Section I sets the stage for conducting research. Sections II through V explain various research designs and how to analyze data from each design, including computer screenshots for clarification. Section VI offers an advanced design learned by undergraduate students in upper-level courses, in an honors program, or attending certain schools. Your instructor will teach the designs and analyses typical of the class, department, or school. Refer to this text for designs and analyses of interest in your current class(es) and in your future training as a researcher.

You may have already learned that the American Psychological Association (APA) governs the research process as well as the way psychologists write papers. Because APA guidelines and writing style form the foundation of our research, this text covers APA style in detail. When it comes to writing in APA style, we relied on the most recent version of the APA manual (6th ed., 2010) while we wrote the chapters.

In addition to weaving APA style throughout the text, we have included in Appendix C a wealth of information on writing in APA style, including an example paper, common mistakes, and helpful pointers.

Beginning in Chapter 1, you will also notice a guide for this book. Tal appears in each chapter and will offer valuable information. Our goal for the tone of the book is friendly, engaging, and accessible. We hope Tal will help us share information with you in a fun way.

Read, think, study, and create. Allow yourself to enjoy asking a research question and finding the answer. By the end of your undergraduate career, you should feel competent as an emerging researcher. The science of psychology needs your help to discover truths about behavior. We hope you accept the challenge.

Acknowledgments

As you venture into the publishing world, one of the greatest truths you will learn is the importance of honest feedback. Every time we publish a manuscript, we receive input from experts, carefully consider their advice, and revise our work. We want to express our deep appreciation to the following reviewers who offered time and talent to improve this textbook.

Alan Albright, University of Memphis
Austin C. Archer, Walla Walla University
Stefanie S. Boswell, University of the Incarnate Word
Eliane Boucher, Providence College
Amy M. Buddie, Kennesaw State University
Gary N. Burns, Wright State University
Mary Jo Carnot, Chadron State College
Sabrina E. Des Rosiers, Barry University
Sarah Estow, Guilford College
Amanda C. Gingerich, Butler University
Paula Goolkasian, University of North Carolina-Charlotte
Joseph G. Johnson, Miami University
Jonathan Kunstman, Miami University of Ohio
Angela M. Legg, Pace University
Nicole Martin, Kennesaw State University
Tim Martin, Kennesaw State University
Darryl Mayeaux, St. Bonaventure University
Chantal Poister Tusher, Georgia State University
Chiara Sabina, Penn State Harrisburg
Jennifer L. Stevenson, Ursinus College
Ashton D. Trice, James Madison University
Lisa A. VanWormer, University of West Florida
Jordan R. Wagge, Avila University
Sally N. Wall, Notre Dame of Maryland University
Guillermo Wated, Barry University

Tammy Zacchilli, Saint Leo University
Carissa A. Zimmerman, Rice University

We also sincerely thank Reid Hester for his encouragement and insights, Cate Huisman for her attention to detail, and Kelly DeRosa for knowing what we wanted before we even asked. Thank you also to Sarah Yeh for bringing Tal to life!

About the Authors

Janie H. Wilson I received my PhD in experimental psychology from the University of South Carolina in 1994. Since that time, I have been teaching and conducting research at Georgia Southern University. In the classroom, I specialize in teaching statistics and research methods.

My research interests include rapport in teaching based on empirical data gathered on the first day of class, electronic communications, interactions with students in a traditional classroom, syllabus design, and the development and validation of the Professor–Student Rapport Scale. My publications include two recent texts with Sage: *An EasyGuide to Research Presentations* (2015) and *An EasyGuide to Research Design and SPSS* (2014). I have had the pleasure of contributing numerous chapters to edited books and have coedited several books related to teaching and learning. I publish extensively on the scholarship of teaching and learning and have offered over 60 conference presentations, including several invited keynote addresses. For 2016, I am honored to serve as the president of Division Two of APA. My primary initiative is sharing the science of psychology with students and the general community.

Shauna W. Joye I earned a BS in biology from Georgia Southern University and a PhD in psychology from Florida State University. During graduate and postdoctoral training, my research and clinical work focused on early childhood learning, attention disorders, temperament, and autism spectrum disorder, with an emphasis on measurement of these constructs. Currently, I am a faculty member at Georgia Southern University, and I examine clinical interventions to enhance self-control, including empirical research in mindfulness. I also work with combat veterans to determine the impact of therapeutic wilderness experiences on wellness. Finally, I continue to pursue a long-standing commitment to teaching and learning through scholarship in that area.

I enjoy working with undergraduate and graduate students who are interested in learning more about the process of research, from study design and analysis to APA-style writing. Outside of teaching at Georgia Southern University, I maintain a private practice where I work as a child and adolescent therapist. My association memberships include the American Psychological Association, Society for Teaching of Psychology, Wilderness Medical Society, and Association for Psychological Science.

FOUNDATIONS OF DESIGN AND ANALYSIS

1

The Scientific Method

Welcome to the science of psychology.

Psychology is a science because the discipline requires rigorous testing of ideas, including carefully designed studies, observable outcomes, and critical thinking. In this chapter we will talk about the scientific method to give you a better idea about what it means to study as a scientist. The **scientific method** is a step-by-step approach to address a research question.

How wonderful that you have the opportunity to study inherently interesting ideas that matter to most people. Your research life will be fun and relevant, and you will quickly realize that every interesting question can be studied in a scientific way. In the history of psychology, researchers have examined how to help people stop smoking, how to enjoy healthy romantic relationships, and the best ways to enhance memory, among other intriguing topics. Psychologists have even studied extrasensory perception in a scientific way, an approach that allowed researchers to debunk the myth. Any topic that allows observable outcomes is a viable focus of psychological research. You will not be bored.

EMPIRICAL DATA

The scientific approach to research questions has been defined in many ways, but all definitions include observable evidence. Observable evidence can also be called *measurable* or **empirical** evidence. At first glance, you might be tempted to think that some areas of interest are not empirical. Topics such as happiness, depression, love, and math knowledge may not seem observable. Perhaps these topics are not directly measurable, but we can certainly bring them to the level of empirical knowledge by being clear about behaviors that reflect happiness, depression, love, and math knowledge.

For example, we cannot see, hear, or smell happiness, but we can decide as researchers that happiness is the number of times a person smiles in an hour. Or we might measure happiness as a person's rating of happiness on a scale from 1 to 5, with 1 representing *very*

Scientific Method.
The scientific method is a step-by-step process of systematically addressing a research question through observation and critical thinking.

Empirical. Empirical refers to observable or measureable behaviors.

unhappy and 5 representing *very happy*. As you can see, to make a concept empirical, scientists must specifically define how the concept is measured. We call this an **operational definition**, which offers enough detail that anyone hearing about the study would know how the researcher measured the concept.

With the scientific method, our goal is to learn something about behavior through empirical research. How do we accomplish this goal? The steps of the scientific method provide a useful structure:

1. Ask a question. What do you want to know?

2. Read, read, read the published literature.

3. Create a method for the study.

4. Collect and analyze data.

5. Answer the research question.

6. Share your findings with others.

Although authors slightly vary the steps listed here, the overall ideas are the same. Let us explain each of the steps and provide some insights from years of teaching undergraduates about psychological research.

STEP 1: ASK A QUESTION

In our experience, students have trouble with this first step. Of all the possible studies that could be conducted, what do you want to study, and what exact question do you have about the area of interest? The first step might seem overwhelming, but a few approaches have helped our students.

Choose a Topic

Start with a broad topic and move forward from there. An enjoyable course in social psychology might narrow your focus to social, and a topic or lecture in social psychology might have been particularly interesting. Suppose the chapter on attribution theory drew your attention, and you want to know what might change attributions when deciding why other people are rude. By starting with a general area of psychology, you can make choices of topics within the area. Reviewing the social textbook, reading class notes, or speaking with the teacher might help clarify ideas for a study.

Another way to begin a topic search is by skimming through a textbook that provides an introduction to psychological science. Begin with the list of chapters in the table of contents to see if a chapter title catches your attention. Next, look within the chapter at

Operational Definition. Researchers use operational definitions to explain variables in enough detail to allow replication of the study.

headings, boxes, and other features around the text. Read details within any section that you like. When you have an idea of exactly what area you want to study, talk with your teacher about how to ask a specific question with a research study.

A third way to pick a research question is to think of the last thing you complained about or found confusing. Maybe someone at a movie theater was loud and obnoxious, and you wondered why in the world someone would act that way. One possible explanation is that darkness helps people hide their identity, allowing them to behave badly without fear of being identified (e.g., Diener, Fraser, Beaman, & Kelem, 1976). Your general question might be, *Do people misbehave when their identity is hidden?*

You can probably think of other ways to find a research question, such as talking with an instructor who conducts research. If available, examine a department website for faculty research interests. E-mail an instructor to find out if you can make an appointment to discuss research ideas. Most faculty members are delighted to give advice on a project as long as the research idea is in their area of expertise.

Ask a Simple Question

The last bit of advice we will offer about asking a question is to keep it simple. Often students are highly motivated and want to ask complex questions. We are always impressed by such motivation, but save the complex questions for later. First you should ask a simple question and learn the marvels of conducting research. After learning the basics, ask more advanced questions. In the real world, researchers usually complete a study and realize they subsequently have more questions based on the results. We build on our prior research projects, expanding knowledge and frequently creating an entire research program.

STEP 2: READ THE PUBLISHED LITERATURE

Asking a research question might seem straightforward, but it is not. When you have an idea of what you want to study, read the literature in the area and fine-tune your research question. You might find a particularly interesting study that makes you think of a follow-up question. Or you might locate a study conducted on a population very different from the group you are considering. You will not be ready to ask a specific research question until you know what unique questions remain.

Locate Research

When you have a research idea, it is time to learn more about the topic. If your question is about bad behavior in the dark, search for publications using terms or phrases such as *loss of identity* and *aggression* (as an example of a bad behavior). Try different combinations of key terms until you find at least one article that (1) is highly relevant to your question and (2) was published within the past few years. Read the entire article, especially the introduction section, to learn other key terms used to explore the topic. After reading a relevant published study, you can rerun your search using key terms such as *deindividuation* and *disinhibition*. You might also learn of a researcher, such as Leon Festinger, who conducted well-known research on your topic.

When you have enough key terms to conduct a thorough search, you should find approximately 50 titles. If your search gives you fewer than 50 options, use fewer search terms and make sure you have not limited the search to terms that appear only in the abstract or title of the publication. On the other hand, if a search returns numerous titles, limit the search by requiring the most relevant key term to appear in the title or abstract. You can also use an author's name as a key term, but relying on one author or set of authors may not yield enough results for a thorough literature review. For most search tools, specifications can be found under "Advanced Search." Through an advanced search, you can also request that the search return only peer-reviewed journal articles. Speak with your instructor about any limitations you should set when searching the literature.

With about 50 relevant titles, systematically click on each title to read the abstract. Reading abstracts will further narrow your pool of articles, because some publications obviously will not be relevant to your research question. However, even if an article makes a broad point, such as deindividuation causing prejudice, you may be able to refer to the article when summarizing the topic at the beginning of your manuscript. Likewise, some articles can be useful at the end of your research paper, when you suggest new avenues for research. We save titles and abstracts into a Word file and indicate which articles might be useful when writing various parts of the manuscript. Be overly inclusive with studies in this phase. You may not use all of the articles in your final manuscript, and that is ok.

If you find an article that is particularly relevant to your research question, you will want to take a look at the reference list. Read any articles that seem related to your study.

Although abstracts should provide excellent article summaries, you must get a copy of the entire article for any paper you reference. Make sure you start your literature review in plenty of time. Frequently you can find abstracts online but will need to request the full article using your school's interlibrary loan system. Read each article, make notes on it, and highlight or underline parts that interest you. Not only will articles give you a lot of information on the area of interest, but they will also provide methodology details, some of which you might want to use in your own study design. Read method sections carefully, and decide if a certain survey or manipulation would help you to answer your research question. It is perfectly acceptable to use ideas from other people's method sections (e.g., their measures) as long as you do not plagiarize. Your instructor probably will want you to add a new component to your study or measure an outcome in a different way, but most researchers begin with measures that have already been used in a research area. Be sure to give credit to authors of a study, even if that means tracking down an original scale (for example) based on a reference in the article you located. Sometimes researchers must play detective to locate surveys and other assessments.

Choose a Specific Question

As you read the published literature, you will continue to polish your research question. The original question might be broad (e.g., *Do people misbehave when their identity is hidden?*) and represent a general theory: *People misbehave when their identity is hidden.* In psychology, a **theory** is an overarching belief about behavior. You will need to narrow the question to create a **testable** idea, meaning an idea for which you can collect data and address the question. You might decide to study behavior in the dark as a way to hide identity. Of course, you would also have to decide how to study misbehavior. A narrow, focused question to test the theory might include any of the following ideas. Notice the level of detail in these testable questions.

- Do muggings increase as the sun sets?
- Do more robberies occur at night versus during the day?
- Do people talk in the dark during a movie more when they cannot be identified than when they have to say their names aloud?

A **hypothesis** emerges directly from a research question and is a specific idea of what we expect results to look like. Change the research question into a statement. Let us examine hypotheses based on the research questions above.

- Increasingly more muggings occur as the sun sets.
- More robberies occur at night than during the day.
- People talk more in a dark movie theater when they remain anonymous versus when they say their names.

Theory. A general way to explain a broad concept is called a theory. Within the structure of a theory, numerous testable hypotheses are possible.

Testable. A hypothesis is testable if it is written in such a way that empirical data can address the question of whether it is true.

Hypothesis. A specific testable question that addresses some part of a theory is called a hypothesis.

In science, we are interested in theories, but we actually test specific hypotheses. The details of how we test our hypothesis are found in the study's method.

You can see that a hypothesis is specific. Researchers state exactly what they expect to find when the data are analyzed. A specific, testable hypothesis is **falsifiable**. That is, an empirical test of the hypothesis will address whether the hypothesis is supported or not. Consider whether the following hypothesis is falsifiable: *If teenagers are given enough freedom, they will choose to spend time at home.* You might collect data and examine the outcome. But what if you failed to find support for your hypothesis? Based on the wording, you could argue that teenagers in your study were not given *enough* freedom. Then you could stubbornly maintain your original belief because the hypothesis was not falsifiable.

Researchers form a testable, falsifiable hypothesis based on the research question, and you have seen the simple relationship between the research question and hypothesis. Merely change the research question into a statement. You might wonder why we bothered spending time on such a straightforward transformation. As you continue reading this book, you will see that statistics rely on forming hypothesis statements. Although the sentence structure is not that of a question, the hypothesis absolutely addresses the research question. Such a simple change in sentence format allows us to analyze data using statistics.

STEP 3: CREATE A METHOD

After reading the published literature and specifying your research question and hypothesis, you can develop a method section for your study. The method emerges from the

Falsifiable. A hypothesis is falsifiable when it has been written in such a way that it can be tested and found either true or false.

research question and is informed by prior publications in the area. First, choose the variables of interest. A **variable** is anything that varies, anything that can take on more than one value. For example, hair color is a variable with several values such as brown, black, red, and blond. Fortunately for scientists, almost everything in the world is a variable. As more examples, depression, happiness, motivation, eye color, and gender all vary.

In the method section, you will discuss exactly which variables will be studied and how. These details allow other researchers to read your work and understand what you are studying, because you operationally defined the variables. Details are important, because the same variable might be defined differently by two researchers. For example, "attending class" is a variable that might be defined with *yes* or *no*. As another option, class attendance can be the number of times students attend class during a term.

Operationally defining variables includes providing information about scales or surveys that you found in the literature and chose to use in your study. Share the reference for the scale to give the authors credit, indicate the number of items, type of items, and perhaps even an example item or two. Some researchers contact authors and ask permission to use their surveys. However, science is meant to be a resource freely shared among members of the community, and most researchers publish survey details to allow reproduction. If an author chooses to sell or otherwise control a survey, usually a crucial detail (e.g., exact wording of items) is omitted from the publication, requiring researchers to contact the author for more information. We always recommend that students use an existing survey, summarize it, and give credit to the authors. As a less desirable alternative, but still a viable option, you can write your own items and provide details in the method section.

The method section will also contain the design of your study. Several designs are available and will be covered in the following chapters. You will learn how to manipulate and measure variables as well as how to analyze the data collected. The method section focuses on design details.

Finally, you should describe the people tested in your study. At the beginning of the method is a section labeled "**Participants**" that describes the people who participate in the research. Here researchers usually provide the number of participants, number of each gender, average age, and a breakdown of ethnicities, including the number of each. Researchers often indicate that the study was approved by the institutional review board (IRB), which means it has been reviewed by a committee concerned with treating participants ethically. You might also want to include information on how participants were recruited for the study, such as via an online sign-up system at your school.

STEP 4: COLLECT AND ANALYZE DATA

Step 4 of the scientific method focuses on the outcome data. Data collection and analysis flow logically from detailing your method section. Researchers think about *what* they want to study and *how* they will study the question of interest. Then the outcome data address the research question.

Variable. A variable is anything that varies. In other words, variables have more than one possible value.

Participants. People who participate in research studies are called participants.

Data collection typically requires interacting with participants. If the interaction will be in person, researchers must be careful to behave the same way for everyone. Standardized behaviors reduce "noise" in the data you collect by making sure any outcomes are based on your research question rather than the mood you were in that day, whether or not you brushed your teeth before talking with the participant, or even what you wore (e.g., a T-shirt with an offensive logo). In our labs, we actually type a script, and all researchers memorize the script before working with participants. We know we have a controlled, standardized procedure when a student researcher in our lab comes to us and says, "I was nervous at first, but now testing participants feels like a habit." We are quick to tell the student that comfort with testing participants is exactly what researchers want. Running a study, when done correctly, should become an automatic process over time.

If participants are tested in a standardized way, data will flow in, and you will soon be able to answer your research question. A caution is that data, such as participant survey packets, pile up quickly. Be sure to enter your data into a computer program regularly and with attention to detail. Keeping your computer data file current allows you to be ready when your instructor calls a meeting and wants to analyze the data or hear how your study is going. You do not want to near the end of the term and realize you have countless hours of data entry ahead of you. Also, sometimes by entering data frequently you might catch a mistake. One of our students once photocopied a measure incorrectly with two items missing. Thankfully, we entered data soon after testing and only had to discard data from eight participants.

When your study is complete and data have been entered into a computer program, you will be ready to analyze the data using an appropriate statistic. The chapters that follow offer details on how to use different statistics and, importantly, which statistic to use based on the design (method) you chose. This text will also explain how many participants should be in your study and other issues related to design and analysis.

STEP 5: ANSWER THE RESEARCH QUESTION

Careful data collection and appropriate statistical analysis will allow you to answer your research question. But remember that the scientific method requires you to define variables in a highly specific way, focusing your question based on operational definitions. Even if the data indicate that your question or idea has no support, a slightly different study on the same variables might, in fact, find support. For example, suppose your general research question was, *Will people give money to charity when they smell a clean odor?* (This question is based on a similar study by Liljenquist, Zhong, & Galinsky, 2010.) Your method would provide further specifics, such as the name of a specific charity and the smell of bleach as the clean odor. As a comparison odor, you might choose lavender. Your specific question becomes, *Will people give more money to a breast-cancer charity when they smell bleach versus lavender?* Stated as a hypothesis, *People give more money to a breast-cancer charity when they smell bleach than when they smell lavender.* If you found no support for bleach causing people to give more money, you do not know if a slight change would reveal an effect. For example, maybe the smell of soap would increase giving.

When your data are analyzed, you will be able to answer your specific research question. Just keep in mind that lack of support merely indicates that your particular approach revealed no effect. A different approach might illustrate support for your broader research question.

Alternatively, sometimes you will find support for your hypothesis. What does this mean? If data analysis indicates a meaningful effect, the effect is true based on the precise method you chose and the exact way you defined your variables. In the bleach example, support would mean people gave more to a breast-cancer charity when they smelled bleach than when they smelled lavender. Congratulations on finding a meaningful effect! But realize that more research is needed to broaden our understanding. Scientists might want to expand the literature by testing different odors, settings, or groups of participants. Researchers publish results, allowing others to read the method, change what they find interesting (e.g., use soap instead of bleach), collect and analyze their data, and report their own findings by publishing and adding to the wealth of scientific knowledge.

STEP 6: SHARE YOUR RESULTS

This step of the scientific method often is taken for granted, but sharing research outcomes is crucial. After all, without other researchers sharing their results, you would not have been able to formulate your study. The most traditional way to share your work is to publish in a peer-reviewed journal. But first, many researchers get feedback on a study by presenting at a conference. As added bonuses, presenting at conferences looks great on your resume, allows you to network with other professionals, and can help you generate ideas for future research.

In summary, the scientific method allows us to ask research questions defined in our own way, empirically test hypotheses, and identify at least one instance in which our research question is supported or not. We should start with a general idea and then examine one specific question, testing a hypothesis. If we find support for our hypothesis, have we "proven" an answer to the question? No. In scientific psychological research, we never prove anything because the possibility of an exception always exists. But we can provide support for the question based on our specific method. Together with the body of research already published, science moves one step closer to forming a cohesive theory.

If we do not find support for our hypothesis, have we proven that our idea is false (i.e., clean smells do not increase charitable contributions)? No. We merely learned that a specific method failed to show support for the original question. It may be that we made a mistake in our study (e.g., we did not keep all variables constant), or perhaps another clean smell, like soap, would have an effect even though bleach did not. Another possibility is that we included some participants who lack a sense of smell. You get the idea.

Although we never *prove* anything through research, the outcome of the scientific method is either support or lack of support for a specific research question (or hypothesis). And that is a worthwhile goal. Every new result from a study in psychology changes the world—or some part of it—forever.

RESEARCH IN PSYCHOLOGY: APA STYLE

In psychology, we use a specific style of writing provided by the American Psychological Association (APA, 2010). APA style gives researchers a framework for the scientific method by standardizing each of the six steps defined above. We know how to ask a specific research question and write it in the form of a hypothesis to be addressed after reading the published literature. When evaluating articles, standard APA style guarantees that readers know exactly where to locate sections of interest. Reading is efficient. When creating a method section, psychologists know the kind of detail that will be expected of them, including operationalizing variables. APA style further dictates the method-section organization of a manuscript.

In Step 4 of the scientific method, we collect data, which usually entails interacting with participants. Psychological scientists concern themselves with the mental and physical safety of participants, requiring a highly ethical approach to data collection. The APA provides guidelines on responsible data collection, such as not pressuring people to be part of a study and making sure people can choose to participate in a study after they know what is expected of them. These and other guidelines are offered in the APA Ethical Principles of Psychologists and Code of Conduct at www.apa.org/ethics/code/index.aspx (2003, with amendments accepted in 2010).

Also in Step 4 of the scientific method, we analyze data. Then we move on to Step 5 to answer our research question using APA format. Rather than use statistical symbols, we use APA symbols or abbreviations. For example, the mean or average of your test scores in a class might be 95. Using a traditional statistics symbol, we might write $\overline{X} = 95$. But the APA symbol for mean is M, so we say $M = 95$. You will find that APA symbols are more logical than statistics symbols, and APA style will be required of you when writing a manuscript. In this textbook, we will rely on APA symbols to keep the focus on APA style.

In addition to using APA symbols, results must generally be reported using two to three decimal places. In most contexts, you will use two decimal places, but in the instances when three decimal places are more appropriate, we will explain why. Fortunately, the statistics package we refer to in this book reports results to three decimal places, so you can use three when needed and round to two when needed. When rounding to two decimal places, look at the third decimal place to know whether to change the value shown in the second decimal place. If the number in the third decimal place is 0–4, the value in the second decimal place remains the same. However, if the number in the third decimal place is 5–9, increase the value in the second decimal place by 1. For example, .334 becomes .33, but .335 becomes .34.

Results answer the research question. APA style provides a format for how to write the details of a statistical analysis such as rounding appropriately and using APA symbols in the results section of a manuscript. A discussion section follows the results section, and here you will speculate on how your specific study and results addressed your research question. Did you find support for your hypothesis? If so, speculate why. If not, speculate why not. Following APA style means the discussion section also places your study into the context of the larger research area of interest. How does your study add to the existing literature? To weave your particular study into the literature, a discussion section involves referring to prior publications. In fact, we usually think of several potential explanations for our results and return to the library for additional articles.

Step 6 of the scientific approach pertains to sharing work with the scientific community. Psychologists follow APA style to prepare a highly organized manuscript with predictable sections of information. From the literature review through the method, results, and discussion, a story emerges about the development and testing of a research question.

Additional features elaborate on the story in some way, including graphs and tables of data, pictures of stimuli, survey items, and other materials viewed by participants. At the end of a manuscript, a reference section details each publication used in the paper to give credit to authors and allow other researchers to access information.

Throughout all manuscript sections, authors are encouraged to use active voice instead of passive voice. For example, rather than write, "Participants were asked to complete informed consent," psychologists write, "Participants completed informed consent." Notice that the verb "completed" engages the reader more than "were asked to complete." As a second example, "Data were analyzed using . . ." could be written as, "I analyzed data . . ." APA style allows the use of *I* and *we* to encourage active voice. Every sentence of a manuscript can be written in active voice, but most journals settle for a good effort. Remember, the goal of APA style is to tell a detailed, organized story in an engaging way.

We highly recommend purchasing a copy of the current *Publication Manual of the American Psychological Association*, usually referred to as the APA manual or APA guide. The APA manual is currently in its 6th edition (2010). As an alternative, you can find websites that show examples of how to write in APA style. Be careful to depend on sites that use the most recent version of APA Style. If you want a book for a quick APA-style reference, try *An EasyGuide to APA Style* (Schwartz, Landrum, & Gurung, 2013). We also included example papers in Appendix C of this book.

SUMMARY

In this chapter we discussed in detail the scientific method, which provides the foundation for research in psychology. Researchers ask a question of interest and read published research to develop the question. A testable research hypothesis emerges directly from the specific research question. We create a method and analyze data to address our hypothesis. As a final step, we share the research with others through presentations and publications, relying on APA style to communicate efficiently.

REVIEW OF TERMS

Empirical

Falsifiable

Hypothesis

Operational Definition

Participants

Scientific Method

Testable

Theory

Variable

PRACTICE ITEMS

1. List the six steps of the scientific method, and discuss what happens in each step.

2. For each of the following terms, give an operational definition.

    a. Affectionate

    b. Depressed

    c. Attractive

    d. Infidelity

    e. Temperature

3. Write a research question and a testable hypothesis for each of the following theories. Notice that a hypothesis merely rephrases the research question into a statement.

    a. Money causes greed.

    b. Old people are wise.

    c. People prefer high-fat foods.

d.   Children lack self control.

e.   Time passes quickly when people are busy.

4. Think of something that you recently saw or heard that you found interesting. Design a simple study, including a specific research question and testable hypothesis, related to this topic.

5. Explain why researchers might use a script when collecting data from participants.

6. Round the following numbers to two decimal places.

a.   67.445

b.   105.017

c.   10.142

d.   0.176

e.   1.003

7. Change the passive sentences to use active verbs.

a.   Participants had been asked to count to 100 before opening their eyes.

b.   While participants were completing the informed consent, the researcher was available for questions.

c.   There were six instructors who were appreciative of their students.

REFERENCES

American Psychological Association. (2003). *Ethical principles of psychologists and code of conduct*. Retrieved from http://www.apa.org/ethics/code/index.aspx

American Psychological Association. (2010). *Publication manual of the American Psychological Association* (6th ed.). Washington, DC: Author.

Diener, E., Fraser, S. C., Beaman, A. L., & Kelem, R. T. (1976). Effects of deindividuation variables on stealing among Halloween trick-or-treaters. *Journal of Personality and Social Psychology, 33*(2), 178–183. doi:10.1037/0022-3514.33.2.178

Liljenquist, K., Zhong, C., & Galinsky, A. D. (2010). The smell of virtue: Clean scents promote reciprocity and charity. *Psychological Science, 21*(3), 381–383. doi:10.1177/0956797610361426

Schwartz, B. M., Landrum, R. E., & Gurung, R. A. R. (2013). *An EasyGuide to APA style* (2nd ed.). Thousand Oaks, CA: Sage.

2

Ethical Research

Conducting research is a privilege. Many groups must be protected, including participants, psychology departments, schools, the discipline of psychology, coresearchers, coauthors, and people who read our publications. When subjects are creatures other than humans, like rats, monkeys, or pigeons, protection includes them as well. We have a responsibility to conduct research ethically. In this chapter, we will explain the many facets of ethical research.

ETHICAL TREATMENT OF PARTICIPANTS

Before we dive into how to protect participants, we would like to explain why we take such care with people involved in research. The history of research is bruised by many atrocities committed in the name of science. As one prominent example, in 1932, black men in rural Alabama joined the Tuskegee Syphilis Study. (These men thought the study cured "bad blood," a term used for syphilis and other diseases.) The men believed they were receiving treatment for the disease, but researchers merely wanted to follow the natural course of syphilis symptoms without any treatment at all. In fact, even when penicillin was established as an effective cure about 15 years later, doctors withheld treatment! They argued that future generations would benefit from the research, and the men's suffering and death contributed to valuable scientific knowledge. The study continued for approximately 40 years, until a doctor read one of the related publications and expressed his outrage. By the time the study ended, many participants died, their wives contracted the disease, and their children suffered because mothers passed the disease to them during pregnancy.

The study served as an example of horrible human suffering in the name of science. Although other examples exist, it was the Tuskegee Syphilis Study that led to the Belmont Report in the late 1970s (National Commission for the Protection of Human Subjects of Biomedical and Behavioral Research, 1979) and to federal laws requiring careful review of all research proposals by those not involved in the research. The Belmont Report details three ethical principles: respect for persons, beneficence, and justice. *Respect for persons* refers to treating all participants with courtesy and fully informing them of the study prior to their participation. People must be free to choose whether or not they want to participate and to what extent. *Beneficence* pertains to creating studies with a high potential for important scientific discoveries and a low potential for harm to participants. Researchers must always consider ways to minimize harm. *Justice* indicates the fair and equal distribution of both positive and negative aspects of a study to all people. For example, researchers should not conduct a potentially harmful study using only disadvantaged groups such as poorer people. Further, if advantages are identified, they must be shared among all people. Based on these three principles, the Belmont Report helps researchers focus on how to conduct ethical research with people.

ASSESSING RISK TO PARTICIPANTS

Obviously your first priority when designing a study is to protect participants. You likely will conduct research that is **minimal risk**. Minimal risk means participants will encounter no more risk than would be expected in everyday life. For example, if you ask students to complete a survey about their attitudes toward college, play a computer game, watch a video, or even eat radishes, such experiences generally would not be considered highly risky. However, if you asked participants to complete a survey about their worst childhood memories, play a computer game with a great deal of violence, watch a video about child abuse, or eat radishes until they feel sick, your study would contain more than minimal risk.

Minimal Risk.
When participants will encounter no more risk than would be expected in everyday life, a study is considered to have minimal risk.

Risk is first assessed by you and your research mentor, but even if you both agree that participants will experience minimal risk, your proposal should be evaluated by an **institutional review board (IRB)**. IRB members heavily rely on the Belmont Report when considering research proposals. Psychologists also refer to the American Psychological Association (APA) Code of Ethics, Principle 8: Research and Publication (APA, 2003).

At our university, IRB approval is required to share study results with the scientific community. Research within a classroom may be considered exempt at your institution, and your instructor will know what is required. Regardless of whether you need to write a full IRB proposal, consider the components in the following list. Each requirement allows you to think about the ethics of your research and protect participants.

Institutional Review Board (IRB).
The IRB is a group of reviewers that evaluates research proposals. Members of the IRB conduct a cost-benefit analysis to determine if the study's benefits outweigh the risks.

A standard IRB proposal includes

- A literature review and references to support the research idea,

- The scientific question to be addressed (hypothesis),

- A description of the people to be tested and how participants will be invited,

- A step-by-step methodology,

- Which statistics will be used to analyze the data,

- How participants and society might benefit from the study,

- Any potential risks to participants,

- Appendices with all materials related to the study (e.g., surveys),

- Information about the personnel who will run the study and have access to the data, and

- Certification that each researcher on the project has completed training in ethics.

If relevant, researchers also provide information about

- Deception of participants,

- Testing of minors (i.e., those under 18 years old),

- Medical procedures, and

- Procedures for working with animals.

In addition to the above elements of your IRB proposal, you will be required to submit an **informed-consent** form that people read and sign before participating. This document allows people to choose freely whether they will participate, which is the Belmont Report's first ethical consideration: respect for persons. The informed-consent form contains some of the same elements as the proposal narrative and is explained in detail later in this chapter.

Members of the IRB committee review each proposal and conduct a cost-benefit analysis. Costs of a study include participants' time and effort as well as any potential harm to participants. Benefits of a study include outcomes such as knowledge of research gained by both participants and researchers and knowledge of the subject area gained if results are shared with the scientific community. IRB members are more likely to approve a study if benefits outweigh costs. Because undergraduate research projects typically offer minimal risk, approval is given based on benefits such as students learning how to conduct research and gaining firsthand knowledge of studies in psychology. A cost-benefit analysis should remind you of the principle of beneficence from the Belmont Report.

In the sections below, we will discuss each part of an IRB proposal to help you prepare your own application prior to conducting research. Keep in mind that some class projects have been submitted by your instructor, and approval has been granted. In any case, you should understand the process designed to protect participants. Throughout your IRB

Informed Consent.
An informed-consent form is a document that describes the study and allows participants to freely choose whether they will participate. If the individual is a child or adult who is not capable of providing informed consent, then this document is signed by a parent, guardian, or other individual legally appointed to care for the participant.

application, write to an audience of professionals, but recognize that not all professionals are in psychology. You must define all terms and explain all theories.

Literature Review

A **literature review** involves reading many studies in the area of interest. Often called the "lit" review, this summary of publications lets IRB members know that you have learned about the subject of interest and inspires confidence in you as a thorough researcher. For the IRB proposal, provide the main points related to your study. What has been published on the same topic? What variables were used? If a particular manipulation you want to use seems risky, perhaps you can reassure your IRB by citing how it was used in a previous study. It is crucial to link with prior literature, and use of your proposed method in other studies helps make the case for use in your study.

It is not necessary to write about all articles you read when preparing your study. In fact, IRB forms may have a page limit. Summarize, but be clear that you have read enough to know what remains to be studied on the topic. Include citations to give authors credit for their work, and provide a reference list.

Hypothesis

Remember the scientific method from Chapter 1. Ultimately researchers want to examine a specific idea, or hypothesis. Provide your hypothesis in the IRB proposal. What is the purpose of your study? What do you expect to find? If you have offered a clear summary of available research, you can easily explain what your study will add to the field and what you expect as an outcome.

The Sample

Describe the **sample** you plan to collect, defined by the group of people you will test in your study. Traditionally, undergraduate research projects use college students in their sample. Only students 18 and older with adequate cognitive abilities can provide their own consent to participate. Researchers in our labs test participants at least 18 years old. However, your mentor may have access to additional populations and allow you to conduct research on participants other than college students 18 years old or older.

You will need to specify any limitations on selecting the sample, such as testing only men or those belonging to one ethnic group. Such limitations require a rationale because uninvolved groups will not be able to benefit from participation (e.g., earn extra credit in a course and gain firsthand experience in psychological research). Recall the Belmont Report's emphasis on justice.

Finally, how will the sample be acquired? Explain the procedure, such as asking psychology students to sign up for studies using an online system or pages on a bulletin board. Will students earn extra credit or course credit for participating? If so, will alternatives be

Literature Review.
A literature review
is a summary of the
available literature
that discusses the
theories and variables
relevant to a study.
The literature review
builds a rationale
for the study and
hypotheses.

Sample. A sample is
the group of people
in a study. The
participants compose
a sample.

offered in case students choose not to serve in studies? It is unethical to require or force students to participate in research. **Coercion** occurs when participants feel pressure to become involved in a study. Some examples of coercion are offering a great deal of extra credit for completing the study, paying students a significant amount of money, asking students repeatedly to participate in the study, or giving the impression that participants must complete the entire study or every item of a survey. In reality, you must give participants whatever they have been offered (e.g., extra credit) even if they skip questions or do not complete the study. To avoid coercion, psychology departments have policies for offering options equivalent to research participation. Some departments require instructors to offer course credit for either serving as a participant or completing a brief written assignment, with both options resulting in the same credit and requiring about the same amount of time and effort from students.

Method

The method should contain details in a step-by-step organization. What will participants experience? In our labs, we encourage students to number the steps of their method to drive home the need for details and organization. Item #1 is always "Participants receive the informed-consent form." The final item always reads, "The researcher thanks participants for their time." If we use a YouTube video, we provide a link. If we have a single survey item, we type the item in the method. For longer materials, such as surveys, we include an appendix. Even if we use a computer program, we describe the program in our method and provide a screenshot in an appendix. The method of your proposal gives IRB members crucial information for a cost-benefit analysis.

Statistics and the Data

An IRB proposal may include planned statistical analyses. Some researchers would argue that data analysis has nothing to do with protecting participants, but just as the literature review demonstrated work ethic, a plan for data analysis shows careful thought. If researchers have no idea how the data will be analyzed, how can they possibly know if the research design (method) will be useful? Perhaps the design cannot answer the research question (hypothesis), and participants will waste their time and energy. The cost of participation may outweigh the potential benefit of a study if the planned analysis will not answer the research question.

This section also may include information about how data will be stored to protect participants' **confidentiality**. Confidentiality refers to when the experimenter knows which data belong to each participant but is careful to report data without disclosing any identifying information. We always promise the IRB that data will be stored in a locked laboratory to protect participants' identities. In fact, whenever possible, we make sure participants are **anonymous**, meaning we have absolutely no knowledge of which participant provided which data. To create anonymity, we identify data by random numbers rather than names, and we keep signed informed-consent forms separate from participant data. Even so, sometimes one of our student researchers tests participants individually. It certainly is possible for the researcher to remember specific behaviors and either see the participant on campus or recall the participant's name. In this case, the researcher understands that participant information must remain confidential. If it becomes necessary to discuss interactions, the student researcher should do so only with a mentor who has been approved as personnel by the IRB.

Last, this section of the proposal may contain details on how long data will be stored and how they will be destroyed when the storage period ends. Length of storage and destruction of the data vary by institution and across time. Consult with your instructor or the IRB to know what is expected of you.

Benefits

In a section on benefits, first consider any potential benefits to the participants themselves. Students of psychology will gain firsthand experience about studies, but often they will not know the study's variables or hypotheses. One way to enhance the educational experience is to explain the study before students leave the lab. If you choose to offer such information, ask participants to avoid sharing details with others.

Confidentiality. Confidentiality is achieved when participants' data remain a secret with the researcher(s).

Anonymous. In research, participants are anonymous if the data do not reflect identity in any way.

A common benefit to participants is course credit. Instructors offer course credit if their students participate because (1) participation may help students learn about research, (2) student researchers in the psychology major need to complete their coursework, which includes testing participants, and (3) gaining knowledge about human behavior is valued by psychology instructors.

Beyond participants, others may benefit from a study. For example, when study results are shared at a conference in the form of a poster or paper, an audience benefits from new knowledge. Further, if results are published (e.g., in a journal), a larger audience has access to new information about human behavior. Publication offers a widespread way to share knowledge, and the source is likely to be available for the foreseeable future. When you plan to share a study in some way, benefits include knowledge gained by society.

Risk

Assessment of risk provides IRB members with potential negative aspects of a proposed study. Will participants be at minimal risk, defined by no more risk than everyday life? If so, researchers must write that participants will be at minimal risk and explain why. IRB committees generally frown on proposals that argue a study contains no risk. Every study has risk, even if the risk involves using participants' time and energy or even boring them with numerous surveys.

Consider whether any portion of your study contains the potential for a negative reaction from participants. What reactions could feasibly occur? What plan do you have to minimize negative consequences? Just as they do with other sections of the IRB proposal, committee members want to know that you are a thorough researcher and have considered the potential cost of your study. For example, you might say that watching a disgusting video could cause participants distress. As an ethical researcher, you could offer on-campus counseling resources to participants as they leave.

Appendices

Risk is further assessed when reviewing study materials, such as surveys. At the end of the proposal, attach all relevant support materials, including surveys, screenshots of computer programs, scenarios, descriptions of equipment used, et cetera. Be sure to give authors credit for their materials, and include all cited publications in your reference section. A complete proposal includes all materials to be seen by participants.

Personnel

In this section of the proposal, IRB members want to know who will be associated with the project. Who will have access to the data? Describe each researcher's role, including the faculty mentor, and explain prior research experience or training. In this section, we also tell committee members that all personnel have completed training in ethics.

Certification of Ethics Training

Most IRB committees require personnel to complete some level of **ethics training** prior to testing participants. Training is usually completed online and includes information to be learned and a quiz of the material. A high score on the quiz is used as an indication that researchers know the material. At our university, failure to perform well requires the researcher to reread the material and test again. When ethics training is successfully completed, a certificate can be printed from the screen or website. Certificates are submitted to the IRB for personnel involved in the project.

Deception

Deception can be divided into active or passive, and IRB committees differ on where they draw the line defining deception in a study. **Active deception** can be defined by telling participants a lie, such as pretending two parts of a single study actually represent two separate studies or telling participants that a **confederate** is a participant. **Passive deception** may include components such as having a confederate act like a participant. The researcher does not actively lie but leaves the participant to draw conclusions. Finally, it is generally not considered deceptive to avoid sharing detailed information about hypotheses or the entire design of the study. For example, researchers do not have to tell each participant every detail of their study just because the participant is in one of multiple possible groups. In our labs, we do offer to summarize the purpose and results when the study is complete, usually at the end of a term. If a participant is interested, we ask for a printed name and e-mail for a later e-mail summary. It is important to remember to follow up at the end of your study. Part of being an ethical researcher is keeping promises.

If active deception is used, **debriefing** is required. Researchers have a responsibility to explain to participants how they were actively deceived and answer any questions before the participant leaves. Some people debrief by handing out a typed sheet explaining the deception, but such a handout can be shared easily with others. In our labs, we ask student researchers to debrief verbally to reduce the chance that the details of our study will be shared with future participants. After all, we need participants to behave normally in our study, and they will not be able to do so if they know the hidden details. Regardless of how you debrief, be sure to ask participants not to share the results of the study with others because it would jeopardize your work. Most people understand the importance of research and are willing to help you when asked politely.

If active deception is not used, debriefing is not required. It is acceptable to thank participants for their time and offer results at a later time for those interested. However, we often choose to tell students a bit about our studies whenever doing so will not compromise the study. For example, we conducted a study on social discomfort by having a confederate act impatient when waiting for a participant to complete a task. Although no active deception was used, and our IRB did not require debriefing, we chose to tell

Ethics Training. Ethics training involves education on how to protect participants and conduct ethical research.

Deception. Deception can be active or passive and occurs when the true nature or purpose of a study is concealed.

Active Deception. Active deception refers to deliberately telling participants a lie during a study.

Confederate. A confederate is a researcher who interacts with participants and pretends not to be a researcher.

Passive Deception. Passive deception is defined as allowing participants to draw their own conclusions, sometimes erroneously, about study components. For example, a confederate may act as a participant but not claim to be a participant, allowing participants to interpret the ambiguous situation.

Debriefing. Debriefing entails telling participants about active deception at the end of a study.

participants that the other person in the room was a confederate trained to be impatient. We assured participants that feeling annoyed with the confederate was a reasonable response. Finally, we asked them not to share details of the study with others, since knowing the other person was a confederate would ruin our results.

Testing of Special Populations

Assent. Assent involves requesting permission for participation from someone in a special population. The person's caregiver must first provide consent.

Special populations include people under 18 years old, adults with an intellectual disability, elderly individuals with decreased cognitive abilities, and any other population without the cognitive capacity to give informed consent. If your mentor has access to special populations of interest to you, you must obtain approval from a parent, guardian, or other legal caregiver such as a conservator. That is, the person legally responsible for the individual must provide informed consent. You should also obtain **assent** from those in the special population, meaning they also agree as best they can to participate.

Obtaining legal approval is difficult for many reasons, and undergraduate research questions likely can be answered using adult participants who are not members of a special population. Keep in mind that "adult" means 18 years or older, so college students who are 17 years old would not be eligible to participate. Some IRB committees allow younger students to participate for the educational experience, but the data must be destroyed. Check with your IRB to determine the policy at your institution.

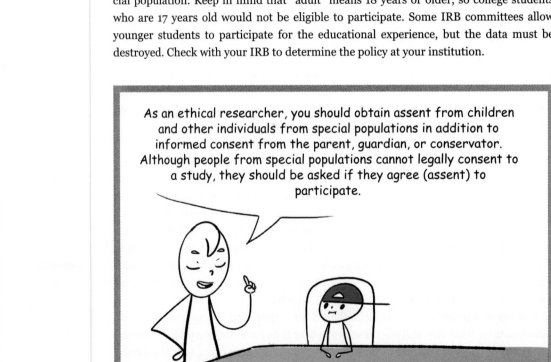

Medical Procedures

Just as few undergraduate studies test minors, medical procedures are uncommon. At times psychologists measure physiological factors, such as heart rate and blood pressure, but because our researchers have no medical training, our lab uses these only as indicators of increased stress. Our IRB understands that we cannot tell participants if they have a medical problem because we are not trained to interpret physiological measures in that way. If you will use any medical procedures, consult with your mentor and IRB committee for guidelines.

Animal Research

Perhaps your institution offers the rare opportunity to test nonhuman animals. If you plan to study nonhuman animal subjects, your institution certainly follows a set of guidelines for ethical treatment. Consult with your mentor and obtain a copy of the *Guidelines for Ethical Conduct in the Care and Use of Nonhuman Animals in Research* from the APA (2012). If you will be conducting research on nonhuman animals, you will submit a proposal to the Institutional Animal Care and Use Committee (IACUC). The IACUC is similar to the IRB, but IACUC members are experts in animal care.

Informed Consent

Informed consent is required of human participants. In other words, participants must know what they will be asked to do, and they must consent before being part of a study. A form for consent contains several parts, many of which also appear in the narrative of the IRB proposal, including

- Personnel on the project and their roles,

- Purpose of the research and summary of what participants will do in the study (e.g., complete surveys),

- Potential risks, even if the risk is considered minimal (e.g., the cost of participants' time),

- How much time is required for participation,

- Benefits to participants and society,

- A promise that data will be kept confidential and how confidentiality will be maintained (e.g., surveys will be locked in a lab and identified by numbers rather than names),

- A statement that participants have the right to ask questions and get answers from the researcher or project mentor,

- A statement that participation is voluntary, and participants can quit any time without penalty,

- Details of compensation, such as course credit, and the fact that alternatives to research are available through individual instructors,

- A stated requirement that participants must be at least 18 years old to give consent,

- Contact information for researchers and, where applicable, the faculty mentor, and

- If active deception is used, a statement that the full purpose of the study cannot be explained at this time, but results will be made available when the study is finished.

Often, the informed-consent form will be dated and signed by participants in a laboratory. Researchers must then keep the informed-consent form separate from each participant's data in order to protect participants' identity. Remember that the data are usually identified by a number, and the number cannot be linked with participants' names. If a study is conducted online, participants will read details about the study, then they may click a button to "Agree" to participate, or the screen might indicate that continuing to the next screen signifies a willingness to participate. If a study is conducted by mail, one option is to provide details of the study in a cover letter, ending with a statement that completing and returning the survey shows consent to participate.

If a study contains any potential for risk, physical or psychological, the informed-consent form must notify participants that they can get help free of charge by contacting the researcher, mentor, or IRB office. Researchers may also provide contact information for a campus counseling center or health services.

On an informed-consent form, researchers generally do not have to specify their hypotheses. Such details easily could **bias** results, making them invalid or inaccurate. Participants may try to support hypotheses or deliberately work against hypotheses, producing invalid results either way. You can always share detailed information with participants when the study is finished, as long as you or others in the lab are not planning to run a related study in the near future.

Before a participant leaves the study, provide a blank copy of the informed-consent form. Remember that this document contains contact information for study personnel as well as various health-service options. Participants may choose to contact those on the form if adverse reactions occur after leaving the study. Negative outcomes are unlikely, but ethical research requires us to be cautious and protect participants.

Bias. When a study contains bias, results are inaccurate due to influences beyond the study variables.

Responses to YouTube

Here's an example of an IRB-approved informed-consent form the authors of this book used in one of their research projects.

Researchers are Drs. Shauna Joye and Janie Wilson, both of whom are psychology professors in the psychology department and conduct research as part of their ongoing scholarship at Georgia Southern University.

Purpose of the Study: The purpose of this research is to examine the potential relationship between watching unsavory YouTube videos and various behavioral tasks such as unscrambling sentences.

Procedures to be Followed: Participation in this research will include viewing YouTube videos, completing surveys, and completing behavioral tasks such as working on unscrambling sentences.

Discomforts and Risks: This study is considered to be minimal risk to participants because students regularly watch YouTube videos and complete paperwork. Some of the videos may be slightly disturbing due to gross topics.

Benefits: The benefits to participants include learning about responses to videos and their ability to complete subsequent tasks. The benefits to society include learning more about responses to popular YouTube videos and the ability to complete subsequent tasks.

Duration/Time Required From the Participant: Participation in this study will take no longer than 45 minutes.

Statement of Confidentiality: The researchers will have access to the data collected in this study. Anonymity will be ensured by coding all data by numbers rather than names. No names will be associated with the data at any time. The data will be kept in a locked storage area in Dr. Shauna Joye's lab in Brannen Hall, located on Georgia Southern University's campus. After seven years, the data will be removed from the area and shredded.

(Continued)

(Continued)

Right to Ask Questions: Participants have the right to ask questions and have those questions answered. If you have questions about this study, please contact the researchers named above, whose contact information is located at the end of this form. For questions concerning your rights as a research participant, contact the Georgia Southern University Office of Research Services and Sponsored Programs at 888-888-8888.

Compensation: If a student is in a psychology course, the student will receive either course credit (i.e., 1.5 credits) or extra credit, depending on the instructor's policy. Alternatives to participating in studies are offered by all professors.

Voluntary Participation: The study is voluntary, and participants are not required to participate. The subjects may end their participation at any time and do not have to respond to questions they do not want to answer.

Penalty: There is no penalty for deciding not to participate in the study. The participants may remove themselves from the study at any time without penalty or retribution. The decision to participate will not jeopardize any relationship with Georgia Southern University. In addition, course grades will not be affected.

The student must be 18 years of age or older to consent to participate in this research study. If consent to participate in this research study and to the terms above is offered, the student must sign and provide the date below.

Each student will receive a copy of this consent form to keep. This project has been reviewed and approved by the GSU Institutional Review Board under tracking number H88888.

Title of Project: Responses to YouTube

Principal Investigator: Dr. Shauna Joye, [email address], 888-888-8888

Other Investigator: Dr. Janie Wilson, [email address], 888-888-8888

_____

Participant Name

_____   _____

Participant Signature   Date

I, the undersigned, verify that the above informed-consent procedure has been followed.

_____   _____

Investigator Signature   Date

TREATING PARTICIPANTS ETHICALLY

IRB approval and informed consent go a long way toward helping researchers conduct ethical studies, but we must also consider the social interaction between researcher and participant. Be on time, polite, and thankful. The day before participants are scheduled to arrive, send them a reminder e-mail of the appointment day, time, and location. Welcome participants to your study even if you had a bad day. If a participant is late, avoid negative comments or body language. If you cannot test that participant because of tardiness, politely say so. You do not have to be a pushover, but you should offer bad news kindly. If you cannot be interrupted by a late participant, post a sign on the door that asks not to be interrupted. Put your e-mail or phone number on the sign for late participants to write down and contact you later.

While testing participants, do not sit close by. Your proximity may cause biased answers, and participants may feel uncomfortable. Do not touch participants, and maintain appropriate eye contact rather than stare (or glance) at body parts in an unprofessional way. You get the idea. Be professional and kind in all interactions. Even when you are conducting an online study, one of the final screens should thank participants for their time.

ETHICS AFTER TESTING PARTICIPANTS

It is tempting to think that ethical considerations stop when participants leave the lab or complete an online survey. Not true. Additional considerations include data entry, data analysis, writing a manuscript, authorship issues, and sharing research with the scientific community.

Data Entry

Enter data into the computer by code only, and be sure codes do not reveal a participant's identity. Check and recheck the data to be sure no errors exist. In addition to simply checking numbers entered from surveys, look over each column of values to see if any numbers are outside of the range of possibilities. For example, if participants rated their motivation on a scale from 1 to 5, the data for motivation should not contain a value of 50. As you read through subsequent chapters in this text, you will gain understanding of how data are entered into the computer for analysis. You will need to follow the step-by-step instructions about how to enter data for various research designs, how to analyze the data correctly, and useful values from the computer output. Errors may result in finding nothing interesting in your study. Or worse, errors might lead you to publish inaccurate results, misleading and potentially harming others.

Data Analysis

Tied to data entry, research goals guide the way researchers analyze data. With careful planning, researchers can use the scientific method discussed in Chapter 1 to address a research question. You should have in mind the statistical analysis (or a few related analyses) that answers the research question. Hopefully you will ask a specific research question, collect data to answer the question, analyze the data, and find support for a new truth about behavior. Many designs and analyses are explained in this book.

"Fishing" in the data indicates that a researcher has no specific hypothesis or analysis in mind. The researcher is willing to run many statistical tests and see what looks interesting. Then interesting results are explained in convoluted ways loosely tied to the original research question. We consider this approach sloppy research. If you run many different tests on the data, you are ignoring the thoughtful approach of the scientific method. Fishing may not be admitted by the researcher, but lack of focus becomes apparent when a manuscript or conference presentation holds a minor result, and the write-up is vague and unfocused.

The temptation to fish for results originates from the desire to find a meaningful outcome. Nothing is wrong with hoping for an interesting answer to your research question. But ethical research requires us to tell the truth based on our specific method. If we run a careful study and find no interesting outcome, we have learned a truth about the world based on our particular method and participants. For example, suppose a professor examined two lecture styles to compare the potential effect on students' grades. Perhaps one lecture style involved the professor talking for 50 minutes, and the other style encouraged student participation. If the researcher found no difference in student grades, the outcome may seem disappointing, but the data must be shared honestly. Telling the truth is always noble.

Unfortunately, journals likely would not publish the lecture study. Why not? After all, it may seem that the value of truth is not diminished by a lack of difference between the groups. However, a journal editor cannot know the reason for this lack of difference. Maybe the researcher ran a sloppy study by failing to keep accurate records of which grades followed each type of lecture. Data may have been entered into the computer wrong. Or perhaps this particular instructor was rude while encouraging student participation, diminishing any possible benefit. Reasons for no group differences are nearly endless. Journal publication usually relies on a careful literature review, a clear research question, a strong method, correct data analysis, and interesting results, to name a few manuscript qualifications.

Writing a Presentation or Manuscript

After data are analyzed, interesting results should be shared with others. As scientists, we understand that the final step of the research process is presenting our work at a conference or submitting a manuscript for publication. Many of us present either a poster or talk at a conference to get feedback from colleagues, and then we write a manuscript for potential publication. Regardless of the method of dissemination, cite others when presenting their ideas. Reference authors who have published in the field and helped build the area of research. You will locate authors early in the research project when conducting a literature review. Instructions on how to cite authors are found in the APA publication manual (2010).

Even when citing the work of others, plagiarism can occur. **Plagiarism** is defined as taking credit for other authors' words or ideas. (For a resource on how to avoid plagiarism, see the APA manual.) We always assume students plagiarize by accident because they do not understand that direct quotes must have quotation marks and give credit to the author(s), or they do not realize rewording an idea does not make the idea their own. Authors get credit for their *ideas* too, not just their exact words.

In our experience, students are more likely to plagiarize when they do not understand a concept and want to make sure they represent it accurately in their paper. Allow yourself time to ask your instructor for help if you do not understand something you have read. A second mistake we have seen our students make is taking notes directly from an article or typing a manuscript while a journal article is open beside them. Writers may have the best of intentions to summarize and paraphrase later, but leaving an article open beside you when writing is asking for trouble. We suggest that you read, turn the article over or close the file, and write what you learned from the article. Of course the authors still get credit for the ideas, but you will be less likely to plagiarize the wording.

Finally, we all tend to make mistakes when we feel rushed. Rushing to complete work often happens after procrastinating. Give yourself time to write a presentation or manuscript, and then leave your best effort alone for a few days. Come back to it with a clear mind, read it from beginning to end, and make edits as you read. If you like to write on hardcopy, print your draft and edit on paper. If you are comfortable using a computer to edit, consider tracking your changes while you work. In Microsoft Word, under Review, click Track Changes, and edit your own paper. Here you can also add notes to yourself or your mentor by clicking New Comment. The program offers two formats when deleting words: Show the words with a line through them, or display the deletion in the right margin. Below you can see how to delete within the paper. Notice that the phrase "with a pen" has a line through it to indicate deletion.

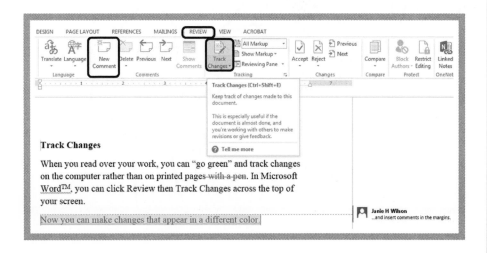

Plagiarism.
Plagiarism is defined as taking credit for the words or ideas of others.

If you prefer to show deletions to the right, under Review, click Show Markup, then choose Balloons and Show Revisions in Balloons. Below, the final word, *later,* was deleted.

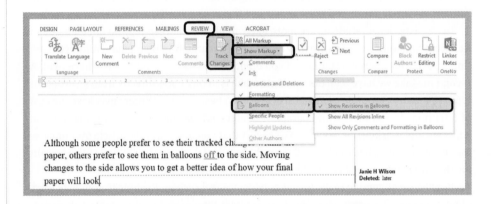

To accept changes in a document, simply right click on the change, and then click Accept in the menu that drops down. Also, if you see any vertical lines to the left of a line of text, that means a change has been made somewhere on that line. Be sure to accept or reject all tracked changes before turning in your final paper.

Authorship Issues

One of the most confusing parts of conducting research as an undergraduate is knowing what warrants authorship. When students conduct their own project, faculty mentors nearly always provide guidance from research idea to final presentation or manuscript. If an instructor is particularly good at subtly encouraging students but letting them accomplish tasks, students may not realize the extent to which the instructor is helping. Rest assured that behind every student project is a professor who helped make the magic happen. If a presentation or manuscript results from the project, the mentor will almost always be a coauthor, although the student is usually first author.

On the other hand, when a faculty member allows students to work with ongoing lab projects, such as a large-scale study designed by the faculty member, coauthorship should not be expected. Perhaps the professor allows students to gain valuable research experience, and the experience might even be in the form of a course with a grade. In our labs, if an undergraduate works on a project from idea to writing, including extensive involvement in all aspects of the project, we discuss the potential for coauthorship openly. Otherwise we are careful to tell students that working in our lab does not warrant authorship. When more than one student works on a project in a significant way, the order of authorship is determined by the professor who mentors the project. We decide who the first author is based on who completes the most work on the project in a useful way.

Presenting and Publishing Research

When your project is complete, ask your instructor if you should present at a conference or write a manuscript for potential publication. Because your work was conducted under the mentor's guidance at a specific school, you need your mentor's permission to share work with the scientific community.

Presenting at a conference is an excellent professional experience. Consider presenting a poster as your first experience. At a subsequent conference, you might present a talk using presentation software such as PowerPoint. The benefits of each type of presentation, as well as preparation instructions for each, can be found in *An EasyGuide to Research Presentations* (Wilson & Schwartz, 2015). The same publication also offers detailed guidance on how to submit a manuscript and respond to various editorial responses.

WHO IS HARMED BY UNETHICAL BEHAVIOR?

In this chapter we spent a lot of time explaining how to be an ethical researcher. It is reasonable for you to wonder what happens when a researcher fails to follow the rules. Some might argue that as long as the participants are not harmed, a poor research ethic harms only the researcher. In a way, that is true. The researcher could lose permission to conduct studies in the future, at least at the current institution, or plagiarism could result in removal from the school.

But negative effects are not limited to the researcher. Failure to follow ethical guidelines damages a mentor's reputation. For example, when student researchers in our department are rude to participants (e.g., arrive late to a study), we often hear about it from a participant, another researcher in the lab, or other professors. As another example, perhaps a student's research gains acceptance into a conference program, but the student fails to show up for the presentation. The mentor who signed the conference form as the advisor will hear the complaint. When our students behave unethically, our research and the research of our future students lose credibility with colleagues.

Because a student's behavior reflects on the department, school, and even the discipline of psychology, every unethical act has the potential to harm reputations. Students who are psychology majors may change their major and pursue a different career path based on a negative research event. Or participants may lose faith in psychology as an ethical discipline that treats people with respect.

We will end this section on the student's responsibility by admitting that others have a responsibility to be ethical as well. Mentors must treat students with respect even while offering constructive criticism. You should realize that your mentor is trying to help you, but obvious rudeness should be discussed privately with the mentor. It is quite possible that your mentor did not intend to be hurtful. If you suspect unethical behavior in other forms (such as seeing someone tamper with data or failing to protect participants' confidentiality), first speak with your mentor to make sure you have not misunderstood. If the situation is not resolved, speak with the department chair about your concerns.

ETHICAL DATA-COLLECTION METHODS

As researchers interested in behavior, psychologists collect information using several methods. In your research project, you likely will want to examine human behavior, requiring another look at the ethics of how to treat participants. Your study might examine laboratory behavior, online responses, or past outcomes such as scores on the Scholastic Aptitude Test. In fact, some methods of data collection do not even let people know they are involved in a study!

In this section, we will explain ways to collect data and the ethics of each method. Throughout this book, we will cover additional research methods. For now our focus is on ethical considerations tied to data collection. Approaches include

- Running studies in a laboratory or online,

- Conducting a study in a natural setting,

- Observing people without their knowledge, and

- Analyzing archival data.

Earlier in the chapter, we focused on traditional laboratory studies. Extending a study to an online environment generally requires the same approach, including an informed-consent document. In such studies, participants know what will happen to them, and they consent to be part of the study. Even in the event of active deception, participants are fully debriefed before the study ends. In other words, people truly are participants because they choose to participate. As long as the IRB has approved the study, following the methodology should result in ethical treatment of participants.

However, not all studies occur in a structured lab or online setting. A step beyond the traditional study is one conducted in the real world or a **naturalistic setting**. Although a researcher might still obtain informed consent and even manipulate variables, data from a real-world study are more applicable to the typical human experience. In other words, a study in a naturalistic setting is higher in mundane realism than a lab study. **Mundane realism** is the extent to which a participant might engage in a specific behavior beyond the study. For example, an instructor could examine the effects of different teaching techniques on students in the classroom. The classroom is a naturalistic setting for students. Such a study would be high in mundane realism because learning in a classroom is often experienced by students outside of a research study. As for ethical considerations, the IRB would need to approve the study, and an informed-consent form could be required by the IRB.

With a naturalistic study, we moved away from the lab and into the real world, but we still collected some type of informed consent, and people clearly served as informed participants. **Observational studies** are those conducted in a naturalistic setting that do not include informed consent. Instead, researchers try to observe people without interfering with their behavior. Because researchers observe behavior in the real world without interfering, the method is high in mundane realism and applicable to real life. The extent to which results can generalize to other settings and populations is called **external validity**. A study high in mundane realism usually has high external validity.

With an observational method, we step on shaky ethical ground. Do researchers have the right to watch people without their consent? The IRB will help you decide what you may observe while safeguarding the privacy of others. In general, if people remain at minimal risk, researchers may observe others as long as the setting is considered public. Interestingly, public places include Internet sources such as social media, allowing researchers to examine information readily available for public viewing. Remember that the IRB makes the decision about what constitutes minimal risk and is ethical research.

A final method of data collection tied to ethics involves viewing existing information or **archival data**. For example, a researcher might want to examine a large database of

Naturalistic Setting. A naturalistic setting is an environment in which participants live their daily lives.

Mundane Realism. Mundane realism refers to the extent to which a study is similar to an activity a person might encounter in everyday life.

Observational Studies. Typically observational studies entail data collection through observation in a naturalistic setting.

External Validity. The extent to which study results can be generalized to other settings and groups is called external validity.

Archival Data, Data collected and stored prior to the beginning of the study are called archival data.

college grade point averages (GPAs) and analyze whether psychology majors differ from music majors. Even if names were removed from the data, the researcher would have access to students' personal information without their permission. In cases such as these, the IRB decides if access will be granted, assuming the person or organization holding the data allows access as well.

DESIGN	PROS	CONS
Laboratory Study	High researcher control	Low external validity
Online Study	High researcher control of study variables; potentially fast data and a large sample	Low researcher control over the study setting
Study in a Natural Setting	Results are obtained in the real world & are more generalizable	Moderate researcher control & moderate external validity
Observational Study	High external validity	Low researcher control
Archival Study	Quick access to data; usually a large sample	Low researcher control

SUMMARY

We hope this chapter revealed some ethical issues encountered by researchers. When designing a study, we must think carefully about the method and be sure we can defend the ethics of our data-collection approach. An IRB proposal provides a useful structure to examine research ethics because the IRB relies on the Belmont Report and the principles of respect for persons, beneficence, and justice. If your project is submitted to the IRB, the committee will conduct a cost-benefit analysis based on many facets of the proposed research and ultimately decide if the project can move from idea to reality. Even if your class project does not require IRB approval, you should reflect on the ethical considerations found in proposals. After a cost-benefit analysis, we hope you welcome the opportunity to excel. Become a model researcher with a strong work ethic and a passion for conscientious, ethical interactions.

REVIEW OF TERMS

Active Deception	Fishing
Anonymous	Informed Consent
Archival Data	Institutional Review Board (IRB)
Assent	Literature Review
Bias	Minimal Risk
Coercion	Mundane Realism
Confederate	Naturalistic Setting
Confidentiality	Observational Studies
Debriefing	Passive Deception
Deception	Plagiarism
Ethics Training	Sample
External Validity	

PRACTICE ITEMS

1. Explain the three ethical principles of the Belmont Report.

2. For each of the following studies about punishment and math performance, take the role of an IRB member. Would you approve the study? Why or why not?

    a. Hayden designs a study to examine the effect of punishment on math performance in adults. She plans to randomly assign individuals to receive either a small shock for incorrect answers or a dime for correct answers each time they complete a math problem. Participants will be given all information about the study prior to participation.

    b. Braydan designs a study examining how much punishment individuals are willing to self-inflict for a monetary reward. She plans to allow adults to administer shocks to themselves for money, with higher voltage resulting in more money earned. She informs them that they can earn up to $300, with voltage high enough to cause a minor burn but no other damage.

   c. Peytan designs a study examining the effect of an unexpected punishment on concentration. Participants are randomly assigned to either receive a small, unexpected puff of air to the face when they get a math problem incorrect, or complete math problems with no punishment. She does not inform participants of the air puff because it is supposed to be unexpected. After the study, Peytan debriefs participants about why she was not able to tell them about the puff of air before the experiment.

3. Which of the following could reasonably be considered minimal risk to participants?

   a. Asking participants to rate the attractiveness of pictures of women in magazines

   b. Asking participants to complete a puzzle

   c. Letting participants believe that they are shocking another person with electricity and telling them they cannot stop

   d. Having a participant watch a video of a mother abusing her child

   e. Asking participants to take a quiz on lecture material

4. List the typical required parts of a research proposal with human subjects that does not use deception, special populations, or medical procedures.

5. Explain why IRB committees might ask about planned statistical analyses.

6. What are some ways you might ensure confidentiality?

7. What is the difference between confidentiality and anonymity?

8. What is the difference between active and passive deception? Which type requires debriefing?

9. What is the age of consent for participants?

10. List the typical required parts of an informed-consent document.

11. In which of the following scenarios are you allowed to *not* give a participant class credit for an experiment?

   a. The student begins the study but must quit because she is distressed by your survey.

   b. The participant skips several questions in the middle of your survey.

   c. The student signs up for the experiment but arrives 30 minutes late, and you do not have time to test the participant.

12. When testing a participant in a lab setting, list positive and negative researcher behaviors.

13. Why is it important to include your research mentor as an author on presentations and publications of your work?

14. Discuss the following five ways to conduct research: laboratory study, online study, study in a natural setting, observational study, and archival study. Include pros and cons of each.

REFERENCES

American Psychological Association. (2003). *Ethical principles of psychologists and code of conduct*. Retrieved from http://www.apa.org/ethics/code/index.aspx

American Psychological Association. (2010). *Publication manual of the American Psychological Association* (6th ed.). Washington, DC: Author.

American Psychological Association. (2012). *Guidelines for ethical conduct in the care and use of nonhuman animals in research*. Retrieved from http://www.apa.org/science/leadership/care/guidelines.aspx

National Commission for the Protection of Human Subjects of Biomedical and Behavioral Research. (1979). *The Belmont report: Ethical principles and guidelines for the protection of human subjects of research*. Retrieved from http://www.hhs.gov/ohrp/humansubjects/guidance/belmont.html

Wilson, J. H., & Schwartz, B. M. (2015). *An EasyGuide to research presentations.* Thousand Oaks, CA: Sage.

CHAPTER

3

Research Designs and Variables

As researchers, we enjoy a wealth of options when choosing research designs and considering statistical analyses. At the heart of design and analysis are the types of variables in our study, from relatively straightforward variables such as eye color to more complex variables like happiness. In this chapter we will discuss research designs and four types of variables. We will also explain how to summarize variables to share results with others.

All designs require a sample. Participants in the sample can report information about themselves (e.g., eye color or happiness), or they can be manipulated in some way (e.g., asked to taste different types of soda in a taste-test study). Whether or not participants are manipulated defines the two design categories in psychology. With no manipulated variable, the study is called a **correlational study**. If a variable is manipulated, the study is called an **experiment**. The word *study* is a general term for either a correlational research design or an experiment. However, a correlational study and an experimental study have specific individual qualities.

CORRELATIONAL DESIGN

A correlational study examines relationships between variables that already exist. For example, if you were interested in looking at the potential relationship between number of hours college students studied for a test and grades on the test, students could report the number of hours they studied and their test grades. In this example neither hours studied nor test grades were manipulated. Participants reported something about themselves that existed prior to the study. Another example would be the potential relationship between college major and life satisfaction. A researcher would not control either college major or life satisfaction. Participants would report their chosen college major and life satisfaction. Take a few minutes to consider the following additional examples of correlational studies.

Correlational Study (Correlational Design). A type of study in which no variables are manipulated is called a correlational study. This type of research design explores relationships between existing variables.

Experiment (Experimental Design, Experimental Study). An experiment is a type of study in which at least one variable is manipulated (the IV), and one variable is measured as an outcome (DV).

- Gender and depression

- Rural versus urban neighborhoods and access to health care

- Age and ability to delay gratification

In most cases, gender and neighborhood are not manipulated, and therefore these variables yield correlational data. Age most certainly cannot be manipulated, and researchers often want to know about changes over time. In fact, changes across years are so important that psychologists turn to two useful approaches for data collection: longitudinal and cross-sectional studies.

Longitudinal Studies

When researchers want to address a research question related to behaviors of a group over time, they conduct a **longitudinal study**. This type of study involves collecting information from the same people, also called a **cohort**. An example might involve measuring children's ability to empathize with other people across years in elementary school. The same group of children, or cohort, would be assessed multiple times. As this example indicates, longitudinal studies can take many years to complete.

Cross-Sectional Studies

Instead of designing a long-term study to collect correlational information, we might design a **cross-sectional study**, which involves studying a sample of participants from several different relevant time periods at once. In the example of children's empathy, we could measure empathy in students currently in grades 1, 2, 3, and 4 of elementary school. We would learn if year in elementary school is related to level of empathy by comparing the four groups of students. Of course, students in each grade might also differ on intelligence, parental guidance, or any number of other variables that might influence empathy. These additional sources of variability are called **individual differences**. Cross-sectional studies offer faster data collection than longitudinal studies, but we might have difficulty addressing our research question due to individual differences across participants. Both methods of data collection are valid approaches to correlational research and involve collecting existing data.

EXPERIMENTAL DESIGN

Often researchers choose to alter participants' experiences rather than simply collect existing information. We choose what participants experience and then see what happens. We watch the outcome. Such a design is called an experiment, the gold standard in psychological research.

Longitudinal Study. A longitudinal study is a type of design that involves data collection from the same people across time.

Cohort. A group of participants with something in common, such as attending the first grade together, is called a cohort.

Cross-Sectional Study. A cross-sectional study involves collecting data across several cohorts at one time. Researchers learn what might occur across a longer period of time for one cohort, but data collection is faster than it is with a longitudinal study.

Individual Differences. Variability across participants inherent to each person (e.g., personality) is called individual differences.

Independent Variable

An experiment contains at least one manipulated variable, called the **independent variable (IV)**. Recall that a variable must vary, so an IV must have at least two **levels** (also called **groups, conditions,** or **treatments**). If we wanted to study aggression in children, we might frustrate them by having them trace a circle while looking only at the reflection of their moving hand in a mirror. This manipulation would represent one level of an IV. In the other IV level, we might have children trace the circle while looking directly at their hand. We would be manipulating what happens to the participants. We would choose the two levels to be experienced "independent" of other factors, such as participants' artistic ability, preference for drawing pictures, intelligence, et cetera. The IV sets the stage for the study. It is the foundation of the experimental design.

Pause to consider the following examples. Remember that an experiment requires manipulation of what happens to participants.

- Ask participants to eat breakfast or skip breakfast.
- Have students study alone for one test and study in groups for a second test.
- Require some participants to drink protein shakes after a workout and others to drink water.

IVs are not limited to two levels. Use as many levels as needed to address your research question.

- Ask participants to eat a large breakfast, small breakfast, or no breakfast.
- Have students study alone, then in a small group, and then in a large group.
- Require some participants to drink 0 ounces of a protein drink, others to drink 4 ounces, others 8 ounces, and still others 12 ounces.

In an experiment, researchers often include a **control group**. A control group is a level of the IV in which participants do not receive the manipulation. A control group offers a baseline against which to compare the manipulated group. Look at the protein-drink example above. Notice the inclusion of a control condition: 0 ounces of a protein drink. This group provides a baseline against which to compare the remaining groups. When you design a study, it is perfectly reasonable to use a control group as a level of your IV, but it is not a requirement. Your research design might instead manipulate people in both groups and have no control condition. As you continue to learn about research, you can decide if you should include a control group in your study.

Dependent Variable

In addition to an IV, an experiment requires a second variable as well. If we are studying frustration and aggression in children, and we have manipulated frustration with the mirror-tracing task, we next have to measure aggression. Aggression is the outcome, or the **dependent variable (DV)**. The DV is still a variable, so we have to make sure it can vary. For example, we might measure aggression by number of physical touches within 30 minutes that appear to have the intent to harm or number of negative verbal comments. We anticipate that the number reflecting aggression will *depend* on the level of the IV experienced by the participant. This expectation is why the DV is named as the "dependent" variable. The DV is not manipulated. We simply measure the same DV across both levels of the IV to see if the groups differ.

Let us return to prior IV examples and add a DV for each. Notice that the DV is the outcome and is free to vary.

- Ask participants to eat breakfast or skip breakfast, and measure alertness.

- Have students study alone for one test and study in groups for a second test, and examine test scores.

- Require some participants to drink protein shakes after a workout and others to drink water, and assess energy level.

Consider the last example above. The IV is whether people drank a protein shake or water, and the DV (outcome) is energy level. Energy is the dependent variable because we hope energy levels *depend* on whether participants drank a protein shake or water.

Cause and Effect

In an experiment, researchers learn powerful information: cause and effect. The IV is the cause, and the DV is the effect. We can return to our example of frustrating children by asking them to trace a circle while watching their hand in a mirror. Recall that the second level of our IV required children to trace a circle while watching their hand directly. Simply tracing a circle should not frustrate children. As the outcome, we measure aggression. In the mirror-tracing study, frustration would be the IV, and aggression would be the DV. If the two groups differed, we would be able to say that frustration caused aggression. Keep in mind what we discussed in Chapter 1 about the scientific method and hypotheses. We might learn that frustration causes aggression *in the specific context of the study and using the specific sample of participants*. Additional research adds evidence in support of a theory: Frustration causes aggression.

> **Dependent Variable (DV).** A DV is the outcome variable in an experiment. The DV is free to vary across all levels of the IV.

RANDOM ASSIGNMENT

You might be thinking about the wealth of variables other than frustration that might explain differences in aggression among children. Perhaps the children differed in personality related to aggression. Or maybe children observed in the afternoon are more aggressive than those observed in the morning. Countless other variables might affect aggression, and it might seem reckless to decide that frustration causes aggression without measuring or manipulating all other variables. But we can solve this potential problem by turning to chance.

When assigning participants to one of the IV levels, researchers use a procedure called **random assignment** (or **simple random assignment**). Random assignment to conditions means everyone in the sample has an equal chance of being put into each level of the IV. By chance, those who simply are aggressive kids will be represented in both levels of the IV. Likewise, random assignment means both of the IV levels will be approximately equally distributed across times of day. For any variable you can consider, random assignment helps to ensure that the variable will be about equally distributed across groups. As an added benefit, chance will result in approximately an equal number of participants in each level of the IV across time.

If you want to be certain groups remain equal in size, a minor adjustment to random assignment can be used in which a participant is randomly assigned to one of the IV levels, and then the next participant is assigned to the remaining level (if the IV has two levels). Only after every level of the IV has been used do you begin again with random assignment to one of the conditions. In an experiment with three IV levels, the first participant is assigned randomly to one of the three levels, then the next participant is assigned randomly to one of the remaining two levels, and the third participant is assigned to the final IV level. For the fourth participant, all three levels are again a possibility, and so on. This procedure is called **block random assignment**.

EXTRANEOUS VARIABLES

Whether you choose simple random assignment or block random assignment to conditions, the procedure helps distribute any differences across IV groups. Some participants will complete the mirror-tracing task, and others will trace the figure without the frustration of a mirror image for guidance. As long as any extra variables (like some children tested by a kind teacher and others tested by a rude teacher) do not vary exactly along with levels of the IV, you do not have a flawed experiment. Such a flaw has a name: A **confounding variable**, often called a **confound**, changes along with levels of the IV. Let us say we assigned everyone in the mirror-tracing group to be tested by a rude teacher and everyone in the simple tracing task to be tested by a kind teacher. At the end of the

Random Assignment (Simple Random Assignment). With random assignment to conditions, each participant in a sample has an equal chance of being put into each IV level.

Block Random Assignment. Block random assignment is a procedure in which a participant is randomly assigned to one of the IV levels, and then the next participant is assigned to one of the remaining levels, and so forth, until all levels have been assigned once. Only after every level of the IV has been used do all IV levels become available again.

Confounding Variable (Confound). An extraneous variable that changes along with levels of the IV is called a confounding variable. This type of variable causes studies to be flawed.

study, we would not know if any effects on aggression were due to the different tracing tasks or the type of teacher who tested. A confounding variable offers an unwanted alternative explanation for results. At the end of a study, we only want one explanation for the outcome, and that single explanation must be based on IV levels.

If we randomly assign participants to conditions, we change what might have been a confounding variable to a nuisance variable. A **nuisance variable** introduces spread (variability) in your DV values but does not ruin a study. Examples of nuisance variables in the mirror-tracing study would include children's aggression as a personality trait, time of day children were tested, and attitude of the researcher, to name a few. Random assignment to IV levels allows chance to about equally distribute any additional variables across both groups. For example, some children using the mirror will be tested by a rude teacher and others by a kind teacher. Likewise, some children tracing the circle without a mirror will be tested by a rude teacher and others by a kind teacher. With a nuisance variable, random variability in DV values is considered "noise" in your data. Sure, noise, or spread in DV values within each level, will make it harder to find out if frustration affects aggression, but differences may still be found. The experimental design is solid.

Although they are not interchangeable terms, together nuisance variables and confounds are called **extraneous variables** because they introduce some type of variability in the data set and are not the focus of the study. Remember that noise created by nuisance variability is just that: a nuisance. The noise from this type of extraneous variable makes it a bit more difficult to see differences across IV groups based on the manipulation of interest (e.g., the tracing task). On the other hand, a confounding extraneous variable creates a serious problem. When a variable changes systematically with the IV levels (e.g., only a rude teacher testing those in the mirror-tracing condition), results will never be clear. Avoid confounds, and let random assignment to conditions equalize the noise from nuisance variables across IV levels.

INTERNAL VALIDITY

Random assignment to conditions eliminates potential confounds associated with individual differences in participants. For example, if you have designed a study to test enjoyment of eating fried chicken versus tofu, you would not want to test vegetarians in the fried-chicken group and chicken farmers in the tofu group. Random assignment of everyone into the two conditions allows random chance to ensure that some vegetarians and some chicken farmers are in both groups. Individual differences associated with attitude toward chicken are reduced to a nuisance variable rather than a confound.

Likewise, random assignment means contextual variables such as time of testing do not become confounds. Suppose you plan to feed everyone tofu in the first half of

Nuisance Variable. A variable that introduces random spread (variability) in your DV values is a nuisance variable. Nuisance variability occurs about equally across all levels of your IV and does not typically ruin an experiment.

Extraneous Variable. Variables that introduce some type of variability in the data set that is not the focus of the study are called extraneous.

the semester and chicken in the second half. A large event could occur at midterm that affects participants' attitudes about fried chicken. Maybe a large-scale recall of chicken is in the news based on rampant salmonella, causing low ratings of fried-chicken enjoyment in the second half of your study. The news event would confound your data because participants were not randomly assigned to conditions. Random assignment would mean about half of your participants in the first part of the semester ate tofu, and half ate fried chicken. Similarly, both groups would be represented in the second half of the term. With random assignment to conditions, the news event would be reduced to a nuisance variable.

Beyond random assignment, confounds can occur in a faulty method. Recall our earlier example of the mirror-tracing task tested by a rude teacher and the simple tracing task tested by a kind teacher. Here a confound has been built into the method. At the end of the study, we would not know whether a group difference was caused by the tracing task or the teacher's personality. Again random assignment would save the day. About half of the participants in each task could be tested by the rude teacher and half by the kind teacher.

When a confound is present in a study, we cannot know if the IV levels truly caused changes in the DV. We lack **internal validity**. Our primary goal in an experimental research design is to find out if our manipulation causes changes in an outcome, making internal validity crucial in experiments.

Internal Validity. Internal validity is the extent to which an IV causes changes in the DV.

LEVELS OF MEASUREMENT

Both experimental and correlational designs rely on studying variables. Correlational designs evaluate relationships between pairs of variables (e.g., body weight and number of minutes people exercise per week). On the other hand, experiments assess the effect of one variable (IV) on another variable (DV). Notice that any research question examines variables.

Remember from Chapter 1 that the scientific method requires researchers to operationally define variables in order to address the research question. Further, the statistic that will be used to analyze variables must be considered when a research design and variables are defined. Without careful thought about both design and statistics, the question of interest may not be answered by the study.

The variables in the design are analyzed using statistics that require us to know the **level of measurement** of each variable. Every variable you could possibly use in a study will represent one of four levels of measurement: nominal, ordinal, interval, and ratio. It is your job to decide the level of measurement for the two variables potentially related in a correlational study and the IV and DV in an experiment. Each variable's level of measurement informs the choice of statistic.

Level of Measurement. A variable's level of measurement defines its scale properties. Levels include nominal, ordinal, interval, and ratio.

Nominal Variable

For a variable to be **nominal**, the levels must represent categories (e.g., the variable of a light-switch position can be "on" or "off"). Another example of a nominal variable is hair color, which can contain several categories such as black, brown, red, and blond. The variable levels are defined by categories or names, but no specific order exists. That is, hair colors cannot be put into any meaningful order to indicate that red hair is "more" than black hair. Do not stretch your imagination to put nominal levels into a meaningful order when no order exists.

In a correlational study, nominal variables might include gender because levels are categories. Recall that a correlational design is defined by lack of manipulation, and gender is not manipulated by a researcher. A second example of a nominal variable not manipulated by the researcher is skin color. Any variable merely defined by categories that are not manipulated can be part of a correlational study.

In an experiment, nominal variables can serve as the IV, the DV, or both. A nominal IV has levels that are categories. For example, if you conducted a taste test for different brands of coffee, the brands would represent categories. As another example, suppose you wanted to examine the potential effect of room color on speed of eating. Various room colors would represent the IV and serve as a nominal variable. Likewise, a DV can provide nominal data. Suppose you wanted to know whether or not students drop a class based on various syllabus formats. Whether or not students drop a class would be a nominal outcome.

Nominal Variable.
Nominal data represent categorical values with no meaningful order.

Ordinal Variable

If the categories of a variable do, in fact, have a meaningful order, the variable illustrates an **ordinal** level of measurement. Examples include days of the week, months of the year, and T-shirt sizes such as small, medium, and large. We would also consider rankings in a spelling bee or taekwondo competition to depict ordinal variables because even though first, second, and third place appear to be numbers, they merely represent categories with a reasonable order. Key terms that might provide a clue for ordinal data are *rank* and *ranked*.

In a correlational study, ordinal variables are not manipulated. We might examine the potential relationship between days of the week and life satisfaction. Participants could rate their life satisfaction Sunday through Saturday. Day of the week is an ordinal variable not manipulated by the researcher. We might also look at class ranking (e.g., junior or senior in college) as a nonmanipulated ordinal variable.

In an experimental design, an ordinal IV would be manipulated. An example would be randomly giving students an A, B, C, or D on a test, regardless of their actual performance, and then measuring their anger. In this design, letter grade is an ordinal variable manipulated by the researcher. Further, an ordinal DV could include T-shirt size after a 90-day weight-lifting program. The outcome of T-shirt size represents the effect of lifting weights.

Interval Variable

Ordinal variables do not have a set distance between them. For example, a person who wins second place in a race might be 2 minutes behind the first-place winner and 25 minutes in front of third place. Conversely, **interval** data have equal intervals between values or increments. An example of an interval variable is temperature. The intervals of interest might be between each degree or between groups of 10 degrees (e.g., 10°F, 20°F, 30°F). Using whichever increments you choose, the thermometer has equal intervals between levels.

Although temperature (e.g., Fahrenheit) is the typical example of interval-level data, in psychology we also analyze **rating items** as interval data. The numbers can have words to define them, or **anchors**. Participants choose a rating by circling a number on the item. A **rating scale** usually is composed of several such items. The most widely used rating scale is the **Likert** scale, which requires participants to choose numbers that correspond with their answers across several items. A single item on a Likert scale is called a Likert item. For example, rating your roommate on cleanliness could be accomplished with a Likert item such as the one below.

Very Messy				Very Clean
1	2	3	4	5

Ordinal Variable. Ordinal data contain categories with a meaningful order but no equal intervals between levels.

Interval Variable. Interval data are characterized by equal intervals between numbers on the scale, but there is no true zero point.

Rating Item. A rating item allows participants to rate their response on a single item with several response options. Options are discrete values with equal intervals between them.

Anchors. On a rating scale, anchors are descriptions given to the numbers.

Rating Scale. Rating scales are used when a researcher wants to collect interval data on a variable of interest, generally using more than one item.

Likert. A Likert item is one that contains a range of values and labels for at least some of the values. A Likert scale is usually composed of more than one Likert item.

The format of a Likert item is up to you. Any number of values can be used, and some or all of the values can have anchors. Keep in mind that offering an odd number of values allows participants to choose a middle value and avoid making a clear statement about their view. If you offer an even number of options, participants must respond on one side of the item or the other.

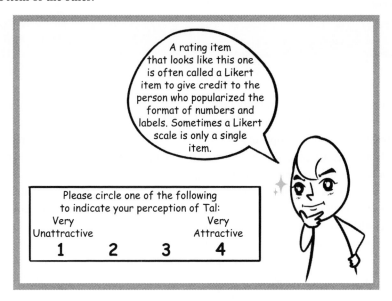

A second type of interval item is a **semantic differential**. A semantic-differential item offers terms with opposite meanings to assess participants' attitudes. Participants provide ratings between one term and the opposite term. For example, you could ask participants to rate their perceptions of research using the following semantic-differential item. Instructions might ask for an X on the blank best representing their perceptions. Each blank below is scored as a value, with options ranging from 1 to 8 on this example.

Of course, formatting is up to you. A semantic-differential item might include a continuous line between the two adjectives, and participants would draw a vertical line to indicate their attitude as shown below. A continuous line represents a **visual analogue** item.

Boring --|------ Engaging

To score the item, a researcher could measure the number of millimeters from the beginning of the line to the participant's mark. Computer-survey programs can provide a number (e.g., from 1 to 100) based on where a participant marks the line using the cursor to slide the mark from left to right.

Semantic Differential. A semantic-differential scale contains terms with opposite meanings and a range of options between the terms. Participants choose from options on this continuum.

Visual Analogue. Visual analogue is a type of rating item not separated into categories. Instead, respondents make a mark on a continuous line to represent their response.

When using any type of rating scale, be careful of wording. If items seem negative, participants might provide inaccurate ratings to appear more positive to the researcher. This response pattern is called **social-desirability response bias** and might be triggered by the following item.

I am racist.

Strongly Disagree					Strongly Agree
1	2	3	4	5	6

To discourage social-desirability response bias, word items to reduce the likelihood that bias will occur. The prior item prompt could be rewritten as, "Sometimes I have negative thoughts about people of a different race." Of course, also give participants privacy when completing the survey, and avoid labeling surveys with participants' names. Anonymity may help reduce social-desirability response bias.

Often the items themselves invoke an attitude that changes ratings on subsequent items. For example, if you asked participants to report their college GPA and followed this request with a series of items rating their intelligence, motivation, and hard work in school, you can see how asking them first to report GPA might alter how they respond to the rest of the survey. Perhaps a student who reports a 2.23 GPA would rate himself or herself as having relatively low intelligence, motivation, and work ethic because the participant is thinking about the poor GPA. We often choose to ask for demographic information such as age, gender, and GPA at the end of a study to avoid influencing responses.

Participants also bring their own response biases to surveys based on their personality. Some people choose only middle values (which is a good reason to use an even number of values for Likert items). Others choose only the most extreme values. And still others refuse to opt for extreme values. Unfortunately, some participants do not bother to read all of the items! As a researcher, you can omit data from participants who do not read items

**Social-Desirability
Response Bias.**
Social-desirability
response bias occurs
when participants
choose responses that
make them appear
more favorable.

by making sure a few items are reverse worded. That way if a participant simply chooses the highest value for all items, you will know the data are useless.

In this section we have discussed several types of written items and surveys. Written items bring the potential for **response bias**, and as you have read, bias comes in many forms. Some biases, such as those of participants who will not use the extreme ends of a scale, do not compromise a study. Other biases, such as not reading the items, can be identified, and a specific participant's data can be removed from the study. Bias such as social desirability can be addressed by careful wording of the items and an assurance of anonymity. Finally, consider the order of items to minimize the potential impact of early items on responses to later items.

Some types of survey items do not use words. Such items can be useful for children and nonverbal participants. One popular visual scale is the Wong-Baker Faces Pain Rating Scale (e.g., Garra et al., 2010) used in hospitals to assess a patient's discomfort. We have modified this single-item scale to assess happiness below.

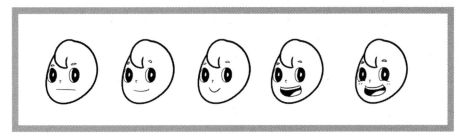

Participants might point to the face indicating the way they currently feel. If you wanted to use such a scale in research, you could assign the numbers 1–5 to the faces, and higher values would indicate more happiness.

You can probably think of additional formats for a rating scale, and likely it would be analyzed as interval data. The goal is to make sure each item can be scored as a number, even if participants see only blanks, a line, or a smiling face. When you score the responses, apply the numbers and record those as your data.

Regardless of whether you choose verbal or nonverbal items, the variable can be used in both correlational and experimental studies. Further, if several items compose a scale, an average rating across items can assess the idea of interest. In a correlational study, temperature, rating scales, and other variables analyzed as interval data would not be manipulated. For example, you might be interested in the relationship between summer temperatures and motivation. Temperature is an interval variable, and it is not manipulated in our example.

In an experiment, consider designs in which the IV or DV represents interval data. If you manipulated the temperature of a classroom, the IV would represent an interval variable. Perhaps your DV could be motivation assessed using a Likert item from 1 to 5, with higher values representing more motivation. Or you might locate an entire scale assessing motivation, and the average rating would provide a DV assessed as interval data. The key component for an experiment is manipulation of an IV and measurement of a DV, and either or both variables could represent interval data.

Ratio Variable

The fourth and final level of measurement for a variable is **ratio**. Ratio variables have equal intervals between levels *and* a zero point that indicates the absence of the quantity measured. For example, amount of money in a bank account represents a ratio variable because money (whether you consider increments of pennies, dimes, dollars, etc.) has equal intervals. Money also has a zero point. Zero means the absence of money. As a second example, the number of days students attend class is a ratio variable. Number of days has equal intervals (e.g., one, two, and three days), and zero means the absence of class days attended. You might be thinking that temperature should be an example of a ratio variable rather than an interval variable, but 0°F does not mean the absence of temperature!

The only difference between an interval variable and a ratio variable is the zero point on the measure. To clearly decide if a variable reaches ratio level, simply ask yourself this question: "Does doubling a value make sense?" Using the bank-account example, does it make sense to say that $10 is twice as much money as $5? Yes. Being able to double a value in a logical way means the scale has an absolute zero point and is a ratio variable. What about data such as height and weight? Again, doubling a value makes sense. Someone who weighs 200 pounds weighs twice as much as someone who weighs 100 pounds. And a building that is 50 feet tall is twice as tall as a building 25 feet in height. We have found that our students identify ratio variables more accurately when we ask the "doubling" question than when we ask them to imagine a zero point.

For a correlational study, variables of interest might include ounces of a drug people take by choice, number of movies people watch each week, and number of minutes using social media. As long as ratio variables are not manipulated, results will assess a potential relationship rather than cause and effect.

For cause and effect, design an experiment. As examples of ratio IVs, we could manipulate how many hours people study, how long people have to wait in line, and the number of times participants are rejected. For DVs, we might measure outcomes such as percentage correct on a test, number of times people complain to others standing in line, and how long people will stay in a negative social situation. The IV, the DV, or both the IV and DV could be ratio variables.

Why Do We Care?

Whether we design a correlational study or an experiment, each variable's level of measurement dictates which statistic to use for analysis. Nominal and ordinal variables are simpler forms of data with no quantity to their levels. For example, brands of breakfast cereal are labels, not numbers. Likewise, months of the year have no quantity and do not allow math such as adding together January and February to equal March. When values can only be named categories, we call them **qualitative** and analyze the data with simpler statistics. On the other hand, interval and ratio variables have values that are numbers with quantity. Not surprisingly, we call them **quantitative** variables. Temperature, rating scales, and money in a bank account can be quantified with numbers such as 90°F, a rating of 5, and $100. Because both interval and ratio variables represent quantities, more sophisticated statistics can be used. After data are analyzed, we can discuss either a relationship between variables or cause and effect, depending on whether we manipulated an IV.

SUMMARIZING VARIABLES: CENTRAL TENDENCY

At each level of measurement, variables must be summarized to communicate effectively and efficiently. Assume you wanted to know about students' performance on Test 1 in your psychology course. You would not likely be interested in knowing all individual test scores, especially if the course contained many students. A summary value would suffice. If scores were percentages correct, the variable would be ratio. Remember to ask yourself the "doubling" question. In this case, it is logical to say that 100% correct is double 50% correct. To express Test 1 scores, a single value would summarize and communicate well.

In this section of the chapter, we will discuss ways to offer a "best" value to summarize data at each of the four levels of measurement: nominal, ordinal, interval, and ratio. Next we will explain how to share information on how spread out the values are in a specific data set.

The best value to represent a data set is called the **measure of central tendency**. The term is a bit misleading because our goal is not necessarily to find the center value in a data set, but to pick one value as the best way to describe the data. A measure of central tendency is particularly important when a data set contains hundred—or thousands—of values. Choosing a single value to represent the data set depends on the variable's level of measurement.

Mode

Recall that nominal data are defined by categorical levels (e.g., brown, blue, or green eyes). As you can imagine, summarizing such data with only one value is a challenge. Suppose our sample contained 10 people with brown eyes, 18 with blue eyes, and 12 with green eyes. The value that occurs most often in this sample is blue eyes, giving us the single value that best represents the sample. The value occurring most often in a data set is called the **mode**, and the mode is used to depict a sample of nominal data. Another way to look at the mode is a "best-guess" value. If a member of the sample walked up to you with eyes closed, what value would you guess for eye color? The best guess would be blue because it is the value that occurs most often in the sample.

It certainly is possible to have two modes in one data set. In a sample with 10 green-eyed people, 10 blue-eyed people, and 6 people with brown eyes, the two modes would be green and blue eyes because they both occur with the highest frequency in the data set.

We have to admit that the mode is a simple measure of central tendency, but nominal data are simple too. With a variable merely represented by named categories, we cannot expect to have an elaborate measure of central tendency. Further, the mode is not really "central" in the data set, but this value is still called a measure of central tendency.

Just as nominal data can have one value that occurs most often, ordinal, interval, and ratio data can have a mode. However, we rarely use the mode with any level of measurement other than nominal. More sophisticated measures of central tendency can be used for the remaining three levels of data.

Median

Median (*Mdn*). A median is the middle value in a data set.

When a variable reaches ordinal level, recall that the categories are in a meaningful order. For example, letter grades are ranked: A, B, C, D, and F or F, D, C, B, and A. Either way, a logical order exists. With ordinal data, our measure of central tendency is the **median (Mdn)**, which is the middle value in a data set. To locate the middle value, we must put all values in sequential order. If letter grades in a data set of 11 students were A, C, B, B, A, C, D, F, B, A, B, we would order them either highest grade to lowest or lowest grade to highest. We have chosen highest to lowest here: A, A, A, B, B, B, B, C, C, D, F. In that line of data, the middle value is a grade of B, which is the median. Remember that our goal is to summarize the data set. In this sample, the best measure of central tendency is the median, which is B. In other words, the single value that represents the sample is a B.

If a data set has an even number of values, you will not be able to pick the middle value. Instead, choose the lower of the two values in the middle. For example, letter grades on the final exam (organized in order) might be A, A, A, B, B, B, C, C, C, C, D, F. The middle values are C and B, therefore the lowest value is C. The median for this sample is a grade of C.

The lower of the two values is chosen because, technically, the median is defined by all values 'at or below' the middle value.

Let us think back to nominal data. Can we use the median to summarize? No, the median cannot be used to summarize a nominal variable because the order of categories is arbitrary. We would not try to put variables such as eye color or gender into a meaningful order. Ordinal data have a meaningful order, and the median is appropriate. The median can also be used to summarize interval or ratio data, but the better choice for those higher-level data is usually the mean. Recall that interval and ratio data are quantitative, meaning the values represent a quantity rather than merely a quality, as is the case with nominal and ordinal variables. The mean provides a measure of central tendency for quantitative variables.

Mean

In most cases, the **mean (M)** is the best measure of central tendency for interval and ratio data. The mean is the mathematical middle of a data set (i.e., the average). Calculate the mean by adding all values in a sample and dividing by the number of values in the sample. For instance, if some classmates rated their boyfriend or girlfriend on a scale from 1 to 10, with higher numbers indicating more kindness, the data set might contain these numbers: 8, 5, 7, 9, 8, 6. To calculate the mean, add the values (sum = 43) and divide by the number of values ($N = 6$). The best value to represent this sample is 7.17 (written as $M = 7.17$). Based on this data set, significant others are rated, on average, as 7.17 in kindness based on a scale from 1 to 10, with higher numbers representing more kindness.

Mean (M). A mean is the mathematical middle of a data set.

When you see a capital N, this means the total sample size. A lower-case n refers to a part of your total sample, such as the number of women (n = 5) in your total sample of N = 10 people.

The mean cannot be calculated for nominal or ordinal data because values have no quantity. It is not possible to add the values of an ordinal variable to find the numerator for the mean formula. The mean as a measure of central tendency is reserved for interval or ratio data.

Outlier. An outlier is
an unusual value in a
data set.

Unfortunately, interval and ratio data cannot be summarized by the mean if the data set contains an unusual number. An **outlier** is a number that is quite different from the remaining values in the data set. For example, we might ask people to report number of tattoos and find these data: 1, 4, 3, 3, 2, 1, 1, 3, 200, 1, 3. As you can see, 200 tattoos is an unusual value in this sample. If we calculated the mean, the outlier would pull the mean upward. Honest communication would suffer if we told people the average number of tattoos is 20.18, because the number does not represent the sample as a whole. We will discuss outliers again in later chapters with specific analyses.

When an obvious outlier (or outliers) is present in a sample, the mean loses accuracy. But we still need a measure of central tendency to summarize and communicate effectively. Without the mean, we fall back to the next best measure: the median. Put the interval or ratio values in order, and report the middle value as the single best representation of the data set. In our tattoo example, we might start with the lower value and order them: 1, 1, 1, 1, 2, 3, 3, 3, 3, 4, 200. The middle value is 3, allowing us to share that 3 tattoos is the best value to accurately represent the sample. Certainly, the median of 3 tattoos does seem to reflect the entire sample better than 20.18 tattoos.

What if the data set contained an even number of values, offering no middle value? With ordinal data, we agreed to choose the lower of the two values. However, interval and ratio data do allow math, which is not to be ignored. Average the middle two values together to represent the median. If number of tattoos included a 12th number, such as 0, order the values, find the middle two values of 2 and 3, average them together, and report the median as 2.50.

The type of variable (nominal, ordinal, interval, or ratio) determines the best measure of central tendency. In addition, the existence of an outlier or outliers in a sample of interval or ratio numbers requires the median to be used as the best single value to represent the data set.

Type of Variable	Best Measure of Central Tendency
Nominal	Mode
Ordinal	Median
Interval & Ratio with outliers	Median
Interval & Ratio with no outliers	Mean

Let's review...

SUMMARIZING VARIABLES: VARIABILITY

In the prior section, we explained the best values to represent samples of nominal, ordinal, interval, and ratio data. Choosing a single measure of central tendency allows you to effectively summarize a data set. Often, a second piece of information completes the snapshot of your sample. In most cases, summarizing data includes a measure of variability. **Variability** refers to how spread out the values are. To clarify why variability is an important second value, consider two samples of amount paid for concert tickets from two websites. On TicketMistress, a sample of ticket prices for a concert includes $24, $30, $31, $23, and $27. On StubSource, ticket prices for the same concert are $15, $27, $7, $39, and $47. The mean for each sample is $27, but the values are much more spread out in the second sample. Which sample gives you more confidence that you would pay close to $27 for a ticket? Because TicketMistress has less variability in the dataset, you could be confident that the concert ticket would cost about $27. With StubSource, you might pay substantially less than $27 or much more. If we only communicated the mean, we would be ignoring the fact that the two samples differ on variability.

Whenever possible, both a measure of central tendency and a measure of variability are used to summarize a data set. The only type of data that will not allow a measure of variability is nominal. Nominal variables merely contain categories with no meaningful order, making spread of values meaningless. For instance, imagine a sample of favorite cookies among a sample of your friends. If the sample included 15 people who love chocolate-chip cookies, 23 who prefer peanut-butter cookies, and 10 who choose oatmeal cookies, it would make no sense to say the spread of cookies was from chocolate-chip to oatmeal. Although no variability measure exists for nominal data, below we will explain types of variability based on the three remaining levels of measurement: ordinal, interval, and ratio.

Range

The **range** is defined by the lowest and highest values in a data set. For example, if glasses of water consumed daily by a sample were 4, 3, 7, 8, 6, and 8, the range would be from 3 to 8 glasses of water. Because this variable is ratio, the values are numbers with meaningful quantity, and we could summarize the range as 5 ounces of water (8 minus 3). However, we argue that reducing the range from two numbers to one number is a bad idea. If we report a range of 5, the data could have ranged from 0 to 5, 1 to 6, 2 to 7, 3 to 8, 4 to 9, and so on. Our goal is to accurately summarize the data set, and reducing the measure of variability from two values to one value is not a compelling reason to lose valuable information.

Although the example of water consumed represented ratio data, the range is generally used with ordinal data. Report both the lowest and highest value as the range. The median and the range are always linked together. Whenever the median is chosen for central tendency, the range must be reported for variability. Recall our earlier example of letter grades: C, B, B, A, F, D, B, B, A, C, and A. Because these values represent ordinal

Variability. Variability represents the spread of values on a variable.

Range. The lowest and highest values in a data set represent the range.

data, the measure of central tendency is the median (*Mdn* = B), and the measure of variability is the range, which is from A to F.

Standard Deviation

**Standard
Deviation (SD).**
Standard deviation
represents an
average variability
around the mean.

The best measure of variability for interval or ratio data *with no outliers* is the **standard deviation (SD)**, which reveals about how far each number in a data set falls from the mean of the sample. Think of standard deviation as the average variability, just as the mean is the average value to represent the sample. We can use the mean value and average variability to paint a clear picture of a data set. As an example, suppose the mean for the number of online videos people watch each week is 34.77, and the standard deviation is 5.06. We can summarize the sample with the mean (*M* = 34.77) and the standard deviation (*SD* = 5.06). As an added bonus, we can add and subtract the standard deviation from the mean to indicate where most of the values in the sample fall.

$$34.77 - 5.06 = 29.71$$

$$34.77 + 5.06 = 39.83$$

With this information, we can let readers know that people watched an average of 34.77 online videos each week, with most people watching between 29.71 and 39.83 videos weekly. We have both our best guess and an indication of how spread out the values are.

The standard deviation is useful because it tells readers where most values likely fall in a sample. It can be used only with interval or ratio variables with no outliers. Recall that data with an outlier (or outliers) require the range as a measure of variability. Again, do not discard valuable information by subtracting the lowest from the highest value. Report both values for the range. Remember that ordinal data also call for the range to illustrate variability. Review the following table as a summary of variability and review of central tendency.

Type of Variable	Best Measure of Central Tendency	Best Measure of Variability
Nominal	Mode	NONE
Ordinal	Median	Range
Interval & Ratio with outliers	Median	Range
Interval & Ratio with no outliers	Mean	Standard deviation

SPSS: SUMMARIZING VARIABLES

When discussing how to summarize nominal, ordinal, interval, and ratio data, we described exactly how each type of data is analyzed. We explained the calculation for the mean so you would understand how to obtain the mathematical center for interval or ratio data. However, the bulk of this textbook will not detail hand calculations. Instead, we will explain the logic behind an analysis and show you how to analyze the data using the most popular computer program in the social sciences: Statistical Package for the Social Sciences (IBM® SPSS® Statistics*). In the following sections, we explain how to analyze the four types of data using SPSS, with screenshots to guide you through the process.

Nominal Data

Let us return to an earlier example of nominal data: eye color. The values in our sample were 10 brown-eyed people, 18 people with blue eyes, and 12 people with green eyes. When you open SPSS, the program will show a box that allows you to work with existing files. At this point, you have none. Click Cancel at the bottom right to remove the box.

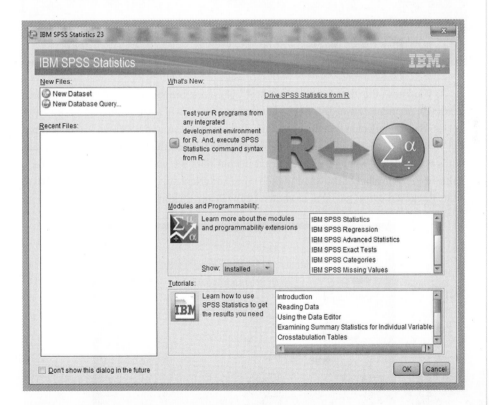

*SPSS is a registered trademark of International Business Machines Corporation.

On the blank spreadsheet that appears, click Variable View at the bottom left.

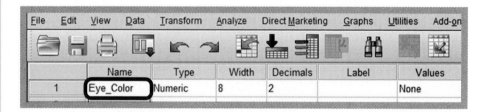

In the column labeled Name (for the name of the variable), type Eye_Color. SPSS does not accept spaces in variable names, so we have added an underscore between the two words. SPSS will automatically fill in the remaining cells to the right.

File	Edit	View	Data	Transform	Analyze	Direct Marketing	Graphs	Utilities	Add-on

	Name	Type	Width	Decimals	Label	Values
1	Eye_Color	Numeric	8	2		None

As you know, this data set contains three eye colors: brown, blue, and green. The program will not analyze words for central tendency, so we will assign numbers to our categories. We might decide that the number 1 = brown, 2 = blue, and 3 = green. In the column for Values, click to the right side of the word None to open the box shown below. Values allow you to define what a 1 will represent in your data set, and so on. In the box, enter a value of 1 for the label of Brown, and then click Add. Next, enter a value of 2 and a label of Blue. Click Add. Label 3 Green, as shown below. After clicking Add, click OK.

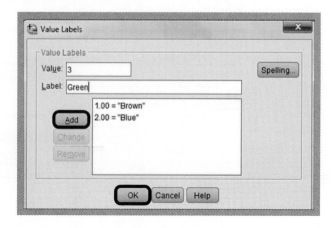

In the Values column, you will see that values have been entered. Now the program will be able to analyze the data, and labels will help you keep track of category names. Click Data View at the bottom left to enter data.

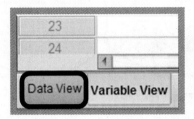

The number 1 represents brown eyes; therefore enter 10 values of 1 under Eye_Color. Continue in the same column and enter 18 values of 2 for the number of people with blue eyes, and then enter 12 values of 3 to depict green eyes. The figure below does not show all 40 values, but you can see the beginning of the data set.

File   Edit   View   Data

	Eye_Color
1	1.00
2	1.00
3	1.00
4	1.00
5	1.00
6	1.00
7	1.00
8	1.00
9	1.00
10	1.00
11	2.00
12	2.00
13	2.00
14	2.00
15	2.00
16	2.00
17	2.00
18	2.00
19	2.00
20	2.00
21	2.00
22	2.00

41 : Eye_Color

Data View Variable View

Values of 1, 2, and 3 help the program analyze the data, but we prefer to see labels on the spreadsheet. To view the labels you entered, click View, and then check the box to the left of Value Labels in the dropdown menu that appears. As shown in the next screenshot, the labels appear on your screen. Remember that labels are for you. Numbers are for the program to analyze. Under those labels are the numbers (1, 2, and 3) that the program needs.

We want SPSS to find the best measure of central tendency for us. But you must tell the computer which measure of central tendency makes sense for nominal data. Nominal data can be summarized only by the mode. To request the mode, click Analyze and then Descriptive Statistics and Frequencies in the dropdown menus. You might be tempted to click Descriptives instead of Frequencies, but only Frequencies will give you the mode. Frequencies will also provide a list of how many times (how frequently) each value occurs in the data set. Although we do not care about that information for the mode, we wanted you to know why this option is labeled "Frequencies."

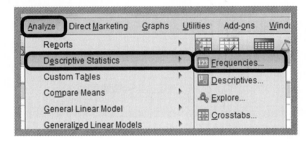

In the box that opens, click on Eye_Color in the left box and click the arrow pointed out below. This will move the variable over to the Variable(s) box to be analyzed. Next click Statistics to choose which measure of central tendency would be most appropriate for nominal data. In the box that opens, check the box to the left of Mode under Central Tendency, and then choose Continue.

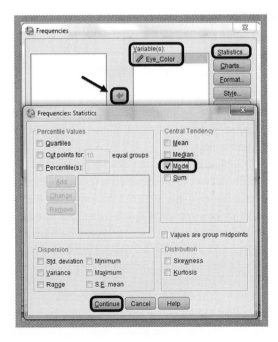

Because we are interested only in the mode for this analysis, uncheck the box to the left of Display frequency tables.

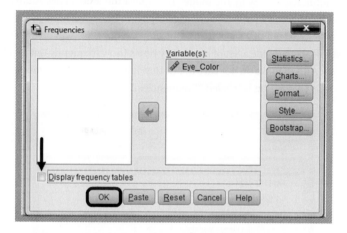

When you click OK, the following output will be produced.

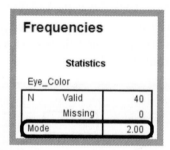

The mode is 2. We know that the level 2 represents Blue eyes; therefore the best guess (measure of central tendency) for this data set of eye color is blue eyes. No measure of variability exists for nominal data.

When the mode of a sample is obvious, the effort required to enter the data into SPSS may not seem worthwhile. But consider a situation in which a researcher has thousands of values. Even when data are entered into SPSS in a random order, the program will reliably produce the mode. Further, now you know how to enter data into SPSS and how to label values. The more familiar you become with this program, the more efficiently you will be able to analyze data for variables across many types of research designs.

Ordinal Data

Let us return to our earlier example of an ordinal variable and analyze the data using SPSS. We examined a sample of students' grades, reporting the median after organizing grades in order: F, D, C, C, B, B, B, B, A, A, and A. Grades ranged from A to F. When grades are entered into SPSS, we do not need to organize them first. We can enter them in any order, such as C, B, B, A, F, D, B, B, A, C, and A, if that is the order of the data set. We have to decide which numbers will represent the letter-grade values. Below we have chosen to represent the letter A with a 1, B = 2, C = 3, D = 4, and F = 5. Label the values as we did in the prior example, and then click OK.

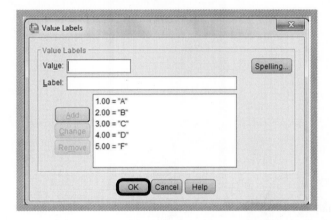

Change to Data View to see the spreadsheet. Enter the numbers corresponding to the correct letter values. Our data include C, B, B, A, F, D, B, B, A, C, and A. In the first cell, a C is represented by the number 3, and so on.

	Test_Grades
1	3.00
2	2.00
3	2.00
4	1.00
5	5.00
6	4.00
7	2.00
8	2.00
9	1.00
10	3.00
11	1.00
12	

As we did before, click View and Value Labels to see the letter grades, allowing the software to analyze the numbers you entered while offering you a more user-friendly label for each value.

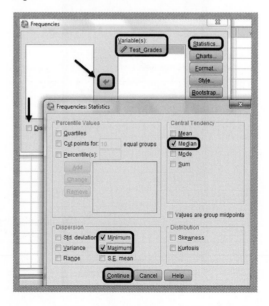

Click Analyze, Descriptive Statistics, and Frequencies. In the box that opens, move Test_Grades to the right side by clicking the arrow in the middle. Remove the check beside Display frequency tables. Click Statistics to open the second box, and then check the small box to the left of Median because ordinal data require the median as the measure of central tendency. For variability, check the small boxes beside Minimum and Maximum. These two values will yield the range. We do not check the box next to Range because we will not report a difference value. Click Continue.

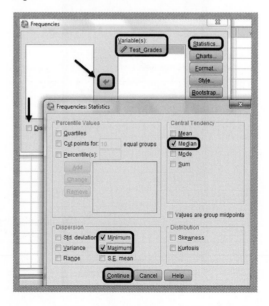

Click OK to view the output, which is shown in the screenshot below. We have circled the median as well as the minimum and maximum values to show you the requested information. Recall that a value of 2 represents a letter grade of B in this sample, so the median is B. The minimum value is a 1, and the maximum value is a 5, which gives us two values for the range. Because we know that a 1 represents A and a 5 represents F, letter grades ranged from A to F.

Frequencies

Statistics

Test_Grades

N	Valid	11
	Missing	0
Median		2.0000
Minimum		1.00
Maximum		5.00

In case you were wondering, we could just as easily have labeled letter grades as F = 1, D = 2, C = 3, B = 4, and A = 5. SPSS would have yielded a median of 4, a letter grade of B.

Interval and Ratio Data

Interval and ratio data with no outliers require the mean (central tendency) and the standard deviation (variability) as summary values, and SPSS does a wonderful job of providing these data. We will analyze an earlier example of people rating the kindness of their boyfriends and girlfriends on a scale from 1 to 10, with higher numbers indicating more kindness. Our small sample contained values of 8, 5, 7, 9, 8, and 6.

Under Variable View, type the variable name: Kindness. Do not label Values with this type of data. With interval and ratio variables, we need to know only what higher numbers indicate in order to understand our output. Because interval and ratio variables are not defined by categories, numbers do not need to represent anything other than the actual values of the variable. In other words, a kindness rating of 1 means a low quantity of kindness. A rating of 10 means a great deal of kindness. Click Data View at the bottom left to see the spreadsheet.

After entering the data under Kindness, click Analyze, Descriptive Statistics, and Frequencies. If you need a reminder of options, look back at the first example in this chapter.

Move Kindness to the right side of the first box, and click Statistics. In the second box, check the small boxes beside Mean and Std. deviation (standard deviation). Choose Continue.

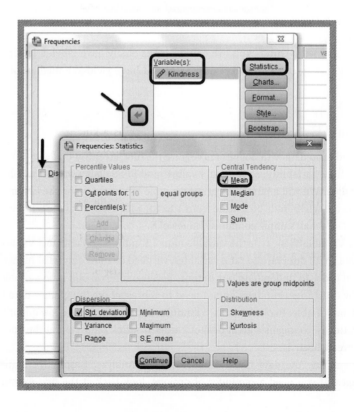

Click OK for output. The figure below shows the mean to be 7.17, and the standard deviation is 1.47.

Frequencies

Statistics

Kindness

N	Valid	6
	Missing	0
Mean		7.1667
Std. Deviation		1.47196

The output tells us that for our sample, the average rating of kindness for boyfriends and girlfriends is 7.17 on a scale from 1 to 10. The average deviation score is 1.47. The central tendency and variability values are sufficient to summarize the sample. As an added bonus, if we add and subtract 1.47 to/from the mean of 7.17, we can tell people where most of the kindness values fell in this sample.

$$7.17 - 1.47 = 5.70$$

$$7.17 + 1.47 = 8.64$$

The single best value to represent our data set is a kindness rating of 7.17 on a scale from 1 to 10, with most values falling between 5.70 and 8.64. In your report, you would write that $M = 7.17$ and $SD = 1.47$. Readers can calculate 5.70 and 8.64 if they are interested.

In real life, computer programs such as SPSS analyze the sample and provide output. Researchers rarely analyze their data using hand calculations. Throughout this text, each time a statistic is introduced, we will discuss the logic of the analysis, and then we will allow SPSS to work with the values. But be careful! You still have to think carefully about what you ask SPSS to do, and you will have to make sense of the output. Software is only the mindless worker. You are the boss.

SUMMARY

When designing studies, researchers choose either a correlational study or an experiment. Correlational research does not include manipulation, relying only on existing data. In contrast, an experimental study involves manipulation of an independent variable and measurement of a dependent variable as the outcome. Regardless of the type of design, all studies use variables: nominal, ordinal, interval, and ratio. Each type of data can be summarized using a measure of central tendency. Except for nominal data, variables must also be summarized with a measure of variability. Central tendency and variability are efficiently provided by SPSS, powerful computer software used by many psychologists.

REVIEW OF TERMS

Anchors

Block Random Assignment

Cohort

Confounding Variable (Confound)

Control Group

Correlational Study
(Correlational Design)

Cross-Sectional Study

Dependent Variable (DV)

Experiment (Experimental Design,
Experimental Study)

Extraneous Variable

Independent Variable (IV)

Individual Differences

Internal Validity

Interval Variable

Level of Measurement

Levels (groups, conditions, treatments)

Likert

Longitudinal Study

Mean *(M)*

Measure of Central Tendency

Median *(Mdn)*

Mode

Nominal Variable

Nuisance Variable

Ordinal Variable

Outlier

Qualitative

Quantitative

Random Assignment
(Simple Random Assignment)

Range

Rating Item

Rating Scale

Ratio Variable

Response Bias

Semantic Differential

Social-Desirability Response Bias   Variability

Standard Deviation (*SD*)   Visual Analogue

PRACTICE ITEMS

1. What is the main difference between a correlational study and an experimental study?

2. List some advantages and disadvantages of cross-sectional and longitudinal designs.

3. In the following study, identify the IV, levels of the IV, and DV. Hakeem wanted to know if people eat more ice cream when they are sad than when they are happy. He designed an experiment and randomly assigned people to watch either a sad video or a funny one. He then allowed participants to prepare a dish of ice cream and weighed the amount taken.

4. What is the difference between a confounding variable and a nuisance variable?

5. How can we increase internal validity and avoid confounds?

6. Describe the difference between a Likert scale and a semantic-differential scale. Give examples of each.

7. What are the four levels of measurement discussed in this chapter?

8. For the following, please indicate the level of measurement.

   a. Miles traveled

   b. Types of sports

   c. Gender

   d. Happiness rated on a 1-to-10 scale

   e. Income (dollars)

   f. Religious preference

   g. Sexuality—straight, bisexual, gay

   h. Time of day—morning, afternoon, evening

   i. Time of day—military time

   j. Length in inches

9. Using SPSS, find the appropriate measures of central tendency and variability for the following data sets, using correct abbreviations where needed.

   a. Depression, with higher numbers indicating more depression: 34, 25, 26, 35, 32, 32, 46, 28

   b. Temperature in degrees Fahrenheit: 102, 87, 21, 92, 98, 97, 101, 84

   c. Types of weather: Stormy, Sunny, Stormy, Light Drizzle, Sunny, Snow, Sunny, Sunny, Snow, Stormy

   d. Places in a race for your school: 2nd, 4th, 3rd, 7th, 8th

   e. Productivity, with higher values indicating more productivity: 5, 6, 4, 8, 7, 7, 4, 5, 9

   f. Gender: Female, Male, Male, Female, Transgender, Female, Female

REFERENCE

Garra, G., Singer, A. J., Taira, B. R., Chohan, J., Cardoz., E. C., & Thode, H. C., Jr. (2010). Validation of the Wong-Baker FACES Pain Rating Scale in pediatric emergency department patients. *Academic Emergency Medicine, 17*(1), 50–54. doi:10.1111/j.1553-2712.2009.00620.x

4

Learning About a Population From a Sample

When conducting research, we follow the scientific method to design studies and address a research question. Selecting a sample is a crucial part of the process because participants show us what is likely to happen in a larger group. We cannot test everyone in a population, but we can learn about a sample. In this chapter, we will discuss ways to select a sample and how we use a sample to guess, or infer, what would likely occur in the larger population from which the sample was chosen.

SELECTING A SAMPLE

As you pose a research question, you will identify which group of people you want to study. This group is called the **population** of interest. For example, if you want to learn about motivation among college students, all college students represent your population. On the other hand, if you want to study aggression among elementary-school children, young children define the population.

It should be obvious that researchers cannot study every person in a population of interest. Instead, we invite a smaller group of people to participate in our study. This smaller group is called a sample (recall this term from Chapter 2), and people who participate are called participants, as defined in Chapter 1. We study a sample and learn a new piece of information, such as college students are more motivated with a supportive instructor, or elementary-school children are more aggressive when they are frustrated. Because a study examines a sample of people from a larger population of interest, researchers assume that the information learned about a sample would be true for the larger population. That is, if we studied a sample of college students and learned that motivation is higher with a helpful instructor, we would assume that a helpful instructor would increase motivation among all college students in the population. **Generalizability** is the extent to which results from a sample likely would be true of the entire population. Recall from Chapter 2 that external validity refers to generalizing results beyond a specific

Population. The group of people a researcher is interested in studying is called the population of interest.

Generalizability. The extent to which results from a sample can be reasonably applied beyond the specific sample in the study indicates generalizability and reflects external validity.

study or setting. We hope for external validity so we can generalize beyond a specific sample to the entire population of interest.

Notice that we *assume* our results would be the same for the entire population. We cannot *know* for certain. After all, we study a sample, not the entire population. We infer from the sample to the population. We use **inferential statistics** to help us make estimates of what would happen in the population based on what we learned from the sample.

Random Sampling

Inferring back to the population from which we pulled the sample works best if the sample represents the population of interest. Such a sample is called, not surprisingly, a **representative sample**. How do we know if our sample represents the population from which it came? Again, we do not know. But we can use a procedure called **random sampling** to increase the chance of selecting a representative sample (also called **simple random sampling** or **random selection**). Random sampling requires everyone in the population of interest to have an equal chance of being selected for the sample. If everyone has an equal opportunity to be invited into the study, it is likely that our sample characteristics will represent the population characteristics. If we are studying motivation in college students, and the entire population of college students generally has a mean motivation of 6 on a scale from 1 to 10, it is highly likely that random sampling will produce a sample of college students with a mean motivation rating of 6. Researchers allow chance to work in their favor. By chance, the motivation value of 6 is the most likely to occur.

Inferential Statistics. Inferential statistics help researchers estimate what would happen in the population of interest based on sample outcomes.

Representative Sample. When a sample has the same characteristics as the population of interest, we call it a representative sample.

Random Sampling (Simple Random Sampling, Random Selection). Random sampling occurs when everyone in the population of interest has an equal chance of being selected for a study.

Cluster Sampling

A second method of random sampling from the population is **cluster sampling**. In this procedure, researchers find a way to put people into groups (or clusters) and randomly choose from the groups. Cluster sampling is a way to randomly sample from the population in a more streamlined way. If you were interested in learning about motivation across all college students, you might first sample by states, perhaps randomly choosing 10 states (or clusters). Within those 10 states you might randomly sample by colleges as clusters, choosing five colleges per state. Within those five colleges, you could randomly select 15 majors. In those majors, randomly select 50 students to contact and ask them to rate their motivation. Several layers of clusters as described here would be called **multistage sampling**, a term used when cluster sampling extends beyond two stages of sampling. Cluster sampling has obvious drawbacks, such as not including a state or college that would provide valuable and unique information. Note that this technique does increase external validity to all college students because it represents random sampling.

Stratified Random Sampling

A third method of random selection involves sampling from specific groups in the population to make sure all relevant groups are in the sample. Sampling important groups (strata) characterizes **stratified random sampling**. Researchers rely on stratified random sampling to obtain representation from different groups within the population. If a researcher wanted to learn about student attitudes toward a tuition increase, the sample should include first-year, sophomore, junior, and senior students. Because seniors usually represent the smallest cohort on campus, random sampling might result in too few from this group. To get a strong representation from all four classifications, the researcher could sample specifically within each group, **oversampling** from the seniors to make sure they are represented in the sample. When you prepare to collect a sample from the population, consider whether specific groups within the population should be represented, decide if you are in danger of selecting too few from the groups, and use stratified sampling to oversample as needed.

Note that stratified sampling and cluster sampling are quite different even though both methods sample using groups. Cluster sampling makes finding participants easier. Randomly selecting from population groups such as churches in a town before contacting participants in the selected churches is easier than randomly choosing from all people in an entire town. Imagine how much easier it would be to locate those who attend a few churches than to trek all over town locating randomly chosen individuals. On the other hand, stratified sampling allows a careful researcher to oversample from specific groups that might otherwise have little representation in the sample.

Cluster Sampling. In cluster sampling, researchers find a way to put people into groups (or clusters) and randomly choose from the groups. This procedure is a way to randomly sample from the population more efficiently.

Multistage Sampling. Multistage sampling occurs when cluster sampling has more than two stages of sampling.

Stratified Random Sampling. Stratified random sampling occurs when we sample from specific groups (or strata) in the population.

Oversampling. Oversampling refers to selecting a larger number of participants from underrepresented groups during stratified random sampling.

Convenience Sampling

As you have read, random sampling from the population can be accomplished in several ways, all of which require both planning and effort. Now let us talk about the sampling method used most often. Do researchers really go out to an entire population of interest and pull a sample? No. Usually a sample is pulled from the nearest group that is part of the population. When a college-student population is needed, researchers generally offer extra credit to students in a course such as Introduction to Psychological Science. Students who sign up are part of the sample. Notice that all students in college do not have a chance to be selected. Random sampling does not happen. Rather, the researchers rely on **convenience sampling**. Convenience sampling is considered a nonrandom sampling technique. Accepting volunteers has been called accidental sampling, but this term seems to indicate that the researcher had an accident rather than sought convenience.

Convenience sampling becomes **quota sampling** if specific segments of the population are targeted. If you wanted to study empathy across different ethnicities, you may want to keep accepting participants in underrepresented groups until you have filled a quota for those groups. Quota sampling ensures that all groups of interest are represented in a convenience sample. Filling a quota based on whoever volunteers remains a nonrandom sampling technique with limited external validity. Although important groups from the population are represented, you cannot know if volunteers reflect the general population.

We do not lose sleep over using a convenience sample because the study outcome can still teach the world an interesting truth about human behavior. Having this type of sample merely limits the extent to which we can say that results apply to all college students. In the motivation example, if our sample came from a specific university, we would write a manuscript that included the sample's origin. Every published manuscript should contain a section that describes the sample. Researchers not only reveal the geographical location of the sample but usually also include, at a minimum, gender, mean age, and ethnicities. When readers know details about the sample, they can think about how well the results might apply to a larger population.

As you can see, sampling from the population can be accomplished in several ways. Simple random sampling is the method most likely to produce a representative sample and allow the best generalizability to the larger population. When subsets of the population may not be chosen to participate, stratified sampling oversamples to gain valuable insights from all important groups. Cluster sampling streamlines random selection by selecting participants in stages. The researcher contacts people in the chosen clusters. Finally, convenience sampling occurs when a researcher accepts any participant from the population of interest. A sample of convenience may lack strong external validity, but it is the method most likely to produce a completed study!

BIAS IN A SAMPLE

Regardless of the sampling method you choose, the sample might not represent the population of interest. In other words, the sample may be biased. Bias can occur either when selecting the sample or during a study, and both can produce questionable results.

Selection bias, also called **sampling selection bias**, can happen when collecting a sample and usually is a problem with nonrandom methods such as convenience sampling. When researchers simply accept any willing participants from a population, the study is in danger of **self-selection bias**. Participants who volunteer may fail to represent the entire population. For instance, if you wanted to study all college students and tested only those who volunteered, the self-selected sample might be more motivated than the population of all college students. In fact, volunteers can differ from the general population in many ways, all of which would reduce external validity (generalizability to the population).

Even if you select a nonbiased sample, bias can occur during a study if some people drop out. Losing participants during a study is called **attrition**, also called **nonresponse bias** to indicate not completing all parts of a study. With attrition, you cannot know if the final sample represents the population of interest. Perhaps you asked elderly people to participate in a study to see if speed walking improved mental function. Soon after the study began, suppose half of the participants quit. It is possible that only physically healthy participants remained, limiting the external validity of results to healthier elderly individuals. If you found an increase in cognitive function after speed walking

Selection Bias (Sampling Selection Bias). Selection bias occurs when we choose participants in a way that alters our results.

Self-Selection Bias. When researchers accept any willing participants from a population, the study is in danger of self-selection bias, indicating that people who volunteer to participate may be different from the general population.

Attrition. Attrition defines the loss of participants during a study. Studies with high attrition rates do not have strong external validity because those who drop out of the study might be different from those who remain in the study.

Nonresponse Bias. Attrition that occurs when participants do not complete all parts of a study may lead to nonresponse bias.

versus no walking, the result may only be true for the physically active segment of the elderly population.

Attrition can also occur in only one of the groups tested, a situation called **differential attrition**. For example, imagine you have two groups: participants asked to eat crickets and those asked to eat bread. Assuming most people do not want to eat crickets, many people in that group likely will drop out of the study. The people who remain in the cricket condition may be quite different from the general population. As a result, differences between the two groups could be due to the type of people remaining rather than your experimental manipulation. What can you do about it? You might examine key characteristics of the two groups, such as motivation, open-mindedness, and sensation seeking. If the two groups do not differ on relevant key measures, you might argue that differential attrition did not compromise your study.

Differential Attrition. Differential attrition occurs when people in one level of a study drop out at a higher or lower rate than participants in the other level(s) of a study.

INFERENTIAL STATISTICS

Now that you understand several ways to select a sample and know the potential for bias, let us turn our attention to the research question. After a sample is selected, we can learn from participants. The information we collect from a sample should give us a good idea of what would be true of the entire population of interest. If we found that a sample of college students in Florida preferred beach vacations over vacations on a mountain trail, we would assume the same preference would be true of all college students in that state. In experiments, we manipulate what participants experience and assess their behavior. If we took a sample of Florida college students to hike the Appalachian Trail, participants might rate mountain vacations higher than the normal population of college students in the Sunshine State. Again we would assume the same result would be true of the entire population of Florida students who hike the trail. We would infer from the sample to the population.

Inferential statistics help us make an inference to the population. Throughout this book, we will explain several inferential statistics designed to address a research question about what would be expected in a population. Ultimately researchers want to know if their sample is different from what is normally found in the world. After all, an unusual outcome is interesting! To find out if our study yielded an outcome different from normal, we rely on SPSS. The software program will do the math, and we will make sense of the output. Inferential statistics and SPSS are powerful tools to address research questions.

If we want to know whether a group is different from normal, we have to know what normal looks like. For practice, let us consider IQ in the normal population, which has a mean of 100 and a standard deviation of 15. Imagine we went out into the world and collected thousands of samples and listed each mean IQ. Because we know the population mean IQ to be 100, what is the most likely sample mean? You guessed it: 100. Most sample means should be 100, but life is messy, so often you will get sample means similar to 100, such as 105 or 98. You are less likely to find a sample mean of 125 or 72 because these values are further from the normal population mean of 100. In fact, the further sample means are from 100, the less likely they will occur. We can visualize the normal population of values with a graph of **simple frequency**, symbolized by f. Simple frequency shows how often (frequently) a sample mean occurs.

We agreed that the most likely IQ sample mean should be 100 because the population mean is 100. A graph would show 100 as the value with the highest frequency, as illustrated by an elevated hump on a curve. Similar values, such as 105 and 98, occur with slightly lower frequencies than 100, as indicated by lower portions of the curve measured against the Y-axis (the vertical axis on the left side of a graph). Values of 125 and 72 occur with even lower frequencies. Consider the simple frequency graph below as an illustration of our discussion.

Simple Frequency
(f). Simple frequency represents the number of times a value occurs.

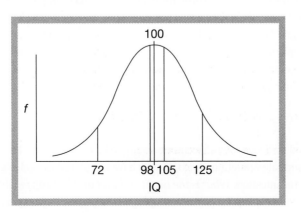

The IQ graph is a picture of the normal population. Normally, a sample's mean IQ is 100, with group mean values further away from 100 less and less likely. Our job as researchers is to locate an unusual outcome. In the IQ example, we might be interested in showing that people who took vitamins during childhood have a higher IQ than normal. We would hope to find a sample mean of people who take vitamins to be far in the right side of our IQ graph.

Regardless of the research question, we begin every study understanding that we may find nothing interesting. That sounds strange, but imagine a situation such as wanting to find out if playing a computer game makes people more intelligent. Suppose a company designs a new computer game and tries to make this claim. Scientific research can find out if playing the computer game actually increases intelligence. We return to the normal population of IQ scores. If the mean IQ of adults is 100, we would have to assume that people in the sample normally have an IQ of 100. Further, we would assume that 100 remains the IQ for people who play the new video game unless we find a value substantially different from 100.

If IQ after playing the game is 100 or near 100, we have found nothing interesting. On the other hand, we might get lucky and discover that the game enhances IQ, increasing the sample's mean IQ to a higher value, such as 105. Would you consider 105 to be very different from 100? Or would 105 be only a little bit different from 100? As a researcher, would you want to tell the world that the new video game enhances IQ? The IQ value of 105 may differ from 100 slightly, indicating that the video game did not truly increase IQ. Instead, such a slight difference may be explained by having a few smart people in the sample. A population mean IQ of 100 ensures that a sample mean of 100 is the *most likely* value to occur. However, life is imperfect, so a sample mean of 105 might not be considered meaningfully different from 100.

Sampling Error

When a sample mean is only a bit different from the population mean, researchers do not take credit for finding anything interesting. A small difference between the sample mean and population mean is called **sampling error**. In the IQ example, sampling error may indicate that a few people in the sample just happen to have high IQs. Even though we use the term sampling "error," the fault is not with the researcher. Randomly pulling a couple of unusual people is part of life. It happens. The good news is that inferential statistics require a sizable difference between the sample mean and population mean before we take credit for finding something interesting.

Sampling Error.
Sampling error occurs when a sample statistic such as the mean does not equal the population value because some unusual people were selected by accident.

Probability

With inferential statistics, we can examine a sample IQ of 105 and find out if it is unlikely to occur in a normal population of people who have not played the video game. With statistics, we ask the question: *What is the likelihood that an IQ of 105 would happen in the normal population of people who have not played the game?* A synonym for likelihood is

probability, defined by the chance of finding a specific result. To rephrase our research question: *What is the probability that an IQ of 105 would normally occur?* Researchers require that the probability, or likelihood, of such a value be rare in the normal population before the value is considered truly different from normal.

Recall the IQ graph of the normal population (below). Would you say 105 is truly different from 100 or merely sampling error? We would argue that a sample mean of 105 is not truly different from the normal population mean of 100.

Probability. In inferential statistics, probability is the likelihood that a result would happen in the normal population.

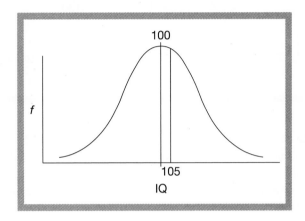

Probability is expressed in a proportion from 0 to 1. Multiplying probability by 100 yields percentage, and percentage ranges from 0 to 100. In psychology, scientists usually rely on a probability of .05 or less before taking credit for an interesting finding. In our example, a probability of .05 would mean that an IQ of 105 would have to happen 5% of the time or less in the normal population. On the other hand, if an IQ of 105 happens more often than 5% of the time in the normal population, we label the value sampling error and move on to another study. We would decide that 105 was not different from normal, and therefore the video game did not make people more intelligent.

Each time we design and run a study in psychology, we find out if our results are different enough from normal to take credit for finding something interesting or unusual. The magic 5% (or a probability of .05) is the tipping point where researchers are willing to say the result is unusual. A value so different from normal is highly unlikely. Of course, it is always possible that an unlikely value—even one that occurs less than 5% of the time normally—represents extreme sampling error. But science has chosen a probability of .05 as the point at which we will take credit for an intriguing discovery. We have to give ourselves credit at some point!

Let us add probability values and percentage to the IQ graph. Below we illustrate the population mean IQ of 100 and IQs at standard deviations of 15 (i.e., 55, 70, 85, 115, 130, 145). The values at the bottom of the graph show the probability of finding sample means of different values. As you can see, the probability of finding a sample IQ above 130 is .023. Because .023 is less than .05, we would agree that a sample mean IQ of 130 is rare.

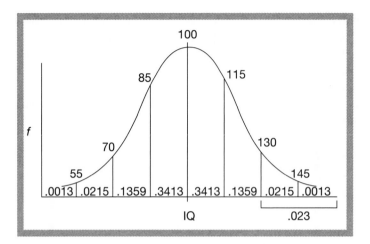

Critical Region.
In a graph of the
normal population,
the critical region
is where values
fall when they are
considered truly
different from
normal.

Our job is to decide if a sample mean is truly unusual. From the graph above, notice that only a few IQ means are shown. How would we make a decision about a sample mean IQ if the value did not appear on the graph (such as a sample mean of 105)? Fortunately, we live in a time with powerful computers. SPSS will calculate which values fall in the rare .05 (5%) ends of the normal graph. The .05 area is called the **critical region** to reflect the importance of finding a highly unusual result.

HYPOTHESIS TESTING

Null Hypothesis.
The null hypothesis
reflects the idea that
a sample will not
differ from the normal
population. Every
inferential statistic
in this book tests the
null hypothesis, and
researchers hope to
reject it in favor of the
research hypothesis.

**Research
Hypothesis.** The
research hypothesis
represents what
we expect to find
in a study. It is the
research question
in the form of a
statement.

We hope you now understand the normal population and know researchers hope to find an unusual result. In every study, with every research question, we consider what would be expected if *nothing* interesting happened. In other words, what would we find if our sample mean was not truly different from the population mean? The **null hypothesis** states what we would expect if nothing interesting happened. In the computer-game study, consider the null hypothesis: *IQ after playing the computer game will not differ from the normal population IQ of 100*. On the other hand, the **research hypothesis**, which reflects the research question, allows us to state our hope: *IQ after playing the computer game will be higher than the normal population IQ of 100*. We hope to reject the null hypothesis in favor of the research hypothesis.

SIGNIFICANCE

When sharing a result, psychologists communicate an unlikely event by saying the result was **significant** (also termed a **significant result**). Significance is a key word that means the result was so unlikely that it would happen 5% of the time or less in the normal population. In our video-game example, a significant effect means IQ after playing the game was so much higher than 100 that it happened less than 5% of the time normally. The game *significantly* improved IQ.

But wait. Could we explain such a rare occurrence by sampling error? Yes, every researcher knows even a significant effect could be explained by extremely bad sampling error. Although it is unlikely, perhaps we simply chose a sample with several highly intelligent people, and their IQ had nothing at all to do with playing video games. After all, unusual events do occur. Including a few participants with incredibly high intelligence would be unlikely, but sometimes unlikely events do happen.

Occasionally, researchers will report a significant finding when, in fact, the result was due to extreme sampling error. This problem is called a **Type I error** (type one). Conversely, at times researchers will say no effect existed when an effect did exist, but the method or sample did not reveal the meaningful effect. This problem is called a **Type II error** (type two). Which is worse? Neither. A Type II error fails to find significance, usually ensuring rejection from journals. A Type I error can get published and mislead readers, but remember that sampling error is not an error on the part of the researcher. It merely happens from time to time. All researchers understand the possibility, and as a community of scientists who publish, we know the truth eventually will emerge as empirical research continues. We follow the rules of hypothesis testing, report significance at the .05 level, and remain humble enough to know that science is not perfect.

Significant (Significant Result). A result that is so unlikely that it would happen 5% of the time or less in the normal population is considered significant.

Type I Error. Type I error is defined by finding a significant result when the result actually does not exist.

Type II Error. Type II error refers to finding no significant result even though the result does, in fact, exist.

Parametric Statistics.
Parametric statistics analyze interval or ratio data and are more powerful than nonparametric statistics. That is, parametric statistics are more likely than nonparametric statistics to reveal a significant outcome, if one exists.

Nonparametric Statistics.
Nonparametric statistics analyze nominal or ordinal data and are not as powerful as parametric statistics. That is, nonparametric statistics are not as likely as parametric statistics to reveal a significant outcome, if one exists.

p-value. The probability value used to indicate the likelihood of a result in the normal population is the p-value. Typically a p-value of .05 or less is considered significant.

Effect Size.
Effect size refers to the strength of a significant effect.

Power. Power is the ability to report a significant result when it is true.

p-VALUES AND EFFECT SIZE

Throughout this text, we will explain research designs and statistics used to analyze them. Researchers are rarely interested in just describing a sample. We use samples to make guesses about the larger population from which they came. Making guesses about populations based on samples requires inferential statistics.

Inferential statistics can be either parametric or nonparametric. The primary difference is the type of data collected, with **parametric statistics** used to analyze interval or ratio variables and **nonparametric statistics** used to analyze nominal or ordinal variables. In general, parametric statistics offer a greater chance of finding a significant outcome, if one exists. In various chapters, we will return to the concept of parametric versus nonparametric for different analyses. You will not be surprised to learn that researchers tend to design studies with data to be analyzed using parametric statistics. After all, when designing a study we want to maximize the likelihood of finding a significant outcome.

We will use SPSS to analyze data from many designs, and all will involve inferential results, including parametric and nonparametric options. Although each analysis begins with the idea that the sample may not differ from normal, we will take credit for an interesting finding if the outcome is so rare that it only happens 5% of the time or less in the normal population. We will take credit for a "significant" result.

Conveniently, SPSS provides the significance value and even calls it "Sig" on the output. We need only to look at the value to see if the probability of a result is .05 or less. If the sig value is .05 or less, we will have confidence that our result is unusual and can take credit for an interesting finding. APA style dictates that we report exact significance values and call them "**p-values**" to communicate probability. Notice that the p stands for probability, so "p-value" literally means "probability value." Researchers also must use three decimal places when reporting p-values. In this text, we will be sure to use three decimal places when reporting p-values in APA-style results sections.

APA style also requires writers to indicate the size of a significant effect. To be clear, if a significant effect (i.e., $p \leq .05$) is found, the **effect size** must be reported. For each inferential statistic in this textbook, we will explain how to obtain effect size as well as values for weak, moderate, and strong effects. Often, effect size can be requested from SPSS and will be on the output. If not, we will show you a simple way to pull some values from the output and calculate effect size.

POWER AND SAMPLE SIZE

It should be obvious that researchers hope to find an interesting result. We hope to find an outcome that occurs 5% of the time or less normally. Assuming we do not have a Type I error, we feel fairly confident reporting a significant finding. The ability to report a significant result when it is true is called **power**. Unfortunately, we never really know for certain that a result is truly different from normal. We can only run a controlled study using the scientific method and use a probability value of .05 or less. For our purposes, power is the ability to say we have a significant effect when we have followed the accepted rules of psychology (e.g., a p-value $\leq .05$).

One key way we can increase power is by using larger samples. A sample of 8,000 participants provides much more power—ability to find significance if it exists—than a sample of 20 people. You should already notice the potential problem here. Researchers can easily test 20 people, but 8,000 participants is an overwhelming number. At what point do we have a large enough sample? The answer is a balance point between increasing power while avoiding an impossibly large sample. And keep in mind that no matter how large a sample is, if no effect exists, one will not be found. A large sample cannot create an effect out of nothing. But a large sample increases the chance of finding *an effect that exists*.

To decide how many people are needed in a study, we must first know the design. Does the study have two groups? Or perhaps the design has three or more groups. Regardless of the design, power analysis will provide a number for how many people should be tested. In this textbook, we will address power analysis for research designs in relevant chapters. Before conducting a study, decide how many people should be in your sample to enhance the chance of finding significance if it exists. In other words, you need to know how many participants are needed to provide power to detect an effect. Without adequate power, you are in danger of making a Type II error: failing to find an effect when it actually exists.

Let us review. Power to find an effect if one exists increases with a larger sample size. If the effect is large, researchers have a good chance of getting a significant result with a smaller sample. If the effect is small, a larger sample might be needed to reveal the effect. Regardless, after an effect is found, APA requires us to calculate the size of the effect.

Showing effect size allows readers to decide if an outcome is meaningful. Certainly, a significant effect may be quite small but still emerge with a large sample. Suppose we asked people to rate the taste of a brand-name cereal and an off-brand version of the same type of cereal, such as fruity circles. If the two cereals are rated as tasting only slightly different, we have a better chance of finding such a difference with a large sample of tasters. We might show that the brand-name cereal indeed tastes significantly better than the off-brand cereal (i.e., $p \leq .05$), but the effect may be small. If taste is rated on a scale from 1 to 100, and the two cereals differed by 1 point on that scale, would it matter? With a small difference of only 1 taste point on a scale from 1 to 100, would you pay a lot more for the brand-name cereal? Probably not. Depending on the statistical test, the actual numbers associated with weak, moderate, and strong effect sizes will differ. Effect size will be addressed in this book with each statistical test.

Sample size and effect size work together to paint a clearer picture of study results. The reader deserves to have this information to decide which results are important in real life. A larger sample size can provide the power needed to find a significant effect. Statistics require information about sample size, and when separate groups are tested, analysis requires the number of people in each group. For this reason, APA style also includes degrees of freedom.

DEGREES OF FREEDOM

Degrees of freedom (*df*) is a term that refers to how many values are free to vary. If you have a group of sample values, most of the values can vary. Let us explain with an example.

Degrees of Freedom (*df*). The number of values free to vary in a data set is termed the degrees of freedom. The *df* are needed when analyzing data using inferential statistics and reporting outcomes in APA style.

Imagine we want to examine the number of tweets per day sent by eighth graders, and the true population mean is 12 tweets daily. Further imagine we collected a sample of eighth graders and asked them how many tweets they send per day. They reported 8, 10, 16, 12, and one other number. What would that number have to be in order to make the sample tweets mean of 12? The final number would have to be 14 for the sample mean to be 12 tweets. In fact, the sample could contain any numbers at all, but one of the values would have to bring the sample mean to 12. That is, all values are free to vary except one value.

As we explain each type of research design and related inferential statistic, we will return to the issue of df and explain the slightly different approach for each statistic. Usually SPSS provides df on the output, and we can use the output value(s) for an APA-style results section. When SPSS does not provide df, we will show you how to obtain the value using related output values. An APA-style results section must always include df to (1) provide information about the number of groups and/or sample size and (2) show values used to calculate final results. Ultimately df are needed to know whether or not an outcome was significantly different from the outcome that would be expected in the normal population.

SUMMARY

Regardless of your research question, answering it will require a sample. In this chapter, we discussed many ways to select participants, including random and nonrandom samples, as well as types of bias that might affect a study. When we conduct a study, our goal is to learn something about a sample and infer that the outcome would be true of the entire population. For instance, if attending yoga classes makes a sample of middle-aged men feel more relaxed, we assume the same would be true for all middle-aged men. To have confidence in a result, inferential statistics will assess the probability of finding a specific level of relaxation in middle-aged men normally, without yoga. If self-reported relaxation is lower after yoga, the value must be so rare that it occurs no more than 5% of the time normally (i.e., $p \leq .05$). Such a rare relaxation outcome would indicate a significant effect, and researchers can take credit for truly inducing relaxation through yoga. If the effect size is moderate or large, changes in relaxation may be worth the effort to engage in the behavior.

REVIEW OF TERMS

Attrition

Cluster Sampling

Convenience Sampling

Critical Region

Degrees of Freedom (df)

Differential Attrition

Effect Size

Generalizability

Inferential Statistics

Multistage Sampling

Nonparametric Statistics

Nonresponse Bias

Null Hypothesis

Oversampling

p-value

Parametric Statistics

Population

Power

Probability

Quota Sampling

Random Sampling (Simple Random
Sampling, Random Selection)

Representative Sample

Research Hypothesis

Sampling Error

Selection Bias (Sampling Selection Bias)

Self-Selection Bias

Significant (Significant Result)

Simple Frequency (*f*)

Stratified Random Sampling

Type I Error

Type II Error

PRACTICE ITEMS

1. What is the difference between random sampling and random assignment?

2. Why is it helpful to study a representative sample when conducting an experiment?

3. What is the difference between simple random sampling and convenience sampling?

4. What might be a drawback of convenience sampling with regard to external validity?

5. For each of the following, name the type of sampling.

   a. Khaleesi believes that owning pets makes 10-year-old children in her neighborhood do their homework. She decides to test this question by randomly choosing 20 children in her neighborhood. (Note that the population of interest is defined by children in her neighborhood.)

   b. Marco wondered if people who listen to classical music while working on a difficult puzzle will perform better than those who do not. He collected data using students in his music class, making sure to invite more Black and Asian individuals to participate since these groups are minorities on his campus.

   c.   Julian wants to know if church attendance and income are related. He goes to a local bank and surveys customers as they leave.

6.   Mary believes that consuming an energy drink will make adults run faster than consuming water. At a local farmer's market, she asks for volunteers. She records how long it takes volunteers to run 100 yards, gives them either an energy drink or water, and then records the 100-yard run again. Please answer the following:

   a.   What kind of sampling is Mary using?

   b.   What are some threats to external validity?

   c.   If Mary finds a p-value of .045, what does that mean?

7.   What is the relationship between probability and percentage?

8.   In inferential statistics, what is the magic number (so to speak) when it comes to deciding whether an effect is significant?

9.   Explain the difference between parametric and nonparametric statistics. Which type of analysis is more likely to find a significant result, if one exists?

10.   For the following studies, please write both a null and research hypothesis.

   a.   Sharon wonders whether adults or children will take more licks to finish a standard-size lollipop. She suspects children will take fewer licks.

   b.   Napoleon likes llamas. He knows that the average weight for a llama is 440 pounds. He wonders if llamas fed kitchen scraps are heavier or lighter than typical llamas but is unsure which way his research might go.

   c.   LaFawnda wants to start Internet dating. She wonders if women will respond more frequently to her messages if she includes a picture of herself.

11.   What is the difference between Type I and Type II error?

12.   What is power, and how can we increase it?

13.   When and why do we report effect size?

14.   Why is it important to report df?

CATEGORICAL VARIABLES AND SIMPLE FREQUENCY

5

One Variable With Frequency Data

Beginning with this chapter, we will introduce research designs that you are likely to use in your own research. As you learned in Chapter 4, you will want to know something about a sample so you can make guesses about what might be true of the larger population. Inference from a sample to a population relies on having a representative sample—which we generally assume we have—and using inferential statistics to analyze data.

RESEARCH DESIGN: CATEGORIZING PARTICIPANTS

The simplest research designs merely group people into categories. As you may remember, categorical data represent a simple, nominal variable. With nominal data, we must analyze values with a nonparametric statistic. Although nonparametric statistics are not as powerful as parametric statistics, sometimes the data call for such analyses. For example, suppose we wanted to know about favorite seasons among adults in Georgia. We could ask adults at a local grocery store to report their favorite season: winter, spring, summer, or fall.

ONE-WAY CHI SQUARE WITH EQUAL EXPECTED FREQUENCIES

For this example, the number of people picking each season represents simple frequency, which was defined in the prior chapter as how frequently a value occurs in a sample. If 40 people chose winter as their favorite season, the simple frequency for winter would be 40. In a design such as this, people are not allowed to pick more than one option. Given no other information, we might expect 25% of the sample to choose each of the four seasons. In other words, a "normal" expectation in this study might be 25% choosing winter, 25% picking spring, 25% saying summer, and 25% indicating fall as their favorite season. If we decided to ask this question of 100 people (our sample), we are saying that 25 people for each season would be our **expected frequency**, or the number we expect to find in each category. To be able to analyze these data, we must expect at least five people per group.

Expected Frequency. The number of people expected to fall in a category of a variable defines expected frequency.

Seasons	Winter	Spring	Summer	Fall
Expected Frequencies	25	25	25	25

Given a normal-population expectation of 25 people choosing each season, our null hypothesis would indicate that we expect to find no difference from 25% expected in each category. For this study, we would state the null hypothesis as follows: *Adults in Georgia prefer all four seasons equally.* Recall from Chapter 4 that inferential statistics test the null hypothesis. We begin each analysis assuming we will find nothing different from the normal population. Sure, we hope to reject the null hypothesis. We hope to reject the idea that our sample is just like the normal population. We want to find something new and interesting!

Notice above that we used the phrase "reject the null hypothesis" when we find something interesting. We also mentioned the phrase in Chapter 4. You might be wondering why we did not say "accept the research hypothesis" instead. Remember from Chapter 1 that one study can only *provide evidence* in support of a research hypothesis but never prove it to be true. If data analysis shows a meaningful effect, the effect is true based on the precise method we chose and the exact way we defined our variables.

We cannot know if every approach to studying the research hypothesis would yield a significant outcome. The best we can do with a significant outcome is say we reject the null hypothesis in favor of the research hypothesis. Together with other studies, we can build evidence for a research hypothesis and ultimately create a foundation for a theory.

In our study of Georgians, we hope to reject the null hypothesis that all seasons will be rated equally often as favorites. It might be reasonable to consider a different outcome because summer is extremely hot in Georgia and winters are mild. Perhaps students in Georgia prefer winter over other seasons, resulting in more than 25% picking winter and less than 25% choosing summer. Let us consider the research question to be addressed: *Do adults in Georgia have an unequal preference for the four seasons?* Changing the question to a statement would represent our research hypothesis: *Adults in Georgia do not equally prefer all seasons.* Our job as researchers would be to collect data and discover if what we found, or **observed frequencies**, differed from the 25% we might normally expect to find. Suppose we collected the following observed frequencies.

Seasons	Winter	Spring	Summer	Fall
Observed Frequencies	40	20	15	25

Our goal now is to find out if what we observed, a 40-20-15-25 split, was different from the 25-25-25-25 split we expected. Sure, the values look different, but remember that the values have to be different enough to reasonably say they are different from the normal (expected) population of 25-25-25-25. We can never just assume that any difference is meaningful. We must rely on probability, as discussed in Chapter 4. If the difference between expected frequencies and observed frequencies is large enough to be very *unlikely* in the normal population, we can take credit for finding something interesting in our sample of Georgians. Otherwise a small difference between observed and expected frequencies might simply reflect sampling error. But how do we find out if the difference is truly unlikely? We turn to inferential statistics.

Frequency data are analyzed using the **chi square** (χ^2) statistic. A χ^2 with one variable is called a **one-way** χ^2. A one-way χ^2 can have two or more levels. In our example, the variable has four levels. Using the one-way χ^2 we can find out if a 40-20-15-25 split across seasons is meaningfully different from a 25-25-25-25 split. In other words, we want to know if what we observe is significantly different from what we expect. Would a split of 40-20-15-25 occur no more than 5% (.05 probability) of the time in the normal population of people from all geographic locations? If the difference between what we expected and what we observed is significant, we will have something interesting to say about adults in Georgia. Our question can be addressed using SPSS.

Observed Frequency. The number of people in a sample who actually fall in each category of a variable defines observed frequency.

Chi Square (χ^2). Chi square is the statistic used to analyze simple frequency data, often defined by how many participants fall in a specific category.

One-Way χ^2 (Goodness-of-Fit Test). The one-way χ^2 is a statistic used to analyze frequency data from one variable of interest, regardless of the number of variable levels.

SPSS: One-Way Chi Square With Equal Expected Frequencies

Open SPSS and go to Variable View to enter Seasons as the variable to be analyzed. Using the steps detailed in Chapter 3, label values as 1 = winter, 2 = spring, 3 = summer, and 4 = fall. Next click OK and move to Data View to enter data.

Under Seasons, type a 1 (winter) in the number of cells representing observed frequencies for winter. We enter a 1 in the first cell and copy/paste the 1 into 39 more cells below to represent the 40 people in the sample who reported winter as their favorite season. Beginning in the 41st cell, enter 20 values of 2 for the 20 people who chose spring as their favorite season, and so on. Make sure you have 100 values when all observed frequencies are entered because the sample contains 100 participants. Below is a screenshot that shows a change in values from 1 to 2 as you continue to enter the data. The picture does not show where values changed from 2 to 3 at cell 61 or from 3 to 4 at cell 76, but you get the idea.

Seasons
1.00
1.00
1.00
1.00
1.00
1.00
1.00
1.00
1.00
1.00
2.00
2.00
2.00

When you are satisfied with data entry, click View, and check the box to the left of Value Labels to see the seasons represented by values. On the screenshot below, 1 now shows as winter, and 2 shows as spring. The remaining 2 levels, summer and fall, continue beneath the first two levels.

To analyze these data, click Analyze, Nonparametric Tests, Legacy Dialogs, Chi-square.

In the box that opens, click on Seasons and move it to the right under Test Variable List using the arrow key between the two boxes. Because we already entered observed frequencies in the spreadsheet, we must tell SPSS what we expected to find. Only then can SPSS analyze a potential difference between what we expected and what we observed. Under Expected Values, the default setting is "All categories equal." In our example, we did indeed expect all categories to have equal frequencies, with winter, spring, summer, and fall having 25 people in each category. Next click OK.

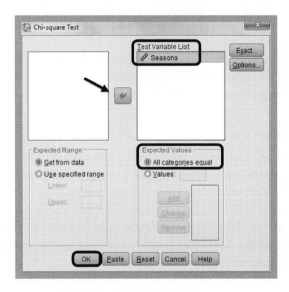

The output is below. We scrolled down a bit in the output to create a screenshot of the main data.

Chi-Square Test

Frequencies

Seasons

	Observed N	Expected N	Residual
winter	40	25.0	15.0
spring	20	25.0	-5.0
summer	15	25.0	-10.0
fall	25	25.0	.0
Total	100		

Test Statistics

	Seasons
Chi-Square	14.000[a]
df	3
Asymp. Sig.	.003

a. 0 cells (0.0%) have expected frequencies less than 5. The minimum expected cell frequency is 25.0.

Observed and expected frequencies appear in the first table. Make sure they reflect the data accurately. Next, look at the Test Statistics table to see the chi-square result as well as degrees of freedom (*df*) and the significance value. You can calculate *df* by subtracting 1 from the number of variable levels (4), which explains *df* = 3 on the output. A significance value of .05 or less indicates an unusual result. In the one-way χ^2, an unusual result means what we observed, 40-20-15-25, was significantly different from what we expected, 25-25-25-25. That is, we did *not* find an equal split across all four seasons when we asked participants in Georgia which season they liked best.

Effect Size: Cohen's *w*

With a significant outcome, we also need to report effect size. Simply begin with the chi-square value (14), divide by the sample size (100), and take the square root to get .37. This calculation is called **Cohen's *w***, and it is reported as *w* = .37. Cohen (1988) indicated that for χ^2, an effect size of .10 is small, .30 is medium, and .50 or beyond is a large effect. We have answered our research question: *Do adults in Georgia have an unequal preference for the four seasons?* Yes, adults in Georgia picked their favorite season in an unusual pattern, with a medium effect size.

Cohen's *w*. When a one-way χ^2 shows a significant relationship, Cohen's *w* provides a measure of effect size.

Recall the null hypothesis: *Adults in Georgia prefer all four seasons equally.* Because we found a significant difference from normal, we can reject the null hypothesis in favor of the research hypothesis: *Adults in Georgia do not equally prefer all seasons.* Again notice that the research question translates smoothly into the research hypothesis. Simply change the research question into a statement to produce the hypothesis.

APA Style for the One-Way Chi Square With Equal Expected Frequencies

As psychologists, we rely on APA style to guide the way we share research. When writing a manuscript, an APA-style method section describes participants and specifies data-collection procedures. Describing participants helps readers decide if results can generalize beyond the sample. Recall that researchers usually report participants' gender, age, and ethnicity. In the following example method section, we report fictional values for demographics and offer procedural details. Carefully examine the method section so you will be able to write your own when needed. Throughout this book, we will present APA-style method and results sections. Our only deviation from APA style will be single spacing some of the lines. You should double space your papers.

Method

Participants

One hundred adults (48 men and 52 women) in a Georgia grocery store participated in this study. Our sample consisted of 39 White, 47 Black, and 14 Latino adults, with a mean age of 46.31 years ($SD = 14.07$). All participants received ethical treatment, and the IRB approved the procedure.

Procedure

The researcher stood near checkout lanes in a grocery store and identified adults as those appearing to be over the age of 18 years and paying for their groceries. The researchers asked participants to report their favorite season: winter, spring, summer, or fall. Shoppers also reported whether they resided in Georgia as well as their age and ethnicity.

Immediately after the method section, we include a results section. To do this, we must return to SPSS output and pull relevant information. We need the χ^2 value, df, sample size, significance value (p-value), and the effect size we calculated. This information tells readers that adults in Georgia showed an interesting pattern of favorite seasons. We also must tell our readers what we expected and what we actually found for each season. Again notice that the SPSS output provides all relevant information. Although the p-value requires three decimal places, χ^2 and Cohen's w require two decimal places. When reporting percentages, you have some flexibility in number of decimal places, just be consistent across all percentages within the results section.

Results

We used a one-way χ^2 to analyze the data on favorite season among adult Georgia residents. What we observed differed significantly from what we expected to find, $\chi^2(3, N = 100) = 14.00, p = .003, w = .37$. Although we expected 25% of Georgia residents to choose winter as their favorite season, 40% chose winter. Further, 20% chose spring rather than the 25% we expected. For summer, only 15% indicated this season as their favorite rather than 25%. Finally, we expected 25% to choose fall as their favorite season, and in fact 25% did choose fall.

Based on the research design of simple frequency data on one variable, we analyzed the data using a one-way χ^2. The SPSS output revealed a significant effect. See that we are not asking if more people like one season compared with another season. We do not compare observed frequencies to each other. Instead, we compare all observed frequencies to all expected frequencies to see if the patterns differ. Do not make the mistake of saying more Georgia residents like winter than any other season. We could only say more people chose winter as their favorite season *than we expected*. Review the results section above and see that the last four sentences compare each expected frequency to each observed frequency.

Power

Recall from Chapter 4 that power is tied to how many participants are needed in your study to have a good chance of finding an effect, if one exists. You should run power analysis before a study to help you plan how many participants to select. If your study fails to reveal significance, one possible reason is a small sample.

For power analysis, researchers often turn to Cohen (1992) or G*Power (Faul, Erdfelder, Lang, & Buchner, 2007), a free program downloadable at www.gpower. hhu.de. For the chi-square analysis, remember that Cohen (1988) suggests .10 for a weak effect, .30 for a moderate effect, and .50 or greater for a strong effect. In general, researchers assume their effect will be moderate (.30) at the $p = .05$ level if they have no other information such as prior research indicating a different effect size. We do not want to assume a large effect because too few participants may be recommended. On the other hand, we do not want to assume a small effect because a huge sample size would be suggested. A medium effect usually is a safe bet if you have no information to suggest otherwise.

We have created a table for your use throughout this book when considering power and the number of participants needed. Values were pulled from Cohen (1992) or calculated using G*Power (Faul et al., 2007). The entire table is located in Appendix A, but here we offer relevant values for the χ^2. Numbers within the table represent total recommended sample size (N).

	Small Effect Size	Medium Effect Size	Large Effect Size
Chi square χ^2			
1 *df*	785	88	32
2 *df*	964	108	39
3 *df*	1091	122	44
4 *df*	1194	133	48
5 *df*	1293	143	52
6 *df*	1363	152	55

The table indicates that we need 122 participants to detect a moderate effect size if one exists with four categories (3 *df*). Had we calculated power before running our study, we would have known that we needed to collect data from 22 more people than we did, for a total of 122 individuals. Because our actual effect size of .37 was higher than .30, we were able to find a significant effect without those additional participants. Power analysis offers a good plan for number of participants. If you get significant results using fewer than the recommended participant number, more power to you.

ONE-WAY CHI SQUARE WITH UNEQUAL EXPECTED FREQUENCIES

In the seasons example, we had no reason to expect anything different from an even split of participants across the four variable levels. We were able to divide the sample equally across winter, spring, summer, and fall. However, an equal split would not be expected in all studies. For example, variables such as wearing braces or not, hair color, and owning a flip-phone versus a more contemporary cell phone would not be expected to have an equal number of people across groups. In other words, we would not expect equal frequencies across all levels of the variables. How would we figure out what to expect in a normal population? We would search published information such as peer-reviewed journal articles owned by the library, or we might look at government publications or websites with recent statistics. Often a bit of research will yield the percentage of people who generally fall in one category or another (e.g., black, brown, red, or blond hair).

Let us consider an in-depth example with unequal expectations across groups. Suppose you spotted a lot of students on your campus smoking cigarettes, and you wonder if smoking on your campus is unusually prevalent. You might want to know how many college students on campus smoke cigarettes based on two categories: Yes and No. If you read available publications and found the national average for smoking cigarettes to be about 18% (as of 2013; Centers for Disease Control and Prevention, 2015), you would begin your study with the expectation that 18% of your sample will report smoking as well. Consider the research question: *Is smoking on my college campus higher than the national average of 18%?* The research question is reflected in the research hypothesis: *Smoking on my college campus is higher than the national average of 18%.* You must begin a study expecting your sample to be normal (i.e., similar to the larger population). An uninteresting outcome would be stated in the null hypothesis: *Smoking on my college campus is the same as the national average of 18%.*

Data collection might involve standing outside of the cafeteria and asking people to report whether or not they smoke. Or you might send students a survey link. No matter how you collect the Yes/No responses, the data will be simple: How many people in a sample reported Yes, and how many people responded with No? Each participant must pick one category or the other, and no individual person can choose both Yes and No. When you have collected answers from members of the population, you can analyze the data.

Remember that when we only have one variable of interest, such as whether or not people smoke, we analyze data with a one-way χ^2. We already know from reading the literature that about 18% of people smoke nationwide, therefore we use that number to calculate expected frequencies. If we decided to collect answers from 200 college students, 18% of 200 is 36 (200 × .18), which is what we would expect to find if our sample is similar to the larger population. For the nonsmoking category, we would expect to find the remaining 164 participants.

Smoking Category	Smoker	Nonsmoker
Expected Frequencies	36	164

Assume you collected data from 200 college students on your campus and found that 45 students reported smoking cigarettes. The other 155 students reported not smoking.

Smoking Category	Smoker	Nonsmoker
Observed Frequencies	45	155

Certainly a 45/155 split is different from the expected 36/164 split, but inferential statistics answer the question "Is the difference from normal different *enough* to be meaningful?" In other words, can we reject the null hypothesis in favor of the research hypothesis? We turn to SPSS for data analysis.

SPSS: One-Way Chi Square With Unequal Expected Frequencies

Open SPSS, click to Variable View, and enter the variable of Smoking. Under Values, label 1 = Smoker and 2 = Nonsmoker. Then click OK and open Data View.

Under the Smoking column, enter 45 values of 1 to indicate 45 people who reported smoking. At the 46th line and in the same column, enter 155 values of 2 to represent 155 people who reported not smoking. Click View and choose Value Labels to see words on the screen rather than numbers. Refer to the first example in this chapter for screenshots, as needed.

To analyze these data, click Analyze, Nonparametric Tests, Legacy Dialogs, Chi-square as you did before. In the box that opens, move Smoking to the right by clicking the arrow button between the boxes. Next click Values under Expected Values. Here you will enter the exact expected frequencies, which included 36 people expected to report smoking and 164 people expected to report not smoking in our example. (In other data sets, expected frequencies may calculate to be decimals rather than whole numbers, and you should round expected frequencies to two decimal places before entering them into SPSS.) Enter 36 in the box next to Values and click Add. Return to the Values box, delete 36 and write 164, then Add this value as well. Be sure to enter expected frequencies in the same order as the data: 1 = Smoker and 2 = Nonsmoker.

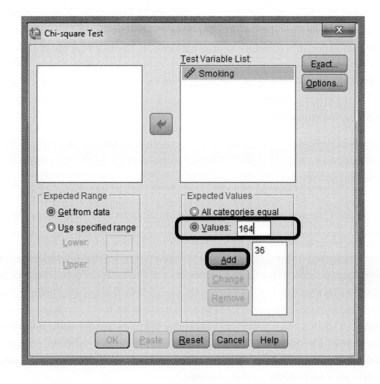

Now that the two expected frequencies have been entered, click Options in the upper right corner. In the new box that opens, place a check to the left of Descriptive. Click Continue and OK, just as you did in the prior example.

In the output below, the table labeled Smoking confirms that we entered the correct data for SPSS to read. Be sure the observed and expected frequencies match your sample data, and note that sample size (N) appears in the first column of values. The final table, Test Statistics, provides a χ^2 value, df, and a significance value, which of course we hope is equal to or less than .05. As you learned, df is the number of variable levels minus 1 ($2 - 1 = 1$ df).

Chi-Square Test

Frequencies

Smoking			
	Observed N	Expected N	Residual
Smoker	45	36.0	9.0
Nonsmoker	155	164.0	-9.0
Total	200		

Test Statistics	
	Smoking
Chi-Square	2.744[a]
df	1
Asymp. Sig.	.098

a. 0 cells (0.0%) have expected frequencies less than 5. The minimum expected cell frequency is 36.0.

The significance value is not at or below .05, which means we cannot say observed frequencies significantly differed from expected frequencies. Our sample did not differ from the normal population of 18% smoking and 82% not smoking. Recall the research question: *Is smoking on my college campus higher than the national average of 18%?* No, the chi-square inferential statistic shows that students on campus do not differ from the expected 18% smoking and 82% not smoking. Did you simply need a larger sample to reveal a significant effect? Not likely. Power analysis called for 88 participants to reveal a medium effect, and the sample actually contained 200! You had a good chance of finding a significant effect if one existed. However, if a small effect existed, you would have needed 785 participants to reveal it. Refer to the power table earlier in the chapter as needed.

APA Style for the One-Way Chi Square With Unequal Expected Frequencies

Once again we turn to APA style to share research. Our method section contains example demographic information for participants and a hypothetical procedure. Notice that we report details on how we operationalized smoking versus not smoking. Results follow immediately after the method section.

Method

Participants

Participants included 200 adults (102 women and 98 men) attending a northeastern college in the United States. Ethnicities included 115 Caucasian, 62 Asian American, and 21 African American individuals with a mean age of 20.02 years ($SD = 3.87$). Two people chose not to disclose their ethnicities. All participants received ethical treatment, and the IRB approved the procedure.

Procedure

Upon entering the study, students completed informed consent. The researcher defined smoking behavior as smoking cigarettes at least 2 days each week for the past 4 weeks. Participants categorized themselves as smokers or nonsmokers based on the researcher's definition. Finally, participants shared demographic information concerning their gender, age, and ethnicity, and the researcher thanked them for their time.

Results

We used a one-way χ^2 to analyze the data of smoking prevalence among college students on a northeastern campus. What we observed failed to differ significantly from what we expected to find, $\chi^2(1, N = 200) = 2.74, p = .098$. We expected 18.0% of our sample of students to report smoking, and our observed frequency of 22.5% illustrated no significant difference from our expectation. Further, we expected 82.0% of our sample to report not smoking, and the observed frequency of 77.5% represented a similar outcome.

SUMMARY

In this chapter, we discussed how to answer a research question that addressed only one variable of interest (e.g., smoking behavior) and the number of participants in each category. For research designs assessing simple frequency in each category, the one-way χ^2 is the best statistic to use. Whether frequencies are expected to be equal or unequal across all levels of a variable, researchers must specify expected frequencies before collecting data. SPSS will analyze the potential difference between expected frequencies and those actually observed in a sample. Researchers generally hope to find an outcome different from expectations.

REVIEW OF TERMS

Chi Square (χ^2)   Observed Frequency

Cohen's w One-Way χ^2 (Goodness-of-Fit Test)

Expected Frequency

PRACTICE ITEMS

1. What is the difference between expected frequency and observed frequency?

2. What is another term for one-way χ^2?

3. What is the minimum expected frequency is needed in each category to be able to use a one-way χ^2?

4. What is the formula for *df* for the one-way χ^2?

5. For the χ^2 analysis, what Cohen's w values represent weak, moderate, and strong effects?

***

For each of the following studies, (a) restate the research question as a research hypothesis, and state the null hypothesis, (b) determine how many participants are needed for adequate power, and (c) enter and analyze the data as well as write APA-style results sections. Be sure to read over the method sections we provided.

6. Gingerich and Lineweaver (2014) found that students who texted during a lecture performed worse on a postlecture quiz, which worries you because you have been observing your classes and calculated that students tend to fall equally into categories of not texting at all (0 texts per hour), texting a little (1–5 texts per hour), texting a moderate amount (6–10 texts per hour), and texting a lot (more than 10 texts per hour). You are interested in seeing if students who know about the Gingerich and Lineweaver study continue to text in class, so you tell your students about these findings. In the next hour, 35 students do not text at all, 40 of them text a little, 37

of them text a moderate amount, and 13 of them text a lot. You want to answer this question: *If students hear that texting during class negatively affects grades, will this change texting frequencies from what normally occurs?*

Method

Participants

   In this study, 125 college students (68% women; mean age = 22.22, *SD* = 2.59) in a single First-Year Experience course participated. All participants received ethical treatment, and the IRB approved the procedure.

Procedure

   At the beginning of a class period with a lecture on how to make good grades in college, the instructor made the statement, "Today we will learn about different factors that can affect grades. For example, a study recently found that students who text during a lecture make lower grades on a quiz." After the statement, the lecture continued as planned for 1 hr. During the lecture, a team of six graduate students noted how many times each student texted.

---

7. According to the Centers for Disease Control (CDC), cancer and heart disease accounted for about half of American deaths in 2010 (CDC, 2014). You are interested in seeing if you can help people get healthier, so you recruit adults and place them on a two-year diet and exercise program. At the end of the two years, you send them all to a doctor who tells you that 41 of them have signs of heart disease, and the other 75 do not. You wonder: *Did my sample of people who were put on a healthy diet and exercise program show lower rates of heart disease than the overall U.S. population?*

Method

Participants

   Participants included 116 adults (66 women and 50 men) recruited from a gym in Greenbow, Alabama. Ethnicities included 89 White, 25 Black, and 2 Asian individuals with a mean age of 32.57 years (*SD* = 10.07). All participants received ethical treatment, and the IRB approved the procedure.

Procedure

Researchers met with participants as a group and explained the diet and exercise program to them. As required, participants stopped eating sugar and increased their fruit and vegetable intake to 3 and 5 servings, respectively. Additionally, all participants agreed to exercise 4 to 5 times each week for 30 min per workout. At the end of 2 years, participants visited their doctors and reported whether they had any signs of heart disease.

8. You came across a news article finding that among historically black colleges and universities (HBCUs), 63.8% of students reported using a condom during their most recent sexual encounter (Bcheraoui, Sutton, Hardnett, & Jones, 2013). You wonder if the same is true for non-HBCU campuses, asking the research question: *Is frequency of condom usage different on non-HBCU than on HBCU campuses?* You anonymously survey 140 college students across 15 non-HBCU campuses (selected randomly) in the United States and find that 84 of your respondents used a condom during their most recent sexual encounter, and 56 did not.

Method

Participants

Students (53 women, 85 men, and 2 nonbinary individuals) from 15 colleges not classified as historically black colleges and universities (HBCUs) in the United States provided survey data anonymously. Students reported their ages, with a mean student age of 18.17 ($SD = 0.87$), and ethnicities included 92 White, 36 Black, 10 Latino, and 2 Filipino individuals.

Procedure

Using a national registry, we divided colleges into HBCU and non-HBCU lists. We then randomly selected 15 colleges on the non-HBCU list. College newspapers on the chosen institutions published a link to the survey. Survey questions included age, gender, ethnicity, and the question, "In your most recent sexual encounter, did you use a condom?"

9. A recent study by Jackson, Steptoe, and Wardle (2015) showed that of women who quit smoking, 10% were able to quit if their partner continued to smoke, 67% gave up smoking if their partner quit at the same time, and 23% were able to quit if their

partners were nonsmokers. These data were collected from married or cohabitating couples, but you are interested in finding out if the same might be true for couples not living together. You ask the research question: *Is the pattern of smoking cessation for women different for couples who live apart than it is for couples living together?* You find a national social media page dedicated to people trying to quit smoking and place an advertisement for participants. You are looking for potential female quitters who are in serious relationships but not cohabitating. You pay participants $10 for completing your survey and find that the following women are able to quit smoking: 4 with smoking partners, 72 with partners who quit smoking at the same time, and 44 with nonsmoking partners.

Method

Participants

We recruited 120 women (mean age = 37.50, *SD* = 10.02). Ethnicities included 60 White, 40 Black, and 20 mixed-race individuals.

Procedure

We posted an advertisement including a link to the two-part survey on a national social media page dedicated to people trying to quit smoking. In the advertisement, we stated that the researchers sought individuals identifying as women, actively trying to stop smoking, and in serious relationships but not cohabitating. Each participant received $10 for completing both surveys. The first survey asked about age and relationship status. The second survey, sent 2 months later, asked whether the women quit smoking.

REFERENCES

Bcheraoui, C. E., Sutton, M. Y., Hardnett, F. P., & Jones, S. B. (2013). Patterns of condom use among students at historically Black colleges and universities: Implications for HIV prevention efforts among college-age young adults. *AIDS Care, 25*(2), 186–193. doi:10.1080/09540121.2012.687864

Centers for Disease Control and Prevention. (2014). Chronic disease prevention and health promotion. Retrieved from http://www.cdc.gov/chronicdisease/overview/

Centers for Disease Control and Prevention. (2015). Current cigarette smoking among adults in the United States. Retrieved from http://www.cdc.gov/tobacco/data_statistics/fact_sheets/adult_data/cig_smoking/index.htm

Cohen, J. (1988). *Statistical power analysis for the behavioral sciences*. Hillsdale, NJ: Lawrence Erlbaum.

Cohen, J. (1992). A power primer. *Psychological Bulletin, 112*(1), 155–159. doi:10.1037/0033-2909.112.1.155

Faul, F., Erdfelder, E., Lang, A.-G., & Buchner, A. (2007). G*Power 3: A flexible statistical power analysis program for the social, behavioral, and biomedical sciences. *Behavior Research Methods, 39*, 175–191. doi:10.3758/BF03193146

Gingerich, A. C., & Lineweaver, T. L. (2014). OMG! Texting in class = U fail: Empirical evidence that text messaging during class disrupts comprehension. *Teaching of Psychology, 41*(1), 44–51. doi:10.1177/0098628313514177

Jackson, S. E., Steptoe, A., & Wardle, J. (2015). The influence of partner's behavior on health behavior change: The English longitudinal study of ageing. *Journal of the American Medical Association Internal Medicine, 175*(3), 385–392. doi:10.1001/jamainternmed.2014.7554

6

Two Variables With Frequency Data

As you read in Chapter 5, the one-way chi square (χ^2) analyzes a design with one variable and at least two levels. Prior to collecting data, expected frequencies might be equal across levels of the variable, or expected frequencies might be unequal across levels, depending on what logically would be expected in a normal population. Remember that the outcome data in a χ^2 reflect how many people fall in each level, or group, of the variable. The χ^2 analyzes only simple frequency data.

RESEARCH DESIGN: TWO CATEGORICAL VARIABLES

A second type of χ^2 analyzes two variables with at least two levels each. Because two variables are in such a design, the statistic is called a **two-way** χ^2. An example of a two-variable design would be whether or not people eat breakfast and if they are underweight, have weight within the normal range, or are overweight. (For more about breakfast and weight, see O'Neil, Nicklas, & Fulgoni, 2014.) The first variable asks a question about breakfast, and participants will fall into one of the two categories. Eating breakfast might be operationally defined as consuming a minimum of 200 calories at least five mornings per week, on average, over the past six months. Next, participants will report their height in inches and weight in pounds for a body mass index (BMI) designation of underweight, normal weight, or overweight, as defined by the Centers for Disease Control (CDC, 2015). Just as with the one-way χ^2, the outcome is frequency, or the number of people who fall into each category. As you know, categorical, or nominal, data are analyzed using nonparametric statistics. In the two-way χ^2, people will fall in one category of the first variable and one category of the second variable.

Other than the number of variables, the two-way design differs from the one-way design in the question it addresses. The one-way design aims to find out if observed frequencies are different from what is expected in the normal population. Is the sample somehow different from normal expected frequencies? On the other hand, the two-way design asks if the two variables are related to each other. As we run a study and begin to analyze data, we always assume the null hypothesis until we can refute it. In the two-way χ^2, state the null hypothesis: *The two variables are not related.* In other words, the two

Two-Way χ^2. A two-way χ^2 analyzes research designs with two variables of interest and an outcome of simple frequency.

variables are independent of each other. Of course, we hope to reject the null hypothesis in favor of the research hypothesis: *The two variables are related*. In our example, the design and analysis would tell us if whether or not people ate breakfast was related to whether they were underweight, normal weight, or overweight. We can state our research question: *Is whether or not people eat breakfast related to their body-weight category?* For a testable hypothesis, we merely change the question to a statement: *Whether or not people eat breakfast is related to their body-weight category.*

Because the two-way χ^2 does not rely on specifying expected frequencies, we do not trouble ourselves with making guesses about how the observed frequencies will look. We merely choose two variables of interest, decide on their levels, and collect observed frequencies. In the breakfast-weight example, participants will report their answer to the two questions (variables).

TWO-WAY CHI SQUARE: 2 × 3 DESIGN

A table of the design is below, and fictional data have been entered for observed frequencies. Imagine we collected information from 250 participants. Note the six boxes, or **cells**, in the design. We call this particular two-way χ^2 a 2 × 3 ("two by three") design because we have two levels of one variable and three levels of the other variable. The six cells are the boxes resulting from a two-way design. In fact, 2 × 3 = 6, which equals the number of cells. A single participant can be listed in only one cell.

Cells. Cells are the boxes of data represented in a two-way design. For example, a 2 × 3 design contains six cells.

	Underweight	Normal Weight	Overweight
Eat breakfast (usually)	20	59	34
Do not eat breakfast (usually)	42	25	70

Power

How many participants will we need? Recall from Chapter 5 that we might assume a moderate effect size and rely on a *p*-value of .05. The only remaining question is the degrees of freedom (*df*) in the design. Whether or not people eat breakfast represents two categories of the first variable (yes or no) and three categories of weight class (under, normal, or overweight). With a two-way χ^2, the *df* value is calculated by subtracting 1 from the number of each variable's levels and multiplying the values. In this example, *df* = (# of breakfast levels – 1) × (# of weight categories – 1) = 1 × 2 = 2. In the table below (and also in Appendix A), χ^2 with 2 *df* relies on 108 participants to find a significant medium-sized effect at the *p* = .05 level.

Chi Square χ^2	Small Effect Size	Medium Effect Size	Large Effect Size
1 *df*	785	88	32
2 *df*	964	108	39
3 *df*	1091	122	44
4 *df*	1194	133	48
5 *df*	1293	143	52
6 *df*	1363	152	55

Note: Numbers in the table represent **total** sample size.

SPSS: 2 × 3 Chi Square

To enter these data into SPSS, open the program and go to Variable View. Enter Breakfast as the first variable (although you could enter weight first because the order does not matter), with 1 = Yes and 2 = No. Enter Weight as the second variable, and label Values of 1 = Underweight, 2 = Normal Weight, and 3 = Overweight. Click OK and change to Data View.

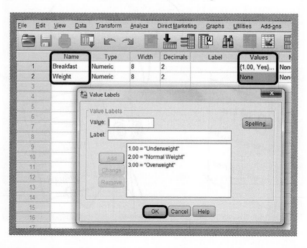

The first cell of your data contains 20 people. We need to enter 20 rows of data to represent people who eat breakfast and are underweight. In the first column, enter a 1 for eating breakfast, and in the second column enter a 1 for underweight. This first row represents the first participant in the first cell. Nineteen more rows depict the rest of participants in the first cell.

	File Edit View Data Transform	

19 : Weight		
	Breakfast	Weight
1	1.00	1.00
2	1.00	1.00
3	1.00	1.00
4	1.00	1.00
5	1.00	1.00
6	1.00	1.00
7	1.00	1.00
8	1.00	1.00
9	1.00	1.00
10	1.00	1.00
11	1.00	1.00
12	1.00	1.00
13	1.00	1.00
14	1.00	1.00
15	1.00	1.00
16	1.00	1.00
17	1.00	1.00
18	1.00	1.00
19		

Now look back over the original data in the six cells. The cell to the right of the first one contains 59 people who eat breakfast and are normal weight. Each row must contain a 1 for eating breakfast and a 2 for normal weight. Enter these 59 rows of 1, 2 under the original rows of 1, 1 that we first entered. It is easiest to enter a 1, 2 and copy/paste the combination 58 more times. End on the 78th row, as shown below.

	File Edit View Data Transform	

79 : Weight		
	Breakfast	Weight
64	1.00	2.00
65	1.00	2.00
66	1.00	2.00
67	1.00	2.00
68	1.00	2.00
69	1.00	2.00
70	1.00	2.00
71	1.00	2.00
72	1.00	2.00
73	1.00	2.00
74	1.00	2.00
75	1.00	2.00
76	1.00	2.00
77	1.00	2.00
78	1.00	2.00
79		

Thirty-four people eat breakfast and are overweight, signified by a 1, 3 combination. Enter these data in the next 34 rows.

File	Edit	View	Data	Transform

114 : Weight

	Breakfast	Weight
96	1.00	3.00
97	1.00	3.00
98	1.00	3.00
99	1.00	3.00
100	1.00	3.00
101	1.00	3.00
102	1.00	3.00
103	1.00	3.00
104	1.00	3.00
105	1.00	3.00
106	1.00	3.00
107	1.00	3.00
108	1.00	3.00
109	1.00	3.00
110	1.00	3.00
111	1.00	3.00
112	1.00	3.00
113	1.00	3.00
114		

The next cell to enter is the bottom left in the data set, which contains 42 participants. Enter a 2, 1 combination per line using copy and paste after entering the first 2, 1.

File	Edit	View	Data	Transform

156 : Weight

	Breakfast	Weight
135	2.00	1.00
136	2.00	1.00
137	2.00	1.00
138	2.00	1.00
139	2.00	1.00
140	2.00	1.00
141	2.00	1.00
142	2.00	1.00
143	2.00	1.00
144	2.00	1.00
145	2.00	1.00
146	2.00	1.00
147	2.00	1.00
148	2.00	1.00
149	2.00	1.00
150	2.00	1.00
151	2.00	1.00
152	2.00	1.00
153	2.00	1.00
154	2.00	1.00
155	2.00	1.00
156		

We have data from only two more cells remaining. Enter 25 rows of 2, 2 to represent the 25 participants who do not eat breakfast and are normal weight. Finally enter 70 rows of 2, 3 combinations for the 70 participants who do not eat breakfast and are overweight.

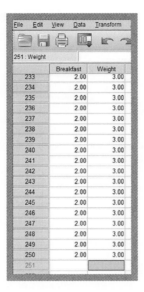

Click View and Value Labels to check the box to the left and reveal the variable labels. To analyze data using the two-way χ^2, SPSS requires a completely different set of options than the one-way χ^2. Click Analyze, Descriptive Statistics, Crosstabs.

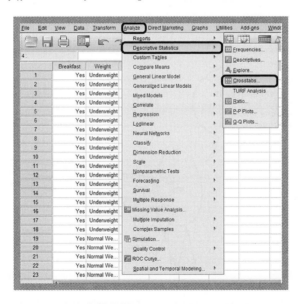

In the box that opens, move Breakfast over to Row(s). We chose to move Breakfast to represent Rows because Breakfast represented rows in our original data table. Then move Weight over to Column(s) to maintain the same format as our original data table. Next click Statistics to set up the χ^2 analysis. Click the box to the left of Chi-square, and also click Contingency coefficient so we can report effect size if we find a significant effect.

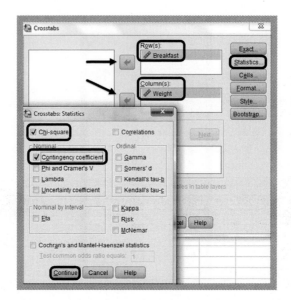

Contingency Coefficient (C). When a two-way χ^2 shows a significant relationship, the contingency coefficient provides a measure of effect size for any design larger than a 2×2.

Effect Size: Contingency Coefficient and Cramer's *V*

The **contingency coefficient** (C) provides effect size for a two-way design larger than a 2×2. Recall that this example is a 2×3 design.

Cramer's *V*. When a χ^2 design larger than a 2×2 reveals a significant outcome, Cramer's *V* provides a measure of effect size that is slightly less conservative than the contingency coefficient.

Some researchers prefer instead to use **Cramer's *V*** for effect size because the contingency coefficient is a more conservative test and can produce a slightly smaller effect size. In SPSS, Cramer's *V* is located beneath the contingency coefficient, so you can use *V* in case your instructor prefers it. Click Continue and choose Cells from the original Crosstabs box. In the new box that opens, click Observed Counts and Row

Percentages. Observed Counts will recreate the data table to make sure we entered everything correctly. Row Percentages will provide the percentage of participants in each row who are underweight, normal weight, and overweight. Percentages allow researchers to communicate the details of their results in a clear way. Click Continue.

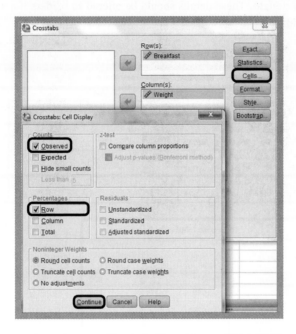

Below is a screenshot of output. The first column is a quick indication that SPSS read 250 rows.

Crosstabs

Case Processing Summary

	Cases					
	Valid		Missing		Total	
	N	Percent	N	Percent	N	Percent
Breakfast * Weight	250	100.0%	0	0.0%	250	100.0%

Let us examine the tables that follow. First we check the basic summary table labeled Breakfast*Weight Crosstabulation to ensure that we entered data correctly. Next, the Chi-Square Tests box provides the χ^2 value, *df*, and any potential significance on the Pearson Chi-Square row. The output also gives effect size in the last table, which can be reported as long as a significant value of χ^2 is found. Remember that any design larger than a 2×2 χ^2 relies on the contingency coefficient or Cramer's *V* for effect size. Recall from Chapter 5 that for χ^2, an effect size of .10 is considered small, .30 is considered moderate, and .50

or beyond is considered a large effect size (Cohen, 1988). Finally, looking back up at the Crosstabulation table, we see the percentages of people who are underweight, normal weight, and overweight among those who eat breakfast (first row of cells). The table also shows the percentages of those who do not eat breakfast and are underweight, normal weight, and overweight. These details should be offered to readers if a significant relationship is found.

Breakfast * Weight Crosstabulation

			Weight			Total
			Underweight	Normal Weight	Overweight	
Breakfast	Yes	Count	20	59	34	113
		% within Breakfast	17.7%	52.2%	30.1%	100.0%
	No	Count	42	25	70	137
		% within Breakfast	30.7%	18.2%	51.1%	100.0%
Total		Count	62	84	104	250
		% within Breakfast	24.8%	33.6%	41.6%	100.0%

Chi-Square Tests

	Value	df	Asymptotic Significance (2-sided)
Pearson Chi-Square	32.021[a]	2	.000
Likelihood Ratio	32.559	2	.000
Linear-by-Linear Association	.628	1	.428
N of Valid Cases	250		

a. 0 cells (0.0%) have expected count less than 5. The minimum expected count is 28.02.

Symmetric Measures

		Value	Approximate Significance
Nominal by Nominal	Contingency Coefficient	.337	.000
N of Valid Cases		250	

Notice that *df* for this example is 2, which is what we used for power analysis based on the calculation: (# of breakfast levels − 1) × (# of weight categories − 1) = 2. The output also shows a significance value (*p*-value) of .000. Because we cannot write that the probability is less than zero, it is customary to write $p < .001$.

The output provides all of the information needed to address the research question: *Is whether or not people eat breakfast related to their body-weight category?* With a significance value of $p < .001$, we can see that whether or not people eat breakfast indeed is related to their body-weight category, with a medium effect size of .34. We reject the null hypothesis that eating breakfast and body weight are *not* related, instead finding support for the research hypothesis: *Whether or not people eat breakfast is related to their body-weight category.* We can also report the percentage of people who fall in each cell to better understand our result. See details in the APA-style results section below.

APA Style for the 2 × 3 Chi Square

An APA-style method section provides details on our sample and procedure, as indicated below for the breakfast-weight example. Immediately following the method, a results section details the appropriate statistical analysis, whether or not the two variables were significantly related, and further details for the reader.

Method

Participants

The sample included 250 participants (137 men, 111 women, and 2 transgendered individuals) with a mean age of 38.55 (SD = 12.27). Ethnicities included Black (n = 99), White (n = 66), Latino (n = 57), and multiracial (n = 28) participants. The university's institutional review board gave approval for the study, and we treated all participants ethically.

Procedure

We distributed a survey link to deans of seven law schools in the Northeast who agreed to send the link to their faculty members. All participants reported whether they regularly ate breakfast, defined as consuming a minimum of 200 calories at least five mornings per week, on average, over the past 6 months. The survey also asked for weight, height, age, gender, and ethnicity of participants. We calculated body mass index (BMI) using the following calculation: (weight in pounds x 703)/height in inches. Participants fell into a category of underweight (BMI less than 18.5), normal weight (BMI 18.5–24.9), or overweight (BMI of 25.0 or higher).

Results

We analyzed these data using a 2 (eat breakfast versus do not eat breakfast) × 3 (underweight, normal weight, and overweight) χ^2. Whether or not participants ate breakfast related to weight category, χ^2(2, N = 250) = 32.02, p < .001, C = .34. Among participants who usually ate breakfast, 17.7% measured as underweight, 52.2% measured as normal weight, and 30.1% fell in the overweight category. Of those who abstained from breakfast, 30.7%, 18.2%, and 51.1% described themselves as underweight, normal weight, and overweight, respectively.

When we share the results of a study, either at a conference or in a publication, other researchers learn valuable information. In the fictional study of breakfast and weight, we would be able to tell others whether or not eating breakfast was related to weight category. Approximately 30% of people who ate breakfast reported themselves as overweight. However, about 51% of those who skipped breakfast reported being overweight.

TWO-WAY CHI SQUARE: 2 × 2 DESIGN

The smallest two-way chi square χ^2 design is a 2 × 2. Let us offer an example for more practice and discussion. Students often ask us if our classes require a term paper, and we suspect that those who want to avoid writing a paper drop our classes when we distribute the syllabus. We could design a study to address our research question: *Is whether or not an instructor requires a term paper related to students' decision to drop the class?* Suppose we located a course called Orientation to College attended by a large number of first-year students. On the first day, we might distribute the syllabus such that half of the students randomly received a syllabus requiring a term paper and the other half saw that they would not write a paper. Then we could see how many students in each group drop the course within the week. Of course, such a study could have some serious consequences for students and would need to be reviewed and approved by the IRB prior to running the study.

Power analysis tells us that the sample should contain at least 88 students based on the *df* calculation: (# of levels paper requirement – 1) × (# of levels of dropping the course – 1) = 1 × 1 = 1, focusing on a medium effect and a *p*-value of .05. Return to the power table earlier in the chapter for specific total samples sizes, or see Appendix A.

Keep in mind that the two-way χ^2 does not rely on specifying expected frequencies before data collection. We do not need to say how many people we expect to fall in each group. We merely collect the data: observed frequencies. Because we have two levels of term paper (with or without) and two levels of dropping (yes or no), the study represents a 2×2 research design. Participants will fall into one of four cells, and remember that each participant cannot be in more than one cell. See observed frequencies below.

	Dropped Class	Did Not Drop
Without Term Paper	34	42
With Term Paper	41	35

Effect Size: Phi Coefficient

The breakfast-weight example showed how to analyze a 2×3 design with categorical data. Any design larger than a 2×2 requires the contingency or Cramer's V to report effect size when a significant relationship is found. However, a 2×2 design is a special case of the χ^2 and requires the **phi coefficient** (φ) for effect size. For our purposes, obtaining the phi coefficient simply means checking the box for phi in SPSS and reporting the effect size when we have a significant outcome in a 2×2 design.

Phi Coefficient (φ). The phi coefficient quantifies effect size when a 2×2 χ^2 reveals a significant relationship.

SPSS: 2 × 2 Chi Square

Following the same steps as the prior example, enter the data into SPSS. Under Variable View, enter Paper as one variable with Values of 1 = Without and 2 = With. The second variable is Dropped, with 1 = Yes and 2 = No. Under Data View, we can enter the data. This time we will click to View Value Labels before entering data to show you flexibility in how SPSS data are entered. Then you can decide whether you like to see value labels as you enter future data sets.

The first cell of the data contains 34 people without a term-paper requirement who dropped the class. Enter 34 combinations of 1, 1 in the first 34 rows to represent this cell. Because we have asked SPSS to reveal value labels, simply enter the 1, 1 combinations using Enter after typing each number. You might instead enter the first row and copy/ paste it into the next 33 rows.

	Paper	Dropped
28	Without	Yes
29	Without	Yes
30	Without	Yes
31	Without	Yes
32	Without	Yes
33	Without	Yes
34	Without	Yes

Continue with the remaining three cells, concluding with 35 rows of 2, 2 to represent students with a term paper who did not drop the course.

	Paper	Dropped
147	With	No
148	With	No
149	With	No
150	With	No
151	With	No
152	With	No
153		

As with the prior example, click Analyze, Descriptive Statistics, Crosstabs to analyze a two-way χ^2. In the box that opens, move Paper to Row(s) and Dropped to Column(s) to follow the format of the data for this example. After you click Statistics, check the box next to Chi-square as well as the Phi coefficient because we have a 2 × 2 design. Click Continue.

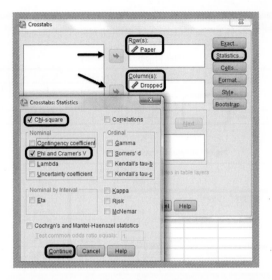

Choose Cells, and in the box that opens, request Observed frequencies. Our data set might best be explained by row (with or without a term paper), so we will ask for percentages by row. Click Continue and then OK.

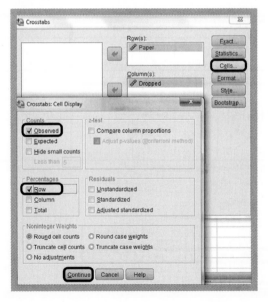

In the first output table, see that you have 152 people in the data set, which is correct. The second table allows you to examine the data by row. Of those required to complete a term paper, 53.9% dropped the class, and 46.1% did not drop. Of those not assigned a term paper, 44.7% dropped the class, and 55.3% did not drop.

Crosstabs

Case Processing Summary

	Cases					
	Valid		Missing		Total	
	N	Percent	N	Percent	N	Percent
Paper * Dropped	152	100.0%	0	0.0%	152	100.0%

Paper * Dropped Crosstabulation

			Dropped		Total
			Yes	No	
Paper	Without	Count	34	42	76
		% within Paper	44.7%	55.3%	100.0%
	With	Count	41	35	76
		% within Paper	53.9%	46.1%	100.0%
Total		Count	75	77	152
		% within Paper	49.3%	50.7%	100.0%

The percentage values seem to support what we thought would happen, but what does the χ^2 reveal? Examine the output tables below for the answer.

Chi-Square Tests

	Value	df	Asymptotic Significance (2-sided)	Exact Sig. (2-sided)	Exact Sig. (1-sided)
Pearson Chi-Square	1.290[a]	1	.256		
Continuity Correction[b]	.948	1	.330		
Likelihood Ratio	1.292	1	.256		
Fisher's Exact Test				.330	.165
Linear-by-Linear Association	1.281	1	.258		
N of Valid Cases	152				

a. 0 cells (0.0%) have expected count less than 5. The minimum expected count is 37.50.
b. Computed only for a 2x2 table

Symmetric Measures

		Value	Approximate Significance
Nominal by Nominal	Phi	-.092	.256
	Cramer's V	.092	.256
N of Valid Cases		152	

In the table labeled Chi-Square Tests, we can see that the *p*-value (Sig) is greater than .05, which means the two variables were *not* significantly related. No meaningful effect exists. With no significant effect, we must ignore effect size (the phi coefficient).

APA Style for the 2 × 2 Chi Square

In an APA-style results section, you might share percentages to describe the four cells in your design, but first you would report no significant relationship. Below we begin with an example method section for this study.

Method

Participants

Participants included 77 women and 75 men, with a mean age of 19.70 ($SD = 2.08$). Ethnicities included 75 White, 40 Black, 27 Latino, and 10 multiracial students in a college orientation course. The university's institutional review board gave approval for the study, and we treated all participants ethically.

Procedure

On the first day of class, the instructor distributed syllabi in two forms: One form contained a requirement to complete a term paper, and the other form offered no paper requirement. Shuffling of syllabi prior to distribution allowed random assignment to conditions. Following the first day of class, the instructor tracked the number of students who dropped the class in each group for a week. To link students with whether or not their syllabus required a term paper, the instructor emailed all students to ask which syllabus they had received. The instructor also requested permission to use their data in a study to be shared with the scientific community. All students agreed and remained in the sample.

Results

We analyzed these data using a 2 (required term paper versus no paper) × 2 (dropped the class or not) χ^2. Whether a professor required a term paper failed to relate with whether participants dropped the course, $\chi^2(1, N = 152) = 1.29$, $p = .256$. Among participants told they would be required to complete a term paper, 53.9% dropped the course, and 46.1% did not drop. Of participants not required to write a term paper, 44.7% dropped the course, and 55.3% did not.

The 2 × 2 design addressed our research question: *Is whether or not an instructor requires a term paper related to students' decision to drop the class?* The answer is no. The two variables were not related. We cannot reject the null hypothesis: *Whether or not an instructor requires a term paper is not related to students' decision to drop the class.* Our inability to find a significant outcome could be limited to the specific sample, instructor, or school. Or perhaps the two variables simply are not related. The research question can be explored further using different approaches, and eventually a clear answer will emerge.

SUMMARY

When researchers design a study with simple frequency as the outcome, the data are analyzed using a nonparametric statistic called the χ^2. You can choose to design a study with one variable and at least two levels or with more than one variable. Either design is useful, depending on the research question. As you learned in Chapter 5, when we design a study with only one variable, a one-way χ^2 compares observations with expectations. What did the researcher expect to find based on the normal population? And what did the researcher actually find in the sample? An unusual outcome is based on observations that do not fit the original expectations, indicating an interesting result. The sample is different from normal.

In this chapter we covered research designs with two variables and an outcome of simple frequency. The smallest two-way design is a 2 × 2 study, but any number of categories can be analyzed with the two-way χ^2. The two-way χ^2 looks for a relationship between two variables. The analysis is not at all focused on laying out expected frequencies prior to data collection. No expectations are communicated. Rather, researchers use observed frequencies to illustrate a relationship, if one exists.

The one-way χ^2 and two-way χ^2 address unique research questions. Although both are called χ^2, be careful to design studies that allow the χ^2 to answer the research question. If you want to know how well the data you collect will fit expectations based on prior research, choose one variable and find out how many people are in each level. Analyze the data with a one-way χ^2. If you want to examine the potential relationship between two variables using simple frequency, rely on the two-way χ^2.

REVIEW OF TERMS

Cells

Contingency Coefficient *(C)*

Cramer's *V*

Phi Coefficient (φ)

Two-Way χ^2

PRACTICE ITEMS

1. What is the difference between a one-way and two-way χ^2?

2. For each of the following, would you use a one-way or two-way χ^2? Specify how many levels of each variable.

   a. Is bedroom color choice (red, blue, green, yellow, pink) related to gender (male, female)?

   b. Does wearing a helmet (yes, no) depend on exposure to education about motorcycle safety (attended motorcycle safety class versus did not attend motorcycle safety class)?

   c. Do approximately 70% of people on the West Coast enjoy surfing and 30% not enjoy surfing?

   d. Is use of a pen or pencil related to whether participants are in math or history classes?

   e. Determine whether college students who transfer to the United States from another country use tutoring services with the same frequency as Americans. Measure use of tutoring services across three categories: no use, some use, and frequent use.

* * *

For each of the following studies, (a) note the type of two-way χ^2 design (e.g., 2 × 2, 2 × 5), (b) state the research question as a research hypothesis and state the null hypothesis, (c) determine how many participants are needed for adequate power, and (d) enter and analyze the data as well as write an APA-style results section. Be sure to read over the method sections we provided.

3. Khanna (2014) found that preschool-age boys (3–6 years old) with high levels of lead in their blood performed worse on cognitive tests than preschool-age girls with elevated lead concentrations. You want to see if higher lead is related to which children move on to the first grade. The research question asks, *Among children exposed to lead, is gender related to whether children are promoted to the first grade?* You collect a sample of 137 6-year-old children from a local school district who all have elevated blood lead levels and find that 68 of 75 girls were promoted, and 56 of 62 boys were promoted.

Method

Participants

Of a group of families whose children evidenced elevated lead concentrations, the parents of 137 preschool children (75 girls, 62 boys) signed consent forms allowing their children to participate in this study. All children attended the same school district. Mean child age was 6.57 years ($SD = 0.37$), and parents chose not to disclose ethnicity. All children received ethical treatment, and the IRB approved the procedure.

Procedure

Parents signed the consent form. One year later, researchers contacted them and asked whether their preschool child advanced to the first grade.

4. Kitayama et al. (2015) showed that aggression is linked with poorer health (e.g., cardiovascular functioning) in the United States but not in Japan, possibly because in the United States, aggression is tied to many other negative factors, such as low income and poverty. In Japan, aggressive outbursts are linked with higher status and *better* health. You wonder if these results are true for other Eastern and Western cultures as well. You ask, *Among people with poor health, do levels of aggression relate with country of origin?* You send out a survey to health departments in Japan, the United States, China, and Canada and ask that they give the survey only to individuals with poor health. In the survey, you ask questions about aggressiveness and assign individuals to either the high- or low-aggression group. You find that 17 of 55 Japanese, 42 of 52 American, 22 of 67 Chinese, and 30 of 45 Canadian participants were highly aggressive.

Method

Participants

Participants ($N = 219$) from Japan, the United States, China, and Canada completed the survey. Participant age averaged 38.4.5 ($SD = 12.40$), and gender varied approximately equally across all four countries (48% Japanese women, 52% American women, 51% Chinese women, and 49% Canadian women). The researcher received no access to ethnicities.

Materials

The Aggression Questionnaire (Buss & Perry, 1992). The Buss-Perry Scale contains 29 items designed to measure aggression, with questions rated on a scale of 1 (*extremely uncharacteristic of me*) to 7 (*extremely characteristic of me*). Psychometric properties indicate good internal consistency and stability over time.

Procedure

Researchers sent a survey link to health departments in the four counties of interest with instructions to send the link only to individuals known to be in poor health. The survey assessed for country of residence, gender, and age. Participants also completed the Aggression Questionnaire, with scores above the median considered "high," and those below the median considered "low."

5. Brooks (2014) examined anxiety and performance after people told themselves either "I am excited" or "I am anxious" and found higher performance when individuals told themselves they were excited. She argued that people should learn to reinterpret anxiety as positive arousal, such as excitement, and that doing so would enhance performance. You wonder what would have happened had she also asked people to tell themselves "I am legendary." You ask yourself, *Does positive self-talk relate with singing performance?* Following the method in the Brooks study, you ask people to tell themselves one of the three statements noted above before singing karaoke on a video game and noting their scores on the game as terrible, okay, or wonderful. In Brooks's study, the effect sizes were large, so you should assume that you will find a large effect size as well. You observe the following simple frequencies.

	Terrible	Okay	Wonderful
I am excited	5	7	12
I am anxious	8	6	5
I am legendary	5	5	10

Method

Participants

College seniors ($N = 63$) participated in this study, with a mean age of 20.75 ($SD = 0.67$). Ethnicities included 25 Asian American, 15 Latin American, 13 African American, and 10 Caucasian American individuals, with gender evenly distributed across groups (52% men). All participants received ethical treatment according to standards established by the university's Institutional Review Board.

Procedure

Participants signed up for the study for extra credit in their Senior Seminar in Psychology course. Those who did not wish to participate received an alternative assignment to earn extra credit. When they arrived in the lab, participants signed the consent form and then learned that they would sing a song using a video-game system. Prior to singing, the researcher randomly assigned participants to say one of the following statements aloud: "I am excited," "I am anxious," or "I am legendary." Immediately afterward, they sang the song *Blank Space* by Taylor Swift for 4 min. The video game gave them a score of poor (terrible), average (okay), or excellent (wonderful).

REFERENCES

Brooks, A. W. (2014). Get excited: Reappraising pre-performance anxiety as excitement. *Journal of Experimental Psychology: General, 143*(3), 1144–1158. doi:10.1037/a0035325

Buss, A. H., & Perry, M. P. (1992). The Aggression Questionnaire. *Journal of Personality and Social Psychology, 63,* 452–459. doi:10.1037/0022-3514.63.3.452

Centers for Disease Control and Prevention. (2015). About BMI for adults. Retrieved from http://www.cdc.gov/healthy weight/assessing/bmi/adult_bmi/ index.html

Cohen, J. (1988). *Statistical power analysis for the behavioral sciences*. Hillsdale, NJ: Lawrence Erlbaum.

Khanna, M. M. (2014). Boys, not girls, are negatively affected on cognitive tasks by lead exposure: A pilot study. *Journal of Environmental Health, 77*(6), 72–77. doi:10.1016/j.jtemb.2015.06.007

Kitayama, S., Park, J., Boylan, J. M., Miyamoto, Y., Levine, C. S., Markus, H. R., . . . Ryff, C. D. (2015). Expression of anger and ill health in two cultures: An examination of inflammation and cardiovascular risk. *Psychological Science, 26*(2), 211–220. doi:10.1177/0956797614561268

O'Neil, C. E., Nicklas, T. A., & Fulgoni, V. L. (2014). Nutrient intake, diet quality, and weight/adiposity parameters in breakfast patterns: National health and nutrition examination survey 2001–2008. *Journal of the Academy of Nutrition and Dietetics, 114*(12), S27–S43. doi:10.1016/j.jand.2014.08.021

7

Examining Relationships

In the previous chapter, we discussed the two-way chi square (χ^2) as a way to find if two variables are related. Chi-square analysis requires simple frequencies in separate groups. The research question asks how many people are in each level across two variables, and data analysis with the χ^2 reveals a relationship between the two variables, if a relationship exists. For example, your research question might ask, *Is money in a person's wallet related to happiness?* The two variables could be whether or not people in a sample have money in their wallets and whether or not they are happy. Data from such a design might consist of the observed simple frequencies in the four cells below.

	Not Happy	Happy
No money in wallet	11	15
Some money in wallet	9	20

Notice that 11 people in the sample were unhappy and reported having no money, 15 people had no money and were happy, and so on. The outcome data are simple frequency counts. The research design called for how many people fell in each of the four categories. Analysis of this design using a two-way χ^2 will tell you if money in a person's wallet is related to happiness. The data above are simple, yielding only frequency counts. Such simple data cannot be analyzed with a powerful statistic based on the definition of power in Chapter 4. We must rely on a nonparametric statistic. Not to worry, a different research design can be analyzed using a more powerful option.

PEARSON'S *r*: SEEKING A RELATIONSHIP

Recall from Chapter 3 the four levels of data: nominal, ordinal, interval, and ratio. Interval and ratio data are defined by math properties and allow advanced data analysis. Your knowledge of measurement levels will serve you well as you design a study based on a more advanced research question: *Is the amount of money people have in their wallets related to happiness such that more money is related to greater happiness?* We still want to know about money, but now we can ask for an exact amount rather than whether or not a person has any money at all. Amount of money in wallets is a ratio variable. We also still want to know about happiness, but this variable can be measured on a rating scale from 1 (*very unhappy*) to 4 (*very happy*). A rating scale represents interval data, a big improvement over simply asking people if they are happy or not (nominal data).

In our example, each participant provides information on both variables. A fictional data set is below.

Dollars in Wallet	Happiness
2	3
10	3
20	2
5	4
12	3
15	4
26	3
5	4
21	2
7	1

Just as with the two-way χ^2, we can find out if the two variables are related. As an added bonus, locating a relationship when one exists is more likely with interval or ratio data as opposed to simple frequency counts because quantitative variables allow a more powerful, parametric statistic. Of course, data analysis must be different to accommodate for interval or ratio data rather than simple frequency counts. To analyze a potential relationship between two interval or ratio variables, we turn to a statistic called **Pearson's r**. The statistic is equally often called the **correlation coefficient** because the analysis examines the potential relationship between two variables, a *co*-relation.

Pearson's r (Correlation Coefficient). Pearson's r is the statistic used to analyze a potential relationship between two interval or ratio variables.

Scatterplot. A scatterplot is a graph that shows all data points in a data set, with one point for each participant.

The Pearson's r statistic indicates the relationship between two interval or ratio variables. Specifically, it measures how related they are in a linear (straight line) way. If the two variables are linearly related, a graph should depict the relationship. A **scatterplot** shows all data points, one for each participant. Usually researchers label the X-axis (horizontal line on the bottom of the graph) with the variable in the first column. The Y-axis (vertical line on the left side of the graph) is labeled with the variable in the second column. Choose values for each axis based on the values in each column. In our example, numbers in the first column range from 2 to 26, and numbers in the second column range from 1 to 4. In the following figure, we graphed data from the 10 participants reporting the money in their wallet and happiness. You will see only nine dots because two participants had identical data.

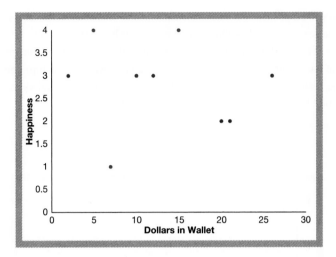

Do the points on the graph appear to fall approximately in a line? If you do not see a linear pattern, you are not alone. We do not see one either. Lack of a clear linear pattern suggests that these two variables are not related. But just to be sure, we should calculate the correlation coefficient. The Pearson's *r* value can range from –1.00 to +1.00, and both the absolute value and sign are important.

The correlation coefficient provides two pieces of information: *direction* of the relationship and *strength* of the relationship. The sign of the *r*-value indicates the direction of the relationship. If the scatterplot shows points in a line pattern from the lower left of the graph to the upper right of the graph, the two variables have a positive relationship.

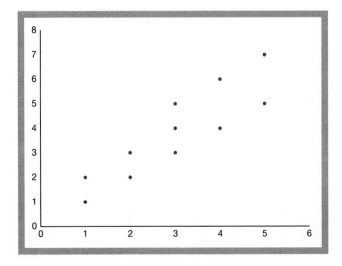

The *r*-value will be positive. As values on one variable increase, so do values on the other variable. The scatterplot below illustrates a positive relationship.

However, if the scatterplot shows an approximate line pattern from the upper left of the graph to the lower right, the two variables share a negative relationship. The *r*-value will be negative. As values on one variable increase, values on the second variable decrease. The scatterplot below represents a negative relationship.

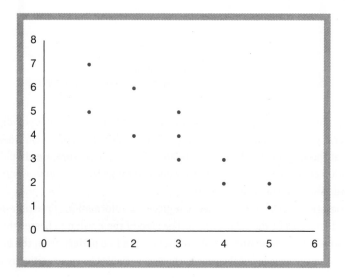

Pearson's *r* also tells the strength of the relationship. Values of either +1.00 or −1.00 for *r* means the two variables are perfectly related. As an example of a perfect positive relationship, numbers on the first variable might increase by 1, while numbers on the second variable increase by 5. For a perfect negative relationship, numbers on the first variable might increase by 3, while numbers on the second variable decrease by 10. In real life, perfect relationships—whether positive or negative—do not exist. Likewise, a Pearson's *r* of 0.00, indicating absolutely no relationship at all between two variables, rarely exists. Life is messy, and two variables will randomly overlap a bit, yielding an *r*-value *close* to .00 but almost never exactly .00.

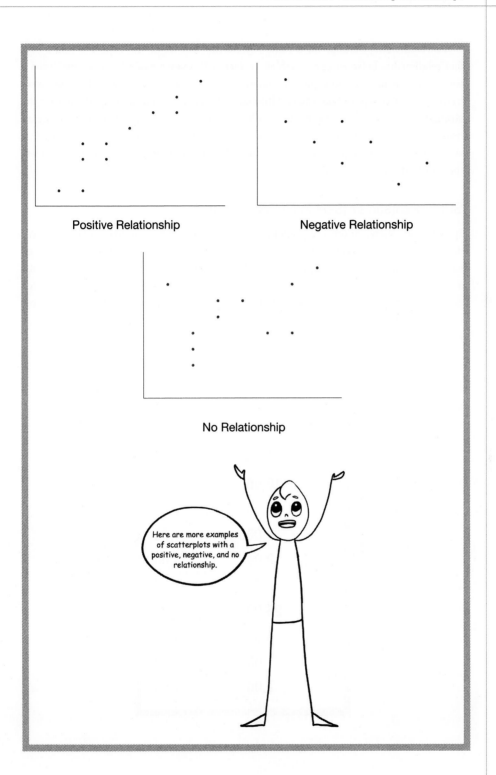

Positive Relationship

Negative Relationship

No Relationship

As researchers, we hope for a value beyond .00, but we do not expect to find a perfect relationship between our variables. In fact, a Pearson's r of $+/-.10$ is considered a weak relationship, $+/- .30$ depicts a moderate relationship, and $+/-.50$ or beyond shows a strong relationship (Cohen, 1992). Although Cohen has given us these guidelines for the strength of a relationship, we know the ultimate test of significance lies in analyzing an r-value to see how unusual it is. If the value is unlikely to occur normally (meaning it is very different from zero), we can take credit for finding an interesting relationship. To test for significance, we turn to SPSS.

SPSS: Pearson's r (Seeking a Relationship)

In Variable View, enter the variable names as you have in prior chapters. We do not typically assign labels to numbers under Values when analyzing interval or ratio data that are not grouped into distinct levels. Enter the two variable names and click Data View at the bottom left of the screen. In Data View, enter values for dollars and happiness, and make sure the data from each participant are on one row together. For example, the first participant reported having $2.00 and a happiness rating of 3.

Dollars	Happiness
2.00	3.00
10.00	3.00
20.00	2.00
5.00	4.00
12.00	3.00
15.00	4.00
26.00	3.00
5.00	4.00
21.00	2.00
7.00	1.00

Click Analyze, Correlate, and Bivariate to request Pearson's *r*.

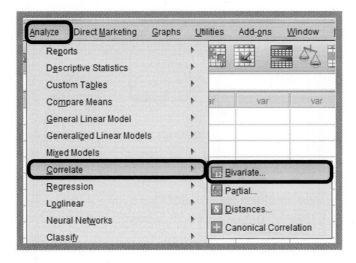

In SPSS, the word 'bivariate' means that you are comparing two variables.

In the box that opens, move both variables over to the right by highlighting each and clicking the center arrow.

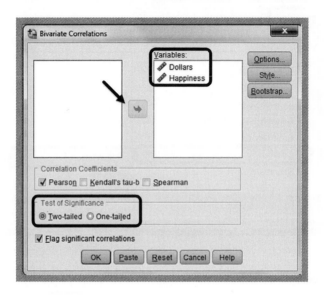

Under Test of Significance, notice your option of a Two-tailed or One-tailed test.

Two-Tailed Test

Recall that for significance, we need a *p*-value of .05 or less. In other words, we need to find an unusual, interesting relationship between money and happiness. Of course, the null hypothesis illustrates no unusual relationship: *Amount of money in wallets and happiness are not related.* Because no relationship would be expected in the normal population, a value of $p \leq .05$ means we found an unusual relationship very different from 0. If we design a study and have no idea whether the *r*-value will be positive or negative, the .05 value must be split across a positive *r*-value (.025) and a negative *r*-value (.025). We split the .05 we have to use. Unfortunately, splitting the .05 sacrifices power because each possible *r*-value direction gets only a .025 (2.5%) chance to occur. This is called a **nondirectional test**. A nondirectional test is also called a two-tailed test. If you have no educated guess about the direction of the relationship, conduct a two-tailed test. Notice that both tails of the distribution below are shaded, and each shaded region is smaller than a one-tailed test (below) because .05 has been divided between two areas. Likewise, if your instructor prefers a conservative approach, rely on a two-tailed test.

Nondirectional Test (Two-Tailed Test). If we have no educated guess about the direction of the relationship, we conduct a nondirectional or two-tailed test.

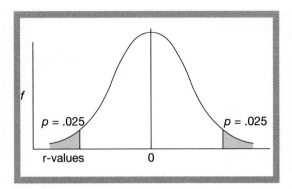

One-Tailed Test

Alternatively, if we have a specific idea (hypothesis) of whether the relationship will be positive or negative, we can gamble all of our .05 allowance on the single direction we expect. We call this approach a **directional test**. In our example, recall the research question: *Is the amount of money people have in their wallets related to happiness such that more money is related to greater happiness?* The research hypothesis specifically states what we hope to find: *Amount of money in wallets is related to happiness such that more money is related to greater happiness.* That is, we expect dollars and happiness to yield a *positive r*-value. Bet all .05 on a positive relationship. A directional test is also called a **one-tailed test**. As indicated in the following figure, this specific one-tailed test is based on expecting the *r*-value to fall in the upper tail of the normal distribution.

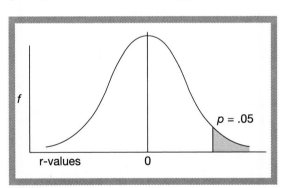

In the money study, we expect money and happiness to show a positive relationship, so we conduct a one-tailed test in SPSS. Click the circle next to One-tailed under Test of Significance. Next, click Options. Options will open a second box that allows you to ask for descriptive statistics. In addition to testing for a significant relationship, you will need to report the mean and standard deviation for variables. After checking the box for these options under Statistics, click Continue.

Directional Test (One-Tailed Test) If we have a specific idea (hypothesis) of whether the relationship will be positive or negative, we have a directional or one-tailed test.

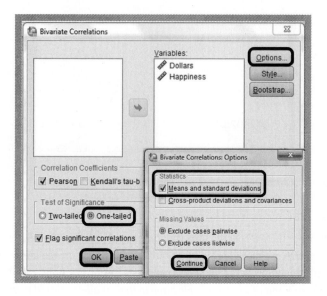

When the box closes, click OK on the original box (Bivariate Correlations) to execute commands. See the output below.

Correlations

Descriptive Statistics

	Mean	Std. Deviation	N
Dollars	12.3000	8.00069	10
Happiness	2.9000	.99443	10

Correlations

		Dollars	Happiness
Dollars	Pearson Correlation	1	-.247
	Sig. (1-tailed)		.246
	N	10	10
Happiness	Pearson Correlation	-.247	1
	Sig. (1-tailed)	.246	
	N	10	10

In the second box of the output, look at the correlation between Dollars and Happiness. The correlation is -.247, and based on a moderate correlation at +/−.30, we might be tempted to think our result shows a meaningful relationship between the two variables. But wait. The *p*-value must be rare, less than .05, to show an unusual relationship between amount of money in wallets and happiness. The significance value is .246, which is not equal to or less than .05. Therefore, the two variables are not related in our sample. Our research question asked, *Is the amount of money people have in their wallets related to happiness such that more money is related to greater happiness?* Now we can answer the research question: *No, the amount of money in the wallet and happiness were not related.* We can also discuss the outcome as failing to reject the null hypothesis: *The amount of money people had in their wallets was not related to their happiness.*

Power

Did we test enough participants to have a good chance of finding an effect if one existed? Recall power analysis from prior chapters. We need to know how many people are required to reveal a significant relationship, if one exists. Based on the table below, we should have included 85 participants for a good chance to show a significant outcome at $p \leq .05$ if a medium-sized effect exists. With our sample size of only 10 people, we had a poor chance of finding a significant outcome even if one was present. We lacked power due to a small sample size, and the potential for Type II error was high (review terms in Chapter 4 as needed). Of course, we used a small sample for the sake of a concise textbook example. Real life requires more.

	Small Effect Size	Medium Effect Size	Large Effect Size
Pearson's *r*	783	85	29

Note: Numbers in the table represent **total** sample size.

Graphs as Figures: Scatterplot

If you are going to include a scatterplot with your results, we prefer Excel for graphing. The final product in Excel is higher quality for publication. In Appendix B, we walk you through how to use Excel for graphing a scatterplot. Although Excel versions differ, the general ideas and formatting options remain fairly constant.

In our current example, if we wanted to include a figure to support our results, we would refer the reader to Figure 1 and offer a scatterplot. Below is a scatterplot for these data created in Excel.

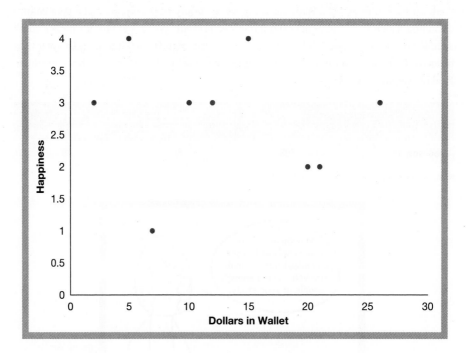

APA Style for Pearson's *r*: Correlational Design

We rely on APA style to report our results, using all circled parts of the SPSS output for this example. As you know, we must report degrees of freedom (*df*) in the results section, and that piece of information is not on the output. We can calculate *df* using *N*, where *N* for correlation refers to number of participants in the sample. For Pearson's *r*, calculate *df* using $N - 2$, which in this case is $10 - 2 = 8$.

Method

Participants

Participants included 10 adults (5 men and 5 women) from a college sample. Ages ranged from 18 to 25 ($M = 21.07$, $SD = 2.35$), and ethnicities included 7 White and 3 Black individuals. We received IRB approval and treated all participants ethically.

Procedure

Students viewed a recruitment flyer placed on campus bulletin boards. Those interested in participating e-mailed the researcher with their availability and received an appointment time. At their appointment, participants reported the amount of money in their wallet as well as their age, gender, and ethnicity. Students also reported current happiness using a rating scale from 1 (*very unhappy*) to 4 (*very happy*). Participants received a $5 gift card for participating in the study.

Results

We examined the potential correlation between amount of money in wallets and ratings of happiness. Participants reported money as number of dollars ($M = 12.30$, $SD = 8.00$) and happiness ($M = 2.90$, $SD = 0.99$). Amount of money in wallets failed to relate to ratings of happiness, $r(8) = -.25$, $p = .246$.

A minor addition to the results section would allow you to include the scatterplot. We might indicate, "As shown in Figure 1, amount of money in wallets failed to relate to ratings of happiness, $r(8) = -.25$, $p = .246$."

In the APA-style results section above, we were careful to use the term *relate* rather than *cause* because neither variable was manipulated. We simply asked participants to report the number of dollars in their wallets and rate their happiness. Because the research design did not manipulate a variable, we could not establish cause and effect. Recall from Chapter 3 that researchers can only learn cause and effect with manipulation of what participants experience. That is, a true independent variable (IV) must be used in the design, and a dependent variable (DV) measures the outcome. With such a design, we can learn the cause (IV) and effect (DV).

PEARSON'S *r*: SEEKING CAUSE AND EFFECT

We could design a similar study with manipulation and a true IV. The research question would change slightly: *Does the amount of money people have in their wallets affect happiness such that more money causes greater happiness?* Notice that the research question indicates cause and effect by using the word "affect" as well as indicating that money "causes" happiness. In the prior example, with no manipulated variable, the research question only used the term "related" to avoid causation language: *Is the amount of money in a person's wallet* related *to happiness such that more money relates to greater happiness?* How might we change the correlational (not manipulated) study into an experimental study?

Let us assume participants entered the study with no money. Suppose we gave people different sums of money and then measured their happiness. We could pull some dollars from a basket and hand cash to each participant. Everyone would get a different amount, depending on what we pulled out. Then we could ask for ratings of happiness as the DV. Our null hypothesis would use cause-and-effect language: *The amount of money in people's wallets does not* affect *their happiness.* The research hypothesis states what we hope to find: *Money in wallets* affects *happiness such that more money* causes *more happiness.* Amount of money in wallets is still a ratio variable, and happiness using a rating scale still represents interval data. Our data might look like the following values. We again use Pearson's *r* to analyze the data, but this time our research design can tell us causation.

Dollars in Wallet	Happiness
5	4
10	2
15	3
21	4
23	4
12	3
1	2
11	3
2	1
17	3
12	2
20	4

Previewing Data With a Scatterplot

We know that we can include a scatterplot in our APA results, but we can also create a scatterplot to provide a quick overview of our data. Given our research hypothesis of a positive correlation, we would expect to see a linear pattern of dots, with the approximate line increasing across the graph from left to right.

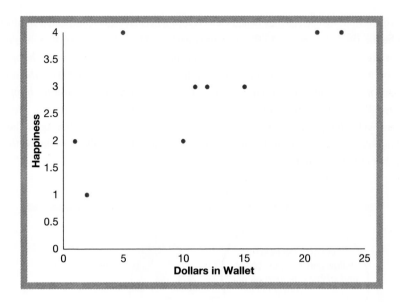

SPSS: Pearson's *r* (Seeking Cause and Effect)

Enter the data into SPSS as shown in the prior example. Remember that we expect a specific direction for the relationship (positive), allowing us to choose a one-tailed test and increase power. Be sure to ask for Descriptive Statistics as well by clicking Options and checking the box next to Means and standard deviations. Click Continue then OK for the output.

Correlations

Descriptive Statistics

	Mean	Std. Deviation	N
Dollars	12.4167	7.21688	12
Happiness	2.9167	.99620	12

Correlations

		Dollars	Happiness
Dollars	Pearson Correlation	1	.688**
	Sig. (1-tailed)		.007
	N	12	12
Happiness	Pearson Correlation	.688**	1
	Sig. (1-tailed)	.007	
	N	12	12

**. Correlation is significant at the 0.01 level (1-tailed).

On the output we can see that Dollars and Happiness correlate at .688 and a significance value below .05. Let us return to the research question: *Does the amount of money people have in their wallets affect happiness such that more money causes greater happiness?* Based on a *p*-value of .007 and a positive *r*-value, we have our answer: *Yes, the amount of money in the wallet affected happiness, with more money causing greater happiness.* We reject the null hypothesis of no effect in favor of the research hypothesis: *Money in wallets* affected *happiness such that more money* caused *more happiness.* Again, because we manipulated the amount of money participants put in their wallets, we know that the amount of money affected happiness ratings.

Effect Size: Coefficient of Determination

Coefficient of Determination. The coefficient of determination is the number that indicates the effect size of a significant *r*-value. To calculate the coefficient of determination, square the *r*-value.

All needed information for a results section is found on the SPSS output. The only exception is the value for effect size. Because this example yielded a significant effect, we must report effect size using the **coefficient of determination**. You already know that a correlation of near or beyond +/−.50 shows a strong relationship (Cohen, 1988), and the Pearson's *r* in this example is .688. Effect size is calculated by squaring the *r*-value. For r^2, .01 is considered a weak effect, .09 is a moderate effect, and .25 is a strong effect. You could have arrived at these values by squaring *r*-values of .10, .30, and .50, which you already knew indicated the strength of *r*.

Although Pearson's r can give you a good idea of the strength of a relationship, r^2 is the best measure for effect size because it is easier to interpret. In our example, the coefficient of determination is $.688^2 = .47$. An effect size of .47 means that the amount of money in wallets overlaps with happiness ratings by 47%. Another way of explaining effect size is to say that 47% of happiness ratings can be explained by the amount of money given to participants. Considering all other variables that likely influence happiness, explaining 47% of happiness by knowing the amount of money people have is impressive.

APA Style for Pearson's r: Experimental Design

Remember, APA style requires information about participants and procedure details related to variables in the research design. The method section operationalizes variables, and the results section reports values from the correlation analysis.

Method

Participants

Participants included 12 adults (6 men and 6 women) from a college sample. Ages ranged from 19 to 24 ($M = 22.17$, $SD = 1.55$), and ethnicities included 7 White, 3 Black, and 2 Latino individuals. We received IRB approval for the study and treated all participants ethically.

Procedure

Students viewed a recruitment flyer placed on bulletin boards on campus. Those interested in participating e-mailed the researcher with their availability and received an appointment time. At their appointments, participants received between \$1 and \$23, with the amount determined randomly. Students also reported current happiness using a rating scale from 1 (*very unhappy*) to 4 (*very happy*). Finally, participants reported their age, gender, and ethnicity, and they received a \$5 gift card for participating in the study.

Results

We examined the potential correlation between amount of money given to participants and their ratings of happiness. Participants reported money as number of dollars ($M = 12.42$, $SD = 7.22$) and happiness on a rating scale from 1 to 4, with higher numbers indicating more happiness ($M = 2.92$, $SD = 1.00$). Amount of money in wallets affected ratings of happiness, $r(10) = .69$, $p = .007$, $r^2 = .47$. The more money people received to put in their wallets, the higher their ratings of happiness.

The APA-style results section above includes the word *affected* rather than *related* because manipulation occurred in this research design. Pearson's *r* is merely a statistical analysis. The way it is interpreted—relationship or cause and effect—depends on the research design. Although the SPSS analysis remains the same, the results section differs based on whether the design was a correlational study or an experiment, using wording specific to each design.

INACCURATE PEARSON'S *r*

Pearson's *r* is a statistic used to analyze two interval or ratio variables with many values. If neither variable is manipulated, Pearson's *r* quantifies a relationship between the two variables. On the other hand, if one variable is manipulated, a significant Pearson's *r* can show cause and effect. Your research question drives your research design and dictates whether you can look for cause and effect. Pearson's correlation coefficient analyzes the data you collect. It is a useful tool.

However, recall that Pearson's *r* only quantifies linear relationships. If the two interval or ratio variables in a research design are related in a linear way, *r* is a fine choice for analysis. Here we will explain several situations that can lead to erroneous results using the *r*-value. Three of the situations lead to an artificially low *r*-value, and two situations create an artificially high *r*-value.

WHEN PEARSON'S *r* FALSELY SHOWS NO RELATIONSHIP

A low *r*-value is likely to be nonsignificant. If the sample size is quite large, a low *r*-value might be significant, but the effect size will be small. Either way, you will be disappointed that the two variables did not relate well to each other, or one variable did not cause changes in the other (with an experiment). But sometimes a low *r*-value is misleading. The three situations in which Pearson's *r* will be low even when a relationship clearly exists are based on (1) outliers, (2) a nonlinear relationship, and (3) restriction of range.

Outliers That Weaken Pearson's *r*

Outlier (for Ungrouped Data). An outlier is a data point that is out of the ordinary. In other words, an outlier is a data point outside of the general relationship pattern.

In psychology, we often want to know what would be true of most participants in a given situation. An **outlier (for ungrouped data)** is a data point based on a participant's response that is far from ordinary. For example, if we measured the potential relationship between number of hot dogs eaten and stomach pain on a scale from 1 (*I feel great*) to 8 (*I feel terrible*), we might find that most people in the sample choose to eat somewhere between 1 and 5 hot dogs. Imagine we happened to get a champion hot-dog eater in our sample who consumes 57 hot dogs and feels great. That participant would be far from ordinary and could obscure a fairly strong relationship by reducing Pearson's r.

Researchers should examine their data to see if the two variables of interest are linearly related by graphing the data. A graph will also show if a clear outlier or two exist in the data set. Consider the following graph of our hot-dog eaters.

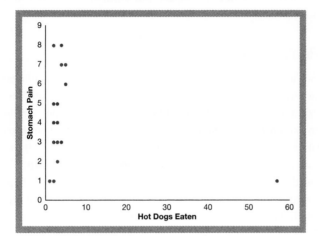

Notice that the outlier obviously deviates from the rest of the data. With the outlier, a one-tailed correlational analysis reveals $r = -.31$, $p = .239$. In this situation, researchers may choose to remove the outlier and rerun Pearson's r. Look at a graph without the outlier.

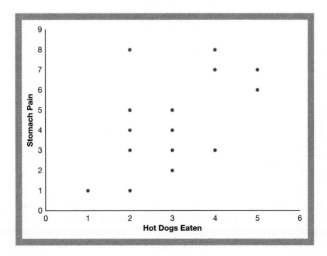

In our example, the r-value is strong without the outlier, with $r = .53$, $p = .041$ (one-tailed test). Of course, ethical considerations require us to report the existence of an outlier, the removal, and the reanalysis. In fact, we recommend reporting the original r-value, providing a graph illustrating the outlier, and providing the subsequent r-value with the outlier removed. It is best to be transparent with readers about your approach to data analysis. An outlier should be visually obvious when graphing, and removing the outlier should be logical. But ultimately readers will decide if your approach was reasonable.

Nonlinear Relationship

Because Pearson's r can only quantify linear relationships, a clear nonlinear relationship will yield a low r-value. For example, romantic partners should spend time together, but most of us also value time with other friends as well as time alone. Suppose we asked a sample of men to report average hours per day spent with their romantic partners and to rate their relationship satisfaction on a scale from 1 (*very unsatisfied*) to 9 (*very satisfied*). Take a look at the fictional graph of a **curvilinear relationship**.

When a relationship is curved rather than linear, we call the shape curvilinear. Relationship satisfaction and time spent with a romantic partner are related in a curvilinear way. Both those who report very little time and those who report a great deal of

Curvilinear Relationship.
When the graph of a relationship is curved rather than a line, we call it a curvilinear relationship.

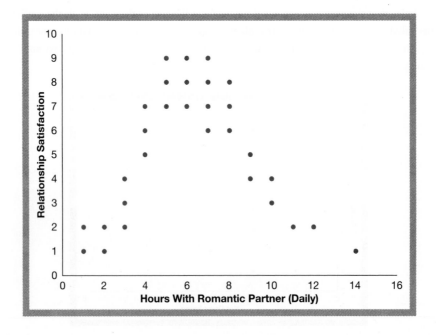

time spent with a romantic partner show less relationship satisfaction. Pearson's r will be low, suggesting no meaningful relation between the two variables. In fact, $r = -.03$ ($p = .882$) in the sample above. However, the graph illustrates a clear nonlinear relationship. Advanced statistics to analyze nonlinear relationships are beyond the scope of this book. But you should make a habit of graphing data to see if a low r-value can be explained by a nonlinear relationship. With a nonlinear pattern, a relationship indeed exists but cannot be captured by our analysis.

Restriction of Range

A final situation in which an r-value may be low even when a meaningful relationship exists is **restriction of range**. For interval and ratio data, variables have a range, such as adult male weights from 120 to 250 pounds and a diet-motivation scale from 1 to 10. Restriction of range occurs when one of your variables has a narrow range of values. For example, if all participants in your sample rated their diet motivation as 8, 9, or 10, the range on that variable would be restricted. The sample would contain no motivation values from 1 to 7. We might expect higher weight to be related to greater motivation to diet as indicated by a positive correlation and as tested using a one-tailed test. Based on a restriction of range, the relationship between diet-motivation ratings and weight among men might be illustrated by the following graph. The r-value for this sample is $-.40$ ($p = .433$), which shows no relationship between diet motivation and weight.

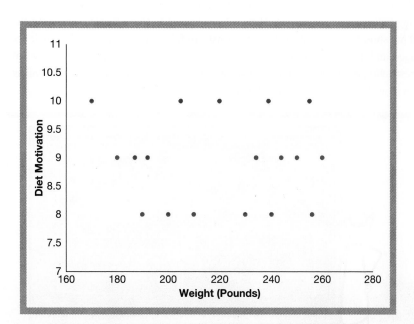

Restriction of Range. Restriction of range occurs when one variable in a data set has a narrow range of values. For example, if you are interested in sleep and grades, restriction of range would be indicated by a sample of participants who all sleep between 7 and 8 hours a night.

When we study interval or ratio variables, we want a wide range of possible values in the sample. If our motivation-weight example contained a wide range of possible motivation values, we might find a meaningful relationship as depicted in the following graph.

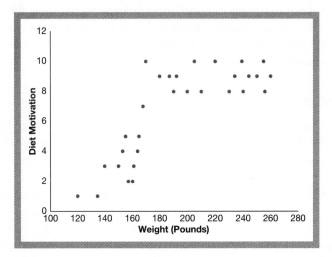

The *r*-value for the sample depicted in the prior graph is .79, with *p* < .001. Notice diet motivation ranges from 1 to 10, a wide range on the rating scale. It is also important that weight contains a wide range of values, or we would have restriction of range on weight.

When a variable is not represented by a wide range of values in our sample, Pearson's *r* may indicate no relationship. How will we know? In this situation, graphing the data will not show the problem. Instead, we must carefully review our variables, their possible ranges, and the spread of values on each (e.g., standard deviation). Logic is the antidote to restriction of range. If you think this problem exists in your sample, try to collect data from more participants until a wider range of values is represented.

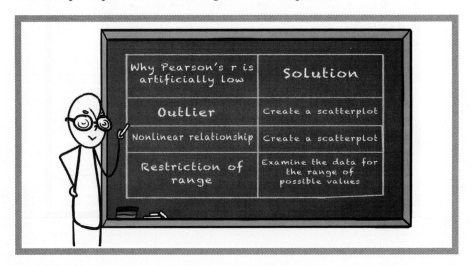

Why Pearson's r is artificially low	Solution
Outlier	Create a scatterplot
Nonlinear relationship	Create a scatterplot
Restriction of range	Examine the data for the range of possible values

WHEN PEARSON'S *r* FALSELY SHOWS A RELATIONSHIP

A strong *r*-value probably will indicate a significant relationship, even when the sample size is rather small. As hard-working researchers, a significant Pearson's *r* with a high absolute value makes us happy. We have something meaningful to report to the world. But we could be wrong. An *r*-value can be falsely high in two situations: (1) restriction of range on a curvilinear relationship and (2) outliers.

Restriction of Range on a Curvilinear Relationship

Remember that a curvilinear relationship cannot be quantified by Pearson's *r*. In our earlier example of daily time spent with a romantic partner and relationship satisfaction, we saw a fictional example in which satisfaction increased across hours spent together, but only to a point, and then satisfaction began to decrease. For a reminder, the graph follows, and the *r*-value was –.03.

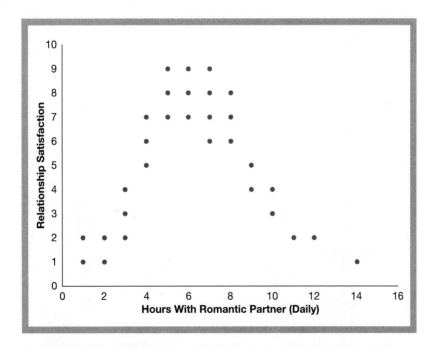

What if we restricted the range on a curvilinear relationship? We might collect a sample of men who see their romantic partners between one and six hours daily. A graph of the sample might look like the following.

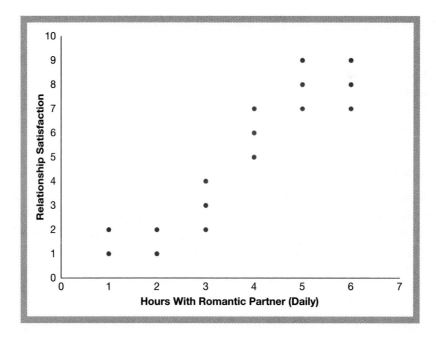

With restriction of range, we would only see a linear relationship between the two variables, and the r-value would be misleading ($r = .92$, $p < .001$). From our data, we might draw the conclusion that the more time people spend with each other, the more satisfied they are with the relationship. Indeed, we could publish this interesting result. Would we be wrong? Yes and no. Our data truly indicate a linear relationship, and over time, more research across the world would address the research question in many different ways, including longer durations of time spent together. Eventually the entire picture would emerge, showing a curvilinear relationship. That is the nature of science and the benefit of an entire scientific community sharing ideas.

Outliers That Strengthen Pearson's r

Just as outliers in the data can reduce Pearson's r, outliers can strengthen the r-value. Either way, researchers usually remove outliers. When unusual data points help to create a linear pattern, we can see the problem by graphing. Let us consider a hypothetical study of television (TV) hours watched daily and college grade point average (GPA). We likely would expect a negative relationship. Notice the outlier in the scatterplot below.

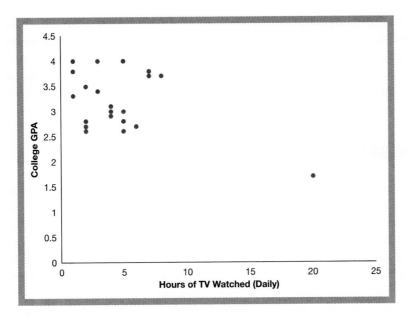

For these data, Pearson's $r = -.47$, $p = .016$, suggesting a significant negative relationship between number of TV hours and college GPA. The more TV watched, the lower the GPA of students in the sample. Most researchers would agree that removal of the outlier paints a clearer and more accurate picture of TV watching and college GPA. When Pearson's r is recalculated without the outlier, $r = .05$, $p = .419$. The scatterplot below illustrates the relationship more honestly.

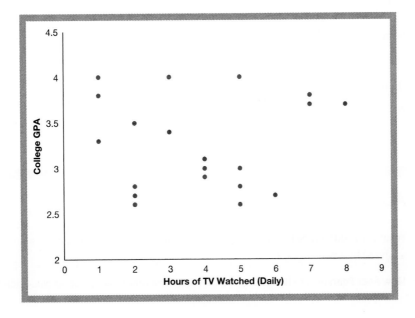

Although it may seem disheartening to find a strong Pearson's r and have to abandon a significant result, always keep in mind that our job as researchers is to communicate the truth. An obvious outlier (or more than one outlier in a large sample) must be removed to show the general relationship pattern, even if that means revealing that no linear pattern exists. At this point in your education, remove only outliers that are obvious in a scatterplot. If you are unsure of whether or not a value is an outlier, talk with your instructor.

SUMMARY

If your research question asks about a relationship between two interval or ratio variables with many values, Pearson's r will analyze the data. The r-value can tell you if the two variables are related, as long as neither variable is manipulated. Alternatively, the r-value can tell you cause and effect as long as one variable is manipulated. Pearson's r does not dictate cause and effect. Pearson's r merely offers an analysis, and you must provide the explanation. At times, the r-value can be artificially inflated or low, and creating a scatterplot reveals the majority of problems that might occur, such as a nonlinear relationship or outliers. A restriction-of-range problem relies on logical evaluation of each variable's range. If no problems are revealed, and the r-value is significant, be sure to report effect size. Pearson's r offers a powerful tool to address a research question about a relationship or cause and effect.

REVIEW OF TERMS

Coefficient of Determination	Outlier (for Ungrouped Data)
Curvilinear Relationship	Pearson's r (Correlation Coefficient)
Directional Test (One-Tailed Test)	Restriction of Range
Nondirectional Test (Two-Tailed Test)	Scatterplot

PRACTICE ITEMS

1. What is the difference between a study design analyzed by Pearson's r and a design analyzed by a two-way χ^2?

2. How does Pearson's r change based on testing for a relationship versus causation?

3. On the following graphs, indicate whether the linear relationship is positive, negative, or so scattered that you cannot determine a relationship.

a.

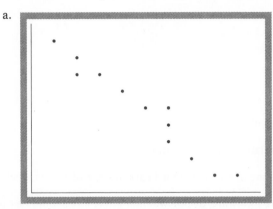

b.

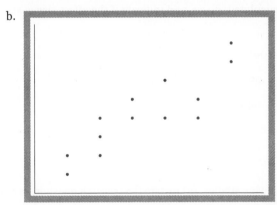

c.

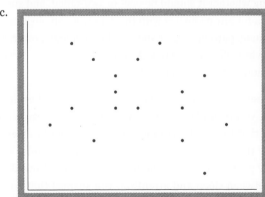

4. Below are examples of *r*-values. Please indicate the direction (positive or negative) and strength (weak, moderate, or strong) of each relationship.

    a. .90

    b. −.31

    c. .17

    d. .02

    e. −.57

    f. .68

5. How do you calculate df for Pearson's r?

6. When can correlation convey causation?

7. What is the name of effect size for Pearson's r, and how is it calculated?

8. For each of the following, decide whether effect size should be calculated. If it should be calculated, do so, and indicate if the effect size is small, medium, or large.

    a. $r = .67, p = .002$

    b. $r = −.12, p = .062$

    c. $r = −.35, p = .049$

    d. $r = .22, p = .822$

* * *

For each of the following studies, (a) restate the research question as a research hypothesis, including whether it should be one- or two-tailed, and state the null hypothesis, (b) check for any problems with the data (e.g., an obvious outlier), (c) determine how many participants are needed for adequate power, and (d) enter and analyze the data as well as write an APA-style results section. Notice that we have written method sections for you to clarify study details.

9. In a review paper on the effects of sleep deprivation and attention (Lim & Dinges, 2008), you read about a positive relationship between sleep and attention such that those who get more sleep have better attention. You decide to study the relationship between these two variables using a sample of high-anxiety participants. Although prior research showed a positive relationship between sleep and attention, you suspect that amount of sleep and attention instead could be negatively related among people with high anxiety. In other words, the relationship might be positive or negative. You ask the research question: *Among people with high anxiety, is amount of sleep related to attention?* In the lab, you ask high-anxiety individuals to

estimate how much sleep they get at night, and then you give them a test of attention with 100 items to recognize. Their attention score will be the number of items they can recall. You collect the following data. Note that the three tables should be entered as two continuous columns in SPSS, and you will have 36 rows in the data file.

Hours Slept	Attention
4	54
4.5	47
5.5	62
5.5	48
6	47
6	60
6	52
6	70
6.5	68
7	70
7	98
7	53

(data continued)

Hours Slept	Attention
7.5	78
7.5	82
7.5	78
7.5	78
7.5	78
7.5	53
8	89
8	90
8	73
8.5	83
8.5	89
8.5	89

(data continued)

Hours Slept	Attention
9	80
9	80
9	94
9	93
9	62
9	76
9.5	76
9.5	82
9.5	92
10	95
10.5	97
11	87

Method

Participants

Participants included 36 college students (20 women and 16 men) recruited through the use of a flyer posted in college residence halls. The flyer specified that those who participated in the study must generally sleep with their televisions on at night. Ethnicities included 10 White, 21 Black, and 5 Asian individuals with a mean age of 21.15 years ($SD = 2.33$). All participants received ethical treatment, and the IRB approved the procedure.

Materials

Attention test. The attention test consisted of a series of 50 neutral pictures shown at 5-sec intervals. Next, participants saw 100 more pictures, 50 of which they saw previously. For each picture, participants indicated whether they had seen the picture before, with scores ranging from 0 correct to 100 correct answers.

Procedure

Participants e-mailed the examiner at the e-mail address provided on the flier. When they arrived at the lab, all participants read and signed informed consent, took the attention test, reported their average number of hours of sleep each night in the last 2 weeks, and provided demographic information.

10. Suppose after you ran a study on sleep and attention, you wanted to find out what other variables might be related to attention. You might read an article by Abdullaev, Posner, Nunnally, and Dishion (2010) linking chronic marijuana use as a teenager to problems with attention in young adulthood. You wonder, *Is use of marijuana positively related to attention problems in college students?* You collect the following data using an attention test based on number of items recalled out of 100 items. In this study, the memory test is provided online through a study link so people can participate anonymously.

Joints	Attention
3	54
3	47
3	45
3	57
3	62
3	48
3	47
2.5	60
2.5	62
2.5	60
2.5	32
2.5	78

(data continued)

Joints	Attention
2	78
2	82
2	88
2	90
2	78
2	78
2	78
2	53
1.5	82
1.5	85
1.5	62
1.5	82

(data continued)

Joints	Attention
1.5	80
1	80
1	81
1	72
1	94
1	93
.5	62
.5	76
.5	80
0	83
0	97
0	60

Method

Participants

Participants included 36 college students (18 men and 18 women) recruited through the use of a flyer posted in college residence halls. Ethnicities included 17 White, 5 Black, and 4 Asian individuals as well as 10 individuals who chose not to disclose their ethnicity, and 20.25 years ($SD = 1.13$) represented the mean age of participants. All participants received ethical treatment, and the IRB approved the procedure.

Materials

Attention test. The online attention test consisted of a series of 50 neutral pictures shown at 5-sec intervals. Next, participants saw 100 more pictures, 50 of which they viewed previously. For each picture, participants indicated whether they had seen the picture before by clicking on the Y key if they had previously seen the picture or the N key if they had not. Scores on this test ranged from 0 to 100 correct answers.

Procedure

Due to the sensitive nature of this project, participants completed the study online to allow anonymity. Participants e-mailed the examiner at the e-mail address provided on the flier and received a link to the study. First, all participants read and agreed to the informed consent by clicking on a button next to the statement, "I give my consent to participate in this study." Next, they took the attention test, reported the average number of joints smoked per week when they were between the ages of 16 and 18, and provided demographic information.

11. Your 25-year-old brother seems to be unable to keep more than a part-time job. He seems happy, but you recall reading a paper finding that unemployed men score lower on the personality trait of agreeableness than those who are employed (Boyce, Wood, Daly, & Sedikides, 2015). You wonder if men who work fewer hours have lower agreeableness than men who work more hours. Using the agreeableness scale of the Big Five Inventory (BFI; John & Srivastava, 1999), you ask men working either full or part time at various establishments in your community to complete the BFI and report about how many hours per week they have worked over the last six months. You ask the research question: *Is agreeableness related to number of hours worked such that more agreeableness is related with more hours worked?* You collect the following data.

Hours Worked	Agreeableness		Hours Worked	Agreeableness		Hours Worked	Agreeableness
			(data continued)			(data continued)	
12	39		20	15		31	41
12	30		20	22		32	16
13	25		20	45		35	38
14	25		20	30		35	26
15	14		23	15		36	20
15	21		25	31		36	41
15	29		26	27		38	30
16	35		27	17		40	41
17	17		29	32		41	27
18	37		29	24		42	31
18	28		30	37		45	23
20	45		30	40		45	12

Method

Participants

Participants included 36 adult men (mean age = 37.51, SD = 10.87) recruited at five local businesses (grocery store, bank, child-care facility, gym, bookstore) by approaching them and asking for participation. All participants received ethical treatment, and the IRB approved the procedure.

Materials

Big Five Inventory (BFI). The BFI is a 44-item scale that assesses personality through the lexical Big Five factors of personality (Openness, Conscientiousness, Extraversion, Agreeableness, and Neuroticism). Participants used a 5-point Likert scale to rate how strongly they agreed or disagreed with statements about their personality. Research on North American samples illustrates strong reliability of the BFI (α = .75 − .90; John & Srivastava, 1999). In this study, we only used the 9 Agreeableness items, with 45 items representing the maximum score.

Procedure

Researchers approached participants in the five locations listed above and asked if they worked at the establishment and would consider participating in a study. After agreement, participants received a premade packet with the consent form, BFI, and demographics form that asked their age, gender, and number of hours worked to complete and mail back to the examiner within 1 week. Of the 47 packets distributed, participants returned 36.

REFERENCES

Abdullaev, Y., Posner, M., Nunnally, R., & Dishion, T. (2010). Research report: Functional MRI evidence for inefficient attentional control in adolescent chronic cannabis abuse. *Behavioural Brain Research, 215*(1), 45–57. doi:10.1016/j.bbr.2010.06.023

Boyce, C. J., Wood, A. M., Daly, M., & Sedikides, C. (2015). Personality change following unemployment. *Journal of Applied Psychology, 4,* 991–1011. doi: 10.1037/a0038647

Cohen, J. (1988). *Statistical power analysis for the behavioral sciences.* Hillsdale, NJ: Lawrence Erlbaum.

Cohen, J. (1992). A power primer. *Psychological Bulletin, 112*(1), 155–159. doi:10.1037/0033-2909.112.1.155

John, O. P., & Srivastava, S. (1999). The Big Five trait taxonomy: History, measurement, and theoretical perspectives. In L. A. Pervin & O. P. John (Eds.), *Handbook of personality: Theory and research* (vol. 2, pp. 102–138). New York, NY: Guilford Press.

Lim, J., & Dinges, D. F. (2008). Sleep deprivation and vigilant attention. *Annals of the New York Academy of Sciences, 1129,* 305–322. doi:10.1196/annals.1417.002

8

Scale Development

Pearson's r is used to quantify a relationship between two interval or ratio variables or, if one variable is manipulated, Pearson's r can help establish cause and effect. Either way, relevant research designs have two interval or ratio variables with several values on each variable. In both of the designs detailed in Chapter 7, Pearson's r addressed a specific research question.

In this chapter, we will talk about how to use Pearson's r to evaluate measures. When you design a study to answer a research question, you often choose published measures as part of your method. Usually a published survey, questionnaire, or scale has been examined in detail by the authors or those who subsequently used the measure. Pearson's r likely provided support for published measures, and you can feel confident that the variables of interest will be adequately assessed. Below we explain the process of making sure a measure is useful. Even if you are not ready to write and evaluate your own measure, you should understand the creation of those you use.

Construct. The concept you are interested in measuring is called a construct.

When we measure a concept of interest, or **construct**, we want to make sure that (a) our measure gives us roughly the same answer each time we use it and (b) we are indeed measuring what we think we are measuring. For example, imagine weighing yourself on a scale that shows your weight as 165 pounds, and then an hour later the scale shows your weight to be 112. Such a scale is not useful because you cannot consistently get the same outcome. Now imagine a different situation: You have a scale that consistently weighs you at 165 pounds, but then you go to the doctor's office and learn you actually weigh 150 pounds. Again, your home scale is not useful. Although it might provide a consistent weight, the scale is inaccurate. When measuring a variable, we must have confidence that the measure is dependable and accurate.

Psychometric Properties. Psychometric properties of a measure include reliability and validity.

Fortunately, numerous measures that exist in the published literature have been carefully constructed, and both dependability and accuracy have been assessed. These and other measures are called the **psychometric properties** of a scale. When such analyses have been conducted, you should be able to find details in published articles. Scales that have been assessed for dependability and accuracy are far more respected that those that have not. Whenever possible, incorporate tested scales in your methodology, and provide references for the scales as well as publications related to the scales' psychometric properties.

PEARSON'S *r* AND RELIABILITY OF MEASURES

Reliability refers to a measure's ability to obtain similar values more than once. For example, if we wanted to examine body image, we might use a 10-item, self-report questionnaire containing items such as, "I feel good about the way my body looks." If the body-image scale is reliable, we should be able to get similar ratings from the same people across two administrations of the scale. That is, if someone has a high score on the first assessment of body image, a second assessment should also yield a high score. A measure that lacks reliability is of little use to researchers because it is not dependable.

Testing for measure reliability comes in several different forms, including test-retest, alternate-forms, and split-half reliability. When measures are highly subjective, we ask more than one researcher to score them, examining reliability of scores between researchers as a measure of interrater reliability. For most measures of reliability, we use the same statistical analysis: Pearson's *r*. However, an important exception, Cronbach's alpha, is explained later in this chapter.

Test-Retest Reliability

An assessment of **test-retest reliability** involves asking participants to complete the same measure twice. For example, if you took a test of statistics knowledge and scored

Reliability. A measure's ability to obtain similar values more than once is called reliability.

Test-Retest Reliability. Test-retest reliability refers to the ability of a measure to result in similar numbers across two administrations of the same test.

98% correct, taking the same test a second time should yield a similar percentage correct. When the entire class takes the test twice, the instructor could use Pearson's r to measure test-retest reliability. In this case, our measure is percentage correct across two time periods, offering ratio data. When collecting data, be sure to write each student's data on a single row as shown below. We added a column for student number to help organize the data.

Student Number	Statistics Test Time 1	Statistics Test Time 2
1	98	95
2	86	82
3	50	43
4	74	79
5	95	97
6	68	66
7	75	65
8	81	79
9	30	40
10	77	85

We would expect the correlation coefficient to be strong and positive. Higher values provide more confidence that the test is a reliable measure of statistics knowledge, with $r = .70$ or higher a typical goal.

To obtain Pearson's r, enter the data into SPSS as shown below. Notice that the student number column is not required because those values are not analyzed.

TestTime1	TestTime2
98.00	95.00
86.00	82.00
50.00	43.00
74.00	79.00
95.00	97.00
68.00	66.00
75.00	65.00
81.00	79.00
30.00	40.00
77.00	85.00

Click Analyze, Correlate, Bivariate.

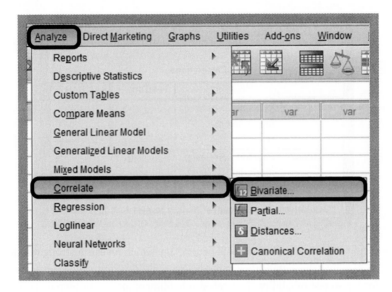

In the box that opens, move TestTime1 and TestTime2 to the right-side box by clicking the middle arrow. Under Test of Significance, click the circle beside One-tailed because we expect a specific direction for Pearson's r: a positive value. Click OK.

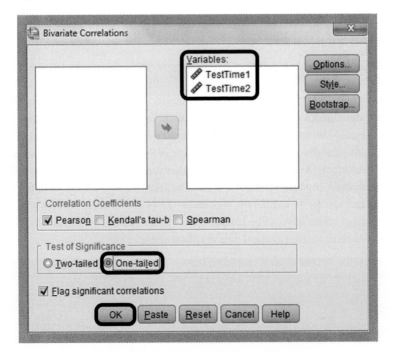

SPSS will provide output as shown below.

Correlations

Correlations

		TestTime1	TestTime2
TestTime1	Pearson Correlation	1	.949**
	Sig. (1-tailed)		.000
	N	10	10
TestTime2	Pearson Correlation	.949**	1
	Sig. (1-tailed)	.000	
	N	10	10

**. Correlation is significant at the 0.01 level (1-tailed).

The output shows a correlation coefficient of .95, which reveals a strong relationship. You will notice that the significance value is less than .001, but we do not focus on the p-value for test-retest reliability. Test-retest reliability of .95 is considered excellent. We can be confident that our statistics test is reliable because it yielded a similar pattern of values across two administrations of the same test. Participants who made a high score at Time 1 also made a high score at Time 2. Those who earned a low score at Time 1 likewise earned a low score at Time 2.

Alternate-Forms Reliability

Alternate-Forms Reliability (Parallel-Forms Reliability). Alternate-forms reliability is established when two different versions of a measure result in similar numbers across two administrations.

A second way to assess a measure's reliability requires asking participants to complete entirely different forms of a measure, called **alternate-forms reliability** (or **parallel-forms reliability**). Using our statistics-test example again, an instructor might test statistics knowledge using two completely separate tests of the same material. Pearson's r could be used to correlate scores across the two tests. Once again, the correlation coefficient should be strong and positive. A Pearson's r of .70 or above indicates acceptable alternate-forms reliability, with higher numbers indicating better reliability.

As an example, suppose a professor wanted to know if one version of a statistics exam yielded scores similar to a different version of the exam. If alternate forms of the test provide similar scores, she can be confident that measurement of her students' statistics knowledge is reliable. Hypothetical data are shown here.

Participant Number	Version 1 of Stats Exam	Version 2 of Stats Exam
1	75	82
2	56	70
3	99	91

Participant Number	Version 1 of Stats Exam	Version 2 of Stats Exam
4	85	90
5	82	85
6	77	83
7	81	76
8	92	95
9	90	88
10	64	72

After providing column headings, enter the data into SPSS and analyze as you did the prior example. Click Analyze, Correlate, and Bivariate. In the next box, move both forms of the test to the right, request a one-tailed test because we clearly expect a specific correlation direction (positive), and click OK. The output below shows an r-value of .90, which illustrates excellent alternate-forms reliability.

Correlations

Correlations

		Version_1	Version_2
Version_1	Pearson Correlation	1	.899**
	Sig. (1-tailed)		.000
	N	10	10
Version_2	Pearson Correlation	.899**	1
	Sig. (1-tailed)	.000	
	N	10	10

**. Correlation is significant at the 0.01 level (1-tailed).

Again, we do not concentrate on the Sig value of .000 ($p < .001$). In fact, with a large sample size, a low r-value could be significant and still not be useful to us. Recall that a high positive r-value is our focus for reliability.

Split-Half Reliability

A third assessment of a measure's reliability using Pearson's r is **split-half reliability**, which involves randomly separating an assessment into two parts. Participants complete the two halves, and their values are assessed using the correlation coefficient (r). Again we would expect strong positive values. Just as with the alternate-forms approach, Pearson's r should be strong and positive, with a value at or above .70 indicating acceptable split-half reliability. Although .70 is adequate split-half reliability, higher is better.

Split-Half Reliability. A measure of reliability based on correlating two randomly selected groups of items is called split-half reliability.

As you have learned, Pearson's r can assess a measure's reliability using three approaches: test-retest, alternate-forms, and split-half reliability. In all three assessments of a measure's reliability, researchers want strong positive Pearson's r-values. Typically, we want to see values above .70 to reflect that we are indeed dependably measuring the construct. The higher the correlation coefficient, the more confidence we can have in the dependability of our measure.

CRONBACH'S ALPHA AND RELIABILITY OF MEASURES

Cronbach's alpha (α). Cronbach's alpha is a measure of a scale's reliability based on all possible split-half estimates.

Internal Consistency. Internal consistency tells us the extent to which items within a scale measure the same construct.

A final assessment of a measure's reliability, **Cronbach's alpha (α)**, assesses the extent to which items within a scale intercorrelate by calculating all possible split-half configurations. A useful and popular way to measure **internal consistency**, Cronbach's alpha ranges from zero to one. Higher positive values on Cronbach's alpha indicate stronger internal consistency, with .70 serving as an acceptable level of reliability. Of course, higher values indicate better reliability. Calculations for alpha can be accomplished by SPSS.

As an example, the brief version of the professor-student rapport scale contains six items (Ryan & Wilson, 2014; Wilson & Ryan, 2013).

	Strongly Disagree				Strongly Agree
1. My professor encourages questions and comment from students.	1	2	3	4	5
2. I dislike my professor's class.*	1	2	3	4	5
3. My professor makes class enjoyable.	1	2	3	4	5
4. I want to take other classes taught by my professor.	1	2	3	4	5
5. My professor's body language says, "Don't bother me."*	1	2	3	4	5
6. I really like to come to class.	1	2	3	4	5

*These two items are reverse scored.

To make sure the scale indeed measures one construct, we would need to test for internal consistency using Cronbach's alpha. A high value for alpha would indicate that the scale items correlate well with each other. Below are data to represent 20 students who completed the brief rapport scale.

Student	Encourages	Dislike	Enjoyable	More	Bother	Like
1	3	3	3	2	3	4
2	3	3	3	1	5	2
3	2	4	2	2	4	2
4	2	4	3	2	4	2
5	3	3	2	3	4	3
6	1	5	1	1	5	1
7	4	2	4	3	4	4
8	3	3	3	3	2	3
9	4	2	4	4	2	4
10	4	2	4	4	2	3
11	3	3	3	3	4	3
12	4	4	4	4	4	4
13	4	2	4	3	4	3
14	5	5	5	5	2	5
15	5	1	4	4	1	5
16	4	2	4	4	2	4
17	3	3	3	3	4	3
18	4	2	3	3	4	2
19	3	1	3	4	2	3
20	3	3	2	3	3	2

SPSS: SCORING AND INTERPRETING MEASURES

Reverse Scoring Items

Four of the items are worded positively such that higher ratings indicate more instructor-student rapport. Two of the items are worded negatively and must be reverse scored after the data are entered in to SPSS. Use of some negative items will show us if participants are just marking every item high (or low) without actually reading them. Enter the six rapport items into SPSS Variable View as shown below. We did not label values because we know that each item response ranges from 1 to 5.

Name	Type
Encourages	Numeric
Dislike	Numeric
Enjoyable	Numeric
More	Numeric
Bother	Numeric
Like	Numeric

Switch to Data View and enter all values as provided by participants. The two negatively worded items must be reverse scored such that 1, 2, 3, 4, 5 ratings by participants become 5, 4, 3, 2, 1 ratings for us so that all items indicate more rapport with higher numbers. After entering data, we can allow SPSS to reverse score the two items (Dislike and Bother) by clicking Transform and Recode into Different Variables.

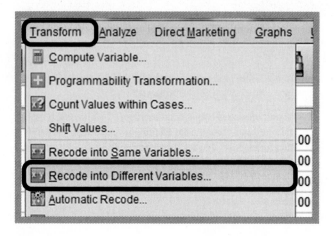

In the box that opens, move Dislike and Bother to the right. Click Dislike under Numeric Variable —> Output Variable to highlight it, then type DislikeR under Output Variable to indicate you are reverse scoring this item. Click the Change button.

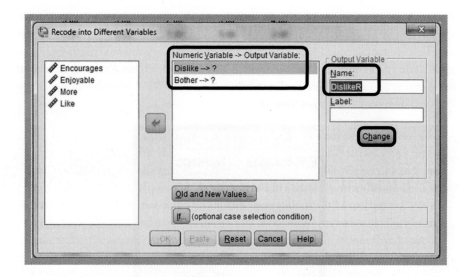

Follow the same procedure for Bother, naming it BotherR for reverse scoring. Click Change, then click Old and New Values.

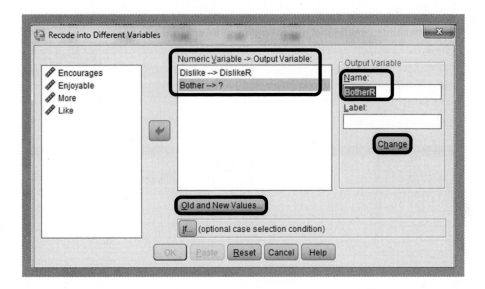

In the box that appears, we will let SPSS know that we want to reverse the scoring of these two items. We want a rating of 1 to be changed to a rating of 5 to allow higher numbers to show more rapport. Type a 1 under Old Value and a 5 under New Value, and click Add.

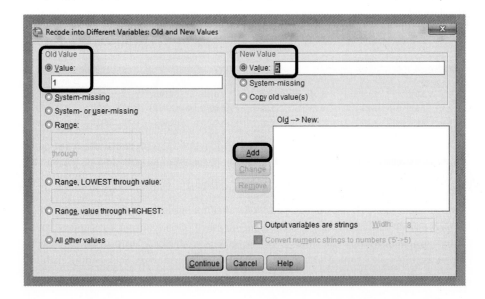

Follow the same procedure for 2 and 4, and so on, clicking Add to change each of the five values. Next click Continue.

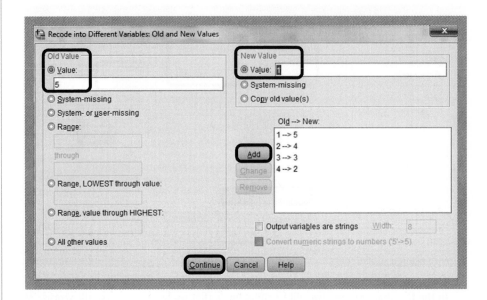

You will return to the prior box. Click OK. SPSS will display a message saying the recoding has occurred. Close that message to see the recoded items on the right side of the data set.

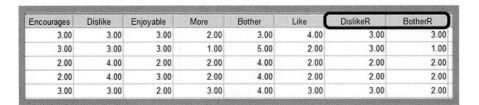

Encourages	Dislike	Enjoyable	More	Bother	Like	DislikeR	BotherR
3.00	3.00	3.00	2.00	3.00	4.00	3.00	3.00
3.00	3.00	3.00	1.00	5.00	2.00	3.00	1.00
2.00	4.00	2.00	2.00	4.00	2.00	2.00	2.00
2.00	4.00	3.00	2.00	4.00	2.00	2.00	2.00
3.00	3.00	2.00	3.00	4.00	3.00	3.00	2.00

Cronbach's Alpha on SPSS

After negatively worded items have been reverse scored, SPSS can provide Cronbach's alpha for the scale as an assessment of reliability. Click Analyze, Scale, and Reliability Analysis.

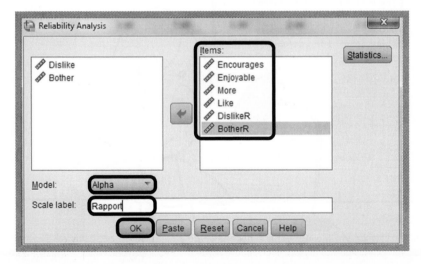

In the box that opens, move the six relevant items to the right. Be careful not to move the old items that were negatively worded. Some researchers choose to delete the old data columns after reverse scoring so they do not get confused. Notice that Alpha, for Cronbach's alpha, is the default statistic (circled in the next screenshot). For Scale label, we have chosen "Rapport." Click OK.

The output below contains an alpha value of .899, or rounded, $\alpha = .90$.

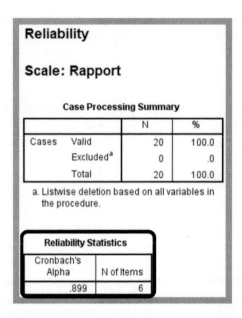

Such a strong Cronbach's alpha indicates that items on the scale are intercorrelated, and we can feel confident that items are consistently measuring a similar construct. As with other forms of reliability we have discussed so far, an alpha of .70 or higher is considered acceptable.

Scoring a Measure

Because Cronbach's alpha demonstrated good internal consistency, we can condense the six items to a single score. After all, the items represent the single construct of rapport. In this data set, we are interested in knowing the average rapport rating per student based on the six rapport items. Click Transform and Compute Variable.

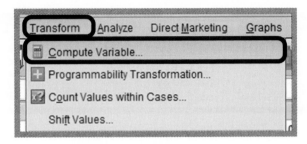

In the box that opens, first name your Target Variable, which simply names the measure. We have chosen Rapport_Avg. Next look at the list of items under Type & Label. We will create a formula to obtain the average of our six relevant items, again ignoring Dislike and Bother because we will be using the reverse-scored items: DislikeR and BotherR. Either use the keys on the pad to create a formula, or type in what you need using your computer keyboard. Begin with an opening parenthesis, and then click the first relevant item—Encourages—over to the right to become part of the formula. Add a plus sign, and then move the second relevant item—Enjoyable—to the right. Continue until you have created the formula in the screenshot below. Enter a closing parenthesis to show where the sum ends. Next, divide the sum of items by 6 to get a mean rapport value for each participant.

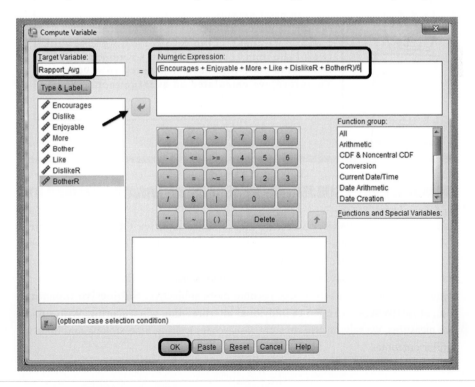

When you click OK, SPSS will provide a message that the average has been computed for each row. The spreadsheet now will show Rapport_Avg as a new column of data.

Encourages	Dislike	Enjoyable	More	Bother	Like	DislikeR	BotherR	Rapport_Avg
3.00	3.00	3.00	2.00	3.00	4.00	3.00	3.00	3.00
3.00	3.00	3.00	1.00	5.00	2.00	3.00	1.00	2.17
2.00	4.00	2.00	2.00	4.00	2.00	2.00	2.00	2.00
2.00	4.00	3.00	2.00	4.00	2.00	2.00	2.00	2.17
3.00	3.00	2.00	3.00	4.00	3.00	3.00	2.00	2.67
1.00	5.00	1.00	1.00	5.00	1.00	1.00	1.00	1.00

Any research design that contains a multi-item measure can be analyzed the same way. Input item values, reverse score negatively worded items, check for internal consistency using Cronbach's alpha, and compute an average value to further analyze. An average value per participant could be used as a DV in a study or serve as a variable to be correlated with other data. For example, the average rapport value could serve as a dependent variable in a study of different teaching approaches. Or perhaps you might be interested in the potential correlation between rapport averages and how many days students attend class in a term.

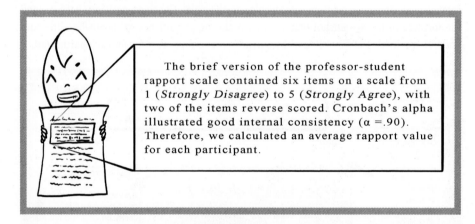

The brief version of the professor-student rapport scale contained six items on a scale from 1 (*Strongly Disagree*) to 5 (*Strongly Agree*), with two of the items reverse scored. Cronbach's alpha illustrated good internal consistency ($\alpha = .90$). Therefore, we calculated an average rapport value for each participant.

RELIABILITY WITH SUBJECTIVE MEASURES: INTERRATER RELIABILITY

Reliability assessments work best when measures are objective. **Objective measures** do not rely on interpretation to score. Good examples would be multiple-choice tests, physiological measures using reliable equipment (e.g., a thermometer or blood-pressure cuff), and even essays scored using a detailed rubric. The reliability of assessments begins to break down as measures become more subjective. **Subjective measures** (e.g., attractiveness) are open to individual interpretation when scoring. With subjective measures, we rely on two or more researchers scoring assessments and hope for similar outcomes.

Objective Measures. When a measure is objective, scores do not rely on interpretation by the researcher. Values on objective measures are usually reliable.

Subjective Measures. When a measure is subjective, scoring is open to each researcher's interpretation.

Suppose we wanted to measure children's kindness on a playground. First we would gather our team of researchers and discuss how we might operationally define kindness. Then we would observe several children and openly discuss scoring of each child's behavior. Only with extensive team training would researchers move forward with individual scoring. After their competence had been established, at least two researchers would score each interaction separately, not discussing their scores with each other. Pearson's r will reveal **interrater reliability** (also called **interobserver reliability**) for subjective scoring. As you probably guessed, the r-value should be strong and positive. Most researchers work toward a correlation coefficient of .90 or higher, but $r = .70$ is considered acceptable.

> **Interrater Reliability (Interobserver Reliability).** Given a subjective measure, the ability of two researchers to score the same construct in the same way is called interrater reliability.

Let us take a few minutes to consider a data set of kindness operationally defined as the number of smiles during a 20-minute recess. The data must include ratings of the same children by two independent researchers.

	Researcher 1	Researcher 2
Sue	3	5
Mari	1	5
Justin	4	6
Nese	2	4
Bubba	5	2
Reagan	4	1
Zeph	6	6
Cal	3	4

(Continued)

(Continued)

	Researcher 1	Researcher 2
Tonya	2	5
Jamilla	1	3
Boris	3	4

We can enter these data into SPSS and identify each researcher in a column. We must take care to match up each child's scores in a row, but we do not need to enter the children's names. In the following screenshot, note that each row represents ratings of the same child by both researchers.

Researcher_1	Researcher_2
3.00	5.00
1.00	5.00
4.00	6.00
2.00	4.00
5.00	2.00
4.00	1.00
6.00	6.00
3.00	4.00
2.00	5.00
1.00	3.00
3.00	4.00

To assess interrater reliability, click Analyze, Correlate, and Bivariate just as we explained in prior examples. In the box that opens, move both Researcher_1 and Researcher_2 over to the right, request a one-tailed test because higher values from the first researcher should relate to higher values from the second researcher (a positive correlation), and click OK. In the SPSS output below, notice the r-value of -.004. An r so weak shows us that interrater reliability is terrible.

Correlations

Correlations

		Researcher_1	Researcher_2
Researcher_1	Pearson Correlation	1	-.004
	Sig. (1-tailed)		.496
	N	11	11
Researcher_2	Pearson Correlation	-.004	1
	Sig. (1-tailed)	.496	
	N	11	11

We cannot rely on the researchers' observations because they perceived different behaviors even though they both watched the same children at the same time. Such a low Pearson's r means that the two scorers were not measuring the construct (in this case, kindness) in the same way, and they should train together again before returning to individual scoring.

If your method includes a subjective measure, you are expected to have more than one researcher score the measure. Be sure to train scorers, practice, score individually, and then analyze interrater reliability using Pearson's r. Research designs with subjective measures require you to assess interrater reliability, and the Pearson's r is reported in the results section.

PEARSON'S r AND VALIDITY

Validity refers to the extent to which a scale actually measures the construct it was meant to measure. A valid self-report scale of creativity, for example, likely contains items related to creative thoughts or behaviors. Such a scale probably does not contain items related to statistical knowledge or aggression. Science offers several ways to assess the validity of a measure, including face validity, content validity, convergent construct validity, discriminant construct validity, and predictive validity.

Face Validity

Researchers assess **face validity** of a scale simply by reading the items. As indicated above, a scale designed to measure creativity should contain items that *appear* to measure creativity. And the scale should not contain items that clearly measure something else.

Validity. A measure's ability to assess the construct of interest is called validity.

Face Validity. When items of a measure appear to assess the construct of interest, items have face validity. Face validity is based on logical thinking rather than a statistic.

Content Validity

Like face validity, researchers assess **content validity** by reading individual items. With content validity, however, the goal is to ensure that *all* aspects of the construct are represented. Using our creativity example, if we want to measure both artistic and musical creativity, then we must include items from each of these domains.

Face validity and content validity are assessed using logic only, not Pearson's *r*. The remaining measures of validity can be assessed using the correlation coefficient.

Convergent Construct Validity

An assessment of **convergent construct validity** relies on locating other measures and comparing them to the scale in question. For example, if we wanted to write a useful self-report scale of depression, we would need to know that our scale actually measured the construct of interest. We might conduct a literature review and locate another scale that is known to be a good depression measure. If we have indeed constructed an acceptable measure of depression, then participants who score high on our new measure should also score high on the established depression scale. That is, Pearson's *r* should be positive and fairly high. Do not expect Pearson's *r* for construct validity to be as high as measures of reliability, but the correlation coefficient should still be above a .50.

Likewise we might locate a scale that measures a similar construct. For example, anxiety is a construct that relates to depression. Because the scale does not assess depression directly, we would not expect an extremely high *r*-value, but we would expect a positive value. The correlation coefficient should still be strong, indicating an overlap of the two constructs.

Convergent construct validity of a measure also can be assessed using scales measuring the *opposite* of a construct of interest. For example, we would expect a scale of happiness to correlate negatively with our depression scale. Values should go in opposite directions, with people scoring high on depression scoring low on happiness. Researchers hope for a strong negative correlation between logically opposite constructs.

Regardless of whether construct validity of a scale is assessed using measures of similar or opposite constructs, Pearson's *r* allows us to measure how well other scales converge on the construct of interest as measured by the scale we have created (or chosen) for our study. If we fail to find convergent validity, we have to question if we have a scale that actually measures the variable of interest.

Discriminant Construct Validity

In addition to knowing that a measure converges with other measures of similar or opposite constructs, you also need to know if the measure *does not* converge with measures of different constructs. **Discriminant construct validity** establishes no relationship between the scale (construct) of interest and completely unrelated constructs. For example, a scale designed to measure depression should not relate well to a measure of introversion. The correlation coefficient should be close to zero. Of course, we already know that *r* will rarely equal exactly zero, but researchers expect an *r*-value close to zero on measures of unrelated constructs.

Predictive Validity

If a measure captures the construct of interest, scores should predict future outcomes, also known as **predictive validity**. Researchers often are interested in behaviors, attitudes, or feelings we might reasonably expect based on score values. Using our depression-survey example, those who score high on depression might be more likely to harm themselves in the future. In this case, psychologists recognize the importance of predictive validity as a chance to intervene before a negative event. A valid scale of depression could allow psychologists to identify people who need help.

As a second example of predictive validity, a valid measure of altruism (helping behavior) might predict empathy toward others. Let us explore the ability of an altruism scale given at age 10 to predict empathy toward others at age 21. On the next page we have a fictional data set with a participant column on the left to remind you to organize the data

Predictive Validity.
The extent to which a measure correlates with a related behavior, attitude, or feeling at a later time is called predictive validity.

by participant. For the sake of this example, we will say scores on the altruism scale range from 1 to 5, with higher numbers meaning more altruism. Empathy might be operationalized using a scale from 1 to 100, with higher numbers meaning more empathy.

Participant Number	Altruism Score (Age 10)	Empathy Toward Others (Age 21)
1	4	85
2	5	87
3	4	76
4	3	54
5	5	92
6	2	67
7	3	70
8	1	43

Predictive validity is a form of 'criterion validity' that indicates how well a measure predicts a future outcome.

A stronger *r*-value indicates better ability to predict from the scale, or greater predictive validity. For our altruism example, we once again enter the data into SPSS, but this time we will enter participant number to help us keep track of which row of data belongs with which participant. Although the participant column will not be analyzed here, often we enter participant data (e.g., age, gender, and ethnicity) to provide details for an APA-style participant section.

Participant	Altruism	Empathy
1.00	4.00	85.00
2.00	5.00	87.00
3.00	4.00	76.00
4.00	3.00	54.00
5.00	5.00	92.00
6.00	2.00	67.00
7.00	3.00	70.00
8.00	1.00	43.00

As we have shown in this chapter, click Analyze, Correlate, Bivariate to open a new box. Then move only Altruism and Empathy to the right side to correlate these two variables. Click beside One-tailed Test of Significance because we have a clear expectation that the two variables will be positively correlated, with higher altruism scores at age 10 predicting higher empathy scores at age 21. Click OK. The output shows Pearson's r, a measure of predictive validity.

Correlations

Correlations

		Altruism	Empathy
Altruism	Pearson Correlation	1	.904**
	Sig. (1-tailed)		.001
	N	8	8
Empathy	Pearson Correlation	.904**	1
	Sig. (1-tailed)	.001	
	N	8	8

**. Correlation is significant at the 0.01 level (1-tailed).

With a Pearson's r of .90, we can see that the altruism scale did a good job of predicting future feelings of empathy. In other words, we demonstrated good predictive validity. If our goal was to predict future empathy, the altruism scale works.

SUMMARY

Pearson's r offers a useful tool to assess reliability and validity. If you create your own measure, you will need to examine its psychometric properties. However, it is unlikely that you will write your own scale during undergraduate years. Instead, recognize the role of Pearson's r and the importance of psychometrics as you choose published measures. Published scales garner more respect if they demonstrate reliability and validity. For your own studies, use Cronbach's alpha to establish internal consistency for multi-item scales. And evaluate interrater reliability for all subjective measures.

REVIEW OF TERMS

Alternate-Forms Reliability
(Parallel-Forms Reliability)

Construct

Content Validity

Convergent Construct Validity

Cronbach's alpha (α)

Discriminant Construct
Validity

Face Validity

Internal Consistency

Interrater Reliability (Interobserver
Reliability)

Objective Measures

Predictive Validity

Psychometric Properties

Reliability

Split-Half Reliability

Subjective Measures

Test-Retest Reliability

Validity

PRACTICE ITEMS

1. Why is it generally more desirable to choose published measures with tested psychometric properties when designing a study rather than create your own measure?

2. What is the difference between reliability and validity?

3. List and describe different types of reliability. Where relevant, please also note what an "acceptable" number is for each.

4. List and describe different types of validity.

5. Lara wanted to know if her measure of creativity has good test-retest reliability. She gave the same measure twice to the same group of people on two consecutive days. Please calculate test-retest reliability and determine whether the outcome is acceptable for Lara's creativity measure.

Time 1	Time 2
56	50
36	32
59	50
60	63
37	39
27	32
89	78

(data continued)

Time 1	Time 2
52	50
78	82
99	90
21	28
57	57
27	29
73	75

6. Geoffrey is teaching a new Child Abnormal Psychology course at his local community college. He tested all students using two versions of his first exam and wants to make sure that the versions are equivalent. Using the following data, calculate the alternate-forms reliability of his two versions of Exam 1 and state whether the reliability is acceptable.

Version A	Version B
98	80
75	78
77	82
78	70
88	90
72	65
54	65
83	90
45	40

(data continued)

Version A	Version B
81	75
76	83
88	90
95	96
76	78
70	64
82	80
68	72
62	47

7. Chas runs the music department at his university. He was tasked with creating a standardized assessment for music majors to see if they leave the program with knowledge taught in the major. He collected the following data representing the total score on the even and odd items of the test. What is the split-half reliability of his music test? Is this number acceptable?

(data continued)

Evens	Odds	Evens	Odds
25	20	42	45
32	30	45	47
36	40	45	49
38	40	46	38
40	40	47	38
40	38	48	45
41	45	50	50

8. Samantha works with survivors of trauma. She has created a measure of sensitivity to emotion that she wants to use in her research, but she has to first make sure the measure has good validity and internal consistency (reliability). The six questions on her measure are rated on a scale from 1 (*strongly disagree*) to 7 (*strongly agree*), with items 2 and 3 reverse scored. Respondents are asked to answer the following questions based on their experiences in the last two weeks.

1. I feel connected with others.

2. I often feel as if I am floating through life.

3. I have trouble making daily decisions.

4. I feel as if I have someone I can call when I am distressed.

5. I am able to fully experience positive emotions.

6. I am able to fully experience negative emotions.

Samantha collected the following data. Please do the following: (a) Discuss the face validity of Samantha's measure, (b) discuss the content validity of her measure, and (c) calculate Cronbach's alpha for her measure and evaluate this number.

Participant	Connected	Floating	Decision	Call	Positive	Negative
1	3	5	4	3	2	4
2	4	5	5	4	1	3
3	5	2	2	4	4	5
4	1	7	6	1	2	1
5	7	2	1	6	5	6
6	3	3	2	2	3	4
7	4	4	4	5	2	3
8	4	5	4	2	2	4
9	6	2	1	4	7	5
10	7	2	2	5	7	7
11	2	5	5	1	1	1
12	3	5	4	4	4	2
13	5	3	5	4	5	6
14	6	1	2	3	6	3
15	7	2	2	7	7	4

9. Pete and Gorbe were given an assignment in their Integrated Research Methods and Statistics course to measure friendliness in strangers by naturalistic observation only. They decided to visit a coffee shop on campus and observe customers as they interacted with the barista. They operationally defined friendliness as number of genuine smiles in the first 20 seconds of interacting with the barista. They collected the following data. Calculate their interrater reliability. Is it acceptable?

Pete	Gorbe
3	3
2	2
5	4
1	0
3	3
6	5
4	4
2	2
0	1

(data continued)

Pete	Gorbe
4	3
1	2
4	4
0	0
0	1
4	4
3	3
1	1

10. Sansa wants to know if her measure of early mathematics skills in preschool predicts math knowledge in the first grade. She gives her mathematics test to a group of preschoolers, waits two years, and then gives them a test of math to assess convergent validity. She also gives them a test of reading skills to assess discriminant validity. Examine both convergent and discriminant construct validity of her measure and state whether each is considered acceptable.

(data continued)

Preschool Math	First-Grade Math	First-Grade Reading	Preschool Math	First-Grade Math	First-Grade Reading
56	55	50	15	30	20
28	29	21	99	85	95
48	58	45	35	45	43
90	81	80	66	60	65
27	36	36	25	20	20
45	68	32	86	78	95
23	15	20	34	45	30
87	88	85	68	72	65
25	26	20	74	82	78

11. Pharrell wants to develop a test of singers' ability to navigate the music industry early in their careers. Based on his knowledge of what he believes singers need to know, he creates the Pharrell Harmony Aptitude Test (PHAT) and then tracks artists over their first year to see how many albums they sell. Calculate the predictive validity of the PHAT and state whether it is acceptable.

(data continued)

PHAT Score	Albums Sold	PHAT Score	Albums Sold
2	50,000	6	110,000
2	2,000,500	7	780,000
3	20,560	7	80,000
3	60,500	7	90,000
3	90,000	8	1,000,000
4	30,000,000	8	1,000,000
4	80,000,000	9	20,000,000
5	560,000	10	75,050
6	110,000,000	10	10,560

REFERENCES

Ryan, R., & Wilson, J. H. (2014). Professor-Student Rapport Scale: Psychometric properties of the brief version. *Journal of the Scholarship of Teaching and Learning, 14*(3), 64–74. doi:10.14434/josotl.v14i3.5162

Wilson, J. H., & Ryan, R. G. (2013). Professor-Student Rapport Scale: Six items predict student outcomes. *Teaching of Psychology, 40*(2), 130–133. doi:10.1177/0098628312475033

9

Prediction

Researchers often ask scientific questions about prediction. For example, does altruism at the age of 10 predict empathy at the age of 21? Can exposure to sweets during the first few years of life predict childhood obesity? Does meditation predict resiliency after trauma? Will exposure to the arts in middle school increase creativity in adulthood? Such questions rely on sound research designs and appropriate analysis for answers.

Our goal in this chapter is to predict one outcome, or **criterion variable**, from one or more **predictor variables**. For the sake of this discussion, we will focus on predictors and outcomes that are related in a linear way. In other words, we might expect higher numbers on a predictor variable to predict higher numbers on the outcome. Or we might expect higher numbers on a predictor variable to predict lower numbers, if the two variables are negatively related. We will restrict our discussion to prediction research questions that rely on interval or ratio variables.

Criterion Variable. A criterion variable is an outcome predicted from another variable or variables.

Predictor Variable. A predictor variable predicts a criterion variable if the two correlate.

PREDICTION AND CORRELATION

The idea of examining linear relationships between two interval or ratio variables should be familiar to you. In Chapter 7 we discussed Pearson's r, and Chapter 8 detailed how to use r-values to build confidence in measures as well as predict based on Pearson's r. In fact, prediction of one variable from another can be possible only when the two variables are related. If two variables show a strong r-value, either positive or negative, you can predict one variable from the other. When designing a study, consider the research question. If you want to know about a potential relationship between two variables, plan to analyze the data using Pearson's r. However, if you want to learn about possible prediction of one variable from another, plan to take the extra step of running a prediction analysis. Planning the appropriate statistic will help you choose useful variables to operationalize and examine.

LINEAR REGRESSION: PREDICTION USING ONE PREDICTOR

With prediction, researchers choose a sample of interest based on a research question such as, *Can we predict childhood obesity from early exposure to sweets?* If we want to learn about childhood obesity, our sample will be composed of children. To find out if we can predict one variable from another, we must have a sample that can provide information on *both* variables. This might seem strange. If we have a sample that offers data on both variables, we do not need to predict anything because the outcome has already happened. It is true that the sample in your study will already have outcome data, but the sample provides information to help other children who are *not* in your sample. As a researcher, your goal is to collect data on both variables from a sample, find out if the two variables are related in the sample, and offer prediction for other children.

First, operationalize the variables of interest. In the question on childhood obesity, the predictor variable is early exposure to sweets. Exposure to sweets can be defined as the average number of high-calorie sweet treats children consume per week when they are between 1 and 3 years old. Obesity, the outcome variable, can be measured by body mass index (BMI) at the age of 10.

Let us point out here that we could collect data in two ways. We could speak with parents of a sample of toddlers to find out the average number of sweets consumed each week, wait seven to nine years, track down those children, and measure their BMI. Sound time-consuming? As another option, we could measure BMI across a sample of 10-year-old kids and ask the parents of those same children to report the average number of sweets per week the children ate when they were toddlers. The first design would give us more accurate data because recall is much better over one week than it is over nine years. The second design will give us an answer faster. Some research projects indeed focus on longitudinal data collection. But for now, we will focus on short-term designs since you likely will be using these designs for your classes.

Correlation First

After collecting data on both variables, analyze the data to see if the two variables are related. You learned in Chapter 7 that Pearson's r examines the potential relationship between two interval or ratio variables. It should come as no surprise that Pearson's r is our first step in analysis. You also likely remember that a scatterplot can reveal problems with Pearson's r, such as outliers. If the correlation analysis shows a meaningful relationship between the two variables, we can predict one from the other.

Specifically, we might write our research hypothesis: *More sweets consumed in early childhood relate to higher BMI in middle childhood.* Of course we also know that statistics are based on assuming the null hypothesis unless results are rare enough to indicate an unusual outcome. In this example, the null hypothesis indicates: *Sweets consumed in early childhood and middle childhood BMI are not related.* We could collect data from a sample of children and find out if sweets and BMI indeed are related. We want to know if we can reject the null hypothesis in favor of the research hypothesis. In the table below, the first column includes participant number to help organize the data, with each row containing values from one 10-year-old participant.

Participant Number	Number of Sweets per Week (Average)	BMI
1	7	21
2	10	23
3	3	20
4	14	26
5	20	32
6	5	17
7	7	24
8	9	22
9	16	34

To enter these data into SPSS, type values by row as they appear in the table.

Participant	Sweets	BMI
1.00	7.00	21.00
2.00	10.00	23.00
3.00	3.00	20.00
4.00	14.00	26.00
5.00	20.00	32.00
6.00	5.00	17.00
7.00	7.00	24.00
8.00	9.00	22.00
9.00	16.00	34.00

Recall from Chapter 7 that participant number is not part of the main analysis. However, your method section will require participant demographics, so when you run your own study, you can enter all participant data into SPSS. Next check to see if the two variables correlate using Pearson's r (see Chapter 7 as needed for a detailed review). Click Analyze, Correlate, and Bivariate.

In the box that opens, move only Sweets and BMI to the right. Under Test of Significance, we can run a one-tailed test because we expect number of sweets and BMI values to be positively related. Remember that a positive correlation means values increase on both variables. As number of sweets increases, so does BMI. You learned in Chapter 7 that the benefit of a one-tailed test is more statistical power to find a relationship if one exists.

Click OK for the correlation output.

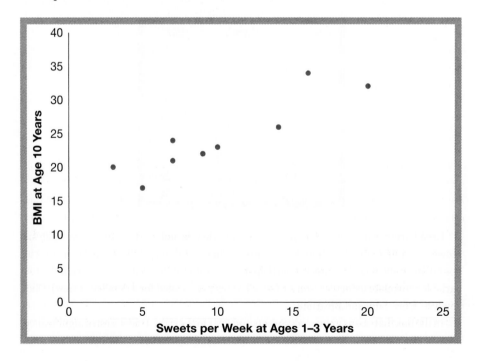

Correlations

Correlations

		Sweets	BMI
Sweets	Pearson Correlation	1	.903**
	Sig. (1-tailed)		.000
	N	9	9
BMI	Pearson Correlation	.903**	1
	Sig. (1-tailed)	.000	
	N	9	9

**. Correlation is significant at the 0.01 level (1-tailed).

The output shows that Sweets and BMI are correlated in a meaningful way with a Sig value of .000 ($p < .001$). And with a correlation coefficient of .90, we can say we revealed a strong relationship.

Sweets consumed in the first few years of life relate to BMI at the age of 10 years, but we need to examine a scatterplot for outliers that might falsely drive the relationship. The scatterplot below shows no obvious outlier.

Linear Regression

Now we know sweets consumed and BMI are related, and the scatterplot shows no obvious outlier. We can continue to use data from our sample of 10-year-old children to predict BMI from sweets. For prediction, we create what is called a **prediction equation**, also termed a **regression equation**. It should make sense that the regression equation is the formula for a line. After all, we are looking at linear relationships. Using the scatterplot above, we can imagine a "line of best fit" that we place on our graph in a way that gets as close to all the data points as possible.

Prediction Equation (Regression Equation). A prediction equation is a formula used to predict one variable from another. In linear regression, the prediction equation is the formula for a line.

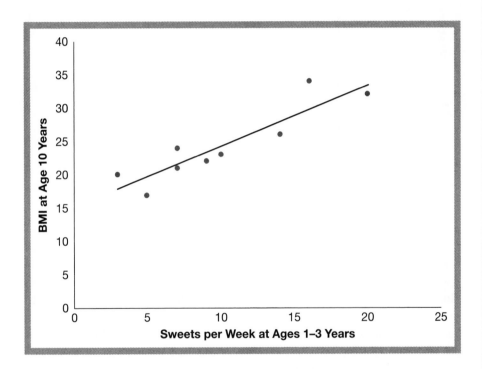

The line of best fit is called the **line of prediction** or a **regression line**. The prediction line shows us what value of BMI to predict based on number of sweets consumed. Simply pick a value such as 5 sweets per week on the X-axis, look at the regression line directly above that value, and move to the left to see what BMI would be predicted from the Y-axis. As shown below, we can expect a BMI of about 20 for a child who consumed 5 sweets per week. The scatterplot with a regression line offers a good way to demonstrate prediction based on several values on the X-axis.

You might recognize that this process does not yield an exact BMI value. As another limitation, the graph allows you to predict based only on a limited range of sweets consumed. What if you located a child who ate an average of 35 sweet treats per week? The value of 35 is not located on the X-axis.

Line of Prediction (Regression Line). The line of prediction or regression line allows prediction of a criterion variable from a predictor, as long as they are related in a linear way.

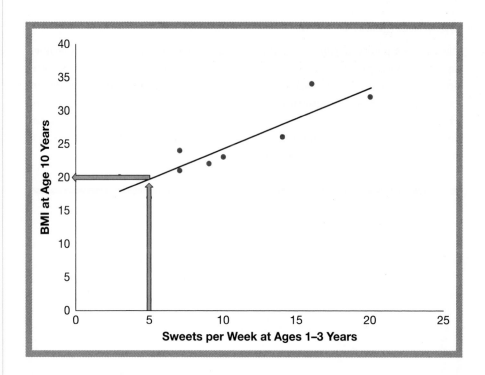

To obtain an exact predicted BMI value for any number of sweets, we turn to the regression equation. The equation allows us to insert any value for number of sweets consumed per week by young kids and predict BMI at age 10. Computer programs such as SPSS provide the two components we need for a regression line: the slope and the Y-intercept. **Slope** tells us the slant of the regression line, including the angle and how much it slants. In the line formula, slope is symbolized by b. In SPSS, b is represented by B and has an associated p-value to indicate whether a variable predicts well. The **Y-intercept** of the line tells us the place at which the line would cross the Y-axis on a graph. In the line formula, the Y-intercept is symbolized by a.

$$Y' = b(X) + a$$

The X in the regression formula above represents the predictor value for an individual person. In the obesity example, the predictor is number of sweets per week. Finally, the Y' in the line formula is the predicted value, or BMI in our example. Using the regression formula, researchers can insert an X value (such as 10 sweets per week) and predict Y' for an individual child (BMI). With a regression formula, we can simply ask parents to report how many sweets their young children eat per week and predict the level of obesity for their children later in life as indicated by BMI. Such information informs parents and allows them to adjust their treat habits.

Slope. The value for slope tells us the slant of the regression line, including the angle and how much it slants. In the line formula, slope is symbolized by b. In SPSS, b is represented by a capital B and has an associated p-value.

Y-intercept. The value for the Y-intercept tells us the place at which the line would cross the Y-axis on a graph. In the line formula, the Y-intercept is symbolized by a.

Error in Predictions

We should caution here that even though we can predict a precise BMI value, we know that prediction is not perfect. Error exists. Prediction analysis yields a value for error, which tells us about how far off we will be each time we predict the outcome from the predictor. In our example, the error term will indicate approximately how many BMI points we might be off in either direction from the BMI predicted for a child. But even with the give and take of error, the predicted value is our best guess based on the data.

The good news is that if the predictor and criterion variable are highly correlated, you will have less error during prediction. In our sweets-BMI example, an r-value of .90 ensures that error is small. We can examine r^2, the coefficient of determination, and know that sweets and BMI overlap by .82 (based on the SPSS output of $r = .903$). In other words, the two variables have 82% of their variability in common, and only 18% of variability in BMI is *not* explained by sweets consumption.

Think about what error might look like with less overlap between the two variables. As a hypothetical example, suppose we wanted to predict the age at which people die from how much time they spend sitting down. The less time people spend sitting, the longer they live, but the correlation is weak (for more information, see van der Ploeg, Chey, Korda, Banks, & Bauman, 2012). With enough participants in a sample, even a weak correlation might be significant. A weak correlation means little overlap, and error will be high. Imagine error was 20 years. If so, we might predict the age of death based on time spent sitting, but our prediction could be off by 20 years in either direction! We might tell a person, "Based on the fact that you sit for 10 hours a day, you are likely to die at the age of 65, give or take 20 years." You see the problem.

When predicting, we want overlap between the two variables of interest, with more overlap enhancing prediction. A positive or negative correlation will work just fine. The absolute value of Pearson's r is important, not the sign (+ or -). The more overlap we demonstrate between variables, the lower the error term, and the better we will be able to predict. Fortunately SPSS will provide all necessary information to address our research questions. In the sweets-BMI example, our research question is, *Can we predict childhood obesity from early exposure to sweets?* We can reword as a statement for the research hypothesis: *We can predict childhood obesity from early exposure to sweets.* And of course the null hypothesis states no effect: *We cannot predict childhood obesity from early exposure to sweets.* With data and SPSS, we will find evidence for one of the two hypotheses.

SPSS: Linear Regression

Because we are interested in the linear relationship between sweets and BMI, the prediction of interest is called **linear regression**. Click Analyze, Regression, Linear.

Linear Regression. When we want to predict one interval or ratio variable from another, we analyze data using linear regression.

In the box that opens, move Sweets to the right under Independent(s) by clicking the arrow in the middle. Then click BMI to the right under Dependent using the arrow. Next click the Statistics button on the right to request Descriptives for each of the two variables. As always, descriptive statistics will be reported in the APA-style results section.

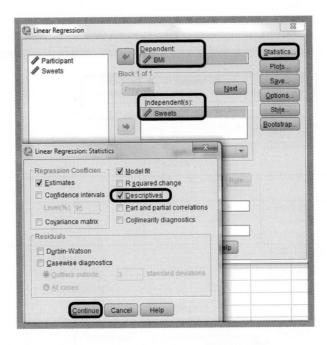

Click Continue to remove the smaller box, and click OK on the final remaining box to get output. Below is the first half of the output, which is where we find our descriptive statistics.

Regression

Descriptive Statistics

	Mean	Std. Deviation	N
BMI	24.3333	5.54527	9
Sweets	10.1111	5.53273	9

Correlations

		BMI	Sweets
Pearson Correlation	BMI	1.000	.903
	Sweets	.903	1.000
Sig. (1-tailed)	BMI	.	.000
	Sweets	.000	.
N	BMI	9	9
	Sweets	9	9

Variables Entered/Removed[a]

Model	Variables Entered	Variables Removed	Method
1	Sweets[b]	.	Enter

a. Dependent Variable: BMI

b. All requested variables entered.

Beneath this information you will find prediction details.

Model Summary

Model	R	R Square	Adjusted R Square	Std. Error of the Estimate
1	.903[a]	.816	.789	2.54540

a. Predictors: (Constant), Sweets

ANOVA[a]

Model		Sum of Squares	df	Mean Square	F	Sig.
1	Regression	200.647	1	200.647	30.968	.001[b]
	Residual	45.353	7	6.479		
	Total	246.000	8			

a. Dependent Variable: BMI

b. Predictors: (Constant), Sweets

Coefficients[a]

Model		Unstandardized Coefficients		Standardized Coefficients	t	Sig.
		B	Std. Error	Beta		
1	(Constant)	15.181	1.851		8.203	.000
	Sweets	.905	.163	.903	5.565	.001

a. Dependent Variable: BMI

Notice under Model Summary the R value of .90. R ranges from 0 to 1 and indicates the ability of a variable to predict an outcome. Just as Pearson's r can be squared to calculate the amount of variability in common for correlation, R^2 illustrates overlap. In this example, R^2 is .816 (rounded to .82), which means the two variables overlap by 82%. Next, under Coefficients, focus on the B column. To the right of (Constant) is 15.181. This value is the Y-intercept (a). To the right of Sweets is .905. This is the slope (b) of the regression line. Together these values create the prediction equation, and we know number of sweets is a good predictor based on a Sig value of .001. We can predict BMI from number of sweets using the equation: $Y' = .91(X) + 15.18$. Note that we round most statistical outcomes to two decimal places. If a specific child consumes 8 treats per week, plug in the 8 for the X value in the equation and predict Y', which is predicted BMI.

$$Y' = .91(8) + 15.18 = 22.48$$

A BMI of 22.48 is considered normal, providing parents with valuable prediction information. Of course, parents should know that 22.48 is a best guess, but error in prediction exists. The SPSS output offers a **standard error of the estimate** in the Model Summary table. In this example, error is 2.55 BMI points, which means each prediction

Standard Error of the Estimate. In linear regression (prediction), the standard error of the estimate indicates about how far off predictions will be from actual outcomes, on average.

can be off by about 2.55 BMI points in either direction around the predicted value. For the child who consumes 8 sweet treats per week, we predict a BMI of 22.48, give or take 2.55, so the child's BMI is likely to fall between 19.93 and 25.03.

Effect Size: Cohen's f^2

Although R^2 does give us a measure of how much overlap we have between the predictor and the outcome variable, researchers tend to report **Cohen's f^2** as effect size. Generally prediction equations contain more than one predictor, but we will use this example to explain Cohen's f^2. Simply pull R^2 from the output and complete the following formula.

$$f^2 = \frac{R^2}{1 - R^2}$$

In this example, the formula contains .816 from the output.

$$f^2 = \frac{.816}{1 - .816} = 4.43$$

Cohen (1992) defined effect sizes for f^2: A weak effect size is .02, a medium effect is .15, and a large effect begins around .35.

APA Style for Linear Regression

We provide a wealth of information in the results section, including the correlation coefficient, descriptive statistics for our variables, and prediction details. But first we describe participants and our procedure.

Cohen's f^2.
When variables significantly predict an outcome, effect size is quantified with Cohen's f^2.

Method

Participants

Participants included nine 10-year-old children recruited by posting a flyer in the main office of 10 elementary schools in Minnesota. The flyer contained a link to the online study. Parents completed the form for their children. The sample consisted of 6 girls and 3 boys with a mean age of 10.53 ($SD = 0.26$). Parents identified all children as Black.

Procedure

After accessing the online study, parents answered questions about their child's current BMI as well as the approximate number of sweet treats the child ate per week from ages 1 to 3 years old. We defined sweet treats as those with a high percentage of calories from refined sugar, such as cake, candy, and ice cream. Parents also reported their child's age, gender, and ethnicity.

Results

We correlated number of sweets consumed between the ages of 1 and 3 ($M = 10.11$, $SD = 5.53$) with BMI at the age of 10 years ($M = 24.33$, $SD = 5.55$). Sweets and BMI related positively, $r(7) = .90$, $p < .001$, $f^2 = 4.43$; therefore, we predicted BMI from sweets consumption ($B = .91$, $p = .001$), with a Y-intercept of 15.18. When predicting BMI from sweets consumed per week, an average of 2.55 BMI points represents our error.

Power

For a good idea of how many participants are needed to illustrate a moderate effect using $p \le .05$, examine the table below. Notice that the required number of participants increases with more predictors.

	Small Effect Size	Medium Effect Size	Large Effect Size
Linear regression			
1 predictor	395	55	25
2 predictors	485	68	31
3 predictors	550	77	36
4 predictors	604	88	40

Note: Numbers in the table represent total sample size.

MULTIPLE LINEAR REGRESSION: PREDICTION WITH TWO PREDICTORS

In simpler studies, such as class projects, you may rely on one predictor. However, most research questions involve more than one predictor. Usually multiple predictors do a better job of predicting an outcome. When we have more than one predictor, we use **multiple linear regression** to analyze data.

Let us continue our discussion of childhood obesity with a hypothetical sample using two predictors. In addition to number of sweets consumed early in life, amount of current exercise should influence BMI. It makes sense that both sweets consumption and exercise would predict BMI better than prediction with sweets alone. You can probably think of additional variables that would enhance prediction, such as genetic influences and number of vegetable servings per week. For now, we will focus on adding average minutes of exercise per week to the equation as a predictor of BMI. We have a new research question: *Can we predict childhood obesity from early exposure to sweets and current exercise?* Take a minute to think about how you would state the research question as a research hypothesis, and consider the null hypothesis of no effect as a comparison. Data collection will help us decide which hypothesis remains.

Multiple Linear Regression. When we want to use more than one predictor to predict a criterion variable, we use multiple linear regression.

Participant Number	Number of Sweets per Week (Average)	Minutes of Exercise per Week (Average)	BMI
1	7	120	21
2	10	90	23
3	3	75	20
4	14	150	26
5	20	138	32
6	5	145	17
7	7	170	24
8	9	93	22
9	16	125	34
10	4	70	11
11	15	89	33
12	5	123	20

SPSS: Multiple Linear Regression

Enter data from the table into SPSS, and be sure to keep the data organized by row. Each row represents data from one participant. Here we have chosen to enter only the two predictors and criterion. We could have entered participant numbers as well as any collected demographics.

Sweets	Exercise	BMI
7.00	120.00	21.00
10.00	90.00	23.00
3.00	75.00	20.00
14.00	150.00	26.00
20.00	138.00	32.00
5.00	145.00	17.00
7.00	170.00	24.00
9.00	93.00	22.00
16.00	125.00	34.00
4.00	70.00	11.00
15.00	89.00	33.00
5.00	123.00	20.00

First correlate each pair of variables to create a table of intercorrelations. Click Correlate, Bivariate, and then move all three variables to the right. We choose to leave the Test of Significance as a Two-tailed test because often we have different expectations for each predictor, with perhaps a directional outcome for one predictor and a nondirectional outcome for a different predictor. With multiple regression, we prefer two-tailed tests for all predictors as the default. Under Options, request Means and standard deviations to describe variables. In this example we are collecting descriptive statistics during correlational analysis rather than later, during prediction analysis. Requesting at either step is fine because the descriptive statistics remain the same. Click Continue and OK.

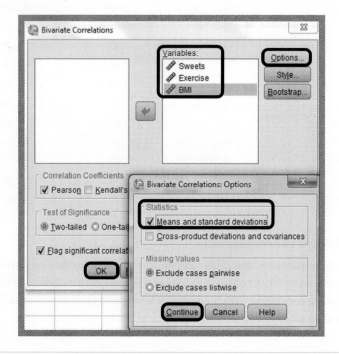

The output provides descriptive statistics and a **correlation matrix**. A matrix of correlations illustrates all possible intercorrelations among variables.

Correlations

Descriptive Statistics

	Mean	Std. Deviation	N
Sweets	9.5833	5.46823	12
Exercise	115.6667	32.01231	12
BMI	23.5833	6.81520	12

Correlations

		Sweets	Exercise	BMI
Sweets	Pearson Correlation	1	.262	.885**
	Sig. (2-tailed)		.410	.000
	N	12	12	12
Exercise	Pearson Correlation	.262	1	.283
	Sig. (2-tailed)	.410		.372
	N	12	12	12
BMI	Pearson Correlation	.885**	.283	1
	Sig. (2-tailed)	.000	.372	
	N	12	12	12

**. Correlation is significant at the 0.01 level (2-tailed).

Create scatterplots for each pair of variables to identify any problems with the data, such as obvious outliers or a curvilinear relationship.

These scatterplots are for your eyes only, so they don't need to be pretty.

Let us move forward with prediction to address the research question. Following the same procedure as the approach used in the prior example, click Analyze, Regression, Linear. In the box that opens, move both predictors under Independent(s), and move the outcome (BMI) under Dependent. We could click Statistics and ask for Descriptives, but remember we already collected descriptive statistics for our variables when we conducted correlation analyses earlier. Click OK for output.

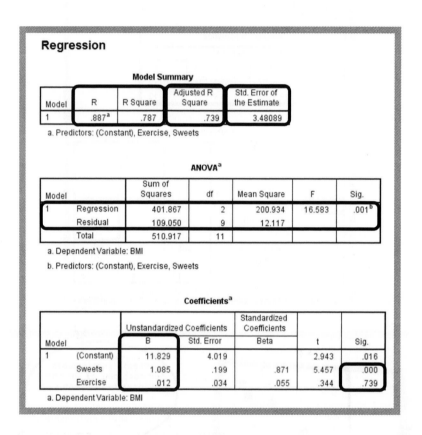

Regression

Model Summary

Model	R	R Square	Adjusted R Square	Std. Error of the Estimate
1	.887[a]	.787	.739	3.48089

a. Predictors: (Constant), Exercise, Sweets

ANOVA[a]

Model		Sum of Squares	df	Mean Square	F	Sig.
1	Regression	401.867	2	200.934	16.583	.001[b]
	Residual	109.050	9	12.117		
	Total	510.917	11			

a. Dependent Variable: BMI

b. Predictors: (Constant), Exercise, Sweets

Coefficients[a]

Model		Unstandardized Coefficients		Standardized Coefficients	t	Sig.
		B	Std. Error	Beta		
1	(Constant)	11.829	4.019		2.943	.016
	Sweets	1.085	.199	.871	5.457	.000
	Exercise	.012	.034	.055	.344	.739

a. Dependent Variable: BMI

With more than one predictor, the R-value now represents the overlap among all three variables (two predictors and the criterion) rather than merely two variables, as in the prior example. R Square shows the exact proportion of overlap among the three variables. However, Adjusted R^2 is a better indicator of overlap when we have more than one predictor. Based on two predictors and an outcome, we will use Adjusted R^2. And of course R^2 allows us to talk about overlap in a more meaningful way: The variables have 74% (or .74 proportion) of their variability in common.

When we have multiple predictors, we need to know if the predictors *as a group* can predict BMI. For this new piece of information, we examine the output table labeled ANOVA. (In Chapter 11, we will discuss the ANOVA in detail, but for now we will merely identify the output table in SPSS.) In the ANOVA table, if the Sig value is equal to or less than .05, we know that a meaningful outcome exists. In this case, a Sig value of .001 means the two predictors *as a group* do predict BMI. When reporting the overall ANOVA result for this example, you will need to report the degrees of freedom (*df*) of 2 and 9 as well as the **F-value** of 16.58 and the significance value of $p = .001$ from the ANOVA table above. *F* is the symbol for ANOVA and is the statistic reported in APA style. In the APA-style results section, you are expected to report the ANOVA values so the reader can see if your predictors as a group work well to predict the outcome. The format is as follows.

$$F(2, 9) = 16.58, p = .001$$

F-value.
F symbolizes the statistical outcome of ANOVA and is the symbol used to represent the statistic in an APA-style results section.

Recall from the previous example that we need to calculate f^2 as a measure of effect size because this value takes into consideration multiple predictors. We completed the formula below using Adjusted R^2 from the SPSS output.

$$f^2 = \frac{.739}{1 - .739} = 2.83$$

An effect size of 2.83 represents a large effect. The equation provides excellent prediction.

After we know the predictors work well as a group, we can move on to the output Coefficients table and examine each predictor individually. Do they both predict well? Or does only one variable significantly predict BMI? Look back at the row for Sweets. All the way to the right, the significance value is .000, allowing us to say that $p < .001$, and Sweets predicts BMI. Now look at the Exercise row. The Sig value to the right is .739, which is above the required .05 needed for significance. Therefore Exercise does not predict BMI.

APA Style for Multiple Linear Regression

Given the correlation matrix and the details of regression analysis, we are ready to share information with readers in APA style.

Method

Participants

Participants included twelve 10-year-old children recruited by posting a flyer in the main office of 10 elementary schools in Minnesota. The flyer contained a link to the online study. Parents completed survey items pertaining to their children. Children's ages ranged from 10.21 years to 10.98 years old ($M = 10.53$, $SD = .26$), and all parents identified their children as White.

Procedure

After accessing the online study, parents answered questions about their child's current BMI as well as the approximate number of sweet treats the child ate per week from ages 1 to 3 years. We defined sweet treats as those with a high percentage of calories from refined sugar, such as cakes, candy, and ice cream. Parents also reported the current number of exercise minutes per week, on average.

Results

We used linear regression to predict BMI from average number of sweets consumed per week and average exercise per week in minutes. See Table 1 for descriptive statistics and correlations among variables.

The two predictors as a group predicted BMI, $F(2, 9) = 16.58$, $p = .001$, $f^2 = 2.83$. Specifically, sweets consumed predicted BMI ($B = 1.09$, $p < .001$), but exercise failed to significantly predict BMI ($B = .01$, $p = .739$). A value of 11.83 represented the Y-intercept, and error in prediction remained at 3.48 BMI units.

Table 1

Descriptive Statistics and Variable Correlations (Pearson's r)

	M (SD)	Sweets	Exercise
BMI	23.58 *(6.82)*	.89*	.28
Sweets	9.58 *(5.47)*	—	.26
Exercise	115.56 *(32.01)*	—	—

Note: N = 12. BMI = Body Mass Index.

*p < .001

In APA style, tables include the sample size somewhere, such as the note we provided under the table. Researchers also define any acronyms in a note below the table. We do not have to spell out mean (*M*) or standard deviation (*SD*) because they are well known symbols. If you have questions about table formatting, see the APA manual (American Psychological Association, 2010).

Note that the correlation matrix found in Table 1 illustrates excellent overlap between sweets and BMI. Therefore it should come as no surprise that sweets predicted BMI well. Likewise, exercise did not correlate well with BMI, and exercise was not a good predictor. When your research design includes multiple predictors, you should provide a correlation matrix. Such details interest readers who want to see how much each predictor overlaps with the criterion variable. In addition, readers want to know how much the two predictors overlap with each other.

The APA-style results section contains all information needed to create the prediction equation if someone wants to predict BMI using the variables as operationalized. Prediction can be accomplished by using sweets consumed as the only X variable. Of course, exercise was removed from the equation by our statistical analysis.

$$Y' = 1.09\left(X_{Sweets}\right) + \cancel{.01(X_{Exercise})} + 11.83$$

We also know that prediction will be off by about 3.48 BMI units in either direction. Considering the range of possible BMI values, our error term is rather small. Prediction should be accurate.

Did we have enough power to locate an effect if one truly existed? With 12 people, you probably recognize a problem. A prediction study with 12 participants lacks power. In fact, based on two predictors, $p \leq .05$, and an assumed moderate effect size, 101 participants would have been needed to uncover a significant effect, if one existed (see the power table earlier in this chapter). Perhaps exercise does predict BMI, but we did not have the power to show it. As a good researcher, you can either collect data from more participants or be careful next time to run power analysis before the study begins.

SUMMARY

Linear regression is an extension of correlation and allows you to answer research questions tied to prediction. When you are interested in predicting outcomes using linear regression, operationally define variables such that they yield interval or ratio data. Decide which variables are predictors, and use several to enhance prediction. Although you can use more than one predictor, each equation allows only one outcome, or criterion. If you want to predict values on a second variable, simply create a second equation. Use the same predictors if you would like.

Prediction is never perfect. The more overlap between variables, the better you will be able to predict. But even a great deal of overlap allows room for error. The error term communicates about how far off you might be when predicting an outcome, and a lower error term is desired. After all, if prediction contains an abundance of error, the predicted value is not useful.

REVIEW OF TERMS

Cohen's f^2

Correlation Matrix

Criterion Variable

F-value

Line of Prediction (Regression Line)

Linear Regression

Multiple Linear Regression

Prediction Equation (Regression Equation)

Predictor Variable

Slope

Standard Error of the Estimate

Y-intercept

PRACTICE ITEMS

1. Why do researchers run a correlation analysis before a prediction analysis?

2. What is the linear regression formula, and what do the different parts of the formula indicate?

3. Why might researchers use more than one variable to predict an outcome?

4. If a specific predictor variable is not significant, do we include it in our prediction equation? Why or why not?

* * *

For each of the following studies, (a) restate the research question as a research hypothesis and state the null hypothesis, (b) determine how many participants are needed for adequate power, and (c) enter and analyze the data as well as write an APA-style results section. Be sure to read over the method sections we wrote for you.

5. You are an industrial/organizational psychologist interested in developing a pre-employment measure of job skills that predicts job performance over time among servers. The owner of a locally owned restaurant, Molly's Place, allows you to collect data at her establishment. At the final stage of an interview process for those seeking employment, you give your test of job skills. One year later, you ask Molly to share these employees' annual performance reviews. You expect the two variables to be positively correlated, allowing prediction. You ask, *Do scores on a preemployment test of job skills predict one-year job-performance scores?*

Test	Performance	(data continued) Test	Performance	(data continued) Test	Performance
60	32	82	42	88	50
60	33	83	38	90	45
62	43	85	32	90	32
65	42	85	35	95	45
75	50	85	45	96	31
78	30	86	47	96	40
80	40	86	48	98	50
80	41	87	46	100	45

Method

Participants

Employees ($N = 24$) who began working at a small restaurant in Lawrence, Kansas, and remained employed for at least 1 year participated in this study. Ethnicities included 20 White and 4 Black individuals with a mean age of 32.04 years ($SD = 10.76$). All participants received ethical treatment.

Materials and Procedure

All employees completed a pre-employment test of job skills, with possible scores ranging from 0% to 100%. One year after their hire date, employees received performance reviews (0–50 points).

6. You read in your psychology class that Hofmann, Wisneski, Brandt, and Skitka (2014) tracked participants over time and found that being the target of a moral or immoral act impacts happiness. You wonder if you can manipulate happiness by sending out kind messages to people, and you expect more positive messages to cause more happiness. You want to know: *Can we predict happiness based on number of positive text messages people receive?* You collect the following data.

| | | (data continued) | | (data continued) | |
Messages	Happiness	Messages	Happiness	Messages	Happiness
0	40	3	41	7	78
0	32	4	58	7	30
0	50	4	51	8	80
1	25	4	27	8	70
1	35	5	25	8	55
1	48	5	88	9	68
2	26	6	69	9	90
2	49	6	90	9	25
2	52	6	75	10	36
3	53	7	85	10	55
3	61	7	95	10	80

Method

Participants

Participants included 33 undergraduate students (mean age = 19.75, SD = 1.25), with gender approximately equally distributed across male (51.5%) and female. Ethnicities included 20 Asian American, 10 Latino American, and 3 African American individuals.

Materials and Procedure

We recruited participants through their Introduction to Psychological Science courses and sent a link to the consent form, which required that students provide their phone number. Based on random assignment, participants received between 0 and 10 positive messages over 10 days. At the end of the 10 days, participants received a text asking them to rate their happiness on a scale of 1-100, with higher numbers indicating more happiness.

7. Hofmann et al. (2014) found that being the target of immoral deeds affected happiness. You wonder, *Can we predict happiness based on number of positive and negative text messages people receive?* Your IRB will not allow you to send personally negative text messages to participants, so instead you send links to negative news stories. Using the same method as the study in the previous item with positive text messages but also adding 0-10 negative messages over 10 days, your DV again is happiness as rated on a scale of 1-100.

Note: In multiple regression, you could expect individual predictors to correlate with the outcome positively, negatively, or either. However, SPSS will not allow you to choose a one-tailed or two-tailed test for *each* predictor, and therefore all bivariate correlations should be run as two-tailed tests.

(data continued)

Positive Messages	Negative Messages	Happiness	Positive Messages	Negative Messages	Happiness
6	0	55	3	7	41
8	1	52	8	10	58
3	6	53	2	1	51
5	2	61	6	4	27
0	4	87	9	7	40
1	5	69	0	2	32
4	8	90	4	8	50
8	3	75	2	5	25
1	0	78	10	0	85
6	7	30	3	6	95
1	9	80	0	10	48
9	2	70	5	5	26
7	4	55	7	8	49
2	10	68	7	1	90
4	6	25	3	9	25
10	9	88	5	3	36
10	3	80	9	3	47

Method

Participants

Participants included 34 undergraduate students ($M = 19.72$, $SD = 1.35$), with gender equally distributed across male (50%) and female participants. Ethnicities included 20 Asian American, 10 Latino American, 2 African American, and 2 European American individuals.

Procedure

Participants learned about the study from their Introduction to Psychological Science instructors and received a link to the consent form. The consent form asked students to provide their phone number. Based on random assignment, participants received between 0 and 10 positive messages and links to between 0 and 10 negative news stories over 10 days. At the end of the 10 days, participants received a text and rated their happiness on a scale of 1-100, with higher numbers indicating more happiness.

8. You have decided to apply to graduate school. Your academic advisor tells you that you must do well on the Graduate Record Examination (GRE) to get into a good school, but you wonder if verbal and quantitative scores predict how well students perform in school. You ask the research question: *Can we predict first-year grade-point average (GPA) in graduate school from GRE verbal and quantitative scores?* You send out a survey to graduate programs at universities in your city and collect the following data from second-year students.

| | | | (data continued) | | | (data continued) | | |
GRE Verbal	GRE Quant	GPA	GRE Verbal	GRE Quant	GPA	GRE Verbal	GRE Quant	GPA
143	146	2.75	152	155	3.57	158	149	4.00
144	140	3.10	152	146	3.74	158	148	3.78
144	149	3.25	152	147	3.22	158	151	3.24
146	146	3.17	153	140	3.98	159	155	3.00
146	144	2.80	153	153	4.00	160	155	3.87
147	151	3.65	153	153	3.90	161	159	3.99
149	144	2.99	153	144	3.24	161	146	3.75
150	155	3.89	154	144	3.35	163	148	3.81
151	140	3.05	155	148	3.33	166	151	3.90
151	148	3.00	155	149	3.31	166	155	4.00
152	141	3.25	155	155	3.45	167	163	4.00
152	144	3.10	156	150	3.88	167	144	3.85

Method

Participants

Participants included 36 second-year graduate students at colleges and universities within a 50-mile radius of Detroit, Michigan. Demographic data indicated a mean age of 25.76 ($SD =$ 2.57) and 69.4% female participants. All participants received ethical treatment in accordance with IRB standards.

Procedure

Graduate-program directors received a request to distribute a survey link to second-year graduate students. Interested participants completed the survey and reported their age, gender, and end-of-first-year GPA as well as their verbal and quantitative GRE scores.

REFERENCES

American Psychological Association. (2010). *Publication manual of the American Psychological Association* (6th ed.). Washington, DC: Author.

Cohen, J. (1992). A power primer. *Psychological Bulletin, 112*(1), 155–159. doi:10.1037/0033-2909.112.1.155

Hofmann, W., Wisneski, D. C., Brandt, D. C., & Skitka, L. J. (2014). Morality in everyday life. *Science, 345*(6202), 1340–1343. doi:10.1126/science.1251560

van der Ploeg, H. P., Chey, T., Korda, R. J., Banks, E., & Bauman, A. (2012). Sitting time and all-cause mortality risk in 222 497 Australian adults. *Archives of Internal Medicine, 172*(6), 494–500. doi:10.1001/archinternmed.2011.2174

GROUPED DESIGNS WITH INDEPENDENT SAMPLES

10

One Variable With
Two Independent Groups

When conducting research, often the research question involves comparing one group with another group. For example, a researcher might want to compare students' self-control after resisting the urge to eat chocolate-chip cookies versus radishes. Or we might examine the sleep quality of college students who text often versus students who seldom text. In the food example, resisting cookies or radishes defines the independent variable (IV; for a reminder of the IV discussion, see Chapter 3). This particular IV contains two levels: Participants will be asked to sit at a table with either cookies or radishes. Notice that because we ask participants to do something, we are manipulating what level they experience. We are controlling what happens to them—with their permission, of course. Manipulation of participants' experiences defines a true IV because an IV requires manipulation.

In our second example, texting little versus texting often, our design might not manipulate which level students experienced. They could come to the study already having texted a little or a lot. Because we would not manipulate the variable of interest, we could not label amount of texting as an IV. Instead, we would call the variable a **quasi-IV** in

Quasi-IV. When variables are not manipulated but are still treated as IVs in an analysis, they are called quasi-IVs. Quasi-IVs yield correlational data and cannot establish cause and effect.

Examples of quasi-IVs are gender, eye color, year in college, and height, which rarely are manipulated.

recognition of the fact that people already exist in a level before they arrive to participate. The texting variable looks like an IV because it contains distinct levels, but it is not.

Although the difference between IV and quasi-IV may seem irrelevant, the distinction matters. As you have read many times, a true IV, defined by manipulating what happens to participants, shows cause. Assuming we run a study carefully, our results will tell us if the IV caused something interesting to happen. Suppose we asked participants to resist eating either cookies or radishes and then measured how long they attempt to solve a complex puzzle to assess persistence (as an indication of self-control on a frustrating task; see Baumeister, Bratslavsky, Muraven, & Tice, 1998, for more information on a similar study). We would hope that the two conditions differ from each other, allowing us to make a statement about whether resistance to cookies or radishes "causes" different durations of persistence on the frustrating task. Perhaps resisting the urge to eat cookies requires more self-control than resisting radishes and wears out people's subsequent self-control. As a result, resisting the cookies might cause less persistence on the puzzle task than resisting the radishes.

Manipulating whether people have to resist cookies or radishes allows us to learn whether or not resisting the different snacks in our study causes different durations of persistence. Our research question is, *Will people who resist cookies persist on a task for less time than those who resist radishes?* By now you should be able to rephrase the research question into the research hypothesis: *People who resist cookies will persist on a task for less time than those who resist radishes.* In this example, time working on a complex puzzle before quitting would be the dependent variable (DV). The IV and DV together would assess cause and effect.

Now let us look again at our quasi-IV example on texting. We could compare sleep quality between students who rarely text and those who often text. We obviously do not manipulate phone use. Participants come to the study already using their phones as they wish. Without manipulation of an IV, we cannot know cause. Likewise, the outcome variable, sleep quality, cannot be an "effect." But sleep quality still represents the outcome variable or DV. If we do not learn cause and effect from a study with a quasi-IV, what do we learn? If sleep quality differs between students at the two levels of texting, we learn that texting and sleep quality are "related." The research question might be, *Is sleep quality related to amount of texting?* And the research hypothesis would state: *Sleep quality and amount of texting are related.*

With a quasi-IV, we use research to identify a meaningful relationship between two variables. The use of the word *relationship* might remind you of correlational designs, and in fact, a study with a quasi-IV is a correlational design. Remember that a correlational design simply means that you collect data that existed prior to your study. Participants come into the study already in a specific level of the quasi-IV.

When you design a study, you need to know whether your IV is a true IV or a quasi-IV. If you use a true IV, your result may tell cause and effect. If you use a quasi-IV, your result may show a relationship between the quasi-IV and DV. Both designs represent useful ways to conduct research. In this chapter, first we will expand on how to run a study with a true IV, including methodology, analysis, graphing, and APA style for both method and results sections. Then we will discuss how to conduct and analyze research with a quasi-IV.

RESEARCH DESIGN: ONE IV WITH TWO LEVELS

In Chapter 3 you learned that if you design a study with a true IV, the study is called an experiment. According to the definition, our snack example characterizes an experiment. Revisit our research question: *Will people who resist cookies persist on a task for less time than those who resist radishes?* Imagine that we randomly assigned some people to sit in front of cookies and other people to sit in front of radishes. Of course, we can prepare ahead of time by deciding the condition for each participant. If we write "cookies" and "radishes" on separate pieces of paper and put them in a cup, we can pick one piece of paper and know which condition will be experienced by the next participant who enters the lab.

With a well-designed methodology and careful attention to random assignment, we are nearly ready to collect data. But first let us define the statistic we need for our snack study. We have two groups with different people in the groups. A two-group design with a DV that is interval or ratio level requires a *t*-test. A **t-test** is a parametric statistic used only when the IV or quasi-IV has two levels. Of course, a quasi-IV is not manipulated, so random assignment to conditions is not possible, but analysis remains the *t*-test. Because our snack example has different people in the two groups, we have what is called an **independent-samples design** (meaning that each person is exposed to only one level of the IV). If we put these two pieces together, we have an independent-samples *t*-test. The **independent-samples t-test** will tell us if resisting cookies versus radishes affects persistence on a task.

t-test. A *t*-test is the statistic used with two levels of an IV or quasi-IV and an interval or ratio DV.

Independent-Samples Design. When we have different people in levels of our IV or quasi-IV (meaning that each person is exposed to only one level), we call the study an independent-samples design.

Independent-Samples t-test (Between-Groups t-test). The independent-samples *t*-test is a statistic used with two different groups of participants in two levels of an IV or quasi-IV with an interval or ratio DV.

Now let us look at some fictional data for our snack study, and remember that the DV is seconds of task persistence. When you look at the data below, notice that not all numbers within a group (column) are the same. You are seeing extraneous variability based on many possible differences in the two conditions beyond the manipulation of resisting cookies or radishes. For example, some people in both conditions may hate to give up on a task, illustrating a personality variable. But no matter. As researchers, we hope extraneous variability *within* each group will be overshadowed by our real interest, which is variability *between* the two groups.

Radishes	Cookies
680	200
755	490
476	510
634	308
725	447
688	380
912	470
560	366
732	592
846	415

SPSS: Independent-Samples *t*-test With an IV

In Variable View, set up names for the data columns. Enter a brief name for your IV in the first cell of the first row. We have named the IV "Snack." Enter a brief name for your DV in the first cell of the second row. We have named the DV "Persistence." Next label the levels of Snack under Values as detailed in Chapter 3. Because Snack represents the IV, and we know the IV has two levels, we must label two categories. Click Values beside Snack, and enter 1 = Radishes and 2 = Cookies. Click OK.

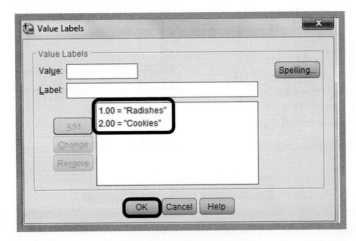

Click to Data View at the bottom of the page to see the column headings you set up for your data. In the first column, enter values of 1 and 2 to indicate which level each participant experienced. In the second column, enter each participant's time to work on the puzzle (in seconds). Click to View Value Labels before or after entering values in the columns.

Snack	Persistence
Radishes	680.00
Radishes	755.00
Radishes	476.00
Radishes	634.00
Radishes	725.00
Radishes	688.00
Radishes	912.00
Radishes	560.00
Radishes	732.00
Radishes	846.00
Cookies	200.00
Cookies	490.00
Cookies	510.00
Cookies	308.00
Cookies	447.00
Cookies	380.00
Cookies	470.00
Cookies	366.00
Cookies	592.00
Cookies	415.00

Click Analyze, Compare Means, Independent-Samples T Test. Although the SPSS term is T Test, researchers generally label the statistic a *t*-test.

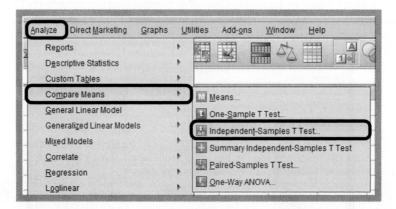

In the new box that opens, click Snack over to Grouping Variable by first clicking on the word Snack and then clicking the arrow to the right. Then click Define Groups, a choice that becomes available when Snack is moved into the Grouping Variable box. In the box that opens, enter a 1 for Level 1 and a 2 for Level 2. We set radishes to be represented by a 1 and cookies to be represented by a 2. Here we are simply telling the computer to read the values of 1 and 2 as IV levels.

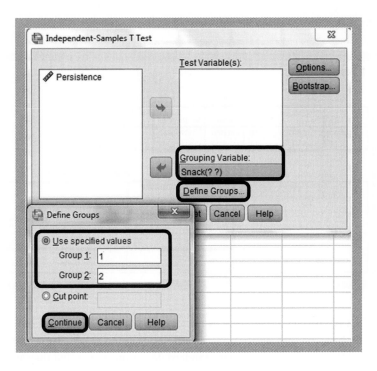

After clicking Continue, see that the Grouping Variable Snack now has a 1 and a 2 in parentheses, showing that the values have been defined for the computer to use. Next move Persistence over to the right by first clicking on the word Persistence and then clicking on the arrow between the boxes. The Test Variable(s) box is where you will always put the DV.

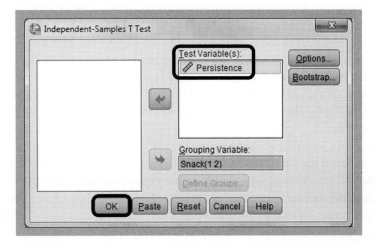

Click OK for SPSS to analyze these data.

T-Test

Group Statistics

	Snack	N	Mean	Std. Deviation	Std. Error Mean
Persistence	Radishes	10	700.8000	127.19347	40.22211
	Cookies	10	417.8000	111.18033	35.15831

Independent Samples Test

		Levene's Test for Equality of Variances				
		F	Sig.	t	df	Sig. (2-tailed)
Persistence	Equal variances assumed	.077	.785	5.297	18	.000
	Equal variances not assumed			5.297	17.684	.000

Our first job is to make sure the two groups do not have wildly different variability. The best outcome would be similar variability, often called "**homogeneity of variance.**" We could look at the two standard deviations to see that they are similar, but a better approach relies on **Levene's test** for similarity of variability (termed *variances,* which is simply standard deviation squared). In the table above we can see that the variances are not significantly different based on an F-value of .077 and a p-value of .785. Therefore we can use the outcome values on the row marked Equal variances assumed.

Focusing on the first row, the output indicates a meaningful difference between the two group means because our significance value is less than .05 ($p < .001$) for a t-value of 5.297. Based on a review of the group means, we can claim that people persist on a task for different amounts of time based on whether they resisted the urge to eat cookies or radishes. In fact, SPSS shows us a p-value of $< .001$, which tells us that such a large difference between groups is seen less than 0.1% of the time in the normal population. The group means show less persistence after resisting cookies than after resisting radishes. We can reject the null hypothesis in favor of the research hypothesis: *People who resist cookies persisted on a task for less time than those who resist radishes.*

In Chapter 4 we explained degrees of freedom (df). For t-tests, the df number indicates how many people were in your study because the formula for df in the independent-samples t-test is $N - 2$. A reader who sees $df = 18$ knows that you had 20 participants in your study. Together with the t-value and p-value, df will appear in the APA-style results section of your paper. Of course, you will also provide specifics about groups, including the mean, standard deviation, and number in each level of the IV.

Homogeneity of Variance. An approximately equal amount of variability in the DV across groups is termed homogeneity of variance.

Levene's Test. Levene's test for equality of variances examines variability in the groups of a research design. If the test shows a significant difference in variability, researchers must report the t-test value from the SPSS output row marked "Equal variances not assumed."

Directional Hypothesis

We designed our study with an expectation that people who resisted radishes would persist longer on the puzzle task than those who resisted cookies. In other words, we had a directional hypothesis. But SPSS ran a two-tailed test by default. A nondirectional hypothesis says we have no expectation for which group would persist longer on the puzzle task. Because we had a directional hypothesis, our result is even more impressive, and the *p*-value will be even better. In this example, a two-tailed *p*-value of < .001 is great, but a more ambiguous result (e.g., *p* = .06) would have required us to adjust the *p*-value for a one-tailed test. With a one-tailed test, simply look at the SPSS Sig column, divide the *p*-value by two and report the new value in your APA-style results section.

Effect Size: Cohen's *d*

At this point the outcome looks good, but we have one more step to take: Calculate the effect size. For an independent-samples *t*-test, effect size is calculated using **Cohen's *d*** (Cohen, 1988). You can do a web search for a Cohen's *d* calculator, but the formula is simple enough to complete without online help. Unfortunately SPSS will not calculate Cohen's *d* for you.

$$d = \frac{M_{group1} - M_{group2}}{SD_{pooled}}$$

Cohen's *d*. When an independent-samples *t*-test is significant, we calculate effect size using Cohen's *d*.

The first mean (M) is the mean for Group 1 (radishes), and the second mean is the mean for Group 2 (cookies). The formula for standard deviation (SD) is below, and the pieces to calculate it can be pulled from your SPSS output.

$$SD_{pooled} = \frac{SE_{pooled}}{\sqrt{\dfrac{1}{n_{group1}} + \dfrac{1}{n_{group2}}}}$$

Independent Samples Test

			t-test for Equality of Means	
t	df	Sig. (2-tailed)	Mean Difference	Std. Error Difference
5.297	18	.000	283.00000	53.42213
5.297	17.684	.000	283.00000	53.42213

On the output, look for Std. Error Difference in the top row to find 53.42213. This number is SE_{pooled} for the numerator. Each n value represents the number per group, which in this example is 10 (radishes) and 10 (cookies). Plug in the pieces to calculate SD_{pooled}.

$$SD_{pooled} = \frac{53.42213}{\sqrt{\dfrac{1}{10} + \dfrac{1}{10}}} = \frac{53.42213}{\sqrt{.1+.1}} = \frac{53.42213}{.447214} = 119.4554$$

Use SD_{pooled} as the denominator in the Cohen's d calculation to complete the equation. Although we have entered each group mean in the numerator, you can see that the Mean Difference has been calculated by SPSS and is shown in the screenshot above (283.00).

$$d = \frac{700.80-417.80}{119.4554} = 2.369085$$

A Cohen's d of approximately +/−.20 is considered a weak effect size, and +/−.50 is a moderate effect size (Cohen, 1988). If Cohen's d reaches +/−.80 (and beyond), the effect is considered strong. In our example, we have a strong effect size. Keep in mind that if no significant outcome exists, it makes no sense to calculate effect size. If the result shows no effect, why would you ask how large it is?

Confidence Intervals

A final piece of information you can offer your reader is the confidence interval for the mean difference between groups. Remember that you wanted to know the difference in persistence between the radish and cookie conditions. How different are they? What difference would likely be found in the general population if people resisted radishes or resisted cookies? A **confidence interval (CI)** gives the reader a range of values that would contain the true population difference between the groups a certain percentage of the time. SPSS provides values for a 95% confidence interval by default, so the range would contain the population difference 95% of the time.

Again, in an independent-samples *t*-test, we are interested in the difference between two groups. Therefore the confidence interval values represent mean *differences*. For example, examine the following SPSS output, which illustrates more of the *t*-test table than we showed you earlier.

> **Confidence Interval (CI)** A confidence interval is a range of values that would contain the true population data a certain percentage of the time.

Independent Samples Test

						95% Confidence Interval of the Difference	
			t-test for Equality of Means				
t	df	Sig. (2-tailed)	Mean Difference	Std. Error Difference		Lower	Upper
5.297	18	.000	283.00000	53.42213		170.76426	395.23574
5.297	17.684	.000	283.00000	53.42213		170.62017	395.37983

Confidence Limits.
Confidence limits
refer to the lower
and upper values of a
confidence interval.

Notice that the 95% confidence interval represents differences between persistence times for the radish and cookie conditions. **Confidence limits** refer to the lower and upper values of the confidence interval. In this example, the lower confidence limit is 170.76, and the upper confidence limit is 395.24. That is, we can be confident that the persistence difference between the two IV levels would fall between these two values 95% of the time in the population of those who experienced the conditions.

You are probably wondering what all of this means. We already know that the two groups differed in their task persistence, and we even know the effect size was large. With standard deviation, we added to the discussion by showing the spread of values within each group. The confidence interval adds another piece of information to our study. Now we know that the true difference between the two conditions in the general population is generally from 170.76 to 395.24 seconds of persistence. We can be 95% confident that the population mean difference will fall between the two confidence limits.

Usually a confidence interval of 95% is used. In the snack example, you could add to your APA-style results section: 95% CI [170.76, 395.24].

Power

We do not need to wonder whether we had enough participants per group to reveal a significant effect. After all, we in fact did find a significant effect. However, our study used a small sample, which was risky. To enhance power, researchers should decide on participant numbers before running a study. The table below shows 128 participants per group to have a .05 chance to reveal a medium-sized effect, if it exists. We only had 20 people in our sample above to simplify for instructional purposes. In the real world, we would want to collect data from at least 128 people, if possible.

	Small Effect Size	Medium Effect Size	Large Effect Size
Independent-samples *t*-test	788	128	52

Note: Numbers in the table represent **total** sample size.

APA Style for the Independent-Samples *t*-test: Experimental Design

Now let us look at example APA-style method and results sections for the snack experiment. Remember that the IV is type of snack, and we have two levels: cookies and radishes. The DV is number of seconds people persist on the puzzle task before quitting. We created characteristics for our hypothetical sample to complete a participants section below.

Method

Participants

Twenty students (10 men and 10 women) at a southeastern university participated in this study. Ages ranged from 18 to 56 ($M = 20.40$, $SD = 5.62$), and ethnicities included 10 Black, 7 White, and 3 Latino participants. The IRB approved this study prior to data collection, and experimenters treated participants in an ethical manner.

Procedure

After completing informed consent, participants sat at a table containing either chocolate-chip cookies or radishes, with type of snack randomly assigned. Participants resisted the temptation to consume the snacks for 10 min. Next, they received a complex puzzle that required tracing an entire figure with a pen without tracing the same line or lifting the pen. In reality, tracing the figure represented an impossible task. Participants attempted to complete the task for as long as they chose, and duration quantified persistence on the task.

Results

We used a one-tailed, independent-samples *t*-test to analyze these data. Type of snack resisted by participants affected the length of time they persisted on an impossible puzzle, $t(18) = 5.30$, $p < .001$, 95% CI [170.76, 395.24], $d = 2.37$. As Figure 1 shows, participants who resisted eating radishes persisted on the puzzle task for a longer duration ($M = 700.80$ sec, $SD = 127.19$, $n = 10$) than those who resisted eating chocolate-chip cookies ($M = 417.80$, $SD = 111.18$, $n = 10$).

Graphs as Figures: Bar Graph

Readers appreciate APA style because the format is standard, concise, and full of useful information. Readers also enjoy pictures of results in the form of graphs, such as the scatterplots used in Chapter 7. Certainly, the results section of our snack example offers the information clearly, but even in this example, a graph may enhance the manuscript. Notice that in the APA-style results section above, we referenced "Figure 1." This figure would be included at the end of your manuscript on a separate page along with a figure title. (For examples of complete manuscripts, see Appendix C.) For *t*-tests, we do not rely on scatterplots. Instead we graph the two group means. Every graph of means must have the word *mean* on the Y-axis, and error bars (e.g., standard deviation) are included. When graphing means, you will choose to use either a bar or line graph, depending on the X-axis variable. If the IV or quasi-IV represents nominal or ordinal data, as in this example, create a bar graph. If the X-axis variable is interval or ratio, create a line graph. Below we show the graph as a figure, and we provide a figure caption for a manuscript. If you want to read step-by-step instructions on how to create this graph in Excel, see Appendix B.

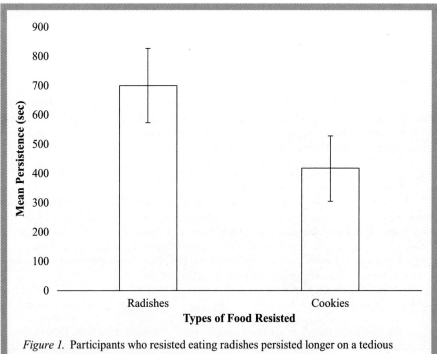

Figure 1. Participants who resisted eating radishes persisted longer on a tedious task than those who resisted cookies. Error bars represent *SD*.

OUTLIERS

Notice that the standard deviation bars in the graph are not large. Of course, we want small error bars because variability within a group reduces our ability to reveal group differences. Large standard deviation bars indicate random individual differences as nuisance variability to the data set. We can examine within-group variability by looking at the graphed deviation bars, the standard deviation on our SPSS printout, or even the raw data within each condition. If we have any reason to suspect a great deal of variability, we should examine each group for outliers.

Remember in Chapter 7 we explained outliers as unusual values in Pearson's *r*. We examined scatterplots to look for any values that were obviously outside of a linear pattern. Locating outliers in Pearson's *r* relied on logic. View the scatterplot, make a case to your reader that the value appears to be an outlier, and remove it before reanalyzing your data. In other words, researchers must be transparent when discussing removal of an outlier.

In a *t*-test analysis, identifying outliers is based on math. Within a group, see if any value falls three or more standard deviations away from the group mean. Because we are looking for outliers within a group, we will call unusual values in a *t*-test **outliers for grouped data**. Use the SPSS output (Descriptive Statistics) to look for outliers by multiplying the standard deviation by 3 and then adding and subtracting that number from the mean to see where the values lie for both 3 *SD above* and 3 *SD below* the mean. Anything outside of that range is considered an outlier.

Let us look at the snack example and focus on the radish condition. For the radish group, the SPSS output shows *M* = 700.8000, *SD* = 127.19347.

Outlier (for Grouped Data). An outlier is an unusual value in a data set. In a single sample of interval or ratio values, an outlier often is defined as a value three standard deviations from the mean.

Group Statistics

	Snack	N	Mean	Std. Deviation	Std. Error Mean
Persistence	Radishes	10	700.8000	127.19347	40.22211
	Cookies	10	417.8000	111.18033	35.15831

If we multiply the standard deviation by 3, we get 381.58. We can add this number to the group mean to get 1082.38 and subtract it from the mean to get 319.22. If any values in that group had been smaller than 319.22 or greater than 1082.38, we would have labeled them as outliers and removed them from the data set prior to the *t*-test analysis.

Just as with outlier removal in Pearson's *r*, you must tell the reader that a data point was removed because it was more than three standard deviations from the group mean. Then analyze the data without the outlier. Of course, we only checked for outliers in the radishes group. Do not forget to check all groups separately for outliers. Although outliers in a *t*-test data set are rare, we should examine the data for points that seem unusual and run the standard deviation calculation when a value is suspect.

USING A QUASI-IV TO ESTABLISH A RELATIONSHIP

Now let us examine a design with a quasi-IV. Recall the example of texting and sleep quality we mentioned earlier. One of many relevant studies was conducted by Murdock (2013), in which students reported on texting behavior, sleep quality, and several additional variables. Among the findings, higher numbers of outgoing and incoming texts related to poorer sleep quality.

Number of Texts	Sleep Quality
Low	5
High	4
High	4
Low	7
High	3
High	5
High	2
High	2
Low	8
Low	9
Low	7
Low	5

For our study, let us say students report how often they text in an average day and rate their sleep quality. We ask them to choose a texting level: low (0–50 texts a day) or high (more than 50 texts a day). Participants rate sleep quality on a scale from 1 to 10, with higher numbers reflecting better sleep quality. Here is the research question: *Are sleep quality and number of texts related such that more texts relate to poorer sleep quality?* The research hypothesis forms a statement: *Sleep quality and number of texts are related such that more texts relate to poorer sleep quality.* And of course, unless the data support the research hypothesis, we must assume the null hypothesis to be true: *Sleep quality and number of texts are not related.*

We can collect data from 12 people for the sake of a concise example, but in real life we would collect data from 128 participants to ensure adequate power. At the left is what they might report. When examining the data, we see no suspected outliers in either the low-text or high-text group.

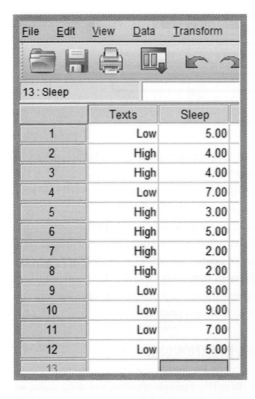

SPSS: Independent-Samples *t*-test With a Quasi-IV

Enter these data into an SPSS file, as shown at left. When labeling values of Texts, we used 1 = low and 2 = high.

We can now analyze the data using the independent-samples *t*-test because number of texts has two groups, and a single interval DV offers the outcome. As with the snack example earlier in the chapter, click Analyze, Compare Means, Independent-Samples T Test (*t*-test).

In the box that opens, Move Sleep under Test Variable(s). Click Texts over to the Grouping Variable and Define Groups as 1 and 2 values. Click Continue.

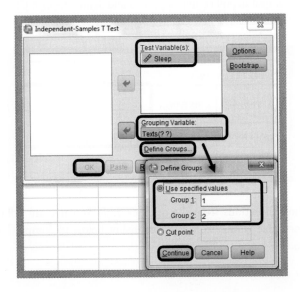

Click OK for output.

T-Test

Group Statistics

	Texts	N	Mean	Std. Deviation	Std. Error Mean
Sleep	low	6	6.8333	1.60208	.65405
	high	6	3.3333	1.21106	.49441

Independent Samples Test

		Levene's Test for Equality of Variances				
		F	Sig.	t	df	Sig. (2-tailed)
Sleep	Equal variances assumed	.285	.605	4.269	10	.002
	Equal variances not assumed			4.269	9.308	.002

Levene's test shows that variability in the two groups can be considered equal, allowing us to examine the *t*-test in the first row. Look at the *t*-test Sig value to see that it is less than .05, indicating that the two groups (low and high texting) indeed differed on sleep quality. Next examine each group Mean under the Group Statistics box to see which group reported better sleep. Do not forget that because we are predicting a direction for this study, we can adjust the *p*-value for a directional test by dividing $p = .002$ by 2 ($p = .001$).

Based on the output, we reject the null hypothesis of no difference in favor of the research hypothesis: *Sleep quality and number of texts were related such that more texts related to poorer sleep quality.* As a reminder, rejecting the null hypothesis means the groups differed *in this particular study.* Science relies on multiple studies to gain confidence in an outcome, and every study serves as an important building block of knowledge.

Return to the output to pull confidence limits and define the 95% CI for the difference between group means.

t-test for Equality of Means

Mean Difference	Std. Error Difference	95% Confidence Interval of the Difference	
		Lower	Upper
3.50000	.81989	1.67317	5.32683
3.50000	.81989	1.65458	5.34542

Finally, follow directions from the prior example to calculate Cohen's *d* for this significant effect. Use values from the screenshot below to complete the steps and obtain $d = 2.46$.

| t-test for Equality of Means | | | |
| Mean Difference | Std. Error Difference | 95% Confidence Interval of the Difference | |
		Lower	Upper
3.50000	.81989	1.67317	5.32683
3.50000	.81989	1.65458	5.34542

As with the previous example, we will use the SPSS output to create a graph in Excel. Remember that the type of graph used (bar or line) depends on the IV or quasi-IV level of measurement. We are analyzing low versus high texts, labels that merely define categories, depicting a nominal variable. Nominal and ordinal X-axis variables require a bar graph. The final graph should include standard deviation as error bars and look like the following figure.

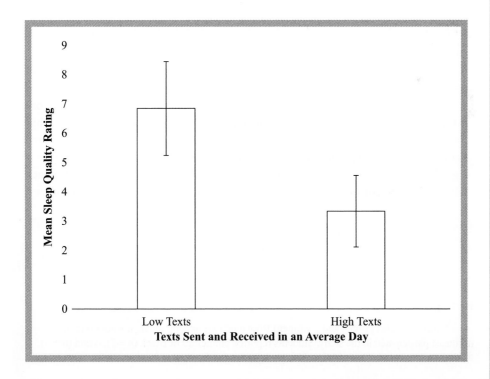

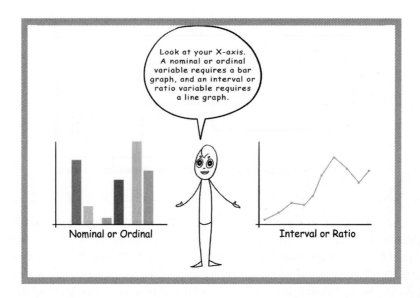

Using the bar graph, together with the SPSS results we obtained, we now turn to APA style.

APA Style for the Independent-Samples *t*-test: Correlational Design

Once again, we offer fictional participant demographics to create a section describing participants. Although we do not provide details about the online survey program, you would provide such details when conducting a study of your own.

In the following results, we again included the confidence interval to offer more information to aid readers. Some authors do not include the confidence interval but focus instead only on significance testing and effect size. Further, although some people argue that a confidence interval should not be offered unless the *p*-value is significant, others urge writers to include the confidence interval in any case. Speak with your professor to see if confidence intervals are required, and if so, when.

Method

Participants

Twelve students (5 men and 7 women) from a private undergraduate institution in the northeast participated in the study. Students reported ethnicities of Black ($n = 5$), Asian ($n = 3$), Native American ($n = 3$), and Other ($n = 1$). Ages ranged from 18 to 28 ($M = 22.75$, $SD = 2.28$).

Procedure

Students who signed up to participate received a survey link. The survey began with informed consent, and students clicked Agree to continue. Participants categorized the number of texts sent and received each day, selecting either low (0–50 texts) or high (50 or more texts). Additionally, they rated average sleep quality over the last 7 days on a scale from 1 to 10, with 1 representing *not at all satisfying* and 10 representing *very satisfying*.

Results

We analyzed these data using an independent-samples *t*-test (low levels of texting versus high levels of texting), with the outcome variable of sleep quality. Level of texting related to ratings of sleep, $t(10) = 4.27$, $p = .001$, 95% CI [1.67, 5.33], $d = 2.47$. Participants who texted at a low frequency rated sleep quality higher ($M = 6.83$, $SD = 1.60$, $n = 6$) than those who texted often ($M = 3.33$, $SD = 1.21$, $n = 6$; see Figure 1).

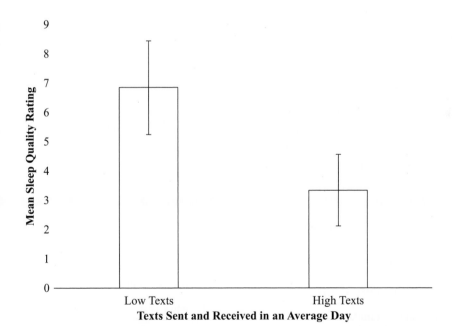

Figure 1. Mean sleep quality ratings based on the number of texts sent and received in an average day. Error bars represent *SD*.

SUMMARY

In this chapter, you learned how to design a study with two distinct groups and different people in the groups. With a true IV, requiring manipulation, participants should be randomly assigned to conditions. A true IV allows us to discuss cause and effect. However, with a quasi-IV, people are not randomly assigned to conditions because they arrive for the study already existing in one group or the other. A quasi-IV allows us to discover if two variables are related. In both types of designs, we discussed examples with two levels of the IV or quasi-IV and only one outcome, or DV. A study with one IV or quasi-IV, different people in the two groups, and one DV of interval or ratio level data requires an independent-samples t-test for analysis.

REVIEW OF TERMS

Cohen's d

Confidence Interval (CI)

Confidence Limits

Homogeneity of Variance

Independent-Samples Design

Independent-Samples t-test (Between-Groups t-test)

Levene's Test

Outlier (for Grouped Data)

Quasi-IV

t-test

PRACTICE ITEMS

1. List three examples of variables that will likely represent quasi-IVs rather than "true" IVs.

2. Can we determine cause and effect using a quasi-IV? Why or why not?

3. What is an independent-samples design?

4. In SPSS, what is the grouping variable? What is the test variable?

5. How do we calculate *df* for the independent-samples *t*-test?

6. For Cohen's *d*, what is considered a weak, moderate, and strong effect size?

7. Because SPSS automatically assumes a two-tailed test, what do we do with our obtained *p*-value to adjust for a one-tailed test?

8. When do we use a bar graph rather than a line graph in communicating our findings visually?

9. How do we identify and remove outliers?

* * *

For each of the following studies, (a) restate the research question as a research hypothesis, including whether it should be one- or two-tailed, and state the null hypothesis, (b) determine how many participants are needed for adequate power, and (c) enter and analyze the data as well as write an APA-style results section. Take a look at each method section we provided.

10. Zhang (2014) found that students who use their laptops to multitask during class (e.g., note taking, surfing web pages, searching for information, and instant messaging) made lower grades on their midterm exam than those who did not use laptops for multitasking. You are interested in seeing if this effect remains if students use their laptops *only* for note taking (and do not multitask). You wonder, *Will participants score higher or lower on a postlecture test when they take notes by hand rather than on a laptop?* Although Zhang found that those using laptops made lower grades, you are unsure if those who use laptops for notes will score higher or lower than those taking notes by hand, since in your experiment, the laptops will not be connected to the Internet. Without the Internet, students are less likely to multitask. You collect the following midterm-exam grades.

| (data continued) | | | (data continued) | |
Laptop	Written		Laptop	Written		Laptop	Written
80	88		54	57		92	91
72	95		80	80		57	90
80	68		68	100		85	89
83	98		90	92		78	78
85	27		62	75		45	79
82	91		95	98		80	83
78	80		90	78		80	94

Method

Participants

Although 42 participants participated in this study, one person's exam score fell more than 3 SD below the mean. Therefore the final sample included 41 individuals ($M = 20.01$, $SD = 2.07$). All participants received ethical treatment.

Procedure

We recruited participants using an advertisement in the university newspaper. As an incentive to try their best, students learned that those who made at least a 90% on the exam would be entered in a raffle to win a $50 gift card to the university bookstore. After participants signed the consent form, we randomly assigned them to view a 1-hr prerecorded video lecture on 100 different ways to cook shrimp and to take notes either using a laptop (with no Internet connection) or by hand. After listening to the video, all participants studied their notes. After 10 min, participants received a list with 200 ways to cook shrimp and indicated which 100 occurred in the lecture.

11. You read an article finding that teenagers who do their own math homework score higher on standardized math exams than teenagers who have an adult help them with their homework (Fernández-Alonso, Suárez-Álvarez, & Muñiz, 2015). You wonder, *Will college students who do their own math homework score higher on their final exams than those who have help?* You recruit students from a large section of a college algebra course and assign them to either do their math

homework at home or go to the campus tutoring center and get help with their homework. You collect the following final-exam scores.

Home	Tutoring Center
58	59
61	60
62	60
65	67
65	72
72	78
72	78

(data continued)

Home	Tutoring Center
73	78
75	79
75	80
80	80
81	81
81	81
82	81

(data continued)

Home	Tutoring Center
85	83
90	90
90	91
91	93
95	93
96	95
98	97

Method

Participants

Forty-two students (20 men, 21 women, and 1 individual who chose not to disclose gender) in a college algebra course at a small liberal-arts university chose to participate. A mean age 19.76 ($SD = 1.00$) represented our sample, and ethnicities included 18 Black, 16 White, and 8 Asian individuals.

Procedure

We randomly assigned participants to complete all of their algebra homework for 2 weeks prior to the final exam either at home by themselves or at the campus tutoring center, where they asked for help as needed. After the final exam, those who agreed to participate in the study received an e-mail requesting their score.

12. Your 16-year-old little sister told you that she identifies as a lesbian, but she worries about coming out at school for fear of becoming a target of bullying. You read an article by Russell, Toomey, Ryan, and Diaz (2014), who reported that coming out in high school was associated with better psychosocial adjustment in young adulthood. Russell and colleagues conducted their study in the San Francisco Bay Area, where people in

the region may exhibit greater acceptance of the gender and/or sexual minority (GSM) community. You are interested to find out whether the same results will occur in a southern sample. You wonder, *Does coming out in high school relate to higher self-esteem in college in the South?* You recruit college students in the GSM community at your school in Georgia by posting flyers in the dining halls and bookstores on campus and contacting the president of your school's gay-straight alliance. To ensure anonymity, participants are sent a link to participate in the study. They report whether they revealed their sexual identity in high school and then completed the 10-item Rosenberg Self-Esteem Scale (Gray-Little, Williams, & Hancock, 1997), for which total scores range from 10 to 40, with higher numbers indicating higher self-esteem.

| | | (data continued) | | (data continued) | |
Revealed	Not Revealed	Revealed	Not Revealed	Revealed	Not Revealed
10	31	28	16	25	38
20	30	26	27	18	20
16	25	15	18	25	28
12	18	15	32	17	11
13	21	21	10	35	30
37	20	18	35	40	15
17	26	38	13	35	17
16	16	21	21	18	31

Method

Participants

Participants ($N = 48$) who identified as gender and/or sexual minorities (GSM) and attended a college in Georgia composed the study sample. Ethnicities included 24 White, 16 Black, 4 Latino, and 2 Asian individuals as well as 2 individuals identifying as mixed race, with a mean age of 18.90 ($SD = 2.66$). GSM identities included 15 gay, 12 lesbian, 6 pansexual, 5 bisexual, 2 transgender, and 2 nonbinary individuals as well as 5 individuals who chose not to disclose their specific GSM identity. One individual identified as both lesbian and transgender.

Materials

Rosenberg Self-Esteem Scale. The Rosenberg Self-Esteem Scale (Gray-Little, Williams, & Hancock, 1997) measures self-esteem using 10 Likert items ranging from 1 (*strongly agree*) to 4 (*strongly disagree*). Five items are reverse scored, and total scores range from 10 to 40, with higher numbers indicating higher self-esteem.

Procedure

We recruited college students in the GSM community at a college in Georgia via flyers posted in the dining halls and bookstores on campus and by contacting the president of the college's gay-straight alliance. To ensure anonymity, participants received a link to participate in the study. They completed the Rosenberg Self-Esteem Scale and then reported their age, ethnicity, current GSM identity or identities, and whether they came out in high school (including to parents and friends).

13. You download Snapchat, a smartphone application that allows you to take and send pictures that "self-destruct" after 1–10 seconds. The next day in class, your instructor tells you about a study by Henkel (2013) in which participants who took pictures of objects at a museum had lower recall for object details than those who did not take pictures. You wonder, *Does the use of Snapchat during a social outing reduce memory of the event?* You survey individuals at a local grocery store to see if they are Snapchat users. Those who have Snapchat are invited to your lab to play board games in small groups for 1 hour. During their visit, half of the participants are randomly assigned to use Snapchat to send photos to the researcher. The next day, you send participants a questionnaire with 15 true-false items asking about other people who were present, games played, and features of the room (e.g., posters on the walls).

Pictures	No Pictures
1	8
4	1
5	4
3	5
7	3
4	8
10	10
6	12

(data continued)

Pictures	No Pictures
8	8
6	9
3	14
7	2
0	4
5	11
9	10
12	7

(data continued)

Pictures	No Pictures
14	9
5	15
4	6
2	10
3	5
7	3
	12
	7

Method

Participants

We recruited adult individuals ($N = 42$) who already owned and used the Snapchat smartphone application on their phones to participate in this study. Individuals included 28 women and 14 men with a mean age of 26.99 ($SD = 6.77$). Ethnicities included 18 Black, 18 White, and 6 mixed-race individuals.

Procedure

We recruited participants from a local grocery store by approaching them as they left the store. We asked if they wanted to participate in a study for a $10 gift card to the grocery store and verified that they owned and used Snapchat. In the lab, participants played board games in small groups for 1 hr. We randomly assigned participants either to use or not use Snapchat during the event. The next evening, all participants received an e-mailed questionnaire with 15 true-false items asking about other people present at the event, games played, and features of the room (e.g., posters on the walls). Participants received 1 point for each correct item, with a maximum score of 15.

REFERENCES

Baumeister, R. F., Bratslavsky, E., Muraven, M., & Tice, D. M. (1998). Ego depletion: Is the active self a limited resource? *Journal of Personality and Social Psychology, 74*, 1252–1265. doi:0022-3514

Cohen, J. (1988). *Statistical power analysis for the behavioral sciences*. Hillsdale, NJ: Lawrence Erlbaum.

Fernández-Alonso, R., Suárez-Álvarez, J., & Muñiz, J. (2015). Adolescents' homework performance in mathematics and science: Personal factors and teaching practices. *Journal of Educational Psychology, 107*(4), 1075–1085. doi:10.1037/edu0000032

Gray-Little, B., Williams, V. S. L., & Hancock, T. D. (1997). An item response wtheory analysis of the Rosenberg Self-Esteem Scale. *Personality and Social Psychology Bulletin, 23*, 443–451. doi:10.1177/0146167297235001

Henkel, L. A. (2014). Point-and-shoot memories: The influence of taking photos on memory for a museum tour. *Psychological Science, 25*(2), 396–402. doi:10.1177/0956797613504438

Murdock, K. K. (2013). Texting while stressed: Implications for students' burnout, sleep, and well-being. *Psychology of Media Culture, 2*(4), 207–221. doi:10.1037/ppm0000012

Russell, S. T., Toomey, R. B., Ryan, C., & Diaz, R. M. (2014). Being out at school: The implications for school victimization and young adult adjustment. *American Journal of Orthopsychiatry, 84*(6), 635–643. doi:10.1037/ort0000037

Zhang, W. (2014). Learning variables, in-class laptop multitasking and academic performance: A path analysis. *Computers and Education, 81*, 82–88. doi:10.1016/j.compedu.2014.09.012

11

One Variable With More Than Two Independent Groups

From the prior chapter, we know that when we design research questions, we often want to know if two groups differ in a meaningful way. Recall that a true experiment requires manipulation, such as asking some participants to resist the urge to eat radishes and others to resist chocolate-chip cookies, and we can establish cause and effect. To minimize potential confounding variables, researchers randomly assign people to the IV levels. A second option involves a quasi-IV that is not manipulated, such as year in school. Participants already exist in a quasi-IV level. Regardless of whether a true IV or quasi-IV is used, ultimately an outcome is measured, such as persistence on a boring task (the DV).

Chapter 10 focused on a two-group design with different participants in the two groups. When your research question involves comparing one group to another, and the DV is interval or ratio data, you can rely on the *t*-test. However, your design may involve more than two groups, and a *t*-test is no longer an analysis option. Let us explore a research question relying on more than two groups.

RESEARCH DESIGN: ONE IV WITH MORE THAN TWO LEVELS

Oppezzo and Schwartz (2014) found a link between walking (versus sitting) and creative thinking. After reading their research and additional publications, we might want to design a similar study. We could examine physical movement using three groups: sitting quietly, walking on a treadmill, and jogging on a treadmill. For this chapter, we will explore designs with different people in the groups. We should randomly assign each participant to one of the three IV conditions and examine cause and effect. To measure creativity, we might ask participants to say different ways that an object might be used. Consider our research question: *Does level of physical activity affect creativity?*

Notice that our research question does not specify which groups will have higher levels of creativity than others among the three groups. The statistical analysis for more than two groups merely assesses whether any of the groups differ. If at least two of the conditions differ from each other in a meaningful way, the outcome will be significant. The research hypothesis remains general: *Level of physical activity affects creativity.*

And of course the null hypothesis states no significant outcome: *Level of physical activity does not affect creativity.*

To ensure approximately equal groups, we could use block random assignment, pulling one condition from the three conditions for the first participant, then pulling one condition from the remaining two groups for the second participant, and assigning the third participant to the remaining group. After returning all three conditions to the mix, we would begin block random assignment again with the fourth participant, and so on. We display the object and assess the DV of creativity based on perceived number of object uses. The study described here might yield the following results.

Sitting	Walking	Jogging
3	7	6
2	5	6
4	8	5
3	9	7
3	10	7
5	6	8
3	5	6
4	3	8
2	8	11
6	6	8
4	7	4
7	12	8
4		

The Sitting condition has one more participant than the other two conditions. Perhaps we pulled from all three groups and randomly assigned this person to the Sitting condition. The remaining two conditions were not used for that round. We ended our experiment with 37 participants. When conducting studies, we tend to use as many participants as possible, ending data collection as needed, such as the end of the term.

SPSS: One-Way, Between-Groups ANOVA With an IV

When analyzing these data, we cannot use a *t*-test because more than two groups exist. Instead, we will ask SPSS to analyze data using the **Analysis of Variance (ANOVA)**, which is a much more flexible statistic and allows more than two groups as well as other designs we will discuss in later chapters. You first heard of the ANOVA in Chapter 9 with multiple linear regression. In regression, ANOVA told us whether the group of variables predicted an outcome, but our ultimate interest was in the individual predictors. Now, in this chapter, ANOVA is our primary focus, so we will spend more time on the details of ANOVA to analyze a grouped variable such as type of physical activity.

To enter these data into SPSS, we follow the steps from Chapter 10, but this time we enter values for three conditions. Under Variable View, enter Movement and Creativity as the IV and DV, respectively. Under Values for Movement, add 1 = Sit, 2 = Walk, and 3 = Jog. Click OK, and move to Data View.

Movement	Creativity
Sit	3.00
Sit	2.00
Sit	4.00
Sit	3.00
Sit	3.00
Sit	5.00
Sit	3.00
Sit	4.00
Sit	2.00
Sit	6.00
Sit	4.00
Sit	7.00
Sit	4.00
Walk	7.00
Walk	5.00
Walk	8.00
Walk	9.00
Walk	10.00

Under Data View, enter 1, 2, or 3 in the first column to represent Sit, Walk, or Jog as the three study conditions. Then enter Creativity values beside each corresponding Movement value. Click View and Value Labels when you want to see Sit, Walk, and Jog in the first column. The screenshot below shows a section of the entered data.

Analysis of Variance (ANOVA). ANOVA is the statistical test used when a variable has two or more levels but usually is reserved for three or more levels of a variable. The outcome for ANOVA is an interval or ratio DV.

We are analyzing data using ANOVA because we want to examine variability between conditions (which we want) and variability within each condition (which we do not want). ANOVA calculates both types of variability to let us know if differences between the groups are much larger than individual differences within each group. When only one IV (types of movement) is used, we have a **one-way design.** With different people in the three groups, the design is **between groups.** Put them together, and you get a **one-way, between-groups ANOVA.**

First, visually check for suspected outliers in each of the three groups. If you find any apparent outliers, calculate the group means and standard deviations to remove values in a condition more than three standard deviations from the group mean. In our data set, no outliers are apparent.

For the one-way, between-groups ANOVA, click Analyze, General Linear Model, Univariate. Do not be concerned that General Linear Model (GLM) seems like a complex term. One type of GLM is the ANOVA we are using to analyze these data. The term *univariate* is used when you have one DV in the research design, so click on Univariate.

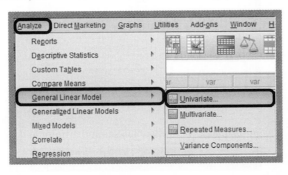

In the box that opens, click Movement over to the right under Fixed Factor(s) using the arrow between the boxes. **Factor** is the term used for an IV or quasi-IV in the ANOVA statistic. Next move Creativity under Dependent Variable using the arrow in the middle. Then click Options to open a box for descriptive statistics and effect size.

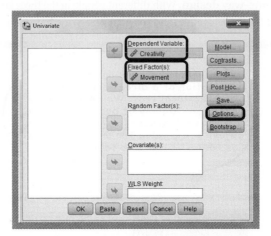

Click Movement over to the right under Display Means for. Then click the box beside Descriptive statistics to get Creativity means and standard deviations for each of the IV levels: Sit, Walk, and Jog. Also click the box beside Estimates of effect size. This request will show the size of an effect if level of movement significantly affects creativity. You should report effect size only when a significant effect exists, but ask SPSS to run the calculation in case you need to know effect size later.

Recall from Chapter 10 that we should examine DV homogeneity of variance across the conditions. We again can use Levene's test by clicking Homogeneity tests in the Options box as shown below. After clicking Continue, the Options box will disappear.

So far, we have asked SPSS to give us three outcomes. We requested descriptive statistics for each IV level. We have also asked SPSS to conduct the ANOVA test to see if level of movement affects creativity (after examining Levene's test), and we have requested effect size. Suppose the ANOVA output shows an effect of movement on creativity based on $p < .05$. A significant outcome tells us something is happening, but we will not know which level of movement causes more creativity than another level of movement. If we want to share useful information with the world, we need to know which groups differ from each other.

We can ask SPSS to gather the information for us using **post hoc** comparisons of means. Post hoc is Latin for "after this" and refers to an analysis conducted after the ANOVA indicates a significant outcome. We look at post hoc analyses only if the main analysis, the ANOVA, reveals a significant effect. Post hoc comparisons pair means in every possible combination. For our example, post hoc includes a comparison of the Sit and Walk means, a comparison of the Sit and Jog means, and a comparison of the Walk and Jog means.

Post Hoc. A post hoc test is conducted following an ANOVA that reveals a significant result. Post hoc mean comparisons reveal which group means differ from each other.

While we are setting up the ANOVA in SPSS, we can ask for post hoc comparisons, knowing that we are allowed to examine those data only if the overall ANOVA is significant. Click Post Hoc as shown below.

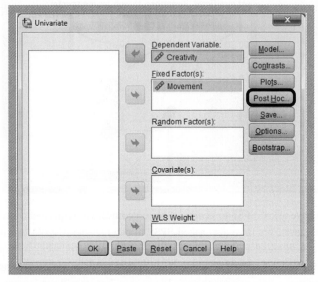

In the box that opens, click Movement over to the right under Post Hoc Tests for. Click beside Tukey for **Tukey's comparisons**, which is a conservative post hoc test. Other options are available for post hoc, and we will offer a second option in the next example. Also keep in mind that your instructor may want you to use a different method of mean comparisons available under the Post Hoc button. Click Continue.

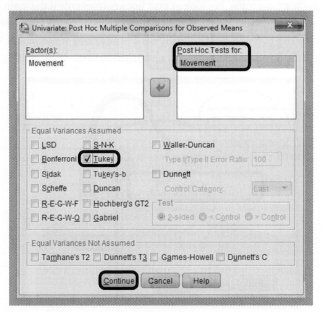

The output follows, which we will show in three separate screenshots. First examine the means and standard deviations for each group. We will need these details for our APA-style results section.

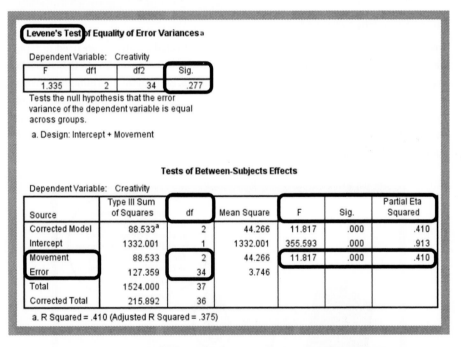

Descriptive Statistics

Dependent Variable: Creativity

Movement	Mean	Std. Deviation	N
Sit	3.8462	1.46322	13
Walk	7.1667	2.44330	12
Jog	7.0000	1.80907	12
Total	5.9459	2.44888	37

Next look at Levene's test for homogeneity of variance. With no significant violation, we can assume approximately equal variability across groups and continue with the examination of the F-test (ANOVA).

Levene's Test of Equality of Error Variances a

Dependent Variable: Creativity

F	df1	df2	Sig.
1.335	2	34	.277

Tests the null hypothesis that the error variance of the dependent variable is equal across groups.

a. Design: Intercept + Movement

Tests of Between-Subjects Effects

Dependent Variable: Creativity

Source	Type III Sum of Squares	df	Mean Square	F	Sig.	Partial Eta Squared
Corrected Model	88.533[a]	2	44.266	11.817	.000	.410
Intercept	1332.001	1	1332.001	355.593	.000	.913
Movement	88.533	2	44.266	11.817	.000	.410
Error	127.359	34	3.746			
Total	1524.000	37				
Corrected Total	215.892	36				

a. R Squared = .410 (Adjusted R Squared = .375)

Look at the Tests of Between-Subjects Effects (ANOVA) table, including degrees of freedom (df), the F-value, the probability value (Sig), and partial eta squared (η^2) for effect size. The Sig value is less than .001, which certainly is beneath the required .05 value needed for significance. Therefore, we know that different levels of movement cause changes to creativity in a meaningful way. We can reject the null hypothesis: *Level of physical activity does not affect creativity*. Instead, we found support for our research hypothesis: *Level of physical activity affects creativity*.

You will see that we have two numbers for *df* in the *F*-test rather than just one *df* value as in the *t*-test. The first *df* number for this example is 2, which quantifies the number of IV levels minus 1 (3 levels − 1 = 2). The second *df* value on the output is 34, which represents the number of participants in the sample (*N* = 37) minus the number of IV levels (3). Reporting both *df* communicates to the reader the number of IV levels and the number of participants in the sample.

Effect Size: Eta Squared

Eta Squared (η^2) Eta squared is the effect size associated with ANOVA. SPSS offers *partial* η^2, which is not a problem because both measures of effect size yield the same value for a one-way ANOVA.

Now that we know level of movement significantly affected creativity, we need to report the size of the effect. **Eta squared (η^2)** represents effect size. According to Cohen (1988), an η^2 of about .01 is considered small, .06 is moderate, and anything around or above .13 is considered a large effect. SPSS does not calculate η^2 but does offer *partial* η^2, and both options quantify effect sizes and yield the same value for a one-way ANOVA. The effect size for this example is .41, a strong effect. Effect size tells us that 41% of creativity can be explained by knowing level of movement.

Post Hoc Comparisons

To learn which groups differ, we must turn to our post hoc comparisons of means.

Post Hoc Tests

Movement

Multiple Comparisons

Dependent Variable: Creativity

Tukey HSD

(I) Movement	(J) Movement	Mean Difference (I-J)	Std. Error	Sig.	95% Confidence Interval	
					Lower Bound	Upper Bound
Sit	Walk	-3.3205*	.77479	.000	-5.2191	-1.4219
	Jog	-3.1538*	.77479	.001	-5.0524	-1.2553
Walk	Sit	3.3205*	.77479	.000	1.4219	5.2191
	Jog	.1667	.79013	.976	-1.7695	2.1028
Jog	Sit	3.1538*	.77479	.001	1.2553	5.0524
	Walk	-.1667	.79013	.976	-2.1028	1.7695

Based on observed means.
The error term is Mean Square(Error) = 3.746.
*. The mean difference is significant at the .05 level.

In the first circled row, Sit and Walk are compared with each other to see if they differ significantly. With a Sig value of .000, they definitely do. Now that we know the two groups are different, we can return to the group means to see which group is higher in creativity than the other group. Return to the first output screenshot to view descriptive statistics. The creativity score for participants who walked was 7.17, and the creativity score for those who sat was only 3.85. So walking causes significantly more creativity than sitting. Now look at the second line where Sit and Jog are compared. A Sig value of .001 indicates a meaningful difference between sitting (3.85 creativity score) and jogging, which showed a mean creativity value of 7.00. The third row on the table simply repeats the comparison of Walk and Sit, so skip it. The fourth row compares Walk and Jog. With a Sig value of .976, we cannot say that these two groups differed.

What have we learned from this study? Return to the research question: *Does level of physical activity affect creativity?* Yes, level of physical movement affected creativity, at least as we operationally defined physical movement and creativity in our study. Further analysis showed us which groups differed in a meaningful way. Post hoc comparisons revealed that both walking and jogging caused more creativity than sitting, but we found no difference in creativity between those who walked and those who jogged.

Confidence Intervals

In Chapter 10, you learned about the confidence interval for a group *difference*. With only two groups, we examined one group difference. In ANOVA, we have more than two groups and therefore multiple CIs for mean differences between groups (in this example, sitting-walking, walking-jogging, and sitting-jogging). If you choose to discuss confidence intervals for each group comparison, look at the final two columns of the Post Hoc Tests table. There you will see the confidence limits for each mean difference at the 95% confidence level.

Knowing the confidence interval for each pair of groups certainly is helpful, and it mirrors the type of confidence interval information we obtained from the *t*-test in Chapter 10. However, when we analyze data using ANOVA on SPSS, the program gives us CIs for each group *mean*, individually. With 95% CIs per mean, we can estimate how many uses people perceive for an object (our measure of creativity) based on their level of activity (sitting, walking, or jogging). When we set up the ANOVA and clicked Options, we asked for Descriptives statistics and Estimates of effect size. Descriptives provided confidence intervals for each individual group rather than differences between pairs of groups. As an example, examine the output below.

Estimated Marginal Means

Movement

Dependent Variable: Creativity

Movement	Mean	Std. Error	95% Confidence Interval	
			Lower Bound	Upper Bound
Sit	3.846	.537	2.755	4.937
Walk	7.167	.559	6.031	8.302
Jog	7.000	.559	5.865	8.135

For most of us, estimating where a population mean would fall makes more sense than discussing potential mean differences. With 95% CIs per mean, we can report how many uses people likely can perceive for an object (our measure of creativity) based on their level of activity.

- Creativity for sitting was 3.85, with 95% confidence limits of 2.76 and 4.94.

- Creativity for walking was 7.17, with 95% confidence limits of 6.03 and 8.30.

- Creativity for jogging was 7.00, with 95% confidence limits of 5.87 and 8.14.

Power

We were fortunate to reveal significant differences between groups, but of course not all of our groups differed from each other. One potential reason for no difference between the walking and jogging conditions is that they, in fact, do not differ when it comes to creativity. A second explanation is that we lacked power to detect an existing effect. According to the table below, we needed at least 159 participants to reveal a significant moderate effect if one existed, and we collected data from only 37 people. Assuming no limitations of time, money, or other issues, researchers would set a goal of 159 participants.

	Small Effect Size	Medium Effect Size	Large Effect Size
One-way, between-groups ANOVA			
2 groups	788	128	52
3 groups	969	159	66
4 groups	1096	180	76

Note: Numbers in the table represent **total** sample size.

APA Style for the One-Way, Between-Groups ANOVA: Experimental Design

In the results section below, we can say "affected" because we used a true IV, defined by manipulation, and therefore know cause and effect. Although we include a graph after the results section as an example, remember that a graph is placed at the end of a manuscript (see Appendix C).

Method

Participants

Thirty-seven students (20 men and 17 women) participated. The sample included 15 White, 12 Black, and 10 Asian students with an average age of 19.72 ($SD = 2.33$). Students chose to participate for extra credit in their Introduction to Psychological Science course, although the instructor offered nonexperimental alternatives for extra credit. Participants received ethical treatment, and the IRB approved the study.

Procedure

Using block randomization, we assigned each participant to one of three conditions: sitting in an office for 30 min, walking on a treadmill in the same office for 30 min, or jogging on a treadmill in the office for 30 min. After exposure to IV groups, participants examined a small wooden dowel with a shovel-shaped structure on one end and a hook on the other end. They listed on paper as many potential uses for the object as they could imagine. People experienced the study individually.

Results

We analyzed these data using a one-way, between-groups ANOVA. Tukey's post hoc group comparisons further analyzed a significant effect ($p < .05$). Level of movement affected creativity, $F(2, 34) = 11.82$, $p < .001$, partial $\eta^2 = .41$. As shown in Figure 1, participants who either walked ($M = 7.17$, $SD = 2.44$, $n = 12$) or jogged ($M = 7.00$, $SD = 1.81$, $n = 12$) showed more creativity than those who merely sat ($M = 3.85$, $SD = 1.46$, $n = 13$). Creativity after walking failed to differ from creativity after jogging ($p > .05$). The 95% CIs for sitting, walking, and jogging reflected limits of [2.76, 4.94], [6.03, 8.30], and [5.87, 8.14], respectively.

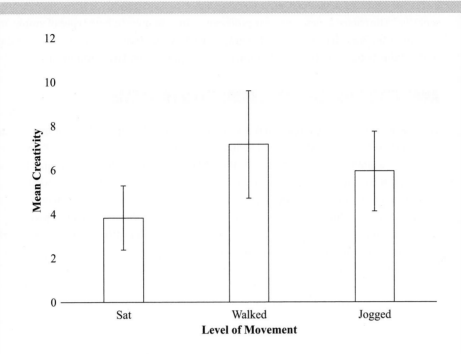

Figure 1. Level of movement affected creativity. Participants who walked or jogged exhibited more creativity than those who merely sat. Error bars represent *SD*.

The results section contains a reference to Figure 1 to efficiently show readers the group differences. As a review of graphing means, pause and examine the IV or quasi-IV. What is the level of measurement? If the variable represents nominal or ordinal data, a bar graph is used. However, if the variable is interval or ratio, a line graph is required. The IV in this example is level of movement, with categories of sitting, walking, and jogging. Because the IV is defined by categories, the variable is nominal and requires a bar graph.

Refer to instructions and screenshots in Appendix B to create your bar graph as shown in the write-up above. We should also point out that a graph of means is not needed when the text portion of your results section contains means and a measure of variability. After all, the two formats offer redundant information, and APA style is concise. However, your instructor may ask for a graph as well as text information in order to help you practice various research components.

As an interesting alternative to graphing means and standard deviations, we could graph means and CIs. That is, the within-group variability bars could represent CIs instead of standard deviations, as long as the figure caption indicated, "Error bars represent CIs." The choice is yours or your professor's. Just do not use *both* types of graphs in a manuscript. We will caution you that graphing CIs using Excel is tricky and beyond the scope of this book. Based on Excel's limitations, we graph standard deviations.

ANALYZING A QUASI-IV WITH MORE THAN TWO LEVELS

The one-way, between-groups ANOVA can analyze one IV or quasi-IV with more than two levels. Actually, the ANOVA can analyze two levels as well, but we generally rely on a *t*-test for a simpler design and turn to the ANOVA with more than two groups. Let us consider a second design and focus on a quasi-IV rather than a true IV. Przybylski (2014) found greater life satisfaction among children who played video games less than 1 hour a day than among children who did not play at all and among those who played much longer than 1 hour a day. Suppose we asked a similar research question: *Do children report different levels of happiness based on how long they play video games?* We might define three groups: no playing, brief play, and longer play. In our study, we might define "briefly" with more specific conditions than Przybylski did. We will include groups who play 1 and 2 hours a day. We will also include comparison groups that play 3 or more hours a day and none at all. In this way, we extend prior research to include different groups. Further, we might examine happiness as an outcome associated with life satisfaction.

After obtaining parental consent, we could visit afterschool programs and ask 12-year-old students approximately how long they play video games each day. They would pick 0, 1, 2, or 3+ hours a day, indicating the time that best describes their habits. Then we could ask all students to complete a scale of happiness, with scores from 1 to 30, with higher numbers meaning more happiness. For adequate power, the table earlier in the chapter specifies that we need 180 participants to find a moderate effect with a four-group ANOVA. Below we have pilot data, so our group sizes are small. We can collect **pilot data** to (1) see if the means are in the expected direction and (2) assess how well our methodology works so we can adjust it if needed. We might find data as shown in the following table.

Pilot Data Pilot data can be collected prior to a study to help determine whether a specific methodology works well. We can also collect pilot data to see if means are in the expected direction before assessing a large sample.

0 Hours	1 Hour	2 Hours	3+ Hours
20	29	18	15
24	25	22	17
18	17	26	25
28	22	12	21
21	23	15	12
19	19	23	20
15	27	21	21
25	26		14
20			

Our job now is to analyze the data using the appropriate statistic. Recall that having different people in each factor level defines a between-groups design, and one factor characterizes a one-way analysis. This example did not include random assignment to conditions or manipulation of what happened to people. Students simply reported what they already do, and their responses placed them in one of the four groups. Regardless, our study is a one-way, between-groups design, and the analysis will be the one-way, between-groups ANOVA.

SPSS: One-Way, Between-Groups ANOVA With a Quasi-IV

First we enter the data, this time setting the Values of hours (of video-game playing) to 0, 1, 2, or 3+ hours. Happiness requires no Values because it is free to vary across all four groups. If no group contains an obvious outlier, click to Data View and enter data, revealing Value Labels when you are ready. In the following screenshot, a portion of the data shows.

Gaming	Happiness
0 hours	20.00
0 hours	24.00
0 hours	18.00
0 hours	28.00
0 hours	21.00
0 hours	19.00
0 hours	15.00
0 hours	25.00
0 hours	20.00
1 hour	29.00
1 hour	25.00
1 hour	17.00

To analyze these data, click Analyze, General Linear Model, Univariate because we again have only one DV: happiness. In the box that opens, click Gaming under Fixed Factor(s) and Happiness under Dependent Variable. Click Options. In the new box that opens, move Gaming over to the right as we showed in the prior example. Also as before, click the boxes next to Descriptive statistics and Estimates of effect size. Remember also to check homogeneity of variance.

Next, instead of asking SPSS to set up post hoc comparisons later, ask for group means to be compared in this box. In the previous example, we decided to use Tukey's comparisons for the post hoc analysis by clicking on the Post Hoc button. Another option is **Least Significant Difference (LSD)**, which is located under the Options tab. For a one-way, between-groups ANOVA, either Tukey's or LSD is an acceptable choice. The LSD comparison is not as conservative as Tukey's, but it is a legitimate option. Remember that your instructor may choose a different post hoc analysis, with many reasonable alternatives.

Least Significant Difference (LSD). Least Significant Difference is a post hoc test for a significant ANOVA factor with more than two levels.

Click Continue to close the box, then click OK in the final remaining box. The first part of SPSS output is shown below.

Univariate Analysis of Variance

Descriptive Statistics

Dependent Variable: Happiness

Gaming	Mean	Std. Deviation	N
0 hours	21.1111	3.95109	9
1 hour	23.5000	4.07080	8
2 hours	19.5714	4.85994	7
3 hours	18.1250	4.35685	8
Total	20.6250	4.54902	32

Levene's test of homogeneity indicates no problem of unequal group variability.

Levene's Test of Equality of Error Variances[a]

Dependent Variable: Happiness

F	df1	df2	Sig.
.250	3	28	.861

Tests the null hypothesis that the error variance of the dependent variable is equal across groups.

a. Design: Intercept + Gaming

Tests of Between-Subjects Effects

Dependent Variable: Happiness

Source	Type III Sum of Squares	df	Mean Square	F	Sig.	Partial Eta Squared
Corrected Model	126.022[a]	3	42.007	2.282	.101	.196
Intercept	13442.377	1	13442.377	730.170	.000	.963
Gaming	126.022	3	42.007	2.282	.101	.196
Error	515.478	28	18.410			
Total	14254.000	32				
Corrected Total	641.500	31				

a. R Squared = .196 (Adjusted R Squared = .110)

The Tests of Between-Subjects Effects table shows ANOVA results, addressing the research question: *Do children report different levels of happiness based on how long they play video games?* A significance value of .101 is larger than the .05 cut-off value allowed. We must say that time spent gaming was not related to happiness *in this study*. We cannot report effect size because no meaningful effect existed. Neither can we look at the post hoc comparisons shown below.

Pairwise Comparisons

Dependent Variable: Happiness

(I) Gaming	(J) Gaming	Mean Difference (I-J)	Std. Error	Sig.[b]	95% Confidence Interval for Difference[b]	
					Lower Bound	Upper Bound
0 hours	1 hour	-2.389	2.085	.262	-6.660	1.882
	2 hours	1.540	2.162	.482	-2.890	5.969
	3 hours	2.986	2.085	.163	-1.285	7.257
1 hour	0 hours	2.389	2.085	.262	-1.882	6.660
	2 hours	3.929	2.221	.088	-.620	8.477
	3 hours	5.375*	2.145	.018	.980	9.770
2 hours	0 hours	-1.540	2.162	.482	-5.969	2.890
	1 hour	-3.929	2.221	.088	-8.477	.620
	3 hours	1.446	2.221	.520	-3.102	5.995
3 hours	0 hours	-2.986	2.085	.163	-7.257	1.285
	1 hour	-5.375*	2.145	.018	-9.770	-.980
	2 hours	-1.446	2.221	.520	-5.995	3.102

Based on estimated marginal means

*. The mean difference is significant at the .05 level.

b. Adjustment for multiple comparisons: Least Significant Difference (equivalent to no adjustments).

It does not make sense to compare specific groups and say they are different after finding a nonsignificant ANOVA.

If your instructor requires CIs, particularly with a nonsignificant result, you may add them as shown in the prior example. If required, examine the Estimated Marginal Means recreated below to obtain CIs surrounding each group mean.

Estimated Marginal Means

Gaming

Dependent Variable: Happiness

Gaming	Mean	Std. Error	95% Confidence Interval	
			Lower Bound	Upper Bound
1 hour	21.111	1.430	18.181	24.041
2 hours	23.500	1.517	20.393	26.607
3 hours	19.571	1.622	16.249	22.893
4.00	18.125	1.517	15.018	21.232

For the sake of example, we will present a line graph illustrating the four group means and standard deviations. Remember that whether you create a line or bar graph depends on the IV or quasi-IV levels. When the X-axis variable is nominal or ordinal, design a bar graph. When the X-axis variable is interval or ratio, a line graph is correct. So far we have created bar graphs because the X-axis variables represented nominal data. In our current gaming example, the quasi-IV is hours spent gaming. The X-axis variable is ratio level, therefore we need to create a line graph. Refer to Appendix B for step-by-step instructions on how to create a line graph for this example.

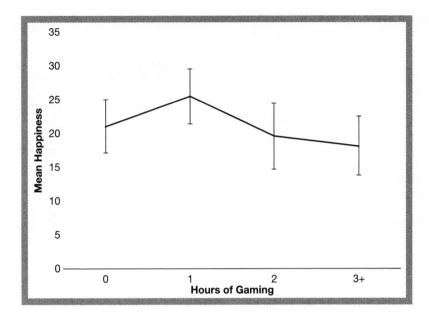

APA Style for the One-Way, Between-Groups ANOVA: Correlational Design

The APA section below contains method and results sections, including all relevant output from SPSS. We have included the mean and standard deviation for each group. However, descriptive statistics lose impact when we already know the groups did not differ.

Method

Participants

Our study included 56 twelve-year-old students (25 boys and 31 girls) in the northeast. We recruited participants from afterschool programs and obtained parental consent for children to complete our survey. The sample included 30 White and 26 Black children.

Procedure

Students reported the average number of hours they played video games each day during the spring school term. Choices for time of playing included 0, 1, 2, and 3 or more hours per day. Next, students reported their overall level of happiness using a scale from 1 to 30, with 1 representing *very unhappy* and 30 representing *very happy*. Researchers explained that higher numbers on the scale indicated more happiness.

Results

   We analyzed these data using a one-way, between-groups ANOVA. Average number of hours spent playing video games each day failed to relate to self-reported ratings of happiness, $F(3, 28) = 2.28$, $p = .101$. As shown in Figure 1, participants who said they played 3 or more hours of video games daily ($M = 18.13$, $SD = 4.36$, $n = 8$) rated their happiness as similar to those who played either 1 ($M = 23.50$, $SD = 4.07$, $n = 8$) or 2 ($M = 19.57$, $SD = 4.86$, $n = 7$) hours daily. Furthermore, students who played 1 hour rated their happiness as similar to those who played 2 hours each day. Finally, students who reported no game playing indicated levels of happiness ($M = 21.11$, $SD = 3.95$, $n = 9$) similar to those of the 3 comparison groups.

   In the APA-style results section above, note that we did not say anything about cause or effect. Instead, we wrote that time playing video games failed to "relate" to happiness. When a variable is not manipulated, the research design is correlational, not experimental. Be careful to use the correct wording for each design. Note also that the ANOVA F-value is followed by $p = .101$ to indicate that we did not find a significant effect. Also on the same SPSS output line is effect size, which we did not report because no meaningful effect existed. Additionally, we chose not to include CIs because the groups failed to differ. The final three sentences contain descriptive statistics for the groups to show the reader details that might be of interest.

   These data addressed the research question: *Do children report different levels of happiness based on how long they play video games?* We failed to reject the null hypothesis: *Children's happiness was not related to how long they played video games.* In our specific study, we defined "never, "briefly," and "a longer period," by asking participants to report whether they play 0, 1, 2, or 3 or more hours daily, on average. We measured happiness using a happiness scale. Based on these operationalized variables and using our specific sample of 12-year-old children in afterschool programs, we did not find support for our research question. The answer to the research question is *No.* But the answer of *No* applies only to this particular test of the research question. We do not know what the answer would be if we allowed people to report exactly how many hours they played video games, including more hours than 3. Only through repeated research can psychologists reveal likely truths about behavior. Numerous studies and many laboratories around the world study research questions using different approaches.

SUMMARY

A one-way, between-groups design is based on one IV or quasi-IV with at least two levels and different participants tested under the factor levels. When the factor contains only two levels, we generally analyze data using an independent-samples *t*-test. We usually reserve ANOVA for designs with more than two factor levels. A *t*-test yields a *t*-value, and ANOVA provides an *F*-value. The overall *F*-test tells us if at least two of the factor conditions differ from each other. If the *F*-test is significant, researchers report effect size and conduct post hoc tests. Post hoc comparisons such as Tukey's and LSD reveal which group means significantly differ from each other. Researchers often choose to include CIs as well, specifying confidence limits. With specific information such as which factor conditions differ, we can share answers to our research questions.

REVIEW OF TERMS

Analysis of Variance (ANOVA)

Between Groups

Eta Squared (η^2)

Factor

Least Significant Difference (LSD)

One-Way, Between-Groups ANOVA

One-Way Design

Pilot Data

Post Hoc

Tukey's Comparisons

PRACTICE ITEMS

1. What are two examples of post hoc tests for ANOVA, and when might you choose one over another?

2. In the one-way between-groups ANOVA, we have two values for *df*. How is each value calculated?

3. With partial η^2, what numbers are associated with weak, moderate, and strong effect sizes?

4. What are the benefits associated with collecting pilot data?

5. When using a quasi-IV rather than a true IV, what do we do differently, if anything, when analyzing data in SPSS?

6. When do we choose to use a line graph rather than a bar graph to visually depict our data?

7. ANOVA in SPSS offers two approaches to CIs. What are they?

* * *

For each of the following studies, (a) state the null and research hypotheses, (b) determine how many participants are needed for adequate power, and (c) enter and analyze the data as well as write an APA-style results section. Please read each method we provided to learn the format of this APA-style section.

8. In your substance abuse class, suppose you read a study by Chen, Wang, and Chen (2014). The authors found support for the "beer goggles" phenomenon, or the idea that with alcohol consumption, other people appear more attractive. Their study was with college students, but you wonder if the same results would occur in a sample of 40- to 50-year-old individuals. You question is, *Among middle-age adults, do various levels of alcohol affect ratings of attractiveness?* If the ANOVA is significant, rely on LSD post hoc comparisons to compare groups.

No Shots	One Shot	Two Shots	Three Shots
1	6	5	10
4	4	7	8
3	1	8	6
2	3	6	6
5	3	4	9
8	2	2	8
6	5	3	7
2	5	3	3
7	7	4	7
3	6	7	8
6	2	10	10

Method

Participants

Participants included 44 middle-age adults (M age = 56.00, SD = 4.99) recruited via a billboard advertisement. Ethnicities included 23 Black, 19 Asian, and 2 White individuals.

Procedure

We assigned individuals to drink 0, 1, 2, or 3 shots of vodka. Everyone drank 4 shots of liquid, but some of the "shots" contained only water with vodka spritzed on the glass rim so the liquid smelled like alcohol. Ten minutes later, participants rated the attractiveness of a gender-neutral stranger's picture on a scale from 1 to 10, with higher numbers indicating more attractiveness.

9. Epley and Schroeder (2014) measured participants' well-being after riding on the subway and found that those who were instructed to talk with a stranger had higher well-being at the end of their commute than those who sat in silence. You wonder if the same results would be true for people talking with a friend versus a stranger.

Your research question is: *Do people differ in happiness after a commute based on different types of interactions with others?* If the ANOVA is significant, rely on Tukey's post hoc comparisons to compare groups. Suppose you collected the following data.

(data continued)

Stranger	Friend	Silence
0	6	0
3	6	1
6	5	0
6	5	2
5	1	3
6	2	3
1	4	2
5	6	1

Stranger	Friend	Silence
2	6	2
3	0	0
4	3	3
1	1	4
2	1	0
6	3	1
	4	4
	5	

Method

Participants

Participants included 45 individuals (28 women and 17 men) with a mean age of 29.55 ($SD = 12.56$). All participants received ethical treatment according to IRB guidelines.

Materials

Modifying the procedure in Epley and Schroeder (2014), participants completed two measures to assess the overall experience of their commute: how happy and how sad they felt after their commute on response scales ranging from 0 (*not at all happy/sad*) to 6 (*very happy/sad*). We reverse scored responses on the sadness item, and then averaged the values on the two items for each participant.

Procedure

We posted a flyer in the Washington, DC, subway system to recruit commuters. Those who called to participate in the study received in the mail a sealed envelope containing a packet to complete at the end of their commute. Participants reported whether they talked with a friend, a stranger, or no one. After completing the survey, participants returned it in the provided addressed and stamped envelope.

10. You are the administrator in charge of the study-abroad program at your college. Although you know that the program provides valuable cultural exposure, you wonder if sending students to Madrid for a semester helps them learn more Spanish than taking a class or using a software program. You decide to track data on a postexperience Spanish exam (worth 100 points) for two years to answer the question: *Do students learn Spanish differently based on their method of learning?* If the ANOVA is significant, rely on Tukey's post hoc comparisons to compare groups. Data follow.

(data continued)

Madrid	Software	Class	Madrid	Software	Class
100	78	70	95	90	85
87	70	85	85	80	47
95	58	87	68	90	80
80	75	78	72	85	70
98	45	65	75	85	95
50	73	98	45	56	85
95	80	71	87	71	54
42	80	85	90	81	78
68	85	72	86	78	79
69	70	80	75	73	70
100	70	75	76		95

Method

Participants

We tracked data from 65 college students across 2 years, with a mean age of 21.02 ($SD = 3.33$). Ethnicities included 30 White, 20 Black, 10 Native American, and 5 Latino individuals. All individuals provided consent for the researcher to access their files.

Procedure

We compared the postexperience Spanish exam scores of students who went to Madrid for a semester with the scores of those who took a Spanish course or used a software program to learn Spanish. Scores on the exam could range from 0% to 100% correct.

REFERENCES

Chen, X., Wang, X., & Chen, Y. (2014). The moderating effect of stimulus attractiveness on the effect of alcohol consumption on attractiveness ratings. *Alcohol and Alcoholism, 49*(5), 515–519. doi:10.1093/alcalc/agu.026

Cohen, J. (1988). *Statistical power analysis for the behavioral sciences*. Hillsdale, NJ: Lawrence Erlbaum.

Epley, N., & Schroeder, J. (2014). Mistakenly seeking solitude. *Journal*

of Experimental Psychology: General, 143*(5), 1980–1999. doi:10.1037/a0037323

Oppezzo, M., & Schwartz, D. L. (2014). Give your ideas some legs: The positive effect of walking on creative thinking. *Journal of Experimental Psychology: Learning, Memory, and Cognition, 40*(4), 1142–1152. doi:10.1037/a0036577

Przybylski, A. K. (2014). Electronic gaming and psychological adjustment. *Pediatrics, 134*(3), 1–7. doi:10.1542/peds.2013-4021

CHAPTER

12

One Variable With
Two Related Groups

In chapters 10 and 11, we discussed one independent variable (IV) or quasi-IV with two or more levels. With both designs, each group contained different people in levels of the IV. As an alternative, some researchers design studies in which they compare people related in some way prior to entering the study, such as siblings. In this chapter, we will discuss examples of **related-samples designs**. Related-samples designs are also called **dependent-samples, paired-samples,** and **matched-pairs** designs. We will focus on an independent variable with only two levels, so you might guess correctly that we will use a *t*-test for analysis. Specifically, we will analyze data using a **related-samples *t*-test**.

Related-Samples (Dependent-Samples, Paired-Samples, Matched-Pairs) Design. A related-samples design is defined by testing the same, similar, or matched participants across IV or quasi-IV levels.

Related-Samples *t*-test. The related-samples *t*-test is the statistical test used when a design has the same, similar, or matched participants in two levels of an IV or quasi-IV with one interval or ratio DV.

Research designs that allow similar people to be measured across all levels of the IV or quasi-IV are powerful. But why? If each pair of participants is similar before arriving at your study, individual differences are minimized. Think about it. Suppose we want to know if giving a speech to an audience causes a larger increase in heart rate than giving a speech to an empty room. If we study pairs of siblings, we can put one sibling in each IV condition. At the end of the study, any differences in heart rate likely could be attributed to the IV conditions rather than individual differences because siblings should have similar heart rates. In comparison, when completely unrelated people exist in the two groups, differences in heart rate could be caused by the IV levels or a lot of potential individual differences such as physical fitness. Sure, you could argue that even sibling pairs can differ on heart rate, but it is reasonable to assume that siblings would not differ as much as two completely random people pulled from a population.

TESTING THE SAME PEOPLE TWICE

Testing pairs of people, with one in each IV level, certainly minimizes individual differences across conditions. But researchers can use an even stronger research design. The same participants can experience *both* IV levels. After all, the person most similar to you is you!

Let us practice using an example with two conditions. Recent evidence suggests that children are more likely to believe information given by an attractive woman than an unattractive woman (Bascandziev & Harris, 2014). The researchers showed preschool children pictures of novel objects, then had two women who varied in attractiveness say different names for the objects. The children picked the woman more likely to be correct, creating a simple frequency DV to be analyzed with a nonparametric statistic. We might design a follow-up study with an interval DV to allow analysis using a parametric statistic, which we know to be more powerful. We could assess children's confidence in each woman's answer on a Likert-type scale from 1 to 7, with higher numbers indicating more confidence.

How sure are you that the woman knows the right name for this object?

I'm sure she does not know						I'm sure she does know
1	2	3	4	5	6	7

Consider the research question: *Do preschool children have more confidence in an attractive woman than an unattractive woman?* Stated as a directional research hypothesis, this question becomes, *Preschool children have more confidence in an attractive woman than an unattractive woman.* The variables must be operationalized, with pictures of an attractive woman and an unattractive woman offering two IV levels.

You might be thinking that beauty is subjective, and you would be right. To make sure we choose pictures of women who most children agree are attractive or unattractive, we could show a small group of preschool children five pictures of women and ask them to order the pictures from least attractive ("ugliest") to most attractive ("prettiest"). The children who rank the pictures are not part of the sample addressing our research question, but they do provide valuable preliminary information when designing the study. We might analyze these data by giving points for each ranking (e.g., 1 point for least attractive and 5 points for most attractive), calculating a mean score for each woman, and choosing pictures with the lowest and highest attractiveness means. The two pictures could then be used in the study.

We have already decided to test the same children twice, asking them to rate confidence in the unattractive and attractive women. Because we can manipulate participants' actions by asking them to look at either the attractive or unattractive woman, the two conditions represent a true IV, and we can examine cause and effect. In prior chapters, random assignment to IV levels helped remove potential confounds, but testing the same people in both conditions means we cannot use random assignment here. Instead, we might ask children to view an unusual object, tell them what the *attractive* woman called the object, and have them circle a number on our confidence scale to indicate how confident they are that the woman correctly named the object. Next, the same children could be asked to view a second unusual object, followed by a label provided by an *unattractive* woman. Children again would rate their confidence using the 7-point scale. We would use a statistic to assess a potential difference between the two conditions.

But wait. Do you see any potential problems with the research design? We have outlined a method in which children always view the attractive woman first and the unattractive woman second. Differences in confidence across the two conditions might be explained by confidence in the women, but other reasonable explanations are possible. For example, children might be bored by the time they view the second woman's picture, causing them to have less confidence in the unattractive woman. Or they might distrust the unattractive woman because they are comparing her with the attractive woman they saw first. Many explanations are possible when the same people are tested more than once in the same order of conditions. In fact, this is such an important concern that researchers have created labels for potential problems.

PROBLEMS WITH TESTING THE SAME PEOPLE TWICE

When the same participants are tested more than once, several problems can be associated with changes in the participant across time. The first manipulation and assessment can change participants' responses to the second manipulation. In general, these problems are called **order effects** because outcomes are impacted by the order of conditions. Order effects are also called **carryover effects** because the effect of one condition carries over to affect the next condition. Order effects occur when participants are influenced during the study by levels of the IV they already experienced. With a two-condition design, an order effect means the first condition influenced responses on the second condition. We do

Order Effects (Carryover Effects). Order effects occur when participants are influenced during the study by levels of the IV they already experienced. With a two-condition design, an order effect means the first condition influenced responses on the second condition.

not want this problem. Returning to our example, if children in the study always view the attractive woman first, their mood might improve across the duration of the study. When they experience the second condition, viewing the unattractive woman, they might rate their confidence in her as high because they are in a particularly good mood. We will not get a clear measure of confidence in the unattractive woman because mood improved in the first condition and carried over to the second condition.

Order effects may be based solely on which condition comes first, but the term also encompasses practice effects and fatigue effects. Alternatively, anything that occurs *between* the first and second manipulation might impact the final DV measure. In other words, people change across time for many reasons that are not tied to our study.

Practice Effect

In some studies, completing a DV the first time allows practice and may improve performance when the DV is completed a second time, defining a **practice effect**. Although practice effects likely would not be a problem in the current study, researchers consider the possibility when DV performance can improve with practice (e.g., quiz performance). Practice effects are a specific type of order effect.

Fatigue Effect

A second type of order effect is fatigue. When participants get tired or bored across a repeated assessment, their performance on the DV may suffer, causing a **fatigue effect**. After the first condition is experienced, and the DV is completed the first time, motivation and energy may decrease. In the current study, children may experience fatigue after examining an ambiguous object and deciding how confident they are in a woman's identification of the object. By the time they see a second object and rate confidence in the second woman, children may not give as much thought to their confidence ratings.

History Effect

Beyond order effects, testing the same people twice allows the possibility of an event between IV levels. A **history effect** occurs when participants change due to anything that occurs across the study. For example, suppose children viewed the attractive woman, and then the fire alarm at school forced everyone to leave the building for 30 minutes. When the children returned, you could continue the study by showing the unattractive woman. You can imagine that children might be affected by the excitement of a fire alarm and standing on the front lawn. A historical event between the two levels can alter outcomes on the second level.

Of course, history is most likely to be a problem when a large event, like a devastating hurricane, occurs between IV levels. Or history effects would be a concern if a long period of time elapses between IV levels, as may be the case in a study that assesses attitudes toward a teacher at the beginning of the term and at the end of the term. Researchers must

Practice Effect.
In some studies, completing a DV the first time allows practice and may improve performance when the DV is completed a second time, characterizing the practice effect.

Fatigue Effect. A specific type of order effect is fatigue. When participants get tired or bored across a repeated assessment, their performance on the DV may suffer, revealing a fatigue effect. After the first condition is experienced, and the DV is completed the first time, motivation and energy may decrease.

History Effect. A history effect occurs when participants change due to anything that occurs across the study. A historical event between exposure to the two IV levels can alter outcomes on the second level.

recognize the potential for history to compromise internal validity, and we might feel less confident that the IV caused changes in the DV.

Maturation

A final potential problem with repeatedly measuring the same participants is maturation. **Maturation** refers to the fact that people age and change over time. Suppose in our example we wanted to examine confidence over time by testing the same children both in preschool and in sixth grade. We would not want to give the attractive condition in preschool and the unattractive in sixth grade, for example, because getting older might change the way children view attractiveness.

Solving Order Problems by Counterbalancing

What is the solution to order effects, history effects, and maturation? Whenever possible, counterbalance the order of conditions. **Counterbalancing** usually is accomplished by randomly assigning people to *order* of IV levels. In our attractiveness example, approximately half of the children should view the attractive woman first and rate their confidence in her answer before moving on to the unattractive woman. The remaining participants should view the unattractive woman first. Counterbalancing the order of IV levels equally distributes any potential order effects. You can be more confident that changes in the DV are due to IV levels rather than which level came first.

Avoiding Confounds

Remember from Chapter 3 that a confound is a variable that changes exactly along with the IV levels. In our example, we have improved our design by counterbalancing the order of conditions, but we still have a potential confound. If the picture of the attractive woman is always shown with one specific ambiguous item, and the unattractive woman is always shown with a second ambiguous item, we will not know if the woman's picture or the item altered confidence ratings. What if the item identified by the attractive woman is simpler, clearer, or somehow familiar to the children? The item could instill confidence. To avoid this potential confounding variable, we could randomly assign which object is paired with which woman. As an alternative, we could systematically pair a specific object with the attractive woman for half of the participants and pair it with the unattractive woman for the other half. As you can see, designing a study requires careful consideration of many details.

RESEARCH DESIGN: ONE IV WITH TWO RELATED GROUPS

Let us examine fictional data from our study of children's confidence in an attractive versus an unattractive woman. We have a DV that ranges from 1 (*I'm sure she does not know*) to 7 (*I'm sure she does know*). Keeping in mind that we tested the same children twice, we must enter confidence values for each child on a separate row. We also have to be careful to put values in the correct column given that the order of conditions varied across participants.

Participant	Attractive	Unattractive
1	5	3
2	6	6
3	7	3
4	4	2
5	6	6
6	5	3

(Continued)

(Continued)

Participant	Attractive	Unattractive
7	6	5
8	7	5
9	6	4
10	7	5
11	4	2

SPSS: Related-Samples *t*-Test (Experimental Design)

To enter these data into SPSS, go to Variable View and label column headings. When we had different people in our groups, we had one column for the IV (or quasi-IV) and one for the DV. With repeated measures, we enter data differently. Now we will give each level of the IV its own column. Label a column for Participant, a second column for Attractive, and a third column heading for Unattractive. We could enter value labels corresponding to our anchors, but labels are not needed to understand the data. Higher numbers reflect more confidence.

Name	Type	Width	Decimals	Label	Values
Participant	Numeric	8	2		None
Attractive	Numeric	8	2		None
Unattractive	Numeric	8	2		None

Go to Data View and enter the data exactly as they are shown in the original data table.

Participant	Attractive	Unattractive
1.00	5.00	3.00
2.00	6.00	6.00
3.00	7.00	3.00
4.00	4.00	2.00
5.00	6.00	6.00
6.00	5.00	3.00
7.00	6.00	5.00
8.00	7.00	5.00
9.00	6.00	4.00
10.00	7.00	5.00
11.00	4.00	2.00

Regardless of whether participants see the attractive or unattractive picture first, confidence rating with the attractive picture is listed first for data analysis, and the confidence rating for the unattractive picture is typed second. You could have entered the data in either order as long as you are careful to put the correct DVs in each column. Click Analyze, Compare Means, Paired-Samples T Test. SPSS refers to this research design as "paired" because the two values for each participant appear on the same row. You learned in Chapter 10 that although the SPSS term is "T Test," researchers generally call the statistic a *t*-test.

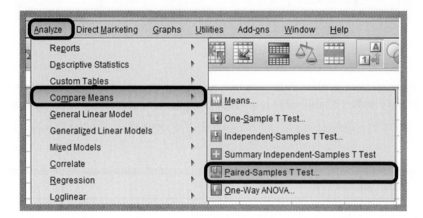

In the box that opens, move Attractive to the right using the arrow. Attractive will appear in the Paired Variables box under Variable 1 beside Pair 1. Next move Unattractive to the right. It will appear beside Attractive, under Variable 2. Clicking OK allows SPSS to compare DV values across the two conditions.

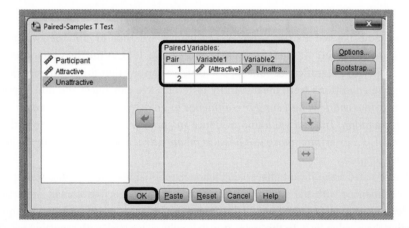

Part of the SPSS output is shown in the following screenshot. From the first table visible, you will need descriptive statistics for the APA-style results section as well as for graphing, if you choose to include a figure.

T-Test

Paired Samples Statistics

		Mean	N	Std. Deviation	Std. Error Mean
Pair 1	Attractive	5.7273	11	1.10371	.33278
	Unattractive	4.0000	11	1.48324	.44721

Further down in the output you will see the *t*-test outcome, degrees of freedom (*df*), and *p*-value. The *df* value is calculated using number of pairs of scores minus 1 (11 − 1 = 10).

Paired Samples Test

Paired Differences						
	95% Confidence Interval of the Difference					
Std. Error Mean	Lower	Upper	t	df	Sig. (2-tailed)
.33278	.98579	2.46876	5.190	10	.000

The table labeled Paired Samples Test shows whether or not the two groups significantly differed. At the far right side of the table, look at the Sig value to see if it is $p \leq .05$. With a significance value of $p < .001$, we can say that the confidence ratings in the two conditions were meaningfully different. We can reject the null hypothesis: *Preschool children had similar confidence in an attractive woman and an unattractive woman.* Instead we found evidence in support of the research hypothesis: *Preschool children had more confidence in an attractive woman than an unattractive woman.*

We revealed a significant effect using a nondirectional test, but because we expected more confidence with the attractive woman than the unattractive woman, we actually needed a directional test. Of course, a directional test has more power and merely requires dividing the *p*-value by 2. In this case, .000/2 is silly, so we stick with reporting $p < .001$. If we return to the descriptive statistics, the means show that children rated more confidence in the attractive woman than in the unattractive woman.

Confidence Intervals

In the same output table showing the *t*-test result, notice the 95% confidence interval for the difference between the two groups (below). Values in the population likely range from a mean difference of 0.99 to 2.47, as shown by the confidence limits for this example.

Paired Samples Test

Paired Differences		
	95% Confidence Interval of the Difference	
Std. Error Mean	Lower	Upper
.33278	.98579	2.46876

Effect Size: Cohen's *d*

With a significant effect, APA style requires effect size. As you learned in Chapter 10, SPSS will not include *t*-test effect sizes. We again turn to Cohen's *d* to communicate the size of an effect if the outcome is significant. The formula for Cohen's *d* with a paired-samples *t*-test is below.

$$d = \frac{M_{group1} - M_{group2}}{SD}$$

The numerator is easily located on the SPSS output. Look at the table for Paired Samples Test. Under Mean you will find the mean difference (Mean), which is one group mean subtracted from the other. Standard deviation (Std. Deviation) is immediately to the right in the table, as shown here.

					95% Confidenc Differ
				Std. Error	
		Mean	Std. Deviation	Mean	Lower
Pair 1	Attractive - Unattractive	1.72727	1.10371	.33278	.98579

Paired Samples Test / Paired Differences

Complete the formula as follows.

$$d = \frac{1.72727}{1.10371} = 1.56$$

Divide the numerator by the denominator to obtain 1.56. Recall from Chapter 10 that a Cohen's d of approximately .20 is considered a weak effect size, .50 is a moderate effect size, and .80 is a large effect size (Cohen, 1988).

APA Style for the Related-Samples t-test: Experimental Design

Although the wording in the results section below does not explicitly say "cause" or "effect," participants were manipulated, allowing a discussion of cause and effect. This example represents a true experiment. The IV was which picture the students viewed.

Method

Participants

Children ($N = 11$) in a 3-year-old preschool classroom in Atlanta, Georgia, participated in this study. Age averaged 3.71 years ($SD = 0.27$), and ethnicities included 5 Black, 4 White, and 2 undisclosed ethnicities. All participants received ethical treatment, and the IRB approved the method.

Materials

Choice of stimuli. Prior to data collection for the study, 7 children from a 3-year-old preschool classroom viewed five pictures of women and ordered them from least attractive ("ugliest") to most attractive ("prettiest"). Pictures received points according to their ranking (e.g., 1 point for least attractive, 5 points for most attractive), and we calculated mean scores for each picture. The pictures with the lowest ($M = 1.49$, $SD = 0.78$) and highest ($M = 4.50$, $SD = 1.05$) scores served as stimuli for the study.

Confidence scale. To assess children's confidence in the woman's answer, we asked them, "Do you think this woman knows the right name for this object?" Children indicated confidence in the woman's object name on a scale from 1 (*I'm sure she does not know*) to 7 (*I'm sure she does know*).

Procedure

We approached parents at the beginning of the school day and asked them to sign a consent form allowing their child to participate in the study. At that time, parents also completed a form indicating demographics for their child. Throughout the day, researchers tested children individually in a quiet room. After asking if the children assented to the study, researchers showed them a picture of a novel object alongside a picture of a woman and indicated a name of the object given by the woman. Children rated their confidence in the object's label. Children next saw a picture of the second woman and answered the same question about a different object's label. We counterbalanced the order of pictured women, providing a random order for each participant. We also randomized which object and object name appeared with each woman's picture. Children received a sticker for participation.

Results

We analyzed these data using a one-tailed, paired-samples *t*-test. Children rated their confidence in a woman's object identification differently based on her level of attractiveness, $t(10) = 5.19$, $p < .001$, 95% CI [0.99, 2.47], $d = 1.56$. When children believed information came from an attractive woman, they rated their confidence in the information higher ($M = 5.73$, $SD = 1.10$, $n = 11$) than when they thought the information came from an unattractive woman ($M = 4.00$, $SD = 1.48$, $n = 11$).

You may have noticed that in a paired-samples *t*-test, the same number of participants will be in both conditions because each participant is tested twice. You will always have the same number of people in both levels, and therefore it is not really necessary to write $n = 11$ for each condition in the APA-style results section. We could have indicated the sample size of 11 once in the results section.

As we have noted before, you may want to include a figure in your manuscript. If so, refer to the figure in the APA-style results section. In this example, the IV is attractiveness based on two categories: a picture of an attractive woman and a picture of an unattractive woman. As you know, categorical data represent a nominal variable. A nominal IV is graphed using a bar graph as shown here.

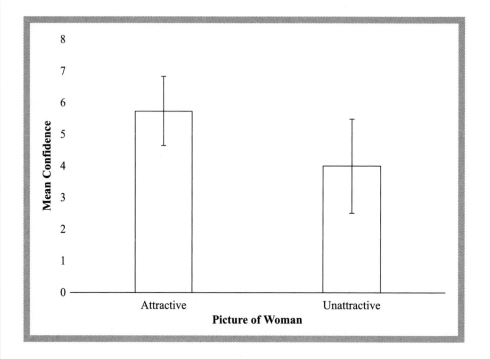

Power

We were fortunate to reveal a significant effect in this study, especially with a small sample size. Power analysis would have revealed the need for 34 participants. In fact, for all paired-samples *t*-tests, you will need 34 participants for adequate power to detect a medium effect size at $p \le .05$, as depicted in the table below. In our example, we used fewer participants for simplicity, but you should strive for enough participants to enhance power.

	Small Effect Size	Medium Effect Size	Large Effect Size
Related-samples *t*-test	200	34	16

Note: Numbers in the table represent **total** sample size. Double the number if you have different people in the IV or quasi-IV levels (e.g., siblings).

RESEARCH DESIGN: ONE QUASI-IV WITH TWO RELATED GROUPS

In the prior example, we examined a related-samples design in an experimental study, but this approach can be used just as easily in a correlational design with no manipulation. Suppose we wanted to know how high-school women feel about their athletic ability currently as compared to how they felt in their elementary-school years. We found an article claiming that among college athletes, comments about gender stereotypes in sports led women to underperform on an athletic task as compared to when a gender-stereotype statement was not made (Hively & El-Alavli, 2014). We might wonder if, over time, girls start to internalize gender stereotypes about sports. Asking high-school girls to think back to their feelings of competence in elementary school might sacrifice accuracy. It would be better to collect information from elementary-school girls, and then have them rate competence again in high school. But waiting is not always realistic. Instead researchers often rely on asking people to recall information.

Based on the research by Hively and El-Alavli (2014), we can devise a research question: *Do high-school girls report less athletic ability for their current age than when they were in elementary school?* The research hypothesis offers a statement: *High-school girls report less athletic ability for their current age than when they were in elementary school.* Is this design an experiment? No. We are merely asking girls to report information and are not manipulating them in any way. This design uses a quasi-IV: elementary-school and high-school time periods. We will not learn cause and effect, but we will learn if time period relates to feelings of athletic competence. Thus, our research design is correlational. We collect two pieces of data from the same people, and analysis will require a paired-samples *t*-test.

Now that we know our research question, design, and planned statistical analysis, we can examine hypothetical data. Below is a table of athletic ability ratings using a scale from 1 to 100, with higher numbers indicating more perceived ability for their age. We have included Participant Number as a column to help keep the data organized by row. Although we would have needed 34 participants for acceptable power, we will use a small data set for a concise example.

Participant Number	Elementary School	High School
1	80	65
2	71	58
3	90	74
4	50	60
5	88	69
6	45	45
7	36	22
8	95	82
9	50	55

SPSS: Related-Samples *t*-test (Correlational Design)

In Variable View, enter Participant, Elementary, and High as the three column headings. Under Data View, enter the data as shown in the above data set (review the prior *t*-test example if needed). Under Data View, click Analyze, Compare Means, Paired-Samples T Test to analyze these data. In the box that opens, click Elementary and High over to the right side. Do not analyze Participant in the *t*-test.

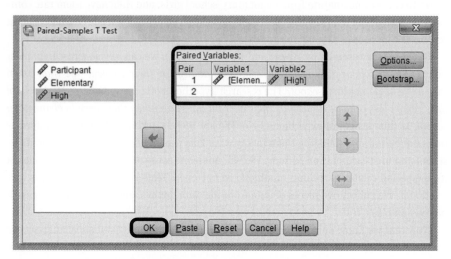

Partial SPSS output is shown below. We have circled the relevant information to compare the two groups and report descriptive statistics.

Paired Samples Statistics

		Mean	N	Std. Deviation	Std. Error Mean
Pair 1	Elementary	67.2222	9	22.25296	7.41765
	High	58.8889	9	17.58156	5.86052

The *t*-test table shows whether or not the two groups significantly differed. Notice also the arrow pointing to the 95% CI.

Paired Samples Test

	95% Confidence Interval of the Difference				
d. Error Mean	Lower	Upper	t	df	Sig. (2-tailed)
3.48807	.28982	16.37685	2.389	8	.044

First we examine the Sig value to see if it is no higher than .05. With a .044 *p*-value, we can say the two groups differed in a meaningful way. We can reject the null hypothesis: *High-school girls reported the same athletic ability for their current age as when they were in elementary school.* Our result provides evidence for the research hypothesis: *High-school girls reported less athletic ability for their current age than when they were in elementary school.*

As you might have realized, we need to divide the *p*-value by 2 because we expected high-school girls to perceive lower athletic ability currently than when they were in elementary school. Thus, our directional *p*-value is .022. Effect size is needed, requiring us to divide the mean difference of 8.33 by the standard deviation of 10.46 to obtain *d* = .80, a large effect size.

APA Style for the Related-Samples *t*-test: Correlational Design

In an APA-style results section, we will report the *t*-value, *df*, *p*-value, confidence interval, and Cohen's *d*. We also need to share with the reader which age group rated their athletic ability higher. Look at descriptive statistics in the first box of the SPSS output to locate means and standard deviations for the two age groups.

Method

Participants

Nine female high-school juniors participated in this study. Ages ranged from 15.07 to 16.98 (*M* = 16.50, *SD* = 0.78), and ethnicities included 7 White and 2 Black individuals.

Procedure

Guidance counselors invited students who worked in the school office to participate. Parents provided informed consent prior to data collection. In addition, students provided assent to participate when they visited the guidance office. Students rated their current perceived athletic ability relative to their peers on a scale from 1 to 100, with higher numbers indicating better perceived ability. Using the same scale, they reflected on their athletic ability relative to their peers when they attended the fifth grade.

Results

We analyzed these data using a directional paired-samples *t*-test. Age level related to confidence in athletic abilities among women, $t(8) = 2.39$, $p = .022$, 95% CI [0.29, 16.38], $d = .80$. Women in high school perceived their athletic abilities to be lower (*M* = 58.89, *SD* = 17.58, *n* = 9) than when they attended elementary school (*M* = 67.22, *SD* = 22.25, *n* = 9).

RESEARCH DESIGN: TESTING DIFFERENT PEOPLE (MATCHED PAIRS)

In the examples above, we tested the same people twice. We can also use the paired-samples *t*-test to assess similar people. One way to pair similar people is to test sibling pairs, as mentioned at the beginning of this chapter. Another option involves matching participants based on some characteristic related to what we are studying. Researchers call the latter approach a matched-pairs design.

Matching Participants

You saw earlier in this chapter that assessing the same people in all conditions has its own set of problems, including order effects. How can researchers capitalize on testing the "same" people across groups but avoid order effects, history, and maturation? Use an exciting compromise: Match pairs of participants first, making them equal on a variable likely to influence your DV. For example, suppose we wanted to examine the potential effect on heart rate of singing a song in front of an audience versus singing alone. The two IV levels would be singing in front of an audience and singing in a room alone, and heart rate would be measured after the song for both conditions. What additional variable might influence cardiovascular responses to singing alone or in front of people? You probably can think of several variables, such as singing ability. After all, someone who is a great singer should be less nervous than someone who cannot carry a tune.

After you have identified a variable that might impact your study but is not the IV or DV, measure participants on that variable. In the singing example, measure singing ability in your sample. Then match up members of your sample into pairs of participants with similar singing ability. Next, randomly assign one member of the pair to sing in front of an audience and ask the other person to sing alone. Not surprisingly, this method is called **matching** because you are matching people on singing ability and then randomly assigning members of the pair to each IV level. Matching is a behind-the-scenes way for you to create a study with less variability based on individual differences, increasing the chance that you will discover a group differences if it exists.

In most cases, participants in the sample are matched for singing ability before they are randomly assigned to experimental conditions. However, it would be perfectly reasonable to randomly assign all participants to conditions and measure their singing ability at the end of the study. Then you could look over the values for singing ability and match people who are similar to each other, making sure one was in the audience group and the other was in the sing-alone group. You might imagine that matching after participants have already participated in your study will force you to drop some people from your study if they have no match at all (maybe they are professional singers or have absolutely no talent). Or perhaps a participant's best match on singing ability was in the same experimental condition. As the researcher, you must decide whether to match people on a potentially important variable before the study or after.

Matching
Matching, or pairing people based on a characteristic you believe will affect the DV, is a behind-the-scenes way to reduce variability, associated with individual differences.

Matching in a Two-Condition Study

We can consider a new example for practice. For this chapter, we will continue our focus on a two-condition study. Recent evidence suggests that taking class notes by hand enhances student test performance over taking notes on a laptop (Mueller & Oppenheimer, 2014). The researchers suggested that students who write out their notes by hand during lecture must process what they are learning to transform the information into fewer words. More effortful thinking about the material results in better retention. We might design a study to test their explanation. If writing with the dominant hand is slower than writing on a computer and thus requires thought and summarizing, writing with the nondominant hand should be even more restrictive. We could ask a new research question: *Do people recall more information when taking notes with their nondominant hand than with their dominant hand?* In the form of a research hypothesis, we would write, *People recall more information when taking notes with their nondominant hand than with their dominant hand.*

The variables must be operationalized, with taking notes using the dominant and nondominant hand offering two levels. Because we can manipulate students' actions by asking them to use either hand, the two conditions represent a true IV, and we can examine cause and effect. The dependent variable is recall of information, which we could measure using a typical test of lecture information. The test will contain 10 multiple-choice items with applied questions rather than simple factual ones because applied questions better assess deeper processing (learning) of the material.

The Matching Process

To first match participants in a meaningful way, we have to consider which individual difference would likely influence the DV of test scores. That is, which characteristic of students might introduce nuisance variability to a study of learning? One possibility is IQ, but if we do not have the time or resources to administer a valid and reliable IQ test, we might use self-reported college GPA as an indicator of intelligence. We could send an email to everyone signed up to participate in our study and ask them to report their college GPA. Then we decide which pairs of students best match on GPA. Matching will not be perfect, but we can match any two GPAs that are reasonably similar. Continuing with our behind-the-scenes preparation, we could randomly assign one person in each pair to one of the two conditions and put the remaining member of the pair in the other condition. When participants show up for our study, we would test them in their assigned condition.

Matching in this way requires keeping track of which two people should be paired. Be careful to avoid placing names on data without IRB approval. Consider using a code to keep track of data. In this example, you might ask students to always write the following code when submitting information to you: *Two-digit birthday month + Number of siblings + First four letters of mother's maiden name.* Of course the IRB must approve all parts of your study, including the code you would like to use. In this example of e-mailing for GPA prior to the study, participants can put their GPA on a Word document along with their code and attach it to the e-mail. Then when they arrive for your study, they can provide their code so you can put them in the correct IV level. Again, the IRB will need to approve any process you consider.

After we have GPAs for each participant, we can match participants into pairs. The following data are GPAs to be matched.

| 2.31 | 4.00 | 3.02 | 3.47 | 2.79 | 3.12 | 3.89 | 2.77 | 2.33 | 2.94 |
| 4.00 | 3.65 | 2.59 | 2.84 | 3.07 | 1.44 | 3.38 | 3.20 | 3.99 | 3.42 |

Notice that we have 20 participants in the sample. With an even number, we have a good chance of matching everyone into pairs. We need to order GPAs from highest to lowest or lowest to highest. Although we could sort these GPAs by looking at them, you will want to allow a computer program to order the values in a larger data set. To order data, enter GPA into Variable View, and then enter GPAs under Data View.

GPA
2.31
4.00
3.02
3.47
2.79
3.12
3.89
2.77
2.33
2.94
4.00
3.65
2.59
2.84
3.07
1.44
3.38
3.20
3.99
3.42

Click Analyze, Descriptive Statistics, Frequencies. In the box that opens, move GPA to the right using the center arrow, and then click OK.

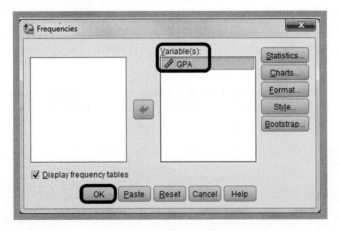

The output shows a table with GPA frequencies and other values. For our purposes, we need the first column of ordered values circled below.

Frequencies

GPA

		Frequency	Percent	Valid Percent	Cumulative Percent
Valid	1.44	1	5.0	5.0	5.0
	2.31	1	5.0	5.0	10.0
	2.33	1	5.0	5.0	15.0
	2.59	1	5.0	5.0	20.0
	2.77	1	5.0	5.0	25.0
	2.79	1	5.0	5.0	30.0
	2.84	1	5.0	5.0	35.0
	2.94	1	5.0	5.0	40.0
	3.02	1	5.0	5.0	45.0
	3.07	1	5.0	5.0	50.0
	3.12	1	5.0	5.0	55.0
	3.20	1	5.0	5.0	60.0
	3.38	1	5.0	5.0	65.0
	3.42	1	5.0	5.0	70.0
	3.47	1	5.0	5.0	75.0
	3.65	1	5.0	5.0	80.0
	3.89	1	5.0	5.0	85.0
	3.99	1	5.0	5.0	90.0
	4.00	2	10.0	10.0	100.0
	Total	20	100.0	100.0	

Notice that 4.00 occurs twice, as indicated by the 2 in the Frequency column, which creates a great match between the two students. Those two participants will be in different conditions. Randomly assign the first person to an IV level, and place the second person in the remaining IV level. Next we will pair students with GPAs of 3.99 and 3.89, and so on, randomly assigning the first person of each pair to an IV level and placing the second person in the remaining condition.

	Nondominant Hand	Dominant Hand
GPA Values Paired	4.00	4.00
	3.89	3.99
	3.65	3.47
	3.42	3.38
	3.12	3.20

Nondominant Hand	Dominant Hand
3.02	3.07
2.94	2.84
2.77	2.79
2.59	2.33
1.44	2.31

You might argue that the final pair of students do not have similar GPAs. Use your best judgment. If 1.44 and 2.31 are too different in your mind, you may choose not to use their data in the final analysis.

When a participant arrives for your study, simply look up the code associated with a specific GPA, and test the participant in the assigned IV level. After testing all participants, GPA values in the table are replaced with test scores, the DV of interest. Analyze the data using the paired-samples *t*-test because the participants have, in fact, been paired.

Nondominant Hand	Dominant Hand
95	98
97	95
92	89
84	80
90	85
82	76
81	80
65	50
71	67
48	43

Again note that our final data set contains the DV of test scores. The GPA values we used to pair students have served their purpose and no longer appear. In a clean SPSS file, enter test scores.

SPSS: Matched-Pairs *t*-test

Under Variable View, label columns with IV levels. Click to Data View to enter data for a paired-samples *t*-test. Click Analyze, Compare Means, Paired-Samples T Test. In the box that opens, move both variables to the right side. If you do not recall the steps, refer to prior examples in this chapter.

SPSS output reveals descriptive statistics in the first table.

T-Test

Paired Samples Statistics

		Mean	N	Std. Deviation	Std. Error Mean
Pair 1	NonDominant	80.5000	10	15.29887	4.83793
	Dominant	76.3000	10	18.17232	5.74659

And both the *t*-test outcome and the 95% confidence interval appear in the Paired Samples Test table.

Paired Samples Test

Paired Differences					
Std. Error Mean	95% Confidence Interval of the Difference		t	df	Sig. (2-tailed)
	Lower	Upper			
1.45144	.91662	7.48338	2.894	9	.018

Based on a Sig value of .018 in the Paired Samples Test table, we know the two groups were meaningfully different. Taking notes with the dominant hand caused significantly different test scores than taking notes with the nondominant hand. We reject the null hypothesis: *People recall the same amount of information when taking notes with their nondominant hand than with their dominant hand.* We revealed support for the research hypothesis: *People recall more information when taking notes with their nondominant hand than with their dominant hand.*

This outcome is good news, but it gets even better. We hypothesized that taking notes with the nondominant hand would require more effortful processing than taking notes with the dominant hand, resulting in higher test scores. As you know, when we clearly expect one group to be higher than the other, we have a directional (one-tailed) test with more power than a nondirectional (two-tailed) test. We divide the nondirectional *p*-value of .018 by 2 to get a directional *p*-value of .009.

Now that we know the two groups differed, calculate effect size using Cohen's *d*. Divide the difference between means (4.20) by the standard deviation (4.59), pulling those two numbers from your SPSS output.

		Paired Samples Test		
		Paired Differences		
				95% C(
	Mean	Std. Deviation	Std. Error Mean	Low
Pair 1 NonDominant - Dominant	4.20000	4.58984	1.45144	.

Cohen's *d* for this example is .92, a large effect. Finally, look at the Paired Samples Statistics table for means to know which group earned higher test scores.

APA Style for the Matched-Pairs *t*-test

We are ready to create an APA-style results section from the output details. First we provide a method section as an example.

Method

Participants

Twenty college students from a men's college in Denmark participated in this study. Nineteen men reported their ethnicity as White, and 1 reported his ethnicity as Black, with a mean age of 19.78 years ($SD = 1.22$).

Procedure

Prior to the study, the researcher e-mailed participants to request their GPA and asked them to provide a unique code based on their mother's maiden name and number of siblings. The code allowed matching of subsequent data from the same participant without compromising anonymity. Researchers matched pairs of participants based on GPA and randomly assigned each person in a pair to each condition. Students participated individually. When they arrived for the study, participants gave the researcher their unique code and watched a 15-min lecture about pineapples while taking notes with either their dominant or nondominant hand. Performance on 10 multiple-choice, applied items constituted the dependent variable.

Results

We analyzed these data using a one-tailed, matched-pairs t-test. Taking notes with the dominant versus nondominant hand affected test scores, $t(9) = 2.89$, $p = .009$, 95% CI [0.92, 7.48], $d = .92$. Students who wrote lecture notes with their nondominant hand earned higher test scores ($M = 80.50$, $SD = 15.30$, $n = 10$) than those who took notes with their dominant hand ($M = 76.30$, $SD = 18.17$, $n = 10$).

Note that we first measured participants on college GPA to pair people by similar GPAs as an indication of similar intelligence. We matched for GPA because the DV was test grades, which reasonably could be influenced by intelligence. Matching first for GPA gave us a better chance of finding an effect of note-taking approaches on test grades. Pairing participants based on a relevant variable offers more statistical power, and you will be more likely to find group differences on your DV if a difference truly exists.

SUMMARY

In this chapter, we explained two-group designs in which either the same people were tested twice or participants were first matched in some way. These designs reduce individual differences and increase the chance of finding a significant study outcome. When the same people are tested twice, several order effects can occur, requiring a solid research design using counterbalancing of conditions. If participants are manipulated with a true IV, researchers can establish cause and effect. If, on the other hand, a quasi-IV is used, we can examine a potential relationship between the quasi-IV and DV. Regardless of whether an IV or quasi-IV is chosen, related-samples designs with two levels are analyzed using a *t*-test.

REVIEW OF TERMS

Counterbalancing

Fatigue Effect

History Effect

Matching

Maturation

Order Effects (Carryover Effects)

Practice Effect

Related-Samples (Dependent-Samples, Paired-Samples, Matched-Pairs) Design

Related-Samples *t*-test

PRACTICE ITEMS

1. What is the difference between a related-samples design and an independent-samples design?

2. Why are related-samples designs considered to be more "powerful" than independent-samples designs?

3. Discuss several problems with testing the same people twice and how you might "solve" those problems.

4. When conducting a study, why might we match participants on a variable rather than have different people in levels of our IV?

5. What effect-size term is associated with the paired-samples *t*-test, and what is considered a weak, moderate, and strong effect?

* * *

For each of the following studies, (a) restate the research question as a research hypothesis and state the null hypothesis, (b) determine how many participants are needed for adequate power, and (c) enter and analyze the data as well as write an APA-style results section. We have written method sections for you as examples.

6. One night when you are in a study group preparing for a final exam, you notice that several of your classmates spend time checking social media pages instead of studying. You read in Panek (2014) that use of social media is related to productivity, with more social media use related to lower productivity. You wonder if access to technology, in general, reduces how prepared students feel after an exam study

session. Based on the Panek study, you think students might feel less prepared. But based on the possibility that cell phones can be used to look up answers to study questions, students might feel more prepared. You ask the research question: *If students have access to their cell phones while studying, will they feel more or less prepared for the exam?* Below, data are presented as pairs of participants with similar GPAs. Higher values for preparation indicate students feel more prepared.

Access to Cell Phones	No Access to Cell Phones
1	0
1	3
2	0
2	4
2	2
3	1
3	1
4	3
4	4
5	0
6	8
7	6
7	5
8	4
8	4
9	5
9	7
10	9
10	10
10	8

Method

Participants

We recruited students ($N = 40$; 50% women, 50% men) in an Introduction to Anthropology class using a flyer posted outside the classroom. Ethnicities included 28 Latino, 5 Black, 5 White, and 2 Chinese individuals, with a mean age of 19.20 ($SD = 2.58$). Researchers entered all participants into a drawing for $25.

Procedure

Students arrived at the study session, which was held in the classroom next door to their regular classroom, 1 hr before a scheduled class exam. At the beginning of the study session, students reported their GPA, and researchers matched them based on this variable. Within each pair, the researchers randomly assigned students to treatment conditions and distributed one of two sheets of paper to each participant. One paper instructed students in the first condition to leave their phones on the table during the study session, and the other paper instructed students in the condition to turn their phones off and place them under the table. At the end of the study session, students rated how prepared they felt for the exam using a scale of 0 (*not prepared at all*) to 10 (*extremely prepared*).

7. You have a daughter with autism spectrum disorder (ASD), which has sparked your interest in treatments for this disorder. Your specific interest is in animal-assisted therapies for ASD. You read a study by Ward, Whalon, Rusnak, Wendell, and Paschall (2014) finding that elementary-age children with ASD who engaged in therapeutic horseback riding scored lower on teacher ratings of ASD impairment. (Higher ratings indicate more impairment.) You wonder if, among older teens with ASD, the same intervention might help reduce self-reported impairment associated with ASD. You ask the research question: *Does horseback riding reduce impairment among high-school-age teens with ASD?*

(data continued)

Participant Number	Pretest	Posttest
1	7	4
2	3	1
3	1	2
4	3	1
5	5	5
6	5	4
7	3	2
8	7	3

Participant Number	Pretest	Posttest
9	2	3
10	3	1
11	4	2
12	6	1
13	4	4
14	6	5
15	4	4
16	2	5

Method

Participants

Participants included 16 teenagers (10 boys, 5 girls, and 1 nonbinary individual) with parent-reported previous diagnoses of autism spectrum disorder (ASD). Ages ranged from 15 to 17 ($M = 16.51$, $SD = 0.97$), and ethnicities included 14 White, 1 Black, and 1 mixed-race individual. In addition to parent consent, researchers obtained child assent prior to both pre- and posttest data collection.

Procedure

Participants reported their impairment on a scale of 1 (*very little impairment*) to 7 (*a great deal of impairment*) before and after a 6-week horseback riding intervention. Although all 16 participants participated in the intervention as a group, each person rode his or her own horse with an instructor present. Participants rode the same horse and worked with the same instructor at each weekly 1-hr session.

8. Hancock, Jorgensen, and Swanson (2013) found several factors related to credit-card use and debt among college students, concluding that early intervention may be the best way to reduce credit-card debt. You ask, *Will first-year college students exposed to a lecture about finances have less credit-card debt one year later than students not exposed to this lecture?* You recruit pairs of twins, assuming that twins will enter college with similar amounts of debt, so you can use a related-samples design. The data in the table below are dollar amounts of debt presented for pairs of twins.

| | | (data continued) | | (data continued) | |
Lecture	No Lecture	Lecture	No Lecture	Lecture	No Lecture
2000	2500	2600	1900	4000	1000
500	600	10100	12010	2000	2500
450	100	460	580	750	1500
150	300	5000	6050	6580	7890
4500	4000	8000	6000	2580	2620
4260	4710	4710	4700	2500	8000
1000	2560	3000	3500	6050	5020

Method

Participants

We recruited 21 sets of twins (12 fraternal, 9 identical) in their first semester of college. Of these, 23 individuals identified as female gender, 18 identified as male gender, and 1 chose not to provide information about gender. Ethnicities included 22 Black, 16 White, and 4 Latino individuals, with a mean age of 18.76 ($SD = 1.01$). Sexual orientations included 32 straight, 8 gay, and 2 pansexual individuals.

Procedure

We recruited participants from a large university in Colorado via posts on Facebook and Twitter. As twins arrived for the study, we randomly assigned them to either the treatment or control group. Those in the treatment group watched a 10-min video lecture about credit-card debt in one room, while those in the control group watched a 10-min video about staying safe on campus in another room. At the end of the spring semester, we asked twins to e-mail their total amount of credit-card debt.

REFERENCES

Bascandziev, I., & Harris, P. L. (2014). In beauty we trust: Children prefer information from more attractive informants. *British Journal of Developmental Psychology, 32,* 94–99. doi:10.1111/bidp.12022

Cohen, J. (1988). *Statistical power analysis for the behavioral sciences*. Hillsdale, NJ: Lawrence Erlbaum.

Hancock, A. M., Jorgensen, B. L., & Swanson, M. S. (2013). College students and credit card use: The role of parents, work experience, financial knowledge, and credit card attitudes. *Journal of Family and Economic Issues, 34,* 369–381. doi:10.1007/s10834-012-9338-8

Hively, K., & El-Alavli, A. (2014). "You throw like a girl": The effect of stereotype threat on women's athletic performance and gender stereotypes. *Psychology of Sport and Exercise, 15*(1), 48–55. doi:10.1016/j.psychsport.2013.09.001

Mueller, P. A., & Oppenheimer, D. M. (2014). The pen is mightier than the keyboard: Advantages of longhand over laptop note taking. *Psychological Science, 25*(6), 1159–1168. doi:10.1177/0956797614524581

Panek, E. (2014). Left to their own devices: College students' "guilty pleasure" media use and time management. *Communication Research, 41*(4), 561–577. doi:10.1177/0093650213499657

Ward, S. C., Whalon, K., Rusnak, K., Wendell, K., & Paschall, N. (2014). The association between therapeutic horseback riding and the social communication and sensory reactions of children with autism. *Journal of Autism and Developmental Disorders, 43,* 2190–2198. doi:10.1007/s10803-013-1773-3

13

One Variable With Repeated Measures: More Than Two Groups

Repeated-Measures (Within-Participants) Design. A research design with the same participants tested under every factor level is called a repeated-measures or within-participants design. Note that an older term for this design is *within-subjects*.

One-Way, Repeated-Measures ANOVA. A one-way, repeated-measures ANOVA is a type of analysis used when we test the same people under every level of a single factor, and the DV represents interval or ratio data.

If a research design has an independent variable (IV) or quasi-IV with two levels, data are analyzed using a *t*-test. If a design has more than two IV or quasi-IV levels, data are analyzed using analysis of variance (ANOVA). Recall that ANOVA allows you to call your IV or quasi-IV a factor, and designs with one factor are called one-way designs. A research design with the same participants tested under every factor level is called a **repeated-measures** or **within-participants design.**

Remember from Chapter 12 that a related-samples design means either the same people are tested under both variable conditions, or people are first matched in some way. A repeated-measures design requires the *same* participants to be tested under all three or more levels of the factor. The ANOVA is not as permissive as the *t*-test, so ANOVA requires the same participants to be tested repeatedly. In this chapter, we will discuss repeated-measures designs with three or more levels. These designs are analyzed with a parametric statistic called the **one-way, repeated-measures ANOVA**.

RESEARCH DESIGN: ONE IV WITH REPEATED MEASURES

Before we create our own hypothetical example, consider a recent article about teacher threats and student performance. Putwain and Remedios (2014) asked high-school students to report how often their teachers tried to scare them with threats of failure if they did not study. Those who reported more threats actually earned lower test scores than those who reported fewer threats. Reading this article might inspire us to design a repeated-measures study in which a teacher tries to motivate students through threats, encouragement, or no comments at all, as a control condition. Such a study contains three levels of a true IV because teacher behaviors can be controlled by the researcher, allowing manipulation of participants. Our research question might be: *Do teacher comments affect students' grades?* The research hypothesis provides a statement of expectation: *Teacher comments affect students' grades.*

We might design a study in which a teacher threatens failure prior to Test 1, encourages students prior to Test 2, and says nothing at all prior to Test 3. Of course, a good design would counterbalance the order of conditions. Otherwise we would never know if differences across conditions were due to other variables such as test difficulty or even a carryover effect of having a threatening teacher at the beginning of the term. With only three IV levels in this study, we could test participants in every possible order:

Threaten, Encourage, Control
Threaten, Control, Encourage
Encourage, Threaten, Control
Encourage, Control, Threaten
Control, Threaten, Encourage
Control, Encourage, Threaten

You might imagine that a teacher would have a hard time being threatening, encouraging, and silent in different orders to students in the same room. To solve this problem, we will have the teacher e-mail students specific notes, depending on their current IV condition. One student would get the first order of IV levels, another student would get the second order, and so on. Using all six possible orders of three conditions presents a bit more work, but it is doable. However, if your IV has four levels, you quickly run into problems when trying to test all possible orders.

With many factor levels, an option often used by researchers is to randomly assign participants to orders. One student might get the first order of conditions, the next student might get the fifth order of conditions, and some orders may not be used in the study. Using this approach, several orders are represented, and order effects are minimized. We will randomly assign participants to orders in our example of teaching approaches. Because we have only three levels and six possible orders, likely all orders will be used.

Whenever possible, researchers should collect or analyze data without knowing which level of the IV was experienced by each participant at a given time. This approach is called being **blind to conditions**. Scoring blind reduces the chance for researcher bias because the researcher has no idea which level of the IV occurred. In the current example, we could reasonably expect the researcher to be blind to IV levels when grading tests. Only after tests are graded would the researcher examine specific e-mails sent prior to the test.

Blind to Conditions (Scoring Blind). Whenever possible, researchers should collect or analyze data without knowing which level of the factor each participant experienced. This approach is called being blind to conditions. Scoring blind reduces the chance for researcher bias because the researcher has no idea which level of the factor is being assessed.

At the end of the study, we must carefully organize the data such that each test grade is matched with the correct IV level. And of course each row of data must represent a specific participant. Data should end up in a table such as the one below.

Participant	Control	Encourage	Threaten
1	72	87	79
2	50	65	52
3	93	95	94
4	65	88	71
5	81	90	80
6	68	77	71
7	52	69	58
8	61	75	68
9	70	83	72
10	67	79	72
11	88	97	94

SPSS: One-Way, Repeated-Measures ANOVA (Experimental Design)

In SPSS, enter each IV level as a separate column heading by typing under Name as explained in Chapter 12. Enter no Values for levels because each column of data will be a separate level in this design, and each level contains ungrouped quantitative data. We have chosen to label our columns: Participant, Control, Encourage, and Threaten.

Click to Data View and enter data. We entered participant numbers to keep track of the rows, but we will analyze only data in the Control, Encourage, and Threaten columns.

Participant	Control	Encourage	Threaten
1.00	72.00	87.00	79.00
2.00	50.00	65.00	52.00
3.00	93.00	95.00	94.00
4.00	65.00	88.00	71.00
5.00	81.00	90.00	80.00
6.00	68.00	77.00	71.00
7.00	52.00	69.00	58.00
8.00	61.00	75.00	68.00
9.00	70.00	83.00	72.00
10.00	67.00	79.00	72.00
11.00	88.00	97.00	94.00

To analyze these data, click Analyze, General Linear Model, and Repeated Measures.

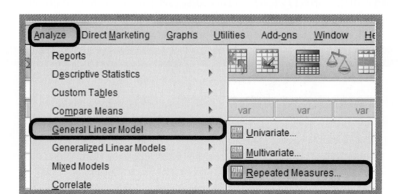

The following box will open, allowing you to define the IV under Within-Subject Factor Name. Remember that *within-participants* is another term for the repeated-measures design, but SPSS uses the older term *within-subject(s)*. Regardless of what SPSS calls this analysis, we know we have a repeated-measures design. Our IV has three levels, and all can be considered types of motivation. We can name the IV "Motivate" as a general term, with specific levels of Control, Encourage, and Threaten. Beside Number of Levels, type the number 3.

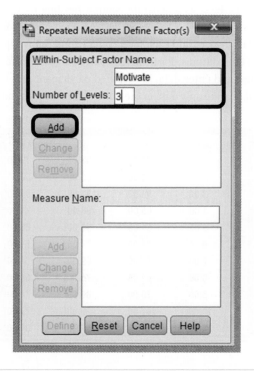

Click Add, and then Define as indicated in the next screenshot.

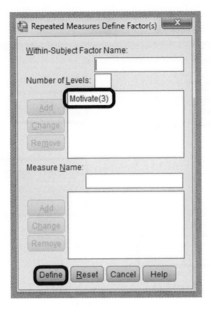

In the next box that opens, define the IV levels by clicking Control, Encourage, and Threaten over to the right side, under Within-Subjects Variables (Motivate).

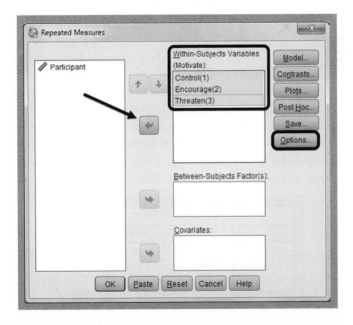

Click Options to request descriptive statistics and effect size for the analysis. Of course, effect size will be relevant only if you find a significant effect, but researchers generally set up the analysis and look at it if needed. Click Motivate to the right under Display Means for. Check the boxes beside Descriptive statistics and Estimates of effect size. Click the box to the left of Compare main effects to obtain post hoc mean comparisons.

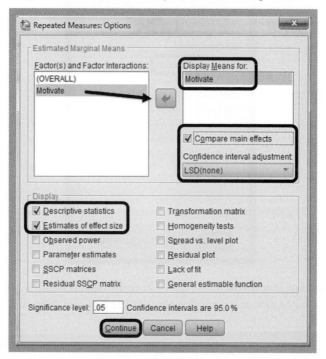

When you click Continue, SPSS will take you back to the first box. Note that we do not click Post Hoc on the right side because (1) we already set up post hoc comparisons under Options, and (2) the Post Hoc option is not available under the button for a repeated-measures ANOVA.

Click OK to see your output and learn if type of teacher motivation affected students' test grades. Here we offer several screenshots to illustrate the majority of output. We will focus on output that is most important to you at this stage in your education. First, Descriptive Statistics are always needed for an APA-style results section.

Descriptive Statistics

	Mean	Std. Deviation	N
Control	69.7273	13.49141	11
Encourage	82.2727	10.29651	11
Threaten	73.7273	12.89256	11

Next, look at the Test of Within-Subjects Effects. This table provides the F-value, degrees of freedom (df), and significance value to let us know if type of motivation affected grades. But first we want to make sure that we are using the correct line for our F statistic.

Tests of Within-Subjects Effects

Measure: MEASURE_1

Source		Type III Sum of Squares	df	Mean Square	F	Sig.	Partial Eta Squared
Motivate	Sphericity Assumed	903.515	2	451.758	47.432	.000	.826
	Greenhouse-Geisser	903.515	1.384	652.833	47.432	.000	.826
	Huynh-Feldt	903.515	1.535	588.683	47.432	.000	.826
	Lower-bound	903.515	1.000	903.515	47.432	.000	.826
Error(Motivate)	Sphericity Assumed	190.485	20	9.524			
	Greenhouse-Geisser	190.485	13.840	13.763			
	Huynh-Feldt	190.485	15.348	12.411			
	Lower-bound	190.485	10.000	19.048			

Sphericity

Typically, you will be able to use the first line ("Sphericity Assumed") for the F-value, but only if you have a *nonsignificant p*-value for Mauchly's test of sphericity. If the test of sphericity is significant, **sphericity** has been violated, which means that variability in a pair *difference* across two levels of the IV is very unlike variability in a pair difference across two other levels of the IV. When we have three groups, such as in this example, the test of sphericity examines differences in pairs between (1) control and encourage, (2) control and threaten, and (3) encourage and threaten. Whenever we conduct a repeated-measures study with more than two groups, we must examine Mauchly's test of sphericity to make sure that $p > .05$. If $p \leq .05$, the pair differences across group comparisons are quite different, violating sphericity.

> **Sphericity.** Sphericity indicates that variability in pair differences across two levels of a factor is very similar to variability in pair differences across two other levels of the factor.

When reporting a significant test of sphericity followed by the correct ANOVA output, use the following format. Be careful to adjust the *F*-statistic *df* using the correct rows in the ANOVA summary table.

Mauchly's test of sphericity showed a significant violation, $\chi^2(df) =$ xx.xx, $p = $ .xxx. Based on Greenhouse-Geisser adjustments, $F(x, xx) = \ldots$

In our example, the test of sphericity is close to a significant violation, but with $p > .05$, we do not have a significant violation.

Mauchly's Test of Sphericity[a]

Measure: MEASURE_1

Within Subjects Effect	Mauchly's W	Approx. Chi-Square	df	Sig.	Epsilon[b]		
					Greenhouse-Geisser	Huynh-Feldt	Lower-bound
Motivate	.555	5.301	2	.071	.692	.767	.500

Tests the null hypothesis that the error covariance matrix of the orthonormalized transformed dependent variables is proportional to an identity matrix.

a. Design: Intercept
   Within Subjects Design: Motivate

b. May be used to adjust the degrees of freedom for the averaged tests of significance. Corrected tests are displayed in the Tests of Within-Subjects Effects table.

What would we have done if $p \leq .05$, indicating significantly different variabilities across group pairs? We would use an adjustment offered by SPSS in the output. Look at the ANOVA summary table below. The first row is Sphericity Assumed. If Mauchly's test had not allowed us to assume sphericity ($p \leq .05$), we would have used the Greenhouse-Geisser row on the ANOVA table instead. Greenhouse-Geisser offers an alternative, conservative test when sphericity has been violated. Refer back to the prior page for APA-style details.

We can use the first lines of data in the box labeled Tests of Within-Subjects Effects. Look at the information on the lines marked Sphericity Assumed as circled below.

Tests of Within-Subjects Effects

Measure: MEASURE_1

Source		Type III Sum of Squares	df	Mean Square	F	Sig.	Partial Eta Squared
Motivate	Sphericity Assumed	903.515	2	451.758	47.432	.000	.826
	Greenhouse-Geisser	903.515	1.384	652.833	47.432	.000	.826
	Huynh-Feldt	903.515	1.535	588.683	47.432	.000	.826
	Lower-bound	903.515	1.000	903.515	47.432	.000	.826
Error(Motivate)	Sphericity Assumed	190.485	20	9.524			
	Greenhouse-Geisser	190.485	13.840	13.763			
	Huynh-Feldt	190.485	15.348	12.411			
	Lower-bound	190.485	10.000	19.048			

Based on a significant p-value of .000 ($p < .001$), we can reject the null hypothesis: *Teacher comments did not affect students' grades.* By rejecting the null, we report evidence for the research hypothesis: *Teacher comments affected students' grades.*

Although significance means at least two groups differ, we do not yet know specifically which groups differ. On the output, look at Pairwise Comparisons for post hoc analysis. Significant comparisons ($p \leq .05$) tell us which groups significantly differ from each other.

Pairwise Comparisons

Measure: MEASURE_1

(I) Motivate	(J) Motivate	Mean Difference (I-J)	Std. Error	Sig.[b]	95% Confidence Interval for Difference[b]	
					Lower Bound	Upper Bound
1	2	-12.545[*]	1.631	.000	-16.180	-8.911
	3	-4.000[*]	.820	.001	-5.828	-2.172
2	1	12.545[*]	1.631	.000	8.911	16.180
	3	8.545[*]	1.364	.000	5.506	11.585
3	1	4.000[*]	.820	.001	2.172	5.828
	2	-8.545[*]	1.364	.000	-11.585	-5.506

Based on estimated marginal means

*. The mean difference is significant at the .05 level.

b. Adjustment for multiple comparisons: Least Significant Difference (equivalent to no adjustments).

As you can see from the Sig column, groups 1 and 2 differ, groups 1 and 3 differ, and groups 2 and 3 differ from each other. Examination of the group means under Descriptive Statistics reveals which groups had higher exam grades than others.

Effect Size: Eta Squared

As you learned in Chapter 11, we use eta squared (η^2) for ANOVA. Recall that an η^2 of about .01 is considered small, .06 is moderate, and anything around or above .13 is considered a large effect. Also recall that SPSS gives us *partial* η^2, which is comparable to η^2.

Confidence Intervals

Notice in the prior screenshot that SPSS provides 95% confidence intervals (CIs) for group mean differences. Although this information is useful, we explained in Chapter 11 that ANOVA in SPSS will also provide 95% CIs surrounding each individual mean. Such confidence limits are more logical, explaining the range of likely population values under each specific condition. Examine the portion of the output below under Estimated Marginal Means.

Estimated Marginal Means

Motivate

Estimates

Measure: MEASURE_1

Motivate	Mean	Std. Error	95% Confidence Interval	
			Lower Bound	Upper Bound
1	69.727	4.068	60.664	78.791
2	82.273	3.105	75.355	89.190
3	73.727	3.887	65.066	82.389

We will add the 95% CIs surrounding each mean to our APA-style results section.

Power

In this example, we have a significant overall effect as well as specific differences between groups. The sample size was quite small, reducing the chance of finding a significant result if one existed. Although we used only 11 participants in the study as a brief example, you would want to follow Cohen's (1992) advice and include approximately 34 people per group for a good chance of revealing a medium effect at the $p \leq .05$ level. Because the same people are tested across the factor levels, 34 is also the total sample size.

	Small Effect Size	Medium Effect Size	Large Effect Size
One-way, repeated-measures ANOVA			
2 groups	200	34	16
3 groups	165	30	12
4 groups	140	24	10

Note: Numbers in the table represent **total** sample size.

APA Style for the One-Way, Repeated-Measures ANOVA: Experimental Design

Let us consolidate methodology and details from the SPSS output in an organized and meaningful way using APA style.

Method

Participants

Eleven students (4 boys, 7 girls) from a ninth-grade mathematics classroom at a private high school in Alaska participated in this study. Ages ranged from 13.57 to 15.02 years ($M = 14.78$, $SD = 3.25$), and ethnicities included White ($n = 6$) and Alaska Native ($n = 5$).

Procedure

Each participant experienced all three levels of the manipulation. For three consecutive exams, students received either threatening (e.g., "If you do not study more, you likely will not pass the next exam"), encouraging (e.g., "You have been doing very well in class, which I am sure will show on the exam"), or neutral (e.g., "Do not forget that the exam is in 3 days") comments regarding the upcoming exam. The researcher counterbalanced the order of messages across students such that each student received a random order of the messages. Exam grades constituted the outcome variable.

Results

We analyzed these data using a one-way, repeated-measures ANOVA. We further analyzed a significant effect using LSD mean comparisons ($p < .05$). Type of teacher motivation affected students' test grades, $F(2, 20) = 47.43$, $p < .001$, partial $\eta^2 = .83$. As shown in Figure 1, when a teacher encouraged students to study, students earned better grades ($M = 82.27$, $SD = 10.30$, $n = 11$) than when the teacher threatened students with poor grades ($M = 73.73$, $SD = 12.89$, $n = 11$) or said nothing ($M = 69.73$, $SD = 13.49$, $n = 11$). Further, students made higher grades after the teacher threatened them than after the teacher said nothing. The 95% CIs for each condition spanned [60.66, 78.79], [75.36, 89.19], and [65.07, 82.39], for no teacher comments, teacher encouragement, and threats, respectively.

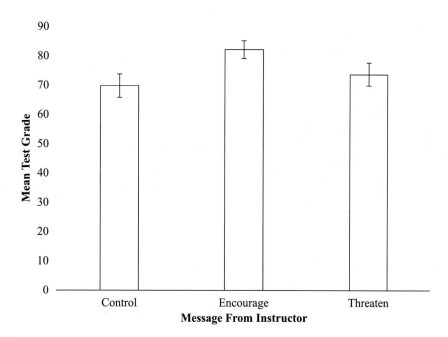

Figure 1. Students encouraged by the instructor earned significantly higher test grades than those threatened or those who received a neutral message. In addition, students threatened by their instructor earned higher test grades than those in the control condition. Error bars represent *SD*.

RESEARCH DESIGN: ONE QUASI-IV WITH REPEATED MEASURES

In the prior example, the design included a manipulated variable, which created an experiment and allowed us to establish cause and effect. Without manipulation, we will not learn cause and effect, but we certainly can establish whether the quasi-IV and DV are related to each other. In this chapter, we will continue to focus on assessing the same participants across all quasi-IV levels. Let us look at an example.

Suppose we are interested in self-esteem across class ranking in high school. We read in a review article by Robins and Trzesniewski (2005) that self-esteem typically decreases in adolescence, but we wonder if this decrease has less to do with age and more to do with year in high school. We could assess self-esteem during the first year, as a sophomore, as a junior, and as a high-school senior. To have a repeated-measures design, we would need to assess the same people across these quasi-IV levels. Our research question would be: *Is year in high school related to self-esteem?* As a research hypothesis, we would state: *Year in high school is related to self-esteem.*

The variable of year in high school is straightforward, but self-esteem must be operationally defined. Fortunately, the available literature offers an established measure: the Single-Item Self-Esteem scale (SISE; Robins, Hendin, & Trzesniewski, 2001). Using this scale, participants rate themselves on one Likert item ("I have high self-esteem") on a 5-point Likert scale from 1 (*not very true of me*) to 5 (*very true of me*).

We might ask seniors to rate their current self-esteem and think back to prior years, reporting what they recall about their self-esteem. Or we might track teenagers through high school, collecting data about their self-esteem across the four years in a longitudinal design. Imagine we did collect data across the four years and obtained the following data set. (Of course, we would have set a goal of assessing at least 24 participants for a real-life study.)

Participant	First Year	Sophomore	Junior	Senior
1	5	5	4	3
2	4	5	5	4
3	4	3	4	2
4	3	3	3	2
5	4	4	4	2
6	4	5	4	3
7	5	5	5	4
8	3	2	3	1
9	4	3	3	3
10	5	5	4	3

SPSS: One-Way, Repeated-Measures ANOVA (Correlational Design)

Enter variables into SPSS. Because this example is a repeated-measures design, be sure to label each column for a quasi-IV level: First_year, Sophomore, Junior, and Senior. We also entered Participant as our first column to help organize the data. Using the same format as in the prior example, click to Data View and enter the data, keeping each participant's self-esteem values on a single row.

To analyze, click Analyze, General Linear Model, and Repeated Measures. In the box that opens, change the Within-Subjects Factor Name to Year and indicate four levels of the quasi-IV. Click Add and Define to tell SPSS the four levels.

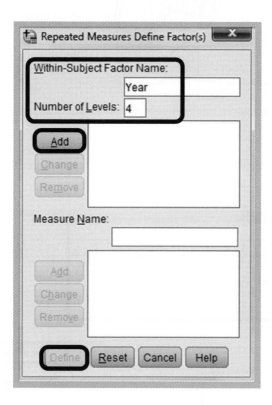

In the new box, move all four levels to the right using the arrow, and then click Options. Under Options, click boxes next to Descriptive statistics and Estimates of effect size, and click the box next to Compare main effects for post hoc comparisons. Refer to the first example in this chapter for step-by-step instructions, as needed.

Click Continue, and then OK for the output. Below we focus on relevant parts of the output. The first screenshot contains group descriptive statistics and the test of sphericity. A *p*-value of .992 tells us sphericity has not been violated.

Descriptive Statistics

	Mean	Std. Deviation	N
First_year	4.1000	.73786	10
Sophomore	4.0000	1.15470	10
Junior	3.9000	.73786	10
Senior	2.7000	.94868	10

Mauchly's Test of Sphericity[a]

Measure: MEASURE_1

Within Subjects Effect	Mauchly's W	Approx. Chi-Square	df	Sig.
Year	.935	.516	5	.992

Tests the null hypothesis that the error covariance matrix of the orthonormalized tra to an identity matrix.

a. Design: Intercept
   Within Subjects Design: Year

b. May be used to adjust the degrees of freedom for the averaged tests of significa of Within-Subjects Effects table.

Below, the ANOVA summary table reveals a significant outcome. With a significance value of .000 ($p < .001$), we can answer our research question: *Is year in high school related to self-esteem?* Yes, the quasi-IV and DV were related. We reject the null hypothesis: *Year in high school is not related to self-esteem.* Our results provide evidence for the research hypothesis: *Year in high school is related to self-esteem.*

Tests of Within-Subjects Effects

Measure: MEASURE_1

Source		Type III Sum of Squares	df	Mean Square	F	Sig.	Partial Eta Squared
Year	Sphericity Assumed	12.875	3	4.292	18.176	.000	.669
	Greenhouse-Geisser	12.875	2.874	4.480	18.176	.000	.669
	Huynh-Feldt	12.875	3.000	4.292	18.176	.000	.669
	Lower-bound	12.875	1.000	12.875	18.176	.002	.669
Error(Year)	Sphericity Assumed	6.375	27	.236			
	Greenhouse-Geisser	6.375	25.866	.246			
	Huynh-Feldt	6.375	27.000	.236			
	Lower-bound	6.375	9.000	.708			

In fact, the effect is large. But exactly how were the two variables related? To offer specifics, we examine post hoc comparisons and group means. The next screenshot reveals which groups were significantly different from each other. On the output, post hoc comparisons are found beneath the ANOVA table.

Pairwise Comparisons

Measure: MEASURE_1

(I) Year	(J) Year	Mean Difference (I-J)	Std. Error	Sig.[b]	95% Confidence Interval for Difference[b] Lower Bound	95% Confidence Interval for Difference[b] Upper Bound
1	2	.100	.233	.678	-.428	.628
	3	.200	.200	.343	-.252	.652
	4	1.400*	.221	.000	.900	1.900
2	1	-.100	.233	.678	-.628	.428
	3	.100	.233	.678	-.428	.628
	4	1.300*	.213	.000	.817	1.783
3	1	-.200	.200	.343	-.652	.252
	2	-.100	.233	.678	-.628	.428
	4	1.200*	.200	.000	.748	1.652
4	1	-1.400*	.221	.000	-1.900	-.900
	2	-1.300*	.213	.000	-1.783	-.817
	3	-1.200*	.200	.000	-1.652	-.748

Based on estimated marginal means

*. The mean difference is significant at the .05 level.

b. Adjustment for multiple comparisons: Least Significant Difference (equivalent to no adjustments).

Take a careful look at the mean comparisons. In the first row, the first and second means did not differ ($p = .678$), indicating that first-year students and sophomores reported similar levels of self-esteem. Likewise, in the second row, groups 1 and 3 failed to differ ($p = .343$). In the third row, groups 1 and 4 differed significantly ($p < .001$). We will not know which group is higher until we look at the group means in a prior screenshot. Examine the remaining circled comparisons: Groups 2 and 3 were not significantly different ($p = .678$), but comparisons between groups 2 and 4 as well as 3 and 4 were significant (both $p < .001$).

Examine the means. Now that we know Group 4 differed from the remaining groups, look for a pattern among the means.

Descriptive Statistics

	Mean	Std. Deviation	N
First_year	4.1000	.73786	10
Sophomore	4.0000	1.15470	10
Junior	3.9000	.73786	10
Senior	2.7000	.94868	10

Specifically, you should see that seniors had lower self-esteem than any younger group. You also know that first-year students, sophomores, and juniors did not differ from each other on self-esteem. These details are an important part of the results to share in your APA-style results section.

Turn to Estimated Marginal Means for 95% confidence intervals around individual group means.

Estimated Marginal Means

Year

Estimates

Measure: MEASURE_1

Year	Mean	Std. Error	95% Confidence Interval	
			Lower Bound	Upper Bound
1	4.100	.233	3.572	4.628
2	4.000	.365	3.174	4.826
3	3.900	.233	3.372	4.428
4	2.700	.300	2.021	3.379

APA Style for the One-Way,
Repeated-Measures ANOVA: Correlational Design

In the method section below, notice that the self-esteem measure contains a report of scale reliability and validity, terms you learned about way back in Chapter 8.

Method

Participants

Ten high-school students (5 girls and 5 boys) participated in this study, with a mean age in the ninth grade of 13.98 years ($SD = 0.57$). Ethnicities included 6 Asian Americans, 3 Caucasian Americans, and 1 Latino American.

Materials

We assessed self-esteem using the Single-Item Self-Esteem scale (SISE; Robins, Hendin, & Trzesniewski, 2001). The SISE consists of 1 item ("I have high self-esteem") rated by participants on a 5-point Likert scale from 1 (*not very true of me*) to 5 (*very true of me*). Robins and colleagues reported strong reliability and construct validity of the SISE.

Procedure

On the first day of school each academic year, participants rated their current self-esteem using the SISE. Parents provided consent prior to each year of data collection.

Results

We analyzed these data using a one-way, repeated-measures ANOVA. LSD comparisons further analyzed a significant outcome ($p < .05$). Year in high school related to ratings of self-esteem, $F(3, 27) = 18.18$, $p < .001$, partial $\eta^2 = .67$. Seniors reported lower self-esteem ($M = 2.70$, $SD = 0.95$, $n = 10$) than juniors ($M = 3.90$, $SD = 0.74$, $n = 10$), sophomores ($M = 4.00$, $SD = 1.15$, $n = 10$), and first-year students ($M = 4.10$, $SD = 0.74$, $n = 10$). (See Figure 1.) Self-esteem of juniors, sophomores, and first-year students failed to differ ($p > .05$). The 95% CIs for self-esteem of each group included first-year students [3.57, 4.63], sophomores [3.17, 4.83], juniors [3.37, 4.43], and seniors [2.02, 3.38].

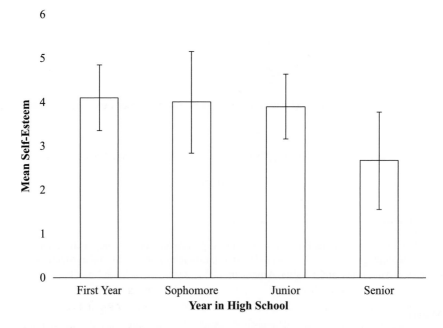

Figure 1. Senior high-school students reported lower self-esteem than first-year, sophomore, and junior students (p < .001). Error bars represent *SD*.

SUMMARY

In this chapter you learned about research designs with one repeated-measures factor containing more than two levels. Such a design is analyzed with ANOVA, which can be called either repeated-measures or within-participants. No matter which name you use, the design requires that the same people experience every level of the factor. When a factor is manipulated, you can address cause and effect. Be careful to counterbalance the order of conditions whenever possible. When a factor is not manipulated, you can address a potential relationship between the factor and DV. Remember that whether or not you manipulate a factor, the analysis remains the same: one-way, repeated-measures ANOVA. However, wording of your APA-style results section must adjust to the type of design used.

REVIEW OF TERMS

Blind to Conditions (Scoring Blind)

One-Way, Repeated-Measures ANOVA

Repeated-Measures (Within-Participants) Design

Sphericity

PRACTICE ITEMS

1. Why is it important to vary the order of IV exposure in a repeated-measures design?

2. What is blind scoring, and why is it useful?

3. How do we use Mauchly's test of sphericity when interpreting SPSS output for the one-way, repeated-measures ANOVA?

4. If sphericity is violated, which F-test do you use?

5. Why must we conduct post hoc analyses with ANOVAs and not with t-tests?

* * *

For each of the following studies, (a) state the research question as a research hypothesis and state the null hypothesis, (b) determine how many participants are needed for adequate power, and (c) enter and analyze the data as well as write an APA-style results section. Include graphs if figures would communicate important outcomes. Be sure to read over the method sections we provided.

6. You read a study about combat veterans using wilderness therapy to recover from psychological distress after deployment (Dietrich, Joye, & Garcia, 2015), and you

wonder if veterans prefer wilderness therapy over other forms of treatment for post-traumatic stress disorder (PTSD). You ask the question, *Do various treatments for PTSD appeal to combat veterans differentially?*

Participant	Wilderness	Medication	Talk
1	9	6	10
2	10	5	8
3	8	3	5
4	5	3	10
5	8	4	7
6	6	8	7
7	9	5	5
8	3	1	3
9	8	9	7
10	6	4	6
11	10	8	9
12	8	6	5
13	10	10	10
14	8	2	5
15	7	1	6

Method

Participants

Participants included 15 individuals (13 men and 2 women) with a mean age of 37.00 ($SD = 15.57$). Ethnicities represented included 11 White, 2 Latino, 1 Black, and 1 Filipino adult. All participants received ethical treatment according to IRB guidelines.

Procedure

We recruited participants via an anonymous survey distributed through Veterans of Foreign Wars (VFW) listservs. The survey defined three types of therapy: wilderness therapy, medication, and traditional talk therapy, with order of presentation counterbalanced. Following each description, we asked veterans to rate the potential for the treatment to help those returning from deployment to transition effectively back to civilian life. Ratings relied on a scale from 1 (*likely not helpful at all*) to 10 (*likely quite helpful*). At the end of the survey, we collected basic demographic information.

7. You wonder, *Are some types of bullying in high school perceived as more harmful than others?* You ask adult participants to rate the harmfulness of high-school physical, verbal, and covert bullying on a scale of 1 to 10, with higher numbers indicating greater potential to cause harm.

Participant Number	Physical	Covert	Verbal
1	2	5	3
2	6	8	4
3	7	6	8
4	5	9	5
5	3	3	1
6	7	8	9
7	4	6	4
8	9	10	8
9	5	8	6
10	9	10	10

Method

Participants

Participants included 10 college students (7 women and 3 men) with a mean age of 20.55 ($SD = 1.56$). Ethnicities included 5 White, 3 Black, and 2 Lebanese individuals.

Procedure

Researchers recruited college students in the student union at a small university in the South. After signing the consent form, participants considered high-school students and reported the perceived harmfulness of three types of bullying: physical (hitting, kicking, tripping, pinching, and pushing, or damaging property), verbal (name calling, insults, teasing, intimidation, homophobic or racist remarks, or verbal abuse), and covert (spreading rumors, negative facial or physical gestures, menacing or contemptuous looks, and other behaviors designed to harm someone's social reputation and/or cause humiliation), with order of conditions counterbalanced. The harmfulness scale ranged from 1 to 10, with higher numbers indicating potential to cause more harm.

8. When you get stressed, you squeeze a stress ball. One day you find yourself wondering if squeezing a stress ball is relaxing only because you believe it will be relaxing (i.e., the placebo effect). You ask, *Does whether a stress ball relieves stress depend on a person's expectations for stress reduction?* You design a study in which participants experience the following factor conditions: Tell them that squeezing a stress ball increases stress, tell them it decreases stress, tell them that stress stays the same, or tell them nothing about the effects of squeezing a stress ball. You measure stress on a scale from −6 (*not stressed*) to 6 (*very stressed*) after participants use the stress ball.

Stress Will Increase	Stress Will Decrease	Stress Will Stay the Same	No Information About Stress Ball
2	−4	0	−5
3	−2	0	−2
3	−1	0	−1
1	0	1	0
1	1	1	1
0	−4	−1	−3
−1	−6	−1	−1
−1	−1	0	0
4	−4	1	−5
3	−2	1	−1
6	0	4	0
1	0	0	0

Method

Participants

We recruited 48 participants with a mean age of 32.05 ($SD = 10.56$). Participants included 30 men, 16 women, and 2 people who did not disclose their gender.

Materials and Procedure

We recruited a community sample of participants by soliciting participation at a local mall restaurant area. When participants arrived in the lab at their assigned time, we asked them to complete informed consent and then handed them a stress ball to squeeze for 30 seconds, saying, "Here is a stress ball." We then asked them to rate their current stress level on an item from −6 (*not stressed*) to 6 (*very stressed*). For the next three trials, we told participants, "This is a different stress ball made of a slightly different material. Based on the material density, this ball should ___," with options of (a) increase stress, (b) decrease stress, or (c) have no effect on stress. These last three trials were counterbalanced across participants. After each trial, participants rated their stress on the 13-point scale.

REFERENCES

Cohen, J. (1992). A power primer. *Psychological Bulletin, 112*(1), 155–159. doi:10.1037/0033-2909.112.1.155

Dietrich, Z. C., Joye, S. W., & Garcia, J. A. (2015). Natural medicine: Wilderness experience outcomes for combat veterans. *Journal of Experiential Education, 38*(4), 394–406. doi:10.1177/1053825915596431

Putwain, D., & Remedios, R. (2014). The scare tactic: Do fear appeals predict motivation and exam scores? *School Psychology Quarterly, 29*(4), 503–516. doi:10.1037/spq0000048

Robins, R. W., Hendin, H. M., & Trzesniewski, K. H. (2001). Measuring global self-esteem: Construct validation of a single-item measure and the Rosenberg Self-Esteem Scale. *Personality and Social Psychology Bulletin, 27*(2), 151–161. doi:10.1177/0146167201272002

Robins, R. W., & Trzesniewski, K. H. (2005). Self-esteem development across the lifespan. *Current Directions in Psychological Science, 14*(3), 158–162. doi:10.1111/j.0963-7214.2005.00353.x

14

Two Variables With Independent Samples

In Chapters 10 and 12, we discussed research designs with one IV or quasi-IV and only two groups. The dependent variable was either an interval or ratio outcome. Designs such as these are analyzed using a *t*-test. An independent-samples *t*-test analyzes data when participants in the two groups have nothing in common when they arrive for your study. Whenever possible, we randomly assign people to the two IV levels. On the other hand, a paired-samples *t*-test analyzes data when participants in the two groups are related in some way (including matched on a variable) or when the same people are tested twice.

In Chapters 11 and 13, we expanded on two-group designs to present larger designs with more than two levels. The analysis changed from a *t*-test to ANOVA. The one-way, between-groups ANOVA analyzes data in which the research design tests different people in factor levels. Again, whenever possible, researchers randomly assign participants to groups. The one-way, repeated-measures ANOVA analyzes data when the same people are tested across all factor levels. Both *t*-tests and ANOVAs are powerful parametric statistics.

RESEARCH DESIGN: TWO IVS WITH INDEPENDENT SAMPLES

In this chapter, we continue to expand on grouped designs. Here we discuss research designs with *two* IVs or quasi-IVs, and each factor must have two or more levels. A **two-way design** indicates two different factors. For example, in the first half of Chapter 11, we examined the potential effect of physical activity (sitting, walking, and jogging) on creativity (listing multiple ways an object can be used). We had one factor with three levels, and the DV was ratio data. Analysis required a one-way, between-groups ANOVA. Suppose now we want to expand our research question to include a second factor: location of activity, with participants inside a building versus outside in a park. The research question changes from *Does level of physical activity affect creativity?* to *Do level of physical activity and location of activity affect creativity?* Notice in this new example, participant location is a second variable of interest. The factor of location has only two levels, which should remind you of a *t*-test, but as soon as a research design has two factors, regardless

Two-Way Design. A two-way design uses two IVs or quasi-IVs, each of which has two or more levels.

of number of levels, an ANOVA is required for analysis. With two factors and different people in conditions, the analysis is called a **two-way, between-groups ANOVA**.

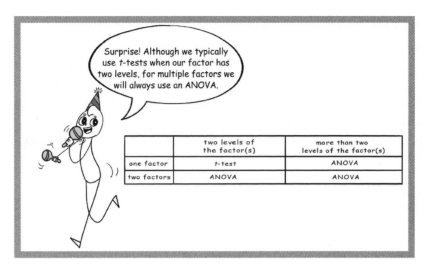

A research design with two factors offers more interesting data than a simpler design. Sure, you could run two separate studies, one with creativity based on level of exercise (like you saw in Chapter 11) and another with creativity based on location. But we often choose to include both variables of interest in one study to obtain an extra piece of information that we would otherwise never know. In addition to uncovering whether exercise and location affect creativity individually, we also find out whether the IVs together affect creativity. This third piece of "bonus" information in a two-way design is called an interaction. An **interaction** tells you if the two factors work together to influence the DV. For example, perhaps type of exercise affects creativity, but only when people are inside a building. Participants located in a park may be highly creative regardless of their level of activity. Only a two-way design can allow you to explore the potential for an interaction.

Let us examine the exercise-location example further. Because both factors are manipulated, we can randomly assign each participant to one level of physical activity and one level of location. This particular example is called a 2 × 3 design based on two levels of one factor and three levels of the other factor. The usual approach is to put the smaller number first rather than calling this a 3 × 2 design. In the following 2 × 3 example, each participant will be placed in one cell of our research design.

	Sitting	Walking	Jogging
Building (Inside)			
Park (Outside)			

Two-Way, Between-Groups ANOVA. A two-way, between-groups ANOVA is a statistic used to analyze two IVs or quasi-IVs with different people in each group and a single interval or ratio DV.

Interaction. In a two-way ANOVA, the interaction indicates if the two IVs or quasi-IVs (i.e., factors) work together to influence the DV.

Before we look at fictional DV values, consider what this design offers. We can find out three pieces of information to share with the world:

- Does level of physical activity (sitting, walking, or jogging) affect creativity?

- Does location (a building vs. a park) affect creativity?

- Do location and level of activity work together to affect creativity?

The first two research questions are called main effects. A **main effect** is the potential outcome of one factor while ignoring the other factor. First this design will tell us if level of physical activity, *regardless of location*, affects creativity. Next we will learn if location, *regardless of level of activity*, affects creativity. The third research question addresses the interaction, and we will be looking to see if the two factors work together in an interesting way to affect creativity.

Because we have three research questions, we will have three research hypotheses:

- Level of physical activity affects creativity.

- Location affects creativity.

- Level of activity and location work together to affect creativity.

Based on practice in prior examples, you should know how to change each research hypothesis to a null hypothesis. That is, what would we expect for each hypothesis if no differences exist? As always, inferential statistics test null hypotheses. If our results allow us to reject a null hypothesis, we can share evidence in favor of a research hypothesis. With a two-way design, we examine three separate hypotheses.

Main Effect. In a two-way ANOVA, the main effect is the potential outcome of one factor while ignoring (or collapsing across) the other factor.

In our creativity example, suppose we randomly assigned participants to one of the six cells in the 2 × 3 design and collected the following data. We might rely on block random assignment to the six cells to make sure we have approximately equal numbers of participants per condition.

	Sitting	Walking	Jogging
Building (Inside)	3	7	8
	4	6	12
	3	8	6
	5	7	5
	2	5	4
	3	4	9
	2	9	
Park (Outside)	7	8	8
	8	9	7
	9	12	10
	4	6	7
	6	11	8
	11	7	10
	6		5

We are ready to analyze these data using a two-way, between-groups ANOVA, which is the statistical analysis for a two-way design when different people are in each cell. Of course, the DV must represent interval or ratio data to allow parametric statistics. Notice how easy it is to collect data, organize it, and turn to analysis because we carefully planned in advance.

SPSS: Two-Way, Between-Groups ANOVA (No Significant Interaction)

For this example, we have chosen to avoid revealing a significant interaction. Instead we will focus on the basics of a two-way, between-groups ANOVA. Later in the chapter we will examine a design that yields a significant interaction.

To organize data in SPSS, first enter variables and define levels under Variable View. The first variable is one of the factors, and the second variable is the remaining factor. You can enter them in either order you like, and be sure to indicate the correct names for each level under Values. For Location, label Values as 1 = Building and 2 = Park. For Activity, 1 = sitting, 2 = walking, and 3 = jogging. The third variable is the outcome (DV of creativity).

Name	Type	Width	Decimals	Label	Values
Location	Numeric	8	2		{1.00, Buildi...
Activity	Numeric	8	2		{1.00, Sittin...
Creativity	Numeric	8	2		None

Click to Data View, and go ahead and ask for View Value Labels. Focus on the first cell of the data: sitting in the building. How many people experienced the study sitting in a building? Seven participants were in this condition. Enter seven values of 1 for Building in the first column. In the second column, labeled Activity, enter seven values of 1 to represent those who sat (Sitting label). This block of seven 1, 1 combinations represents the first cell of data for those who sat inside a building. In the third column, enter their creativity scores as shown below.

Location	Activity	Creativity
Building	Sitting	3.00
Building	Sitting	4.00
Building	Sitting	3.00
Building	Sitting	5.00
Building	Sitting	2.00
Building	Sitting	3.00
Building	Sitting	2.00

Next, how many people completed the study in the building while walking? Again, seven people are in this cell. In SPSS, enter seven values of 1 under Building and seven values of 2 under Activity. Enter the creativity scores for this cell in the third column as shown below.

Location	Activity	Creativity
Building	Sitting	3.00
Building	Sitting	4.00
Building	Sitting	3.00
Building	Sitting	5.00
Building	Sitting	2.00
Building	Sitting	3.00
Building	Sitting	2.00
Building	Walking	7.00
Building	Walking	6.00
Building	Walking	8.00
Building	Walking	7.00
Building	Walking	5.00
Building	Walking	4.00
Building	Walking	9.00

Enter data for the third cell across the top of the original data set, representing jogging in a building (containing six people). Then enter the bottom, left cell depicting participants sitting in a park (with seven people). Continue entering data under the same three columns you used for the first two cells. We offer a screenshot to illustrate.

Building	Walking	9.00
Building	Jogging	8.00
Building	Jogging	12.00
Building	Jogging	6.00
Building	Jogging	5.00
Building	Jogging	4.00
Building	Jogging	9.00
Park	Sitting	7.00
Park	Sitting	8.00
Park	Sitting	9.00
Park	Sitting	4.00
Park	Sitting	6.00
Park	Sitting	11.00
Park	Sitting	6.00

Complete data entry by filling in the final two cells in the original data set.

Park	Sitting	6.00
Park	Walking	8.00
Park	Walking	9.00
Park	Walking	12.00
Park	Walking	6.00
Park	Walking	11.00
Park	Walking	7.00
Park	Jogging	8.00
Park	Jogging	7.00
Park	Jogging	10.00
Park	Jogging	7.00
Park	Jogging	8.00
Park	Jogging	10.00
Park	Jogging	5.00

Click Analyze, General Linear Model, and Univariate. Recall that the word Univariate indicates one outcome. In this example, our single DV is Creativity.

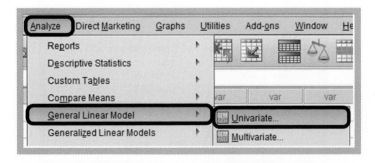

In the box that opens, move Location and Activity, the two IVs, to the right under Fixed Factor(s). Move Creativity, the DV, to the right under Dependent Variable. Then click Options.

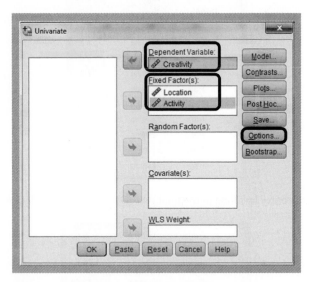

The box that opens will allow you to move Location, Activity, and Location*Activity to the right under Display Means for. Request Descriptive statistics and Estimates of effect size by checking the boxes to the left of those options. Click Continue, which will return you to the prior box.

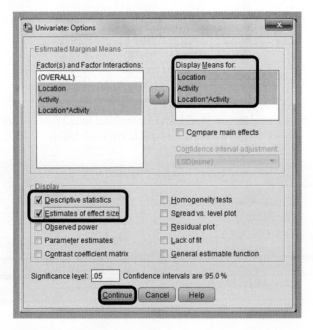

Choose Post Hoc to set up comparisons between group means. Click only Activity to the right because this IV has three levels and requires post hoc analysis to tell us which pairs of means differ. However, Location has only two levels, and a significant effect means those two groups differ. Put a check beside Tukey to analyze the three levels of Activity, and click Continue and then OK.

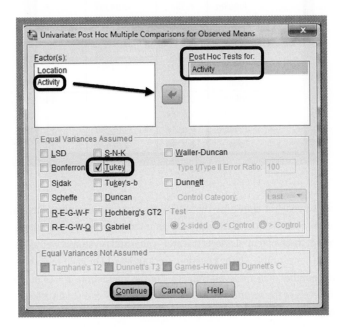

The output should look like the next several screenshots. The first picture shows Descriptive Statistics, which we will need when we discuss which groups showed higher creativity than others.

Descriptive Statistics

Dependent Variable: Creativity

Location	Activity	Mean	Std. Deviation	N
Building	Sitting	3.1429	1.06904	7
	Walking	6.5714	1.71825	7
	Jogging	7.3333	2.94392	6
	Total	5.6000	2.66359	20
Park	Sitting	7.2857	2.28869	7
	Walking	8.8333	2.31661	6
	Jogging	7.8571	1.77281	7
	Total	7.9500	2.11449	20
Total	Sitting	5.2143	2.75062	14
	Walking	7.6154	2.25605	13
	Jogging	7.6154	2.29269	13
	Total	6.7750	2.65530	40

The second screenshot shows us the ANOVA test examining the potential for a main effect of Location, a main effect of Activity, and an interaction between Location and Activity. Notice that each of these potential effects has an F-value and p-value as well as specific degrees of freedom (df). (For example, df for Location are 1 and 34.) For each main effect, the first df value shows the number of factor levels minus 1. For the interaction, $df = $ (# of levels of the first factor $-$ 1)(# of levels of the second factor $-$ 1). For all three F-tests (main effects and the interaction), the second df value is calculated by subtracting the number of cells from N: $40 - 6 = 34$.

Dependent Variable: Creativity

Source	Type III Sum of Squares	df	Mean Square	F	Sig.	Partial Eta Squared
Corrected Model	129.951[a]	5	25.990	6.093	.000	.473
Intercept	1860.106	1	1860.106	436.091	.000	.928
Location	53.058	1	53.058	12.439	.001	.268
Activity	53.897	2	26.948	6.318	.005	.271
Location * Activity	22.049	2	11.024	2.585	.090	.132
Error	145.024	34	4.265			
Total	2111.000	40				
Corrected Total	274.975	39				

a. R Squared = .473 (Adjusted R Squared = .395)

Effect Size: Eta Squared

Partial eta squared (η^2) provides effect size, but this information is relevant only if the effect is significant as indicated by a p-value less than or equal to .05. Recall that effect sizes for partial η^2 are .01 for weak, .06 for moderate, and .13 (or higher) for strong (Cohen, 1988).

Post Hoc for a Main Effect

If a significant main effect of activity exists, we will also need to look at post hoc comparisons on the screenshot below to see exactly which groups differed among the three levels.

Post Hoc Tests

Activity

Multiple Comparisons

Dependent Variable: Creativity

Tukey HSD

(I) Activity	(J) Activity	Mean Difference (I-J)	Std. Error	Sig.	95% Confidence Interval	
					Lower Bound	Upper Bound
Sitting	Walking	-2.4011*	.79547	.013	-4.3504	-.4518
	Jogging	-2.4011*	.79547	.013	-4.3504	-.4518
Walking	Sitting	2.4011*	.79547	.013	.4518	4.3504
	Jogging	.0000	.81007	1.000	-1.9850	1.9850
Jogging	Sitting	2.4011*	.79547	.013	.4518	4.3504
	Walking	.0000	.81007	1.000	-1.9850	1.9850

Look over all of the SPSS output to address the following questions:

1. Does location affect creativity? If so, what is the effect size? Which group is higher than another?

2. Does activity level affect creativity? If so, what is the effect size? Among the three pairs of means, which means are significantly different from each other?

3. Do location and activity interact to affect creativity? If so, what is the effect size? What are the details of the effect?

Here are the answers:

1. Yes, location affects creativity. The effect size is .27. The group means show us that creativity is higher in a park than in a building regardless of whether a person is sitting, walking, or jogging.

2. Yes, activity level affects creativity. The effect size is .27. Post hoc analysis tells us that creativity while sitting differs from creativity while walking or jogging no matter where the activity happened. The group means tell us that creativity while walking or jogging is *higher* than while sitting. Walking and jogging did not differ.

3. No, location and activity do not interact to affect creativity. The *p*-value in this row is .090, showing a nonsignificant effect. Therefore, effect size is irrelevant, and no further analysis is needed.

Recall our original research question: *Do level of physical activity and location of activity affect creativity?* The answer is *yes*, physical activity affects creativity, and location of activity affects creativity. However, the two variables do not work together to affect creativity. In other words, we did not find evidence for an interaction.

Confidence Intervals

Data analysis revealed two significant main effects, and we could share 95% confidence intervals in two ways. First, we have the option of sharing confidence intervals for each *comparison* between two means. But notice that SPSS provided confidence intervals only for activity level because we ran post hoc analyses. We do not have output for the confidence interval when comparing the two locations of the study. No problem. Recall from Chapter 11 that the ANOVA statistic on SPSS provides confidence intervals surrounding each mean, creating a more intuitive range of values for what the population should look like under that condition. Confidence intervals surrounding each mean for Location and for Activity are shown in the following screenshot.

Estimated Marginal Means

1. Location

Dependent Variable: Creativity

Location	Mean	Std. Error	95% Confidence Interval	
			Lower Bound	Upper Bound
Building	5.683	.463	4.742	6.624
Park	7.992	.463	7.051	8.933

2. Activity

Dependent Variable: Creativity

Activity	Mean	Std. Error	95% Confidence Interval	
			Lower Bound	Upper Bound
Sitting	5.214	.552	4.093	6.336
Walking	7.702	.575	6.535	8.870
Jogging	7.595	.575	6.428	8.763

Power

Although we revealed two significant main effects, we failed to demonstrate an interaction effect. One potential explanation for the lack of an interaction effect is that, in fact, type of activity and location did not interact to affect creativity. But a second explanation could be lack of power. Researchers should consider how many participants are needed for an 80% chance of showing an effect at the $p \leq .05$ level. Given no other information, we would assume a moderate effect size, if one exists. As mentioned in Chapter 11, an η^2 of .01 is considered small, .06 is moderate, and anything around or above .13

is considered a large effect (Cohen, 1988). For each main effect, we must consider the number of factor levels. The table below indicates a total of 128 participants when we have two groups and a total of 159 participants with three factor levels.

The interaction is our new piece of information in this chapter. The interaction contains cells, and our 2 × 3 design has six cells. In the table below, see that 211 participants are needed in our sample, to be divided approximately equally across the six cells.

For the sake of brevity in this textbook, we did not provide data for 158 participants. But when you conduct your own studies, be sure to consider power and sample size prior to data collection.

	Small Effect Size	Medium Effect Size	Large Effect Size
One-way, between-groups ANOVA			
2 levels	788	128	52
3 levels	967	159	66
4 levels	1096	180	76
Two-way, between-groups ANOVA			
Main effects	See one-way between-groups ANOVA		
Interactions			
2 × 2 = 4 cells	1096	180	76
2 × 3 = 6 cells	1290	211	86
2 × 4 = 8 cells	1443	237	97
3 × 3 = 9 cells	1510	249	102
3 × 4 = 12 cells	1691	279	116
4 × 4 = 16 cells	1894	314	131

Note: Numbers in the table represent **total** sample size.

Graphing a Main Effect

Our example revealed two significant main effects, both of which could be graphed and added to the APA-style results section. In this example, we will focus on the main effect of activity level. What level of measurement is activity level? The levels are sitting, walking, and jogging, which are categories, making activity a nominal variable. Recall that a nominal or ordinal X-axis variable requires a bar graph. Collect the three group means from the SPSS output and graph as shown in the APA-style results section below. Include standard deviations using error bars.

APA Style for the Two-Way, Between-Groups ANOVA With Main Effects

We created a participants section for you and expanded details for the procedure. The results section organizes data from the SPSS output.

Method

Participants

Forty students (20 men and 20 women) participated. The sample included 12 White, 12 Black, and 10 Asian students with an average age of 19.72 (SD = 2.33). Students chose to participate for extra credit in their Introduction to Psychological Science course, although the instructor offered nonexperimental alternatives for extra credit. Participants received ethical treatment, and the IRB approved the study.

Procedure

Using block randomization, we assigned each participant to one of six conditions: sitting, walking, or jogging either in an office or in a small park for 30 min. Inside, participants walked or jogged on a treadmill; outside, they walked or jogged around the perimeter of a park. After exposure to groups, participants examined a small wooden dowel with a shovel-shaped structure on one end and a hook on the other end. They listed on paper as many potential uses for the object as they could imagine. People experienced the study individually.

Results

We analyzed these data using a 2 × 3 (location × activity level), between-groups ANOVA. Location affected creativity, $F(1, 34) = 12.44$, $p = .001$, partial $\eta^2 = .27$. Participants tested in a park exhibited more creativity ($M = 7.95$, $SD = 2.11$, $n = 20$) than those tested in a building ($M = 5.60$, $SD = 2.66$, $n = 20$). The 95% CIs for creativity among those in the park spanned [7.05, 8.93] and for those in the building, limits ranged from [4.74, 6.62]. In addition, activity level affected creativity, $F(2, 34) = 6.32$, $p = .005$, partial $\eta^2 = .27$. As seen in Figure 1, participants who walked ($M = 7.62$, $SD = 2.26$, $n = 13$) and those who jogged ($M = 7.62$, $SD = 2.29$, $n = 13$) evidenced more creativity than those who merely sat ($M = 5.21$, $SD = 2.75$, $n = 14$). Participants who walked and those who jogged showed similar levels of creativity ($p > .05$). The 95% CIs for sitting, walking, and jogging reflected limits of [4.09, 6.34], [6.54, 8.87], and [6.43, 8.76], respectively. Location and activity level failed to interact to affect creativity, $F(2, 34) = 2.59$, $p = .090$.

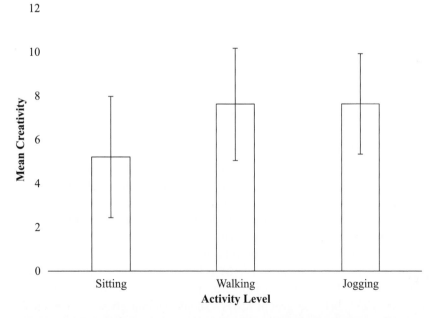

Figure 1. Walking and jogging resulted in higher levels of creativity than sitting. Error bars represent *SD*.

RESEARCH DESIGN: ONE IV AND ONE
QUASI-IV WITH INDEPENDENT GROUPS

The following study differs from our previous example in several ways. As a design difference, we include one ratio IV, which will affect graphing. Another design difference is the use of a second, quasi-IV that is not manipulated. Thus, our research design is quite different even though the two-way, between-groups ANOVA will again be used to analyze the data. A final key difference in the following example is a significant interaction to demonstrate post hoc analysis of cell differences.

In this design, we will ask the research question: *Do gender and number of trust violations affect subsequent reported trust?* Haselhuhn, Kennedy, Kray, Van Zant, and Schweitzer (2015) conducted a series of experiments and found that violations of trust disrupted subsequent trust among women less than among men, perhaps due to the value women place on maintaining relationships. We could expand their study to see if the same pattern of results would be true if more than one trust violation occurred. In addition, whereas Haselhuhn and colleagues examined trust violations by strangers, we will ask participants to focus on a trust violation perpetrated by a friend.

Our general research question was shown above: *Do gender and number of trust violations affect subsequent reported trust?* But remember that a two-way design actually contains three research questions:

- Does gender relate to reported trust?

- Does number of trust violations affect trust?

- Do gender and number of trust violations affect trust?

Of course, each question can be written as a research hypothesis, countered by a null hypothesis of what to expect if no differences exist.

Our quasi-IV is gender of the participant (we cannot randomly assign participants to a specific gender). In this example, members of our sample self-reported identifying as either male or female. Our second variable of interest is a true IV because we will manipulate number of trust violations by a friend, assigning participants randomly to one of three levels: a control condition of no trust violation, one trust violation, and two trust violations. The DV is level of trust on a rating scale from 1 to 7, with higher numbers indicating more trust in the friend. Based on our prior example, we know a 2×3 between-groups ANOVA should contain 211 participants to enhance our ability to find an interaction, if one exits. The following fictional example depicts far fewer participants than you would test in real life. Assume we collected the following data.

	No Trust Violations	One Trust Violation	Two Trust Violations
Male Participants	6	2	1
	7	5	3
	5	4	2
	7	3	4
	7	5	1
	6	4	4
	6	3	3
	5	2	
Female Participants	7	5	5
	6	4	4
	7	6	4
	5	6	5
	6	7	6
	6	5	6
	7	4	3
		5	

SPSS: Two-Way, Between-Groups ANOVA (Significant Interaction)

To analyze these data, use the same approach as we used in the first example from this chapter. Label column headings with the quasi-IV, IV, and levels of each under Values. Label the third column with the DV: Trust. Under Gender, we labeled Values of Men = 1 and Women = 2.

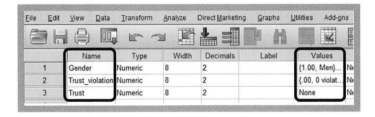

For number of trust violations, we chose to label no violations as 0, one trust violation as 1, and two trust violations as 2. Normally we label the first value with the number 1, but it seemed more logical in this example to begin labeling with a 0 because the first group experienced 0 trust violations. Any number you choose will work as long as you enter the correct values for each part of the data set.

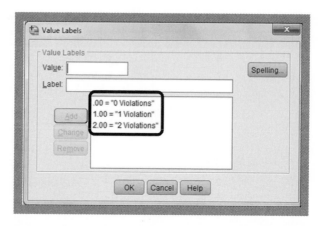

After labeling values for the two factors, click to Data View to enter data as explained in the prior example. Remember to enter one cell from the data at a time. Below is a screenshot illustrating the first 21 cells, which illustrate the bulk of data for Men, including all levels of trust violations. Continue entering data in the three columns until all six original data cells are represented.

Gender	Trust_violations	Trust
Men	0 Violations	6.00
Men	0 Violations	7.00
Men	0 Violations	5.00
Men	0 Violations	7.00
Men	0 Violations	7.00
Men	0 Violations	6.00
Men	0 Violations	6.00
Men	0 Violations	5.00
Men	1 Violation	2.00
Men	1 Violation	5.00
Men	1 Violation	4.00
Men	1 Violation	3.00
Men	1 Violation	5.00
Men	1 Violation	4.00
Men	1 Violation	3.00
Men	1 Violation	2.00
Men	2 Violations	1.00
Men	2 Violations	3.00
Men	2 Violations	2.00
Men	2 Violations	4.00
Men	2 Violations	1.00

After all 45 participants' Trust values have been entered, click Analyze, General Linear Model, Univariate. In the box that opens, move Gender and Trust_violations to the Fixed Factor(s) box, and move Trust to the Dependent Variable box using the arrow keys in the middle. Then click Options just as we demonstrated in the prior example.

In the Options box, click all variables to the right using the arrow button. Check the boxes next to Descriptive statistics and Estimates of effect size. Request a comparison of main effects using the LSD methods of comparing group means. As you know, Tukey's would be fine as well, or your instructor might ask for a different post hoc comparison. We choose LSD for this example to remind you of options.

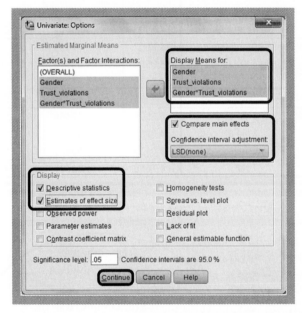

When you click Continue, the box will disappear. Click OK for output. The screen shot below shows Descriptive Statistics, which we will need to explain directions of group differences.

Descriptive Statistics

Dependent Variable: Trust

Gender	Trust_violation	Mean	Std. Deviation	N
Men	0 violations	6.1250	.83452	8
	1 violation	3.5000	1.19523	8
	2 violations	2.5714	1.27242	7
	Total	4.1304	1.86607	23
Women	0 violations	6.2857	.75593	7
	1 violation	5.2500	1.03510	8
	2 violations	4.7143	1.11270	7
	Total	5.4091	1.14056	22
Total	0 violations	6.2000	.77460	15
	1 violation	4.3750	1.40831	16
	2 violations	3.6429	1.59842	14
	Total	4.7556	1.66727	45

Remember, a two-way ANOVA produces three valuable tests, complete with individual F-values, degrees of freedom, p-values, and effect sizes.

On the next page, we focus on key elements from the output.

Tests of Between-Subjects Effects

Dependent Variable: Trust

Source	Type III Sum of Squares	df	Mean Square	F	Sig.	Partial Eta Squared
Corrected Model	79.365[a]	5	15.873	14.414	.000	.649
Intercept	1007.004	1	1007.004	914.468	.000	.959
Gender	20.448	1	20.448	18.569	.000	.323
Trust_violation	51.039	2	25.520	23.175	.000	.543
Gender * Trust_violation	8.120	2	4.060	3.687	.034	.159
Error	42.946	39	1.101			
Total	1140.000	45				
Corrected Total	122.311	44				

a. R Squared = .649 (Adjusted R Squared = .604)

Pairwise Comparisons

Dependent Variable: Trust

(I) Trust_violation	(J) Trust_violation	Mean Difference (I-J)	Std. Error	Sig.[b]	95% Confidence Interval for Difference[b]	
					Lower Bound	Upper Bound
0 violations	1 violation	1.830*	.378	.000	1.067	2.594
	2 violations	2.562*	.390	.000	1.773	3.352
1 violation	0 violations	-1.830*	.378	.000	-2.594	-1.067
	2 violations	.732	.384	.064	-.045	1.509
2 violations	0 violations	-2.562*	.390	.000	-3.352	-1.773
	1 violation	-.732	.384	.064	-1.509	.045

Based on estimated marginal means

*. The mean difference is significant at the .05 level.

b. Adjustment for multiple comparisons: Least Significant Difference (equivalent to no adjustments).

First look at the Test of Between-Subjects Effects for ANOVA results. Check for the three potential outcomes.

1. Do we have a main effect of gender? It may seem odd to call this a main "effect," given that we did not manipulate participant gender, but *main effect* is a general term used to imply significance. We will be sure to avoid cause-and-effect terms when we write the APA-style results section.

2. Do we have a main effect of trust violation? If so, we will need to examine post hoc comparisons to see exactly which groups differ because we have more than two groups.

3. Do we have an interaction effect? In other words, do gender and trust violation interact to affect trust? If at least one of our variables is a true IV, we can use cause-and-effect terminology to discuss the interaction.

Here are the answers:

1. Yes, gender is related to subsequent trust. Because gender contains two levels, we know from the group means that women are more trusting than men, with an effect size of .32.

2. Yes, number of trust violations affects subsequent trust. Trust violation was defined by three levels, requiring us to examine post hoc comparisons. We learned that no violations resulted in significantly more trust than either one or two trust violations, with an effect size of .54.

3. Yes, gender and number of trust violations interacted to affect subsequent trust, with an effect size of .16. Note that we can say "affect" because one of the variables is a true IV, indicating cause and effect. An interaction effect presents a unique problem: We must compare cells. With six cells, we have nine cell comparisons to examine, which we will explain in the section following confidence intervals.

Recall that 95% confidence intervals surrounding each group mean communicate what should be found in the population for that condition. With three significant effects, be prepared to report many confidence intervals. We will explain them here but not include them in our APA-style results section for this data set. If your instructor wants you to add them, follow the format of the previous example. Another option is to create a table of descriptive statistics and confidence intervals for each group. A final option is to graph means and the confidence intervals that surround them, but recall that graphing confidence intervals in Excel is not intuitive.

For the main effect of gender, examine Estimated Marginal Means (left) for confidence limits surrounding men and women, individually. In the output box to the left, notice the confidence intervals for each mean associated with number of trust violations. Finally, SPSS provides 95% confidence intervals surrounding each *cell* mean to explain the interaction.

Estimated Marginal Means

1. Gender

Dependent Variable: Trust

Gender	Mean	Std. Error	95% Confidence Interval	
			Lower Bound	Upper Bound
Men	4.065	.219	3.622	4.509
Women	5.417	.224	4.963	5.870

2. Trust_violations

Dependent Variable: Trust

Trust_violations	Mean	Std. Error	95% Confidence Interval	
			Lower Bound	Upper Bound
0 Violations	6.205	.272	5.656	6.755
1 Violation	4.375	.262	3.844	4.906
2 Violations	3.643	.280	3.076	4.210

3. Gender * Trust_violations

Dependent Variable: Trust

Gender	Trust_violations	Mean	Std. Error	95% Confidence Interval	
				Lower Bound	Upper Bound
Men	0 Violations	6.125	.371	5.375	6.875
	1 Violation	3.500	.371	2.750	4.250
	2 Violations	2.571	.397	1.769	3.374
Women	0 Violations	6.286	.397	5.483	7.088
	1 Violation	5.250	.371	4.500	6.000
	2 Violations	4.714	.397	3.912	5.517

Examining the Interaction

Use the SPSS Descriptive Statistics table to recreate the design with cell means. We like to insert cell standard deviations and cell sample size (n) values to have everything in one place when we are ready to explain the interaction in APA style. Include confidence intervals for cells means as desired. For the interaction, n refers to the number of participants in each cell.

	No Trust Violations	One Trust Violation	Two Trust Violations
Male Participants	$M = 6.13$	$M = 3.50$	$M = 2.57$
	$SD = 0.83$	$SD = 1.20$	$SD = 1.27$
	$n = 8$	$n = 8$	$n = 7$
Female Participants	$M = 6.29$	$M = 5.25$	$M = 4.71$
	$SD = 0.76$	$SD = 1.04$	$SD = 1.11$
	$n = 7$	$n = 8$	$n = 7$

We will need to examine cell means and decide which pairs significantly differ. Each pair of cells horizontal and vertical to each other are reasonable comparisons. Diagonal cells are *never* compared. A difference between diagonal cells could be explained either by gender or by trust violations. In other words, we would learn nothing of value because we would not know which variable meaningfully influenced the DV. For example, if we compared men with no trust violations to women with two trust violations, a difference between these cell means would fail to explain *why* the groups differed. By comparing only horizontal or vertical cell means, we will know exactly why a DV differed because levels of only one factor vary. In this example, we have nine cell mean comparisons to make.

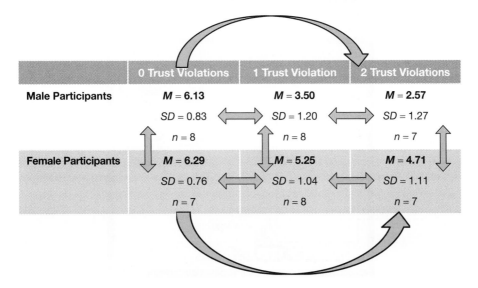

Post Hoc for an Interaction

Unfortunately, SPSS will not conduct post hoc comparisons of cells using drop-down menus. We will show you how to write a bit of code to get the job done.

Click Analyze, General Linear Model, Univariate. Instead of clicking OK as you did previously, click Paste.

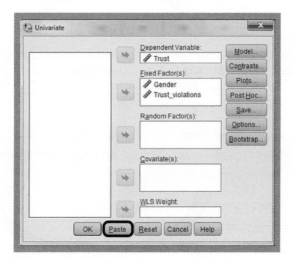

SPSS code is revealed. We can ask the software to compare male and female participants across each level of Trust_violation by typing a C as indicated below. A menu will appear, allowing you to choose COMPARE.

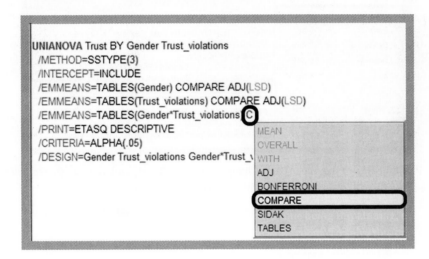

Add "gender" in parentheses.

```
UNIANOVA Trust BY Gender Trust_violations
 /METHOD=SSTYPE(3)
 /INTERCEPT=INCLUDE
 /EMMEANS=TABLES(Gender) COMPARE ADJ(LSD)
 /EMMEANS=TABLES(Trust_violations) COMPARE ADJ(LSD)
 /EMMEANS=TABLES(Gender*Trust_violations) COMPARE(gender)
 /PRINT=ETASQ DESCRIPTIVE
 /CRITERIA=ALPHA(.05)
 /DESIGN=Gender Trust_violations Gender*Trust_violations.
```

In addition to examining gender differences across the three levels of Trust_violations, we need to assess potential trust violations across genders. Only with both types of comparisons can we obtain all nine post hoc tests needed. After pressing Enter at the end of the new line of code to add a blank line, highlight and copy the line you just edited.

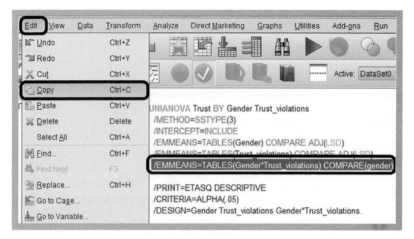

Paste the line in the open space. Change Gender to Trust_violations as shown below. The newest line of code will conduct different cell comparisons.

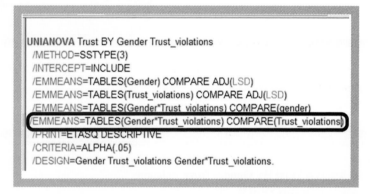

On the menu at the top of your screen, click Run and then All.

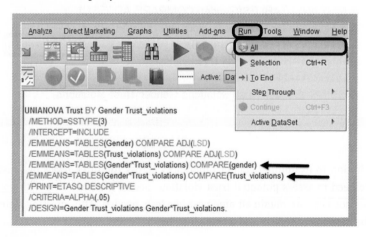

SPSS will add to your output, and many of the tables will be repeated from the original analysis. Your goal is to locate Pairwise Comparisons for the interaction in two tables. One table will compare male and female participants across each level of Trust_violations. A different table will compare zero, one, and two trust violations across each gender.

First, we will look at gender across trust violations. You will know you are looking at the correct table because the top left of the first column will say Trust_violations.

Pairwise Comparisons

Dependent Variable: Trust

Trust_violations	(I) Gender	(J) Gender	Mean Difference (I-J)	Std. Error	Sig.[b]	95% Confidence Interval for Difference[b]	
						Lower Bound	Upper Bound
0 Violations	Men	Women	-.161	.543	.769	-1.259	.938
	Women	Men	.161	.543	.769	-.938	1.259
1 Violation	Men	Women	-1.750*	.525	.002	-2.811	-.689
	Women	Men	1.750*	.525	.002	.689	2.811
2 Violations	Men	Women	-2.143*	.561	.000	-3.277	-1.008
	Women	Men	2.143*	.561	.000	1.008	3.277

Based on estimated marginal means

*. The mean difference is significant at the .05 level.

b. Adjustment for multiple comparisons: Least Significant Difference (equivalent to no adjustments).

Examine this table. With no trust violations, did male and female participants differ? With a Sig value (*p*-value) of .769, these two cells failed to differ. Do you see a gender difference for one violation? The *p*-value is .002, so we do see a gender difference. Finally, we see a gender difference for two violations ($p \leq .001$). Let us stay organized and put the *p*-values on the chart below. Notice that not only do we know whether these particular cell means differ from each other, we know which mean is higher in each pair.

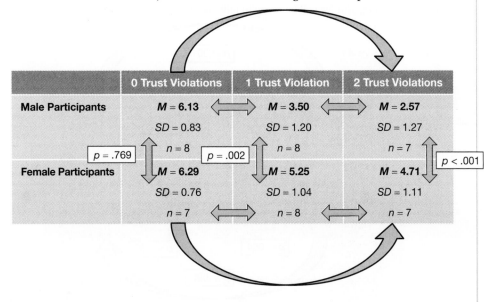

	0 Trust Violations	1 Trust Violation	2 Trust Violations
Male Participants	*M* = 6.13	*M* = 3.50	*M* = 2.57
	SD = 0.83	*SD* = 1.20	*SD* = 1.27
	n = 8	*n* = 8	*n* = 7
Female Participants	*M* = 6.29	*M* = 5.25	*M* = 4.71
	SD = 0.76	*SD* = 1.04	*SD* = 1.11
	n = 7	*n* = 8	*n* = 7

p = .769   *p* = .002   *p* < .001

Next, the other new Pairwise Comparisons table will compare Trust_violations across Gender. You will know you are looking at the correct table because the top left of the first column will say Gender.

Pairwise Comparisons

Dependent Variable: Trust

Gender	(I) Trust_violations	(J) Trust_violations	Mean Difference (I-J)	Std. Error	Sig.b	95% Confidence Interval for Differenceb	
						Lower Bound	Upper Bound
Men	0 Violations	1 Violation	2.625*	.525	.000	1.564	3.686
		2 Violations	3.554*	.543	.000	2.455	4.652
	1 Violation	0 Violations	-2.625*	.525	.000	-3.686	-1.564
		2 Violations	.929	.543	.095	-.170	2.027
	2 Violations	0 Violations	-3.554*	.543	.000	-4.652	-2.455
		1 Violation	-.929	.543	.095	-2.027	.170
Women	0 Violations	1 Violation	1.036	.543	.064	-.063	2.134
		2 Violations	1.571*	.561	.008	.437	2.706
	1 Violation	0 Violations	-1.036	.543	.064	-2.134	.063
		2 Violations	.536	.543	.330	-.563	1.634
	2 Violations	0 Violations	-1.571*	.561	.008	-2.706	-.437
		1 Violation	-.536	.543	.330	-1.634	.563

Based on estimated marginal means

*. The mean difference is significant at the .05 level.

b. Adjustment for multiple comparisons: Least Significant Difference (equivalent to no adjustments).

Recall that this table resulted from the SPSS code to compare number of trust violations across gender. For men, no violations and one violation differed ($p < .001$), as did no violations and two violations ($p < .001$); however, one and two violations failed to differ ($p = .095$). For women, no violations and one violation did not reach the required .05 level ($p = .064$), and neither did one violation and two violations ($p = .330$). Among women, we can see that no violations and two violations differed ($p = .008$). Add these p-values to the following diagram, and we will be ready to talk about the interaction details.

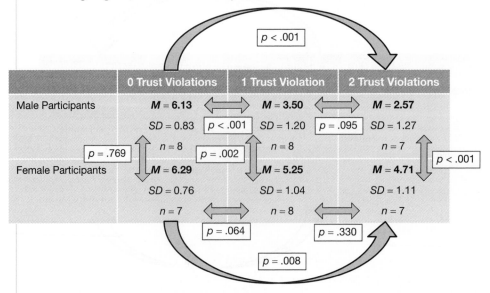

We will admit that the figure above is cluttered, but the payoff is worth the work. When you have a significant interaction, the results of your study often become more interesting. An interaction means gender and number of trust violations work together to affect subsequent feelings of trust. In this example, the interaction details tell us that men report reduced trust after one or two trust violations compared with none. Men's level of trust in a friend does not differ between one and two trust violations, perhaps indicating that one violation is plenty to ruin subsequent trust. The pattern differs for women. Two trust violations significantly reduce trust as compared with no violations. One violation is not sufficient to reduce trust in a friend for women.

It is also interesting to note that men and women reported the same level of trust in a friend in the absence of a trust violation. However, male participants reported less trust than female participants after either one or two trust violations by a friend. This suggests that men are less forgiving than women after even one trust violation. Of course, we do not make speculations in our results section, but we would talk about potential explanations in the discussion section of our paper.

Graphing an Interaction

With a significant interaction, graphing helps communicate results to readers. When graphing the interaction, both gender and number of trust violations must be represented in a single graph. One of the factors is placed on the X-axis, and the remaining factor is explained in a legend. The Y-axis represents the dependent variable, as you have seen before. Label the Y-axis as Mean Trust to indicate cell means on the DV.

The type of graph used, bar or line, depends on which of the two factors you place on the X-axis. If number of trust violations is used on the X-axis, a line graph is required because the variable represents ratio data. Below is the final graph with number of trust violations on the X-axis. In Appendix B, we use step-by-step screenshots to show you how to graph this interaction using Excel.

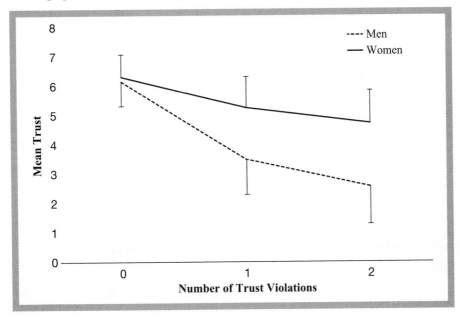

If you instead chose to label the X-axis with gender, you would need a bar graph because gender is a nominal variable. In this case, number of trust violations would appear in the legend as shown below. Again, refer to Appendix B for detailed instructions on how to create this bar graph for the interaction.

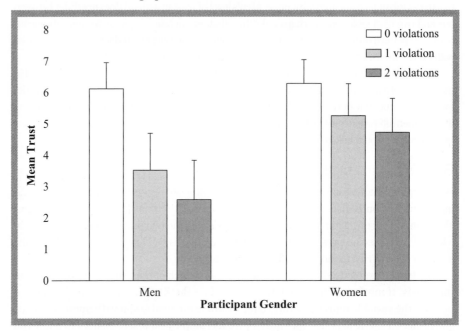

A figure caption provides guidance on interpreting either graph.

Figure 1. Gender of the participant and number of trust violations by friends interacted to affect reported level of trust ($p < .05$). Men and women reported equal levels of trust when friends did not violate their trust. But men and women diverged when trust violations occurred, with subsequent trust from men declining more than trust from women across violations. Error bars represent *SD*s.

Notice that the same figure caption applies to both graphs because the data remain the same. They merely are illustrated in different ways. Researchers must choose only one of the interaction graphs to use. When adding an interaction graph to your paper, decide which graph provides the better illustration.

APA Style for the Two-Way, Between-Groups ANOVA With an Interaction

The following APA-style method and results sections communicate the three results and their details. Notice that we also refer to the interaction graph. We did not choose to enter all confidence intervals in the results section because this example contained 11 confidence intervals, each with corresponding confidence limits. If your instructor asks for confidence intervals, refer to prior chapters and your SPSS output under Estimated Marginal Means.

Method

Participants

Forty-five Amazon MTurk workers (23 men and 22 women) participated in exchange for 25 cents. Ethnicities included 50% White, 30% Black, and 20% undisclosed ethnicities, with a mean age of 32.50 years ($SD = 12.53$). The IRB reviewed and approved this study.

Procedure

After reading a short summary of the study, participants clicked on a link to the study. They first read a scenario in which they asked a close friend, who happened to be an expert in electronics, to mail them a refurbished cellular phone. Participants in the control condition (no trust violations) learned that the phone arrived the next day and worked well. Participants in the one-trust-violation condition read that the phone arrived broken. After complaining, the friend replaced it with a working phone. Participants in the two-trust-violations condition learned that the friend replaced a broken phone with another broken phone. Eventually the friend sent a third phone that worked. We programmed the online system to randomly show each participant one of the conditions.

Next, all participants read a scenario indicating that they asked the same close friend to send them a refurbished computer. They rated their trust in the friend's ability to send a fully functional computer on a scale from 1 (*very little trust*) to 7 (*a great deal of trust*).

Results

We analyzed these data using a 2 × 3 (gender × trust violations), between-groups ANOVA. Both the main effect of trust violations and the interaction between gender and trust violations (below) required post hoc analyses. We analyzed these significant effects using LSD mean comparisons ($p < .05$). Participant gender related to ratings of trust, $F(1, 39) = 18.57, p < .001$, partial $\eta^2 = .32$. Overall, women reported more trust in their friend ($M = 5.41, SD = 1.14, n = 22$) than did men ($M = 4.13, SD = 1.87, n = 23$). In addition, number of trust violations by a friend affected trust ratings, $F(2, 39) = 23.18, p < .001$, partial $\eta^2 = .54$. Participants who did not experience a trust violation reported more trust ($M = 6.20, SD = 0.77, n = 15$) than those who experienced one trust violation ($M = 4.38, SD = 1.41, n = 16$) or two trust violations ($M = 3.64, SD = 1.60, n = 14$); trust ratings in the latter two groups failed to differ ($p > .05$).

Participant gender and number of trust violations interacted to affect trust ratings, $F(2, 39) = 3.69, p = .034$, partial $\eta^2 = .16$. Men ($M = 6.13, SD = 0.83, n = 8$) and women ($M = 6.29, SD = 0.76, n = 7$) reported the same level of trust in a friend in the absence of a trust violation. Conversely, male participants reported less trust than female participants after either one ($M = 3.50$, $SD = 1.20$, $n = 8$; $M = 5.25$, $SD = 1.04$, $n = 8$, men & women, respectively) or two ($M = 2.57$, $SD = 1.27$, $n = 7$; $M = 4.71$, $SD = 1.11$, $n = 7$, men & women, respectively) trust violations by a friend. Across men, one or two trust violations reduced trust as compared with none, but one violation failed to differ from two. For women, two trust violations produced significantly lower trust ratings as compared with no violations. One violation failed to differ from the remaining conditions. (See Figure 1 for the interaction between participant gender and number of trust violations.)

SUMMARY

In this chapter we discussed a research design with more than one IV or quasi-IV and an interval or ratio DV. Each factor had two or more levels, and our design assessed different participants in each cell (completely between-groups). A two-way design can include two IVs, two quasi-IVs, or one of each and allows analysis with ANOVA and provides three potential outcomes: two main effects and an interaction. Any combination of main or interaction effects is possible. For main effects, variables with more than two levels require post hoc comparisons to find out exactly which groups differ. Because an interaction always has at least four cells (i.e., a 2×2 design), significance demands post hoc comparisons of cell means. We can write simple SPSS code for post hoc comparisons of the interaction, and graphing communicates outcomes well.

REVIEW OF TERMS

Interaction	Two-Way, Between-Groups ANOVA
Main Effect	Two-Way Design

PRACTICE ITEMS

1. What is the difference between a one-way and two-way design for data analyzed using ANOVA?

2. Without looking back in the chapter, add the following terms to all relevant boxes below: ANOVA, *t*-test.

	Two Levels of the Factor(s)	More Than Two Levels of the Factor(s)
One Factor		
Two Factors		

3. What are the three primary outcomes we get from a two-way ANOVA?

4. Why does an interaction, if significant, tell us "more" about our data?

5. With partial η^2, what numbers are associated with weak, moderate, and strong effect sizes?

* * *

For each of the following studies, (a) provide the research and null hypotheses for each question to be tested, (b) determine how many participants are needed for adequate power for main effects and the interaction, and (c) enter and analyze the data as well as write an APA-style results section. Include graphs if figures would communicate important outcomes. Be sure to read over the method sections we provided.

6. Thomas and Millar (2013) found that people were typically happier with experiential purchases (e.g., a vacation) than material purchases (e.g., a new outfit). You wonder if there might be a social aspect to spending money that also impacts happiness with a purchase. Specifically, you want to know if purchasing an experience versus purchasing an item impacts how happy that purchase makes a person, and you also want to know whether making the purchase alone or with a friend impacts happiness. You randomly assign participants to one of four conditions: (1) purchase an item alone, (2) purchase an item with a friend, (3) purchase an experience alone, and (4) purchase an experience with a friend. You wonder, *Do type of purchase and whether an item was purchased with a friend affect happiness with the purchase?* Because this example is a two-way design, the general research question actually contains three questions.

   • Does type of purchase affect happiness with the purchase?

   • Does making a purchase alone versus with a friend affect happiness with the purchase?

   • Do type of purchase and whether the purchase is made alone or with a friend interact to affect happiness?

   You ask participants to indicate how happy the purchase made them feel on a scale of 1 (*not happy*) to 9 (*very happy*). Analyze these data, including LSD mean comparisons as needed.

Participant Number	Type of Purchase	How Purchased	Happiness
1	Experiential	With a Friend	3
2	Experiential	With a Friend	5
3	Experiential	With a Friend	7
4	Experiential	With a Friend	6
5	Experiential	With a Friend	8
6	Experiential	With a Friend	2
7	Experiential	Alone	5
8	Experiential	Alone	3
9	Experiential	Alone	6
10	Experiential	Alone	7
11	Experiential	Alone	7
12	Experiential	Alone	5
13	Material	With a Friend	4
14	Material	With a Friend	8
15	Material	With a Friend	6
16	Material	With a Friend	5
17	Material	With a Friend	7
18	Material	With a Friend	3
19	Material	With a Friend	3
20	Material	Alone	1
21	Material	Alone	2
22	Material	Alone	3
23	Material	Alone	3
24	Material	Alone	1
25	Material	Alone	3

Method

Participants

We recruited 25 college students (mean age = 19.77, SD = 2.37) via their Introduction to Psychology course. Ethnicities included 15 Black, 6 White, 2 Asian, and 2 Latino individuals (15 men and 10 women).

Procedure

We brought participants into the lab and gave them $20 to buy either an item or an experience (e.g., a movie) either alone or with a friend. They made their purchase based on their assigned condition within the next week and returned to the lab. During their second visit to the lab, we asked participants to rate how happy the purchase made them feel on a scale from 1 (*not happy*) to 9 (*very happy*).

7. You read an article by Cohen, Nisbett, Bowdle, and Schwartz (1996) concluding that Southern men were more likely to respond to an insult than Northern men, and you wonder if the same is true of Southern women, including men as a gender comparison group. You are also interested in expanding the research question to include those raised in the Midwest. Using Cohen and colleagues' method of having a confederate deliberately bump into individuals and call them "assholes," you ask the question: *Do gender and where people were raised relate*

	North	South	Midwest
Men	6	10	4
	6	9	5
	5	4	6
	8	8	7
	9	8	10
	2	9	1
	3	7	2
	7	8	7
	5	8	6
	4	5	1
Women	10	7	5
	8	7	4
	6	8	3
	10	6	7
	9	8	2
	5	1	1
	4	2	1
	8	6	6
	5	6	4
	1	2	1

to aggression after an insult? This general question contains three outcomes to be tested:

- Does gender relate to aggression after insult?

- Does where people were raised relate to aggression after insult?

- Do gender and location of childhood interact to relate to aggression after insult?

Aggression scores are presented below, with higher numbers indicating more aggression. Analyze these data, including LSD mean comparisons as needed.

Method

Participants

We recruited 60 undergraduate students via an advertisement in the university newspaper. Ages ranged from 18 to 26 ($M = 22.49$, $SD = 2.33$), with 30 individuals who identified as men and 30 who identified as women. Ethnicities included 28 White, 18 Black, 10 Latino, and 4 Native American individuals.

Materials

Story narrative. All participants read the following story: Jordan and Peytan worked together late every day this week on a project for work. Neither of them has slept much lately. They spent nearly every waking hour working together on this project, even eating meals together. Jordan knows that Peytan is married but has begun to send flirtatious text messages to Peytan. One night, Peytan leaves the phone at home, and Peytan's spouse sees a text message from Jordan that says, "Hey you, you looked great in those jeans this morning." Peytan's spouse drives over to Peytan's work to deliver the phone and sees Jordan in the parking lot.

Procedure

We scheduled an appointment with each participant to take part in the study. Prior to each appointment time, a female confederate sat on a bench outside the lab door. When the participant started walking down the narrow hall, the confederate stood and walked toward the participant while looking down at a sheet of paper. When they got close to each other, the confederate bumped into the participant's shoulder and then muttered "asshole" to herself (but loud enough for the participant to hear) as she continued to walk down the hallway.

In the lab, participants signed the consent form, read a gender-neutral story about potential infidelity, and rated their likelihood to aggress against Jordan if they experienced the story as Peytan's spouse. Participants rated aggression on a scale from 1 (*very unlikely to aggress*) to 10 (*very likely to aggress*). Before leaving the study, participants reported demographic information, including the region of the country where they spent their childhood.

8. School can be stressful. You saw a pharmaceutical commercial stating that stress is bad for your health, and you wonder what the research says. You find an article by Keller and colleagues (2012) arguing that individuals with *both* a great deal of reported stress as well as a belief that stress is bad for health had an increased risk for premature death. Because school is stressful and you do not want to die prematurely, you wonder if there is a way to improve health among those who are stressed, such as engaging in meditation. You will also assess the impact of a message explaining that stress can be helpful versus a control condition. You design a 2 (education versus no education) × 3 (zero, three, or six weeks of

	Zero Weeks Meditation	Three Weeks Meditation	Six Weeks Meditation
Education	10	10	0
	16	14	1
	5	17	1
	6	5	2
	10	6	2
	12	8	5
	13	10	8
		11	
No Education	5	1	4
	6	6	5
	6	7	5
	8	7	6
	10	10	8
	12	10	8
	15	11	10
	16		

meditation training) study to answer the question: *Do meditation and education about stress affect physical health?* As you know, the study actually consists of three research questions:

- Does education about stress affect physical health?

- Does meditation affect physical health?

- Do education and meditation interact to affect physical health?

Because you do not have 70 years to wait for people to die, for your DV you measure number of days a person suffers from a physical illness in the six months after program completion. Analyze any relevant significant effects using LSD mean comparisons.

Method

Participants

We recruited 44 healthy adult individuals (22 men and 22 women) using flyers posted in a small town square. Ethnicities included 50% Black, 25% White, and 25% Asian individuals, with a sample mean age of 36.77 ($SD = 10.24$). All participants received ethical treatment.

Procedure

We randomly assigned participants to education or no education as well as 0, 3, or 6 weeks of meditation training. Those in the education group watched a video indicating that stress can be good for individuals' health if it is seen as a way to get people motivated to achieve goals. Those in the no-education group watched a documentary about whales. Meditation groups met once weekly for 1 hr, during which participants focused on mindfulness meditation. We asked participants to track on a calendar how many days over the next 6 months they felt sick for at least half of the day. At the end of the 6 months, we e-mailed participants and asked for their total number of sick days.

REFERENCES

Cohen, J. (1988). *Statistical power analysis for the behavioral sciences.* Hillsdale, NJ: Lawrence Erlbaum.

Cohen, D., Nisbett, R. E., Bowdle, B. F., & Schwartz, N. (1996). Insult, aggression, and the Southern culture of honor: An "experimental ethnography." *Journal of Personality and Social Psychology, 70*(5), 945–960. doi:10.1037/0022-3514.70.5.945

Haselhuhn, M. P., Kennedy, J. A., Kray, L. J., Van Zant, A. B., & Schweitzer, M. E. (2015). Gender differences in trust dynamics: Women trust more than men following a trust violation.

Journal of Experimental Social Psychology, 56, 104–109. doi:10.1016/j.jesp.2014.09/007

Keller, A., Litzelman, K., Wisk, L. E., Maddox, T., Cheng, E. R., Creswell, P. D., & Witt, W. P. (2012). Does the perception that stress affects health matter? The association with health and mortality. *Health Psychology, 31*(5), 677–684. doi:10.1037/a0026743

Thomas, R., & Millar, M. (2013). The effects of material and experiential discretionary purchases on consumer happiness: Moderators and mediators. *Journal of Psychology, 147*(4), 345–356. doi:10.1080/00223980.2012.694378

Appendix A

Power Analysis Table

This table gives the sample sizes recommended to have an 80% chance of finding a small, medium, and large effect with $p \leq .05$. Specific effect sizes are located in relevant chapters. **Numbers in the table represent *total* sample size.**

	Small Effect Size	Medium Effect Size	Large Effect Size
Chi square χ^2			
1 *df*	785	88	32
2 *df*	964	108	39
3 *df*	1091	122	44
4 *df*	1194	133	48
5 *df*	1293	143	52
6 *df*	1363	152	55
Pearson's *r*	783	85	29
Linear regression			
1 predictor	395	55	25
2 predictors	485	68	31
3 predictors	550	77	36
4 predictors	604	88	40
Independent-samples *t*-test	788	128	52
One-way, between-groups ANOVA			
2 levels	788	128	52
3 levels	969	159	66
4 levels	1096	180	76
Related-samples *t*-test	200*	34*	16*
One-way, repeated-measures ANOVA			
2 levels	200	34	16
3 levels	165	30	12
4 levels	140	24	10
Two-way, between-groups ANOVA			
Main effects	See one-way between-groups ANOVA		
Interactions			
2 × 2 = 4 cells	1096	180	76
2 × 3 = 6 cells	1290	211	86
2 × 4 = 8 cells	1443	237	97
3 × 3 = 9 cells	1510	249	102
3 × 4 = 12 cells	1691	279	116
4 × 4 = 16 cells	1894	314	131

*Double this number if you have different people in the IV or quasi-IV levels (e.g., siblings or matching).

Note: Table values were obtained from Cohen (1992) and G*Power (Faul, Erdfelder, Lang, & Buchner, 2007; download this free program at www.gpower.hhu.de).

Appendix B

Graphing in Excel

We rely on Excel to create all types of graphs because the program is intuitive and provides clear figures. In this appendix, we offer step-by-step instructions on how to graph scatterplots, simple bar and line graphs, and figures to illustrate interactions using a PC. If you use a Mac, search for Internet tutorials to create similar graphs and figures. You will notice that we link our examples to graphs appearing in text chapters. Let us begin with Chapter 7 and scatterplots.

SCATTERPLOTS

In Chapter 7 we presented an example of dollars and happiness. Actually, we presented two examples on these variables, but here we have chosen to focus on the first data set.

Dollars in Wallet	Happiness
2	3
10	3
20	2
5	4
12	3
15	4
26	3
5	4
21	2
7	1

A	B
2	3
10	3
20	2
5	4
12	3
15	4
26	3
5	4
21	2
7	1

We will show you details on how to create a scatterplot of these data. A scatterplot represents interval or ratio variables when we seek a linear relationship. The data are generally analyzed using Pearson's *r*.

Open Excel and enter data from the example into two columns. We entered dollars in the first column and happiness values in the second column, and we were careful to keep data together by row since each row represents a single participant.

Highlight all of the numbers and click Insert. Next look for the scatterplot icon as shown below and click the arrow to the right of the icon to reveal several options. From these options, choose the first one as indicated in the following screenshot.

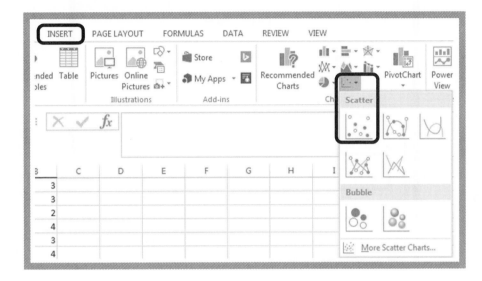

When you click on the scatterplot graph, a picture of your data appears in the middle of the spreadsheet. You will want this graph to appear in its own sheet, so right click on the graph and select Move Chart.

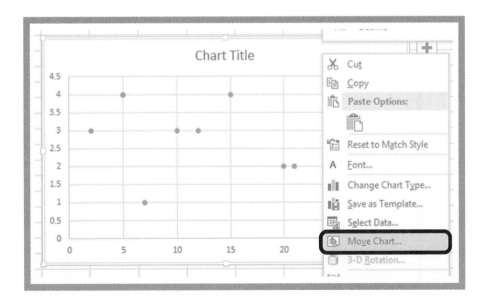

In the box that opens, select the circle to the left of New sheet, and then give the graph a relevant name so you can find the file whenever you need it. Click OK.

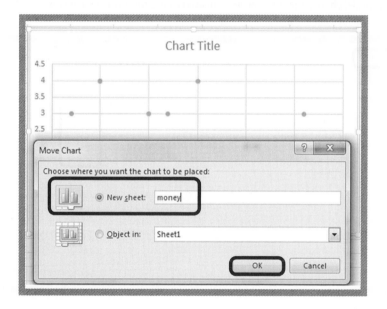

The graph appears on a separate sheet. You will need to delete extra information to present a clear and concise graph. Click the title, horizontal lines, and vertical lines on the graph and Delete.

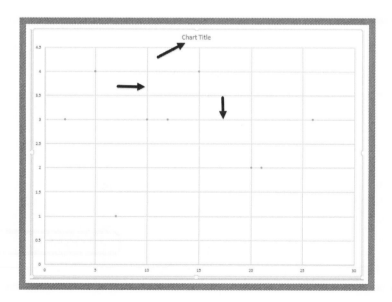

Next, click anywhere inside the graph to reveal buttons on the upper right side of the figure, as shown below. Check the box to the left of Axis Titles. Although we do not want a chart title on the top, we do want labels for our X-axis and Y-axis.

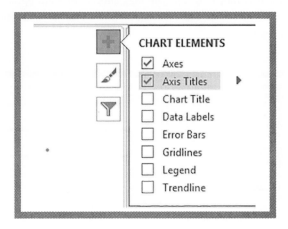

Click on the Y-axis and type Happiness in the open bar near the top of the page. Hit Enter. Follow the same instructions for the X-axis, and label it Dollars in Wallet.

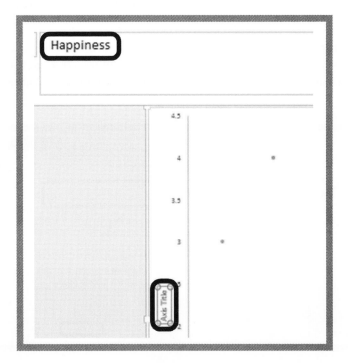

Again click on one of the axis labels. Below we show the Y-axis. Right click to open boxes that allow you to choose Font. The box in the screenshot below appears, and you can change Font style to Bold and Size to 20 points. We chose these formatting options because we like the way they look, but you may choose different options as long as the graph remains simple and clear. Click OK, and follow the same instructions to make the X-axis label more readable.

Notice that the numbers against the X-axis and Y-axis are difficult to read. We can enlarge them by right clicking on the numbers of an axis and again choosing Font to format. Enlarge the numbers on both axes to make them more visible. Click OK after each change.

Click on one of the data points inside of the graph to open a formatting bar on the right side of your screen. The bar should be labeled Format Data Series as shown below. We want to change the color and size of the markers because tiny blue markers (the default) are not highly visible. Click the paint bucket and MARKER. Under BORDER, click Solid line, change the color to black, and increase the marker size to 5 points. Click FILL and again choose a Solid fill and change the color to black.

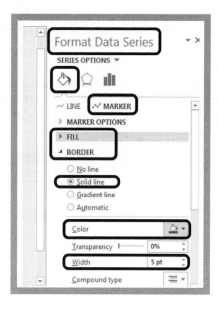

Close Format Data Series to view the graph.

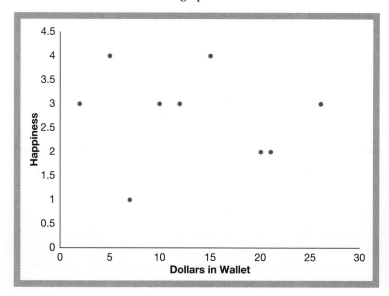

The graph should look familiar because we introduced it in Chapter 7 to illustrate the first data set. Now you know how to create one for yourself. You can include a figure in your APA-style manuscript or simply check for problems in the data set such as an outlier.

BAR GRAPHS

When graphing data separated into groups, such as data analyzed using a t-test or ANOVA, the IV or quasi-IV on the X-axis defines the type of graph to create. An X-axis variable that represents nominal or ordinal data must be graphed using a bar graph. However, when the X-axis is labeled with an interval or ratio variable, a line graph is required.

In Chapter 10 we discussed an example of resisting the urge to each radishes or cookies, with the expectation that resisting radishes would be easier. Resisting cookies would require effort, causing participants to persist for fewer seconds on a subsequent tedious task. As a reminder, the data are below.

Radishes	Cookies
680	200
755	490
476	510
634	308
725	447
688	380
912	470
560	366
732	592
846	415

The SPSS descriptive statistics from Chapter 10 are presented below.

T-Test

Group Statistics

	Snack	N	Mean	Std. Deviation	Std. Error Mean
Persistence	Radishes	10	700.8000	127.19347	40.22211
	Cookies	10	417.8000	111.18033	35.15831

Note that radishes and cookies are the two IV levels, and type of snack represents nominal data. Nominal data on the X-axis require a bar graph. We showed the final bar graph in the first half of Chapter 10, but below we will create it in Excel using step-by-step instructions.

For the snack example, we begin by entering IV level names in cells A1 and B1. Underneath the labels, in cells A2 and B2, we enter the group means from the SPSS output.

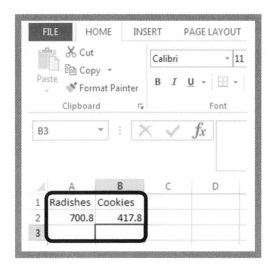

Highlight the four cells and click Insert. Look for the bar graph icon as shown below and click the arrow to the right of the icon to reveal several options. Choose the first option under 2-D Column.

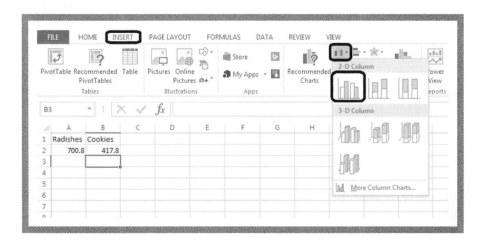

As with the scatterplot example, a graph will appear within the spreadsheet. Move the figure to its own page by right clicking on the graph and choosing Move Chart. In the new box that opens, click the circle to the left of New sheet, name the file, and then click OK.

The graph will now appear as its own page. Here we will format the graph by removing superfluous information, adding labels, formatting font sizes, removing color, and most importantly, adding error bars (standard deviation) to each group as an indication of how much spread of values exists within a group.

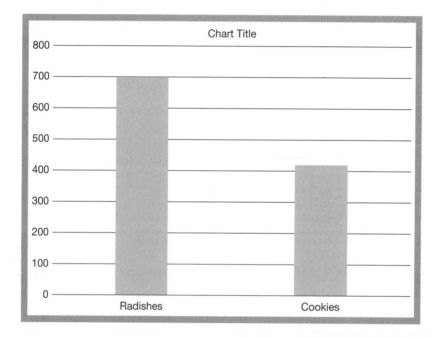

Left click on the Chart Title and press the Delete key on your keyboard. Remember that Chart Titles are not used in APA style. Remove the many horizontal bars across the graph as well to omit clutter.

Below we continue to make the graph more reader friendly by adding axis titles and enlarging their font as well as enlarging numbers on the Y-axis and Radishes and Cookies on the X-axis. Again return to the scatterplot example if you are unsure of what steps to take.

Next we will add error bars to the graph by returning to the + option on the upper right side of the graph. Hover over Error Bars until another box opens. There click More Options.

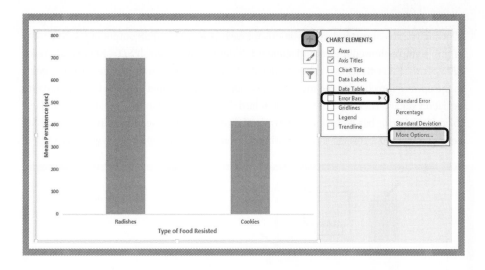

A bar on the right side of the screen opens, offering a wealth of formatting options to Format Error Bars.

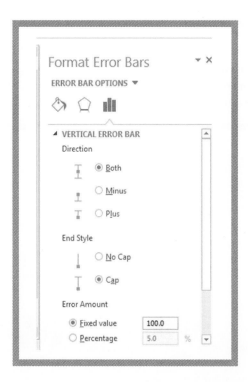

On the bottom of the right panel, click Custom and Specify Value. A small box opens, allowing you to enter standard deviations for each group. The SPSS output at the beginning of this example showed means and standard deviations, with Radish $SD = 127.19$ and Cookie $SD = 111.18$. Enter these two values under Positive Error Value to create the error bar going in the upward direction on the mean bars. Be sure to put a comma between the two standard deviation values. Then type the same standard deviation values under Negative Error Value to create the error bar going in the downward direction on the mean bars. In the screenshot below, we use two arrows to show you where the error bars will appear when you click OK.

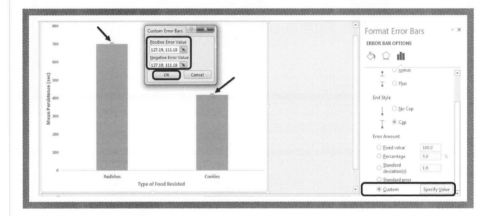

Notice the standard deviation error bars on the graph below. Error bars illustrate average variability within each group. Larger error bars indicate a great deal of variability, and smaller error bars represent little variability within each group. Because participants within a group are treated the same, we hope for small error bars.

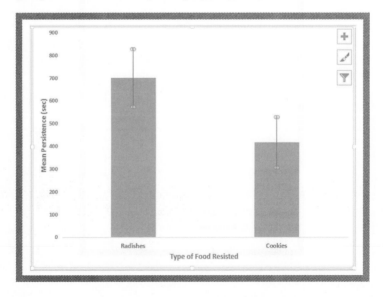

Finally, we need to change the bar colors to white. Right click once on either of the mean bars, and the right-side panel will offer options to format the bars. Click on the icon of the paint bucket.

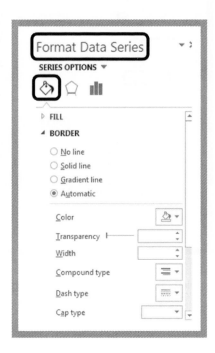

Under the paint bucket, click Fill and choose No Fill.

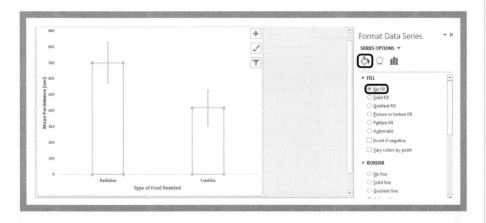

Be careful! If you stop here, your graph will show no mean bars. The inside turns to no fill, and the border also disappears. To create black borders, click Border and choose Solid Line. Change the color to black.

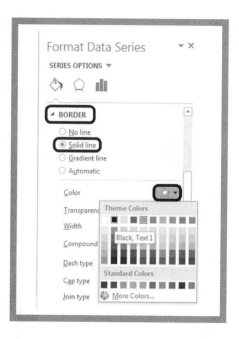

Now your graph is complete. To insert the graph into a Word document, right click on one of the axis margins and choose Copy, then Paste into Word.

You can use the graph as a figure to support an APA-style results section. Every graph of means must have the word "mean" on the Y-axis, and error bars (e.g., standard deviations) are included. Below we show the graph as a figure and add a figure caption for a manuscript.

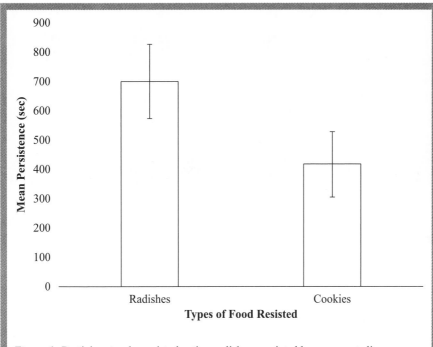

Figure 1. Participants who resisted eating radishes persisted longer on a tedious computer task than those who resisted cookies. Error bars represent *SD*.

Notice that the vertical line for the Y-axis is missing in the graph above, which is the default in Excel for this type of graph. If your instructor wants you to add a line for the Y-axis, simply right click on the axis numbers and choose Format Axis. Next, click on the bucket symbol then the little arrow next to Line. Choose the option for Solid line and change the color to black.

LINE GRAPHS

The final type of simple graph we will show you is a line graph. In Chapter 11, we offered an example of gaming and happiness, with people reporting video-game playing of 0, 1, 2, or 3+ hours. Because the quasi-IV represented ratio data, we must create a line graph.

0 hours	1 hour	2 hours	3+ hours
20	29	18	15
24	25	22	17
18	17	26	25
28	22	12	21
21	23	15	12
19	19	23	20
15	27	21	21
25	26		14
20			

SPSS output illustrated the means and standard deviations per group needed for graphing.

Descriptive Statistics

Dependent Variable: Happiness

Gaming	Mean	Std. Deviation	N
0 hours	21.1111	3.95109	9
1 hour	23.5000	4.07080	8
2 hours	19.5714	4.85994	7
3 hours	18.1250	4.35685	8
Total	20.6250	4.54902	32

Enter group labels and means into Excel. When group labels are numbers (such as hours of gaming in this example in the first row), you might need to format the cells for text so the program does not read them as numbers. The values need to be words to label the X-axis correctly. Highlight the first row, right click on the highlighted portion, and choose Format Cells.

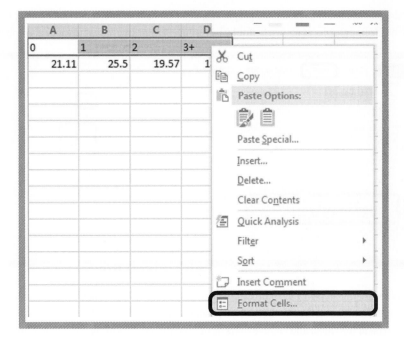

Click Text for the format of the cells as shown in the following image. Click OK.

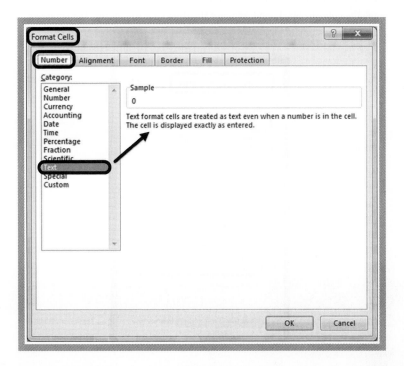

Now you are ready to create the graph. Highlight all eight cells (rows 1 and 2), click Insert, and choose line graphs as shown below by hovering over the arrow next to the line graph icon.

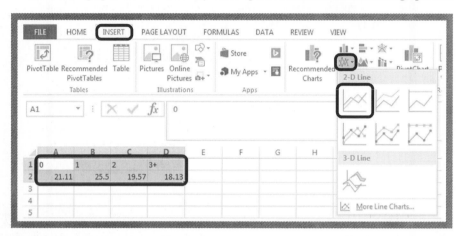

Following the steps for graphing in the bar-graph example (above), remove the title and remove the horizontal lines from the background of the graph. Use the + button to add Axis Titles, type in the titles, and change fonts as needed to make them readable. Your line graph will have a blue line. Click on the blue line to open the panel of options on the right side of the screen. Under Format Data Series, choose the paint-bucket icon. Then click beside Solid line, change the color to black, and increase the thickness to 5 points (or whatever thickness makes the graph most visible for your reader).

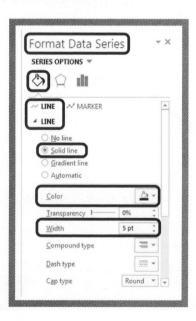

To add error bars, click the + button again on the upper right side of the graph to open options for Error Bars, then More Options. On the right of your screen, click Custom to enter standard deviation values for each mean. Be sure to separate each standard deviation with a comma. Include standard deviation bars above *and* below the means as shown below. Refer to the bar graph example above for step-by-step instructions as needed.

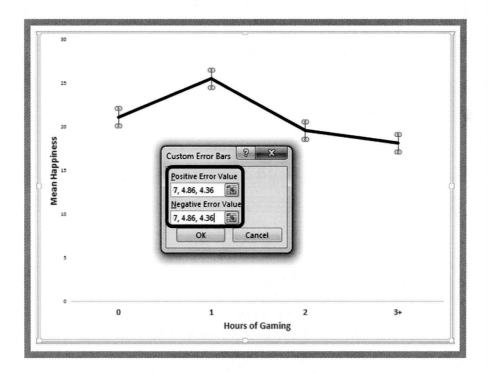

Click OK for Excel to create standard deviation bars on the graph. See that the specific standard deviation value for each group goes upward one standard deviation from each mean and downward one standard deviation from the mean. These error bars communicate the amount of spread in happiness for each quasi-IV group: 0, 1, 2, and 3+ hours of gaming per day.

For a line graph, as well as any graph included in a manuscript, the goal is to maximize readability. After all, the goal of any research project is to share results with other people. Scatterplots and simple graphs with one IV or quasi-IV communicate clearly and efficiently.

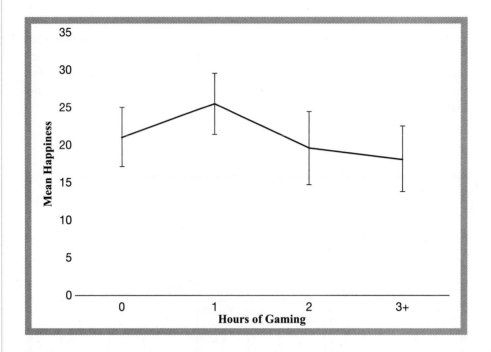

INTERACTION GRAPHS

In Chapter 14, we explained a higher-level grouped design called a two-way, between-groups ANOVA. The term *two way* means the research design contains two IVs or quasi-IVs (or one of each). When graphing, we often want to include both factors in one figure. This type of graph can be a bit tricky, but we will explain in this section exactly how to create this figure to enhance your manuscript.

To begin, let us return to the example from Chapter 14. We examined the potential interaction between participant gender and number of prior trust violations on current level of trust in a person. The DV was level of trust on a rating scale from 1 to 7, with higher numbers indicating more trust in the friend. Our original data are below.

	No Trust Violations	One Trust Violation	Two Trust Violations
Male Participants	6	2	1
	7	5	3
	5	4	2
	7	3	4
	7	5	1
	6	4	4
	6	3	3
	5	2	

	No Trust Violations	One Trust Violation	Two Trust Violations
Female Participants	7	5	5
	6	4	4
	7	6	4
	5	6	5
	6	7	6
	6	5	6
	7	4	3
		5	

SPSS output contained the means and standard deviations, which have been reproduced below.

Descriptive Statistics

Dependent Variable: Trust

Gender	Trust_violation	Mean	Std. Deviation	N
Men	0 violations	6.1250	.83452	8
	1 violation	3.5000	1.19523	8
	2 violations	2.5714	1.27242	7
	Total	4.1304	1.86607	23
Women	0 violations	6.2857	.75593	7
	1 violation	5.2500	1.03510	8
	2 violations	4.7143	1.11270	7
	Total	5.4091	1.14056	22
Total	0 violations	6.2000	.77460	15
	1 violation	4.3750	1.40831	16
	2 violations	3.6429	1.59842	14
	Total	4.7556	1.66727	45

When graphing the interaction, both gender and number of trust violations must be represented in a single graph. One of the factors is placed on the X-axis, and the remaining factor is explained in a legend. The Y-axis represents the dependent variable, as you have seen before, and only group means are graphed.

In Excel, type the factor levels you want to appear on the X-axis in the first row (we have chosen number of trust violations), and then type the six cell means as shown below. The second row contains means from male participants across trust violations.

Row 3 contains means from women. See that we put Men and Women labels in the first column; these will become our legend labels. We recreated the six cells of the 2 × 3 design. Next, across the top, highlight zero, one, and two trust violations, and right click to choose Format Cells to make them read as text to label the X-axis. Review the line-graph example above for more detailed instructions if you need them.

Highlight all cells as shown below, and click Insert and the line-graph icon. From the options, the first graph is fine.

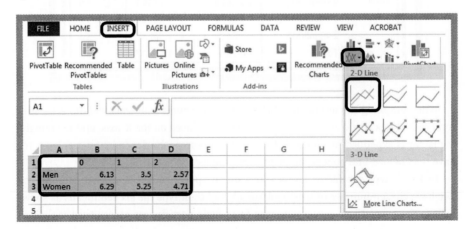

When you click the line-graph option, the following graph appears.

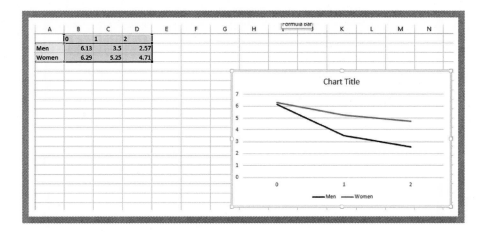

Move the graph to a new sheet and then clean up the graph as explained in prior examples. Delete the title and horizontal lines across the background. Insert axis titles, and enlarge fonts as needed for readability.

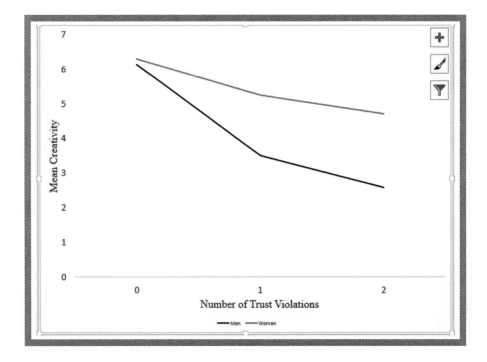

Click on the legend at the bottom marked Men and Women. Drag the legend to the upper right corner.

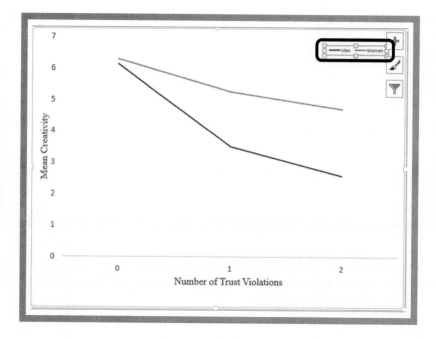

Right click on the legend to enlarge the font size.

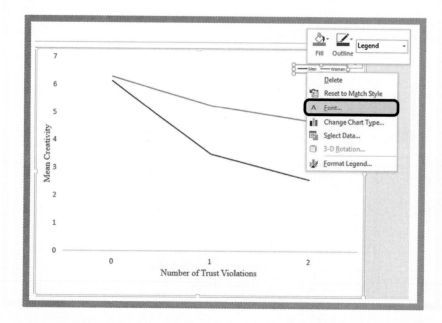

The details are up to you. Enlarge the box as needed by clicking on the edges. You can also change to a larger font size. The goal is readability.

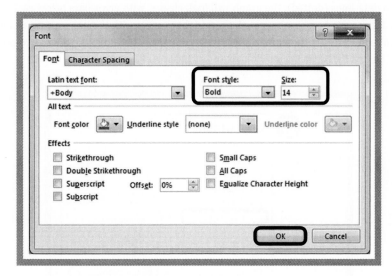

Change the lines to black, thicken them, and set one to be a dotted line so you can tell them apart.

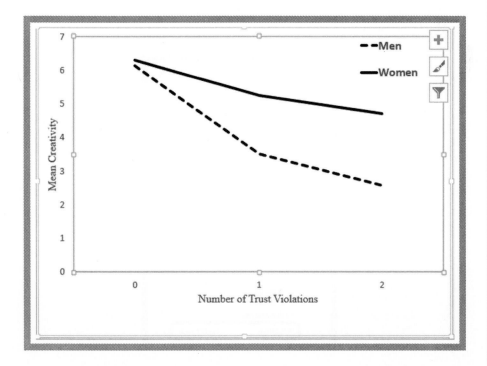

Our final goal is to add error bars to each of the lines. We will begin with the data for men across number of trust violations. Because the men are represented by the lower of the two data lines (dotted), the graph will look clearer with error bars below each group mean. If the error bars went upward, they might overlap with the line for women and be hard to read. Click on the line for men, then click the + button and tell Excel to provide More Options for Error Bars.

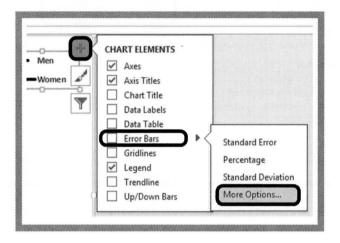

Under Format Error Bars, click Minus for downward bars, and Custom to enter standard deviation for each cell (group). Click Specify Value.

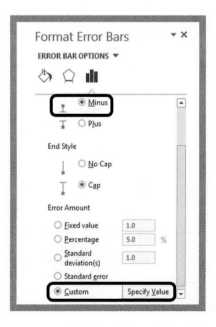

Return to your table with the six cell means and standard deviations. Notice that the trust means for men are 6.13, 3.50, and 2.57. The standard deviation values across these cells are 0.83, 1.20, and 1.27.

	No Trust Violations	One Trust Violation	Two Trust Violations
Male Participant	*M* = 6.13 *SD* = 0.83 *n* = 8	*M* = 3.50 *SD* = 1.20 *n* = 8	*M* = 2.57 *SD* = 1.27 *n* = 7
Female Participant	*M* = 6.29 *SD* = 0.76 *n* = 7	*M* = 5.25 *SD* = 1.04 *n* = 8	*M* = 4.71 *SD* = 1.11 *n* = 7

Enter the standard deviation values for error bars on the line for men, and click OK.

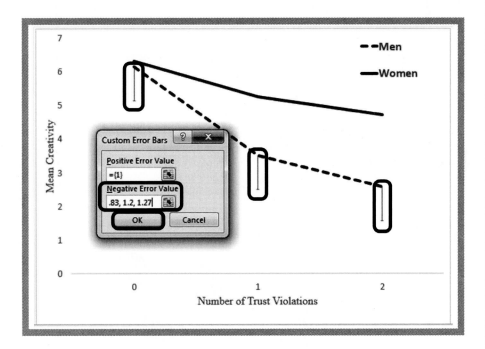

Follow the same procedure for female participants, with standard deviation values of 0.76, 1.04, and 1.11, except this time, designate the error bars as positive instead of negative.

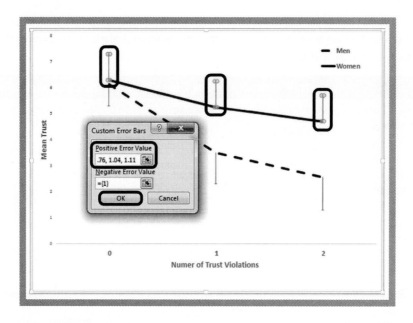

The graph is finished! We have designed a study based on a research question, collected data, analyzed the data, and organized it in a meaningful way to communicate efficiently. A graph does an excellent job of conveying a lot of information quickly.

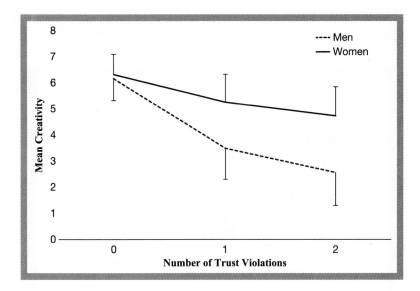

A figure caption provides guidance on interpreting the graph.

Figure 1. Gender of the participant and number of trust violations by friends interacted to affect reported level of trust ($p < .05$). Men and women reported equal levels of trust when friends did not violate their trust. But men and women diverged when trust violations occurred, with subsequent trust from men declining more than trust from women across violations. Error bars represent *SD*.

If we had instead chosen to place gender on the X-axis and number of trust violations in the legend, we would enter the data as shown below. Highlight all 12 cells and Insert a bar graph (what SPSS calls Column). With the nominal variable of gender now on the X-axis, we must create a bar graph.

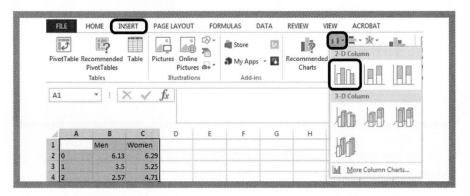

If you notice that SPSS has created a graph with number of trust violations on the X-axis (as it sometimes does), we need to adjust the figure.

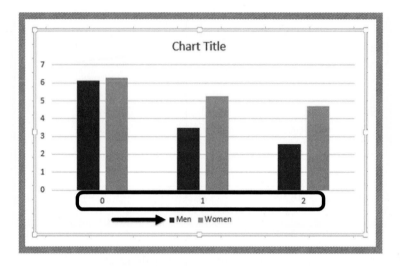

Right click on the graph and click Select Data.

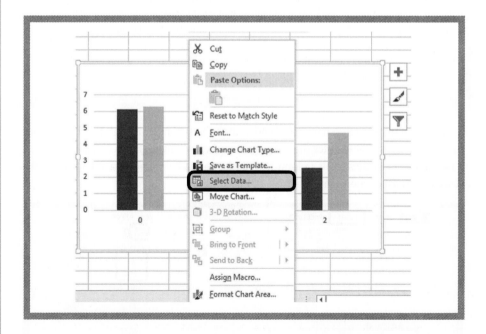

In the box that opens, click Switch Row/Column to put Men and Women on the Horizontal Axis. Click OK.

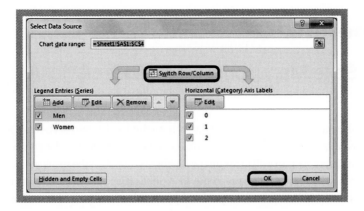

Now you can continue to format the graph as detailed in this section. Because you are creating a bar graph, refer also to the section on Bar Graphs (above) as needed. After completing all format changes, the graph should look like the following. Again, a bar graph was required because we changed the X-axis variable to gender, and gender represents nominal data. Notice in the graph below, error bars only go up and not down. We used this format because several of the bars are filled with a color, so an error bar would not be visible to readers.

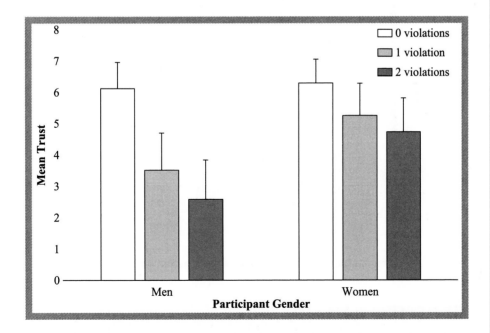

Researchers choose only one graph to represent the interaction, often creating both options and choosing the one that better tells the story. Is it clearer to see the line graph with number of trust violations on the X-axis or a bar graph with participant gender on the X-axis? You decide.

Appendix C

APA-Style Manuscript Guidelines

In this book, you learned how to write APA-style method and results sections. The purpose of this appendix is to provide you with some guidelines for writing the entire APA-style manuscript. This appendix will focus on the highlights. For all of the specifics about writing a manuscript in APA style, please read the APA publication manual, which is currently in its 6th edition (2010). New versions are written regularly, so be sure to follow the most current manual.

KEY ELEMENTS IN APA-STYLE WRITING

The APA publication manual provides great information about the different sections of a manuscript. We want to highlight what we think are some of the more important or nuanced aspects of writing a research paper.

The Basics

When you open your document to begin typing, go ahead and set up your formatting. Most programs do *not* have APA-style settings as the default. Change your margins to one inch on all four page margins, and set the page to double spacing. Add page numbers to the top right of the page, usually within a header.

As for the actual writing, we learned somewhere in our past to think of the paper as an hourglass. We start with general information in the introduction to introduce the topic to readers, offering few specific study details until we move toward studies that are highly relevant to our own study. By the time we near the end of our introduction, the story should be tightly related to our study. In the final paragraph of this section, we write what we will examine and what we expect to find—our research hypothesis. Without creating a page break, we continue with our method section, detailing our sample, our materials, and exactly how we operationalize variables. Of course, the results section follows the method, and our results are specific to our study. Next, in the discussion section, we restate our findings, speculate why we found them, and then relate them back to the literature as a whole. We put our study and results back into the larger story surrounding our topic.

Title Page

The title of your paper should give the reader a good idea of what your paper covers. We prefer to avoid passive titles such as those starting with "The Effects of...." Just below your title, add author names and affiliations. All parts of the title page are written in regular font (i.e., not bold, underlined, or italicized).

Abstract

The abstract is a brief summary of your entire paper. Include about two sentences summarizing each section of your paper (introduction, method, results, and discussion). Most abstracts do not include any references because you will be providing citations in the body of the paper. If you use an abbreviation, you will need to spell it out the first time. Convention is that abstracts should be 150-250 words, though journals will have their own instructions on abstract length.

Introduction

For many students, the introduction is the most difficult section of the paper to write because it is where you justify why you are conducting your study based on the current literature. The APA publication manual outlines four purposes of the introduction: introduce the problem, explore the importance of the problem, describe relevant scholarship, and state research hypotheses within an overview of the research design.

The goal of the introduction is to lead the reader through your logic. Why is the topic important? What studies have already been conducted in this area? You are not required to give an exhaustive account of all publications, but include enough studies that readers feel like they understand the topic of your study. Make a case for what is available in the current literature, what is missing, and how you will fill that void. At the end of the introduction, summarize your method very briefly and then give the reader your hypotheses.

Method

By now we hope you have been practicing writing method and results sections as you worked your way through this book. Based on many examples, you already know that the method is where readers locate information about participants, recruitment, ethics, any materials used in the study, and a detailed description of what happened during the study (i.e., the procedure).

Results

This section is where you will present your own findings. Explain how the data were analyzed, report the results of inferential statistics, and provide descriptive statistics of your variables. Refer to figures and tables as needed. If you choose to include confidence intervals, do so in the results section. Note that APA style requires effect size and encourages confidence intervals. Report whatever you or your instructor believe is needed to tell the reader your story. As a caution for this section, we find that students have a difficult time leaving their conclusions *out* of the results. Make sure you only state the facts, not your opinion. Do not worry—you will be able to speculate in your discussion section.

Discussion

In this section, first give a very brief summary (one or two sentences) of the results without including any statistical data. It is important here not to just restate sentences from your results section but instead reword your results in a more conversational manner. Talk about how your findings relate back to your hypotheses and the literature as a whole. Speculate about why you might have found your specific results, and be sure to refer to other publications in support of your speculation. You may refer to articles already mentioned in your introduction section, but often you will locate new articles to support your potential explanation. How might you test your explanation in a future study? Finally, explain some limitations of your study.

Unfortunately you might end up with nonsignificant results when conducting your own undergraduate research. This is okay! You will just have to spend extra time in the discussion section speculating why you might not have found a significant outcome. For example, discuss power and whether you had enough participants to reveal an effect, if one indeed existed. Reflect on your data-collection practices, your operational definitions, the potential for a biased sample, et cetera. Each explanation should lead you to suggestions for how to improve the study in the future.

References

References should start on a new page with the word "References" centered at the top of the page, not bolded, underlined, or italicized. All references should be in alphabetical order with digital object identifiers (DOIs) when available.

Tables, Figures, and Appendices

Tables, figures, and appendices should be placed at the end of the paper, after the references, in that order. Tables and figures are labeled numerically (e.g., Tables 1, 2, & 3) and separately (e.g., Figures 1 & 2). Appendices are labeled with capital letters, in alphabetical order (Appendix A, B, C, & D). For information on formatting tables, figures, and appendices, please see the APA publication manual and the Purdue Online Writing Lab. If you choose to use a table or figure to represent data, the same values generally do not appear in the text of your results section.

COMMON MISTAKES AND TIPS FOR WRITING

Over the years, we have compiled a list of common writing mistakes and writing tips. We hope they help you write a great manuscript!

- Use active language throughout the paper. A statement such as, "There were five participants" can be reworded as, "Five students participated."

- Include transition words and phrases between ideas. Searching *transition words* on the Internet will give you a list of terms, including words/phrases such as *however, in addition to, further, for example, similarly, in contrast, specifically, although,* and *whereas.* Transition terms allow you to take readers by the hand and lead them through your paper.

- Avoid using *due to, utilize,* and *in regards to.* These phrases are too flowery and rarely add to the paper. Instead, try *because of, use,* and *regarding.* Similarly, we avoid the term *one* to represent a person, as in "One should avoid using fancy words." Remember that we write with the goal of communicating with readers. Our *ideas* should impress readers, not our highbrow writing style.

- When using words such as *this* and *these,* each word must be followed by what you are discussing (e.g., "these pointers improve readability").

- The word *while* is a time word, so it can be used in the method with a statement such as, "While participants rubbed their bellies, they also tapped their heads." However, you would not use *while* in this sentence: "While prior research found. . . . " Instead, say, "Although prior research found. . . . "

- The words *female* and *male* are adjectives, and the words *men* and *women* are nouns. It is okay to refer to a participant as a *woman* or a *female participant,* not as a *female* if no modified word comes next.

- Some authors suggest adding effect sizes (and sometimes confidence intervals) even when *p*-values are not significant. We do not do this because we feel it is misleading to the reader. However, we recognize that the debate continues. If your instructor prefers adding supplemental information when you fail to reject the null hypothesis, so be it!

- Make sure to clear your paper of any "widows" or "orphans," which are single lines of text at the top/bottom of the page. Typically, word processing programs do this for paragraphs but not for headings. Review general formatting of your paper after all of the writing is complete and you are ready to turn in your masterpiece.

EXAMPLE PAPER WITH COMMENTS

In the pages that follow, you will see a paper based on a *Teaching of Psychology* publication by the authors of this book in which we examined whether the first day of class affects student motivation and ratings of the course and instructor. We say "affects" because we manipulated IV levels. The sample publication included here has been simplified for illustrative purposes. For the full version, which also includes student outcomes across the semester, please use the following: doi10.1080/00986280701700151.

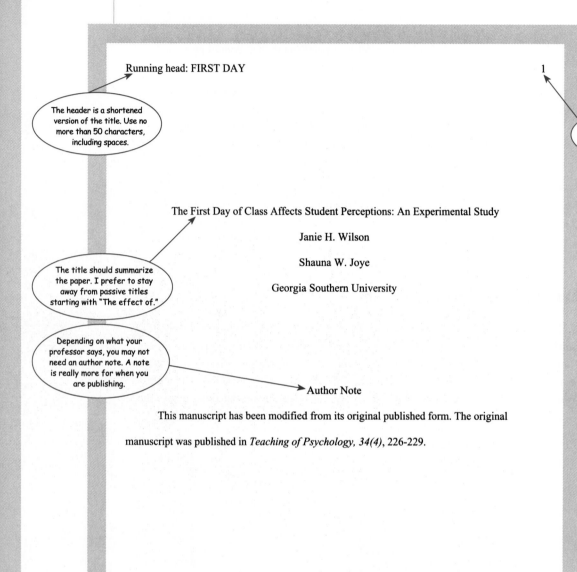

Running head: FIRST DAY   1

The header is a shortened version of the title. Use no more than 50 characters, including spaces.

Page numbers go in the top right corner.

The First Day of Class Affects Student Perceptions: An Experimental Study

Janie H. Wilson

Shauna W. Joye

Georgia Southern University

The title should summarize the paper. I prefer to stay away from passive titles starting with "The effect of."

Depending on what your professor says, you may not need an author note. A note is really more for when you are publishing.

Author Note

This manuscript has been modified from its original published form. The original manuscript was published in *Teaching of Psychology, 34(4)*, 226-229.

FIRST DAY   2

Abstract

Teaching experts assert that the first day of class impacts students, setting important expectations and class tone. However, no empirical research supports this supposition. We randomly assigned students ($N = 27$) to view a video of their professor either providing a positive or negative first-day experience. Students with the positive experience reported better attitudes and more positive expectations at the end of the first day. Students also reported higher motivation to succeed in the course (all $ps < .01$). Our study provides experimental evidence that the first day of class influences student perceptions and motivation.

Do not indent the abstract paragraph.

It's good to include your sample size somewhere in the abstract.

Notice that the words "Running head" appear only on the first page of the manuscript.

Use 1-inch margins and 12-point Times New Roman font throughout the paper.

- *Do not bold the word "Abstract."*
- *The abstract is a brief summary of the paper, so make sure to include sentences summarizing all sections of the paper (intro, method, etc.).*

FIRST DAY   3

The First Day of Class Affects Student Perceptions: An Experimental Study

According to accepted teaching experts, the first day of class requires careful preparation and execution (e.g., Duffy & Jones, 1995; McKeachie, 2002). Duffy and Jones (1995) suggested that instructors use the first day of class to cover the syllabus, help students get to know each other, and introduce students to the process of learning. Similarly, McKeachie (2002) suggested using the first day to get acquainted and establish course goals as well as cover the syllabus, the textbook, and even some lecture material. McKeachie insisted that teachers use the first day in its entirety to communicate the importance of class time. In fact, Nilson (2003) and Wolcowitz (1984) argued that the first day of class sets expectations that persist across the entire term. For example, excitement about the course on the first day prevents motivation problems later in the term (Wolcowitz, 1984). Although few instructors would disagree with the intuition that the first day, like every day of class, is important, our study responds to Henslee, Burgess, and Buskist's (2006) call for more scientific inquiry into accepted teaching beliefs by examining the effects of a positive or a negative first day on several variables.

A wealth of research indicates that teacher behaviors predict student attitudes toward the teacher and the course as well as motivation and even grades (e.g., Wilson, 2006). If the first day of class is indeed crucial, experimental manipulation of teacher behavior on the first day might impact these same student outcomes. Our study focused on whether the first day of class affects students' expectations, attitudes, and motivation. In this study, we defined a positive first-day experience by students' preferences identified by Perlman and McCann (1999) and Henslee et al. (2006) and a negative first day by students' dislikes (Henslee et al., 2006; Perlman & McCann, 1999). We expected students with the positive first day to report a better attitude toward the

---

Annotations:

You will be tempted to bold the title, but do not.

When we write "e.g.," we mean "for example." This abbreviation means what we are offering is an example of many possible examples. When we write "i.e.," we mean "that is," and we will give complete information. Another way to think of i.e. is "in other words."

Introduce your study at the end of the introduction, and include your research hypotheses.

Inside parentheses, use the "&" sign in citations with more than one author. Outside the parentheses, like here, spell out the word "and" in citations with more than one author.

With three, four, or five authors, you write out all their names the first time (shown in the paragraph above). After that, you use the term "et al." for all authors except the first one. With six or more authors, you can use the term "et al." with the first author's name the first time the study is referenced. With only two authors, you use both of their names every time.

course and their instructor, rate their instructor as more effective, and report feeling more

motivated by the instructor than those who experienced a negative first day.

Method

Headings for the Method, Results, and Discussion are bolded and centered.

Participants

Subheadings (i.e., Level 2 headings) are bolded and flush to the left. If you need to use a sub-subheading (Level 3 heading), indent 0.5" from the left, bold, and use lower case letters except for the first word.

Students in a summer course of introduction to psychology participated in this

experiment. Fifty-six students attended the first day of class. Because eight of these students

indicated they had heard of the instructor previously or knew the instructor, we removed them

from the data set. Twenty-seven students [23 women and 4 men with an average age of 20.30

When a sentence begins with a number, always spell out the number.

$(SD = 1.51)$] chose to complete surveys. Ethnicities included 20 White, 5 African American, 1

Asian, and 1 biracial student. All students received three extra credit percentage points on their

Use two decimal places for most numbers.

final grade for participation.

Materials and Procedure

Using a course roster, a graduate assistant randomly assigned students in the course to

experience either a positive or negative first day of class as defined by student preferences. The

instructor (first author) never obtained information regarding names and condition assignments.

Student preferences (i.e., learning about the course, grading standards, work required) for the

first day characterized the positive condition. Student dislikes (i.e., beginning course material,

using full class time, assigning homework) defined the negative condition.

If the procedure is simple, you may choose to add it to the materials section with this combined title, or you might just use "Procedure" and include simple materials such as a single-item rating scale.

On the first day of class, two female graduate students in their early to mid-twenties

waited for students in the classroom. When it was time for class to begin, they explained that the

professor was out of town at a conference but had prepared a video. They further explained that

projection problems necessitated moving half of the class to another room so everyone could sit

near the front of the classrooms. One graduate student called out names to join her in another room (with no explanation offered as to why specific names were called out), where they experienced the positive first day. Students who remained in the original classroom received the negative first-day experience.

After settling into their respective classrooms, students saw a video of either a friendly professor who covered information on the syllabus for 15.5 min or the same professor avoiding emotional tone while covering the syllabus. In the former condition, students left the classroom immediately following the video presentation and after completing evaluations. In the latter condition, students viewed the video followed by a film segment from the History Channel and received a homework assignment based on the film segment before completing evaluations. These activities required them to remain for the entire class period.

At the end of the first day of class, students rated their response to the statements "The instructor is likely to motivate me to do my best work" on a scale from 1 (*strongly disagree*) to 5 (*strongly agree*); "Rate the course (so far) as a whole" from 1 (*poor*) to 5 (*excellent*); and "Rate the overall effectiveness of your instructor" from 1 (*poor*) to 5 (*excellent*). Participants also rated their attitude toward the professor on a scale from 1 to 7 (*strong positive attitude toward the professor*).

Scale anchors are always italicized.

Results

Review this results section to see how much you have learned! Remember that independent-samples *t*-tests were explained in Chapter 10.

We analyzed these data using one-tailed, independent-samples *t*-tests. Outcomes included student ratings of the course and the professor as well as motivation. Students with the positive first-day experience reported higher ratings than students with a negative first day for the variables of attitude toward the course, $t(25) = 5.85$, $p = .004$, Cohen's $d = 5.78$, attitude toward the professor, $r(25) = 5.47$, $p = .008$, Cohen's $d = 4.99$, perceived effectiveness of the professor,

FIRST DAY   6

$t(25) = 7.10$, $p = .010$, Cohen's $d = 6.14$, and motivation, $r(25) = 4.79$, $p = .008$, Cohen's $d =$

5.65. Table 1 shows descriptive statistics for all dependent variables.

Numbers that indicate tables or figures are always written as numerals. If you have tables and figures, number them consecutively but separately. For example, you might have Figures 1, 2, and 3 and Tables 1 and 2.

Begin your discussion with a brief review of at least one of your results. Then you can move on to discuss the result. Be sure to bring in research to support your potential explanation.

Discussion

The first day of class influenced students by the time they left the classroom. Students

with the positive first day reported better attitudes toward the course and the teacher than those

who experienced the negative first day. They also reported higher motivation after a positive first

day as defined by student preferences. These outcomes support the assertion from Wolcowitz

(1984) that a positive first impression spurs student motivation. A student-centered first day

(Perlman & McCann, 1999) likely facilitated rapport (Wilson, 2006).

This study marks the first known experimental manipulation of the first day of class

based on research reports of student preferences (Henslee et al., 2006; Perlman & McCann,

1999). As such, we altered several aspects of the first-day experience: length of class period,

lecture, homework, and emotional tone. The negative effects of the first day conceivably

occurred due to any of the components we altered or a combination of all aspects of the first-day

environment. Future research should isolate which variables impact students most strongly and

whether effects are moderated by factors such as student or instructor gender, ethnicity, or age, to

name a few. Additional limitations of our study included not matching for academic ability prior

Often a discussion will contain a separate section on Limitations in which you discuss, well, the limitations of your study. In this manuscript, limitations are discussed without using a separate heading.

to assigning students to conditions; however, we found that students in the conditions did not

differ on grade point average. The two groups might have differed in additional ways, such as

trait motivation, a baseline we did not measure. Instead, we relied on random assignment to

conditions to distribute individual differences uniformly across the two groups. Finally, we

recognize that this study employed a rather small N, perhaps limiting our ability to reveal differences across student evaluations of the course and instructor. Indeed, although not significantly different, the majority of means supported our predictions.

Our study provides experimental evidence that the first day of class influences student perceptions and motivation. With this possibility in mind, how should instructors structure the first day? We recommend learning what students like and dislike to create a positive first-day experience (e.g., Perlman & McCann, 1999). Although we do not subscribe to the consumer model, respecting students' preferences might reduce their stress and enhance their motivation. After all, the first day brings a wealth of new, and perhaps overwhelming, information: Students must learn a new schedule, location, teacher, colleagues, and the syllabus. Perhaps we as instructors should use the first day to ease students' minds rather than fill them.

End the discussion with a statement about the importance of your study. Such an ending redirects the reader from limitations back to the primary results and why they are important.

FIRST DAY   8

References

Duffy, D. K., & Jones, J. W. (1995). *Teaching within the rhythms of the semester.* San Francisco:

Jossey-Bass.

Henslee, A. M., Burgess, D. R., & Buskist, W. (2006). Students' preferences for first day of class

activities. *Teaching of Psychology, 33*, 189-191. doi: 10.1207/s15328023top3303_7

McKeachie, W. J. (2002). *McKeachie's teaching tips: Strategies, research, and theory for*

college and university teachers (11th ed.). Boston: Houghton Mifflin.

Nilson, L. B. (2003). *Teaching at its best: A research-based resource for college instructors* (2nd

ed.). Bolton, MA: Anker.

Perlman, B., & McCann, L. I. (1999). Student perspectives on the first day of class. *Teaching of*

Psychology, 26, 277-279. http://dx.doi.org/10.1207/S15328023TOP260408

Wilson, J. H. (2006). Predicting student attitudes and grades from perceptions of instructors'

attitudes. *Teaching of Psychology, 33*, 91-95. doi:10.1207/s15328023top3302_2

Wolcowitz, J. (1984). The first day of class. In M. M. Gullette (Ed.), *The art and craft of*

teaching (pp. 10–24). Cambridge, MA: Harvard University Press.

Book titles are italicized.

Include dois as often as possible. They can be in this format or the format in the Perlman & McCann reference below.

Journal volume numbers are also italicized. If each issue of a journal volume begins with page 1, you must also include the volume issue in parentheses, with the volume in italics and the issue not italicized. For example: *Journal Title, 14*(3), 123-132.

For book chapters, make sure to include the page numbers here.

APA reference style indents every line of text after the first line. This format is called a hanging indent.

Only the first word of a title is capitalized unless a colon is used. With a colon, also capitalize the first word after the colon.

Notice no use of italics for the title of a journal article.

9

Table 1

Means and Standard Error of Measurement by Group

Dependent Variables	Positive First Day (n = 13)		Negative First Day (n = 14)	
	M	*SEM*	*M*	*SEM*
Attitude toward course	3.90	.23	2.82	.13
Attitude toward instructor	6.10	.41	4.44	.23
Instructor is effective	4.20	.29	2.82	.13
Instructor motivates me	4.40	.22	3.29	.17

Note. For all variables, higher numbers indicate more favorable outcomes.

[Annotation callouts:]

Notice the use of horizontal lines only. APA style does not include vertical lines in tables.

A brief title explains what is found in the table.

Do not be concerned that within-group variability is illustrated with standard error of the mean (*SEM*). You learned to rely on *SD*, which is also entirely appropriate as a measure of variability. *SEM* is *SD/n*.

Source: Joye, S. W., & Wilson, J. H. (2015). Professor age and gender affect student perceptions and grades. *Journal of the Scholarship of Teaching and Learning, 15*(4), 126–138.

EXAMPLE PAPER WITHOUT COMMENTS

We have also included a second example paper by both authors published in the *Journal of the Scholarship of Teaching and Learning* that examines how professor age and gender affect student perceptions and grades. Again we use "affect" because we manipulated IV levels. We have made some minor edits to the paper to enhance readability for this text. For the full paper, please use the doi 10.14434/josotl.v15i4.13466.

Professor Age and Gender Affect Student Perceptions and Grades

Shauna W. Joye

Janie H. Wilson

Georgia Southern University

Abstract

Student evaluations provide rich information about teaching performance, but a number of factors beyond teacher effectiveness influence student evaluations. In this study, we examined the effects of professor gender and perceived age on ratings of effectiveness and rapport as well as academic performance. We also asked students to rate professor attractiveness as a potential explanation for group differences. Participants ($N = 308$) saw a picture of either a young or old male or female professor while listening to an audio lecture. Students reported greater perceived rapport and attractiveness with the female relative to the male professors and for younger versus older professors. However, students perceived the male professors as more effective than the female professors. An interaction revealed that among female professors only, participants rated the younger version as more attractive than comparison conditions. Thus, age and gender bias likely impact student evaluations of teaching. Our study also revealed higher quiz grades in the older-female condition.

Keywords: student evaluations, professor age, professor gender, rapport, student grades

Professor Age and Gender Affect Student Perceptions and Grades

Student evaluations help professors consider changes such as teaching style, course

content, and classroom policies in an effort to help students learn and retain information. Perhaps

the opportunity for reflection offers the most powerful benefit of evaluations. At many colleges,

evaluations determine raises, promotions, tenure, and even teaching awards. In support of

widespread use, data

effectiveness (e.g., M

However, nu

For example, variabl

the course, and reas

instructor's control.

other factors affecte

variability in evaluat

evaluations also resi

size, classroom setup

contextual issues suc

student evaluations.

student and contextu

with the course and

Unfortunatel

themselves, such as

remain unchangeabl

cultural norms relate

be kind (Ebert, Steffens, & Kroth, 2014), agreeable, open, and contentious (Löckenhoff, 2014),

and society expects both men and women to be competent (Löckenhoff, 2014). In the teaching

realm, Kierstead, D'Agostino, and Dill (1988) found that whereas male professors earned high

student evaluations if they demonstrated competence, female professors earned the same high

ratings only if they demonstrated both competence and warmth. Similarly, society associates

positive perceptions with youth (Danziger & Welfel, 2000). In the classroom, Horner, Murray,

and Rushton (1989) found a negative correlation between instructor age and ratings of teaching

effectiveness ($r = -.33$). Likewise, Wilson, Beyer, and Monteiro (2014) used images of young

and old adults and found that older professors received more negative ratings on perceptions of

friendliness and rapport than younger professors. An interaction between gender and age showed

that students rated an older woman as less organized than a younger woman, although male

professors were rated the same regardless of age.

Perhaps tied to age, attractiveness relates with positive perceptions. Allport (1954)

asserted that society wants to believe in a just world. Individuals want to believe that people get

what they deserve. Relatedly, people believe that physically beautiful people somehow earned

beauty by embodying good qualities (i.e., "what is beautiful is good;" Dion, Berscheid, &

Walster, 1972). Specifically in research on the scholarship of teaching and learning, more

attractiveness links with higher overall student ratings (e.g., Riniolo, Johnson, Sherman, &

Misso, 2006), higher ratings of teacher effectiveness (Felton, Mitchell, & Stinson, 2004), better

course quality (Felton, Koper, Mitchell, & Stinson, 2008), higher grades (Gurung & Vespia,

2007), and perceptions of being more approachable, likeable, and providing a more enjoyable

class (Gurung & Vespia, 2007). In a large-scale study of online ratings of professors ($N = 2281$),

Freng and Webber (2009) found that even after controlling for a number of other factors, professor attractiveness still accounted for 8% of the variance in student ratings. Hamermesh and Parker (2005) suggested that more positive ratings may relate with more learning if students focus more intently on attractive professors, remaining more engaged and earning higher grades.

As the above studies indicate, student perceptions fluctuate based on instructor gender, age, and attractiveness. However, the bulk of research asks students to evaluate professors with whom they have int

associated with a nu

potentially covary w

interactions may act

the absence of positi

more positive attitu

Exposure Effect; Za

of variables such as

In an attemp

variables, Goebel an

look at photographs

friendliness and poo

rated the more attrac

to give too much wo

instructor beauty inf

is provided. When e

Wilson and c

students photograph

attractive than older professors, revealing a bias toward youth. This societal perception remains pervasive, with youth typically seen as more attractive (Bargh, Chen, & Burrows, 1996; Zebrowitz, Olson, & Hoffman, 1993). Because attractiveness relates with higher teaching evaluations, older professors may suffer.

Of course cultural expectations of attractiveness across the lifespan differ for men and women. A youthful appearance among women is particularly valued, with younger women seen as more attractive than older women (Sarwer, Grossbart, & Didie, 2003). Although Wilson and colleagues (2014) found higher student ratings of attractiveness for younger professors, the effect was driven by ratings of female pictures. In an interaction, students rated younger female professors as more attractive than older female professors, but this effect was not seen for male professors. Based on these data, older female professors may experience the most bias in teaching evaluations if they are seen as unattractive by a society valuing youth.

Interestingly, even when beauty cannot be assessed, instructor age and gender influences student evaluations. Arbuckle and Williams (2003) showed students a computer-generated gender-neutral stick figure presenting a 35-minute lecture in a gender-neutral voice. They asked students to identify the stick figure as either male or female and old or young as well as evaluate the lecture. Of the four possible professor age/gender groups, when students perceived the stick figure as a young male professor, they rated the figure as speaking more enthusiastically and using a meaningful tone of voice.

The available literature suggests that instructor gender and age influence evaluations even when students have only a picture or a stick figure on which to base judgments. Researchers might argue that such studies have limited external validity. Conversely, classroom studies may fluctuate based on the ongoing, dynamic nature of professor-student interactions, reducing internal validity. In the current study, we provided photographs of professors as well as

additional classroom-related information in the form of a lecture. Students viewed photographs

of either a male or female professor who was either young or old, listened to and completed a

quiz on a brief lecture, and then rated the professors on attractiveness, effectiveness, and rapport.

Our hypotheses follow:

1. We expe
   effective
   age, than

2. We expe
   ratings o

3. Finally,
   instructo
   is enhanc

Participants

In this study,

participated. Our sar

minorities including

response to this dem

old (*SD* = 2.79). Our

psychology course,

instructor allowed cr

management system

received IRB approval prior to running the study and treated all students ethically. Of the

original 340 participants, 308 completed the entire survey and remained in the data set.

Materials

Materials consisted of two pictures of "instructors" chosen from a web search of publicly

available pictures. Digital alterations made both images appear older (i.e., wrinkles and lighter

hair color), for a total of four images. We used black-and-white, high-quality pictures of the head

and neck only.

For the lecture, participants heard a three-minute audio file about the history of Bedlam

Hospital in London. A 16-year-old boy prepared the audio file, and digital alteration increased

the sound frequency to create a gender-ambiguous audio that could feasibly represent both ages

and genders of "instructors." At the beginning of the Qualtrics survey, students read that they

would hear a file that was digitally altered. Thus, we explained the artificial sound of the file,

allowing students to "buy in" to the gender implied by the instructor's picture they viewed.

Before the lecture began, students read that they would be quizzed on lecture material. A 10-

item, true-false quiz assessed learning based on lecture content.

Students rated their perceptions of professor effectiveness using measures from both

Goebel and Cashen (1979) and Wilson and colleagues (2014). These included seven items of

teacher effectiveness, including the teacher encouraging questions, expecting good work,

assigning too much work, being organized, explaining concepts, behaving in a friendly manner

toward students, and overall being a good teacher. For each item, ratings ranged from 1-5, with 1

representing *Strongly Disagree*, 2 indicating *Disagree*, 3 rating *Neither Agree nor Disagree*, 4

representing *Agree*, and 5 indicating *Strongly Agree*. Based on prior research, we did not

consolidate these items but instead used them as separate measures of teacher effectiveness.

Students also completed the Brief Professor-Student Rapport Scale. The scale contains

six items that assess student perceptions of rapport with an instructor. Five-point ratings range

from *Strongly Disagree* to *Strongly Agree*; two of the items are reverse scored. We altered the

wording slightly by asking students to rate how they thought the professor in the picture *would*

behave rather than indicate how an existing professor did, in fact, behave. For example, "My

professor makes clas

brief version of the s

of rapport (Ryan &

including student mo

course, and learning

ratings in data analy

Students rate

you think this instru

Attractive. Students

item: "How old do y

Procedure

Participants

clicking the bottom

pictures randomized

or older adult woma

iconic Play button. I

altered. Instructions

the material immedi

After listening to the lecture and completing the quiz, students rated the seven professor

assessments used by Goebel and Cashen (1979) and Wilson and colleagues (2014). Next,

participants completed the Brief Professor-Student Rapport Scale. The picture remained above

the scale when completing ratings. On the next page, the picture again appeared at the top, and

students indicated perceived age of the instructor and attractiveness. Lastly, students provided

basic demographic information about themselves.

Results

Manipulation Check

We intended to create the impression of young versus old male and female professors.

Our manipulation check revealed that we created the intended perceptions based on a significant

difference between assume ages of professors, $F(1, 304) = 148.13, p < .001$, partial $\eta^2 = .33$.

Students rated the digitally-altered "older" pictures as older ($M = 43.49, SEM = 0.49, n = 151$)

than the unaltered "younger" pictures ($M = 35.46, SEM = 0.49, n = 157$). However, we also

noted that instructor gender influenced assumed age, $F(1, 304) = 17.99, p < .001$, partial $\eta^2 = .06$,

with men viewed as older ($M = 40.72, SEM = 0.55, n = 158$) than women ($M = 38.00, SEM = $

$0.61, n = 150$). Further, instructor gender and aging of pictures interacted to affect assumed age,

$F(1, 304) = 9.87, p = .002$, partial $\eta^2 = .03$. Students perceived the aged pictures to be older than

the younger pictures for both the male professor (M for old $= 43.86, SEM = 0.69, n = 76$; M for

young $= 37.82, SEM = 0.71, n = 82$) and the female professor (M for old $= 43.12, SEM = 0.70, n$

$= 75$; M for young $= 32.88, SEM = 0.53, n = 75$). Additionally, students guessed that the young

male professor was older than the young female professor. Pictures of the older male and female

instructors failed to differ ($p > .05$).

Collapsing Data

Although our manipulation check revealed that images altered to communicate an older

professor did cause students to estimate a higher age relative to the younger images, the

perceived ages differed by only 2.84 years based on variability within conditions. Further,

students perceived the male instructor to be older than the female instructor, particularly in

pictures intended to

similar in age. Beca

and perceived age re

2003), we divided p

instructor as up to 4

the entire data set).

Of the group

years old or younger

look older, 66 stude

less. Of female pictu

perceived age, with

than 40. Finally, 59

participants perceive

The final ana

perceiving an older

an older female prof

Primary Analysis

We analyzed these data using a 2 (gender of professor) X 2 (perceived age of professor),

between-groups MANOVA. Dependent variables of interest included seven items related to

teacher effectiveness as well as the Brief Professor-Student Rapport Scale (Wilson & Ryan,

2013), attractiveness rating, and quiz grades in percent correct.

Omnibus tests allowed us to further examine effects for gender of the instructor pictured,

perceived age of the instructor, and the interaction (below, all $p < .05$). Gender of the instructor

affected scores on student perceptions of the instructor's ability to explain material well, $F(1,$

$304) = 3.86$, $p = .05$, partial $\eta^2 = .01$, brief rapport $F(1, 304) = 12.54$, $p = .001$, partial $\eta^2 = .04$,

attractiveness, $F(1, 304) = 88.53$, $p < .001$, partial $\eta^2 = .23$, and quiz grades, $F(1, 304) = 4.30$, p

$= .039$, partial $\eta^2 = .01$. Regardless of perceived age, students rated the male instructor as better

at explaining the material ($M = 3.41$, $SEM = 0.08$) than the female instructor ($M = 3.16$, $SEM =$

0.09). However, students assumed more rapport with the female instructor ($M = 3.42$, $SEM =$

0.05) than the male instructor ($M = 3.17$, $SEM = 0.04$), and students rated her as more attractive

($M = 4.74$, $SEM = 0.10$) than the male instructor ($M = 3.48$, $SEM = 0.09$). Finally, students

earned higher grades on the lecture quiz when they viewed a female professor ($M = 59.04$, SEM

$= 1.27$) versus viewing a male professor ($M = 55.43$, $SEM = 1.19$).

Perceived age of the instructor, regardless of gender, affected student perceptions of

professor-student rapport, $F(1, 304) = 13.84$, $p = .001$, partial $\eta^2 = .04$, attractiveness, $F(1, 304) =$

19.21. $p = .001$, partial $\eta^2 = .06$, and quiz grades, $F(1, 304) = 7.79$, $p = .006$, partial $\eta^2 = .03$.

Students rated younger instructors as more attractive ($M = 4.40$, $SEM = 0.09$) than older

instructors ($M = 3.82$, $SEM = 0.10$) and assumed more rapport with the younger instructor ($M =$

3.23, $SEM = 0.05$) than the older instructor ($M = 2.93$, $SEM = 0.06$). Interestingly, students scored significantly higher on a quiz of the lecture material if they believe the lecture to come

from an older professor ($M = 59.66$, $SEM = 1.30$) versus a younger one ($M = 54.81$, $SEM =$

1.15).

An interaction between instructor gender and age further explained attractiveness and

quiz-grade, $F(1, 304) = 11.83$, $p = .001$, partial $\eta^2 = .04$, and $F(1, 304) = 4.93$, $p = .027$, partial η^2

$= .02$, respectively. /

the younger picture

$SEM = 0.15$). Rating

outcome, students e

woman ($M = 63.39$,

compared with the o

and female instructo

Our first hyp

study as more effect

supported. Of the se

serves as the cleares

in favor of male inst

professor would ear

this effect would no

hypothesis. Attractiv

effects for gender an

rapport), but these v

hypothesis that the younger female professor would inspire higher grades. In fact, participants

who perceived an older female professor scored higher on the quiz.

Students expect male professors to be effective in their work but expect female professors

to spend time building supportive relationships with students. According to Kierstead et al.

(1988), male professors earned better student evaluations if they demonstrated competence, but

students required female professors to demonstrate both competence and warmth to obtain the

same high ratings. Unfortunately, failure to behave as gender roles dictate (according to students)

results in greater hostility toward female professors, in particular (Sprague & Massoni, 2005),

and may also result in poorer evaluations. Professors who behave in a way to support

expectations receive higher student evaluations.

In our study, perhaps we can explain higher rapport ratings for female professors by

higher ratings of attractiveness. Goebel and Cashen (1979) found that students perceived more

attractive professors as friendlier, more encouraging, more organized, less likely to give too

much work, and better professors overall than unattractive professors. Perhaps people do not

expect women to be warm; instead, they expect attractive people to be warm. To test this

potential explanation, we examined the correlations between attractiveness and rapport based on

the female pictures, $r(148) = .24$, $p = .003$, and male pictures, $r(156) = .23$, $p = .003$, both of

which yielded significant relationships. However, these correlational values were in the weak-to-

moderate range. Certainly, attractiveness explains some variability in rapport, but we cannot say

with confidence that gender of the professor failed to further explain student ratings of rapport.

Likewise, students rated younger professors as more attractive and warmer (higher

rapport) than older professors. In fact, perceived age correlated negatively with rapport, $r(306) =$

$-.27$, $p < .001$, and ratings of attractiveness, $r(306) = -.31$, $p < .001$. These results align with societal norms. Lucăcel and Băban (2014) asked participants in their twenties about perceptions

on aging and found that the majority of people in their sample held a negative perception of old

age and the aging process. Similarly, individuals under 35 years do not believe that older people

can be as effective as younger workers (Abramson & Silverstein, 2004). Our study suggests that

students do not discard ageist attitudes at the classroom door. Students expect older professors to

be less effective teac

        In addition to

expected attractiven

Hamermesh and Par

However, we found

the lecture. This resu

the younger woman.

perceived to be over

        An older wor

work ethic. Students

Indeed, based on a s

scores for those perc

women than younge

although perceived a

.16, *p* = .006, this co

.27, *p* = .001. For ma

to reach significance

perceived age of the female professor, activating a schema for "mother" may explain higher

grades.

        Taken together, results of the current study reveal the impact of professor gender and age

on student evaluations of teaching and grades. As instructors, we would benefit from minimizing

potential negative effects reported here and maximizing benefits associated with professor

gender and age. For example, Legg and Wilson (2009) found that when students received an

emailed welcome message one week prior to the first day of class, motivation, attitudes toward

the instructor, and retention benefitted. Although students may be able to guess a professor's

gender based on a name, an email can attenuate the impact of age.

        Professors can also improve students' early impressions on the first day of class. For

example, professors might offer what students consider an "ideal" first day, which includes

covering the syllabus in a welcoming manner, avoiding homework, and ending class early.

Although some may argue that ending class early on the first sets a "lazy" tone for the remainder

of the course, Wilson and Wilson (2007) found that following students' wishes for the first day

of class improved both student motivation and end-of-term grades. As another first-day activity,

welcoming students by shaking hands increased ratings of instructor skill and ability to motivate

students (Wilson, Stadler, Schwartz, & Goff, 2009). We should caution that this effect occurred

for female professors only; for male professors, the opposite effect was seen. Certainly, many

approaches can enhance students' perceived effectiveness related to female instructors and

rapport related to male instructors as well as older professors.

        How does the current study inform the use of teaching evaluations for professor tenure,

promotion, raises, and awards? Traditional measures focus on student perceptions, not student

performance. As a result, older female professors may experience a disadvantage. The practice of

PROFESSOR AGE AND GENDER   17

rewarding or punishing faculty based on student evaluations may represent an unfair approach if

biases exist. In the case of the older female professor, she may embody a highly effective teacher

when helping students learn even if her teaching evaluations remain relatively low.

Potential Limitations and Suggestions for Future Research

A potential limitation in this study includes the fact that most students in our sample

attended an introduc

expectations of othe

bias, whether explic

D'Mello, & Sackett,

students beyond tho:

Students who

lecture. We recogniz

our external validity

heavily on perceptio

In the richness of cl:

social interactions, p

empirical study allow

information illustrat

tenure, promotion, r

students, discrimina

PROFESSOR AGE AND GENDER   18

References

Abramson, A., & Silverstein, M. (2004). *Images of aging in America 2004*. Retrieved December
    18, 2014, from http://assets.aarp.org/rgcenter/general/images_aging.pdf

Allport, G. W. (1954). *The nature of prejudice.* New York: Addison-Wesley.

Arbuckle, J., & Williams, B. D. (2003). Students' perceptions of expressiveness: Age and gender
    effects on teacher evaluations. *Sex Roles, 49*(9/10), 507-516. doi:
        10.1023/A:1025832707002

Bargh, J. A., Chen, M., & Burrows, L. (1996). Automaticity of social behavior: Direct effects of
    trait concept and stereotype activation on action. *Journal of Personality and Social
    Psychology, 71*(2), 230-244. http://dx.doi.org/10.1037/0022-3514.71.2.230

Bornstein, R. F. (1989). Exposure and affect: Overview and meta-analysis of research, 1968-
    1987. *Psychological Bulletin, 106,* 265-289. http://dx.doi.org/10.1037/0033-
    2909.106.2.265

Danziger, P. R., & Welfel, E. R. (2000). Age, gender, and health bias in counselors: An
    empirical analysis. *Journal of Mental Health Counseling, 22,* 135-149.

Dion, K. E., Berscheid, E. & Walster, E. (1972). What is beautiful is good. *Journal of
    Personality and Social Psychology, 24*(3), 285-290. http://dx.doi.org/10.1037/0033-
    2909.110.1.109

Ebert, I. D., Steffans, M. C., & Kroth, A. (2014). Warm, but maybe not to competent?–
    Contemporary implicit stereotypes of women and men in Germany. *Sex Roles, 70*(9-10),
    359-375. doi: 10.1007/s11199-014-0369-5

PROFESSOR AGE AND GENDER   19

Felton, J., Koper, P. T., Mitchell, J., & Stinson, M. (2008). Attractiveness, easiness, and other

   issues: Student evaluations of professors on Ratemyprofessors.com. *Assessment and*

   Evaluation in Higher Education, 33(1), 45-61. doi: 10.1080/02602930601122803

Felton, J., Mitchell, J., & Stinson, M. (2004). Web-based student evaluations of professors: The

   relations between perceived quality, easiness, and sexiness. *Assessment and Evaluation in*

   Higher Educ

Freng, S., & Webbe

   "hotness" ma

   10.1080/009

Goebel, B. L., & Ca

   of teachers:

   http://dx.doi.

Gurung, R. A. R., &

   learning. *Tea*

Hamermesh, D. S., &

   putative peda

   10.1016/j.ec

Horner, K. L., Murr

   teaching effe

   http://dx.doi.

Kierstead, D., D'Ag

   Bias in stude

   344. http://d

PROFESSOR AGE AND GENDER   20

Kock, A. J., D'Mello, S. D., & Sackett, P. R. (2015). A meta-analysis of gender stereotypes and

   bias in experimental simulations of employment decision making. *Journal of Applied*

   Psychology, 100(1), 128-161. http://dx.doiorg/10.1037/a0036734

Legg, A. M., & Wilson, J. H. (2009). Email from professor enhances student motivation and

   attitudes. *Teaching of Psychology, 36*, 205-211. doi: 10.1080/00986280902960034

Löckenhoff, C. E., Chan, W., McCrae, R. R., De Fruyt, F., Jussim, L., De Bolle, M., …

   Terracciano, A. (2014). Gender stereotypes of personality: Universal and accurate?

   Journal of Cross-Cultural Psychology, 45(5), 675-694. doi: 10.1177/0022022113520075

Lucăcel, R., & Băban, A. (2014). Young peoples' perspective regarding aging. *Cognition, Brain,*

   Behavior. An International Journal, 18(2), 151-161.

Marsh, H. W., & Roche, L. A. (1997). Making student evaluations of teaching effectiveness

   effective: The critical issues of validity, bias, and utility. *American Psychologist, 52*(11),

   1187-1197. http://dx.doi.org/10.1037/0003-066X.52.11.1187

Remedios, R., & Lieberman, D. A. (2008). I liked your course because you taught me well: The

   influence of grades, workload, expectations, and goals on students' evaluations of

   teaching. *British Educational Research Journal, 34*(1), 91-115. doi:

   10.1080/01411920701492043

Riniolo, T. C., Johnson, K. C., Sherman, T. R., & Misso, J. A. (2006). Hot or not: Do professors

   perceived as physically attractive receive higher student evaluations? *The Journal of*

   General Psychology, 133(1), 19-35. doi: 10.3200/GENP.133.1.19-35

Ryan, R., & Wilson, J. H. (2014). Professor-Student Rapport Scale: Psychometric properties of

   the brief version. *Journal of the Scholarship of Teaching and Learning, 14*(3), 64-74.

PROFESSOR AGE AND GENDER   21

Sarwer, D. B., Grossbart, T. A., & Didie, E. R. (2003). Beauty and society. *Seminars in*

Cutaneous Medicine and Surgery, 22(2), 79-92.

Sprague, J., & Massoni, K. (2005). Student evaluations and gendered expectations: What we

can't count can hurt us. *Sex Roles, 53*(11/12), 779-793. doi: 10.1007/s11199-005-8292-4

Wilson, J. H., Beyer, D., & Monteiro, H. (2014). Professor age affects student ratings: Halo

effect for you

10.1080/875

Wilson, J. H., Stadle

The impact c

Teaching an

Wilson, J. H., & Rya

outcomes. *Te*

Wilson, J. H., & Wil

experimental

10.1080/009

Zajonc, R. B. (1968)

Psychology l

Zebrowitz, L. A., Ol

across the lif

http://dx.doi.

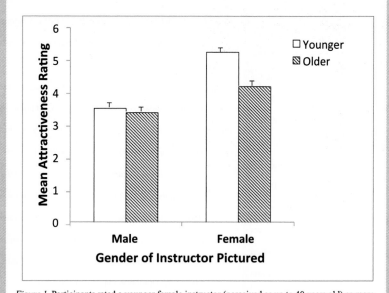

Figure 1. Participants rated a younger female instructor (perceived as up to 40 years old) as more

attractive than an older version of the same instructor. Perceptions of male instructors did not

differ based on age. Error bars represent *SEM.*

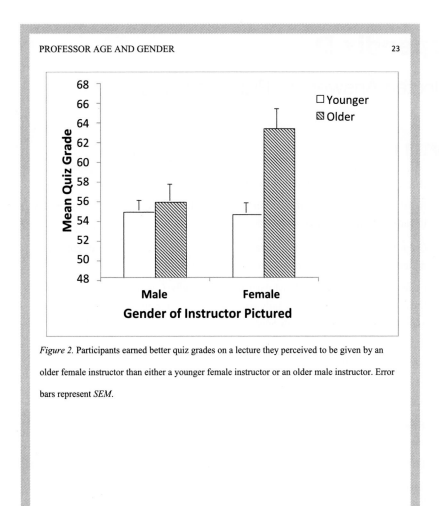

PROFESSOR AGE AND GENDER   23

Figure 2. Participants earned better quiz grades on a lecture they perceived to be given by an

older female instructor than either a younger female instructor or an older male instructor. Error

bars represent *SEM*.

Source: Wilson, J. H., & Wilson, S. B. (2007). Methods and techniques: The first day of class affects student motivation: An experimental study. *Teaching of Psychology, 34,* 226–230.

Appendix D

Selected Answers to Practice Items

CHAPTER 1

1. a. *Ask a question.* State what it is I want to know.

   b. *Read the published literature.* Conduct a literature review of everything related to aspects of my research question.

   c. *Create a method.* Choose my variables as well as figure out how I am going to define them and how I can test my research question.

   d. *Collect and analyze data.* Treat participants ethically. Consistently test participants the same way to avoid accidentally affecting outcomes. Enter data regularly, and analyze data using appropriate statistics.

   e. *Answer the research question.* Refer to outcomes from statistical analysis, and write the result in APA style.

   f. *Share my results.* Present my research at conferences and publish results when possible.

3. a. Research question: *Are people less likely to give money to charity as their income increases?*

      Testable hypothesis: *People are less likely to give to charity as their income increases.*

   b. Research question: *Do people over age 65 give better advice than adults between 25 and 35 years old?*

      Testable hypothesis: *People over age 65 give better advice than adults between 25 and 35 years old.*

   c. Research question: *Will grocery sales show a higher percentage of fatty foods purchased than healthier foods?*

      Testable hypothesis: *Grocery sales will show a higher percentage of fatty foods purchased than healthier foods.*

   d. Research question: *Compared to adults, will children be less able to resist consuming a dessert when they are urged to avoid eating?*

      Testable hypothesis: *Compared to adults, children will be less able to resist consuming a dessert even when they are urged to avoid eating.*

e. Research question: *Will people report that a shorter amount of time has passed when they work on a puzzle than when they sit in silence?*

Testable hypothesis: *People will report that a shorter amount of time has passed when they work on a puzzle than when they sit in silence.*

5. If you use a script, you will not forget parts of the procedure or accidentally explain instructions differently across participants.

7. a. Participants counted to 100 before opening their eyes.

b. While participants completed the informed consent, the researcher remained available for questions.

c. Six instructors appreciated their students.

CHAPTER 2

1. *Respect for Persons:* Treat all individuals with respect, and inform them of the study prior to participation so they can choose whether to participate.

Beneficence: Conduct only studies that have the potential to add to the scientific literature without causing undue harm to participants.

Justice: Make sure all people in a study are impacted both negatively and positively in the same manner.

3. a. Asking participants to rate the attractiveness of women in magazines

b. Asking participants to complete a puzzle

e. Asking participants to take a quiz on lecture material

5. If a researcher does not know how to analyze data from a study, the researcher has wasted participants' time and valuable research resources. Also, lack of an analysis section indicates that the researcher has not carefully considered how the research question will be answered.

7. When data are anonymous, participants' answers are in no way linked with any identifying information. When data are confidential, the researcher knows individuals' answers but keeps that information a secret to protect their identity.

9. Participants can give consent to participate if they are 18 years old or older unless they are in a special population requiring consent from a caretaker.

11. c. The student signs up for the experiment but arrives 30 minutes late, and you do not have time to test the participant.

13. Without the research mentor, you most likely would not have been able to conduct the research.

CHAPTER 3

1. In a correlational study, no variables are manipulated, and we generally cannot learn cause and effect. In an experiment, at least one variable is manipulated, and we have an opportunity to learn cause and effect.

3. a. IV: Type of video
   b. Levels of the IV: Sad and funny
   c. DV: Weight of ice cream in the bowl

5. Random assignment to conditions generally reduces extraneous variables to nuisance variables.

7. The four levels of measurement for variables are nominal, ordinal, interval, and ratio.

9. a. $M = 32.25$, $SD = 6.65$
   b. $Mdn = 94.5$, Range = 21 to 102 (Note that 21 is an outlier, requiring the median and range to describe the sample.)
   c. Mode = Sunny (Note that no measure of variability exists for nominal data.)
   d. $Mdn = $ 4th place, Range = 2nd to 8th place
   e. $M = 6.11$, $SD = 1.76$
   f. Mode = Female (No measure of variability exists for nominal data.)

CHAPTER 4

1. Random sampling occurs when everyone in the population has an equal chance of participating in the study, whereas random assignment refers to the way participants are assigned to groups after they are already in the study.

3. In simple random sampling, everyone in the population of interest could be in my sample. In convenience sampling, I draw from a readily accessible sample that belongs to the population of interest.

5. a. Simple random sampling
   b. Quota sampling
   c. Convenience sampling

7. Percentage is probability multiplied by 100. In inferential statistics, researchers tend to use probabilities to communicate findings.

9. In general, parametric statistics analyze interval or ratio data, whereas nonparametric statistics analyze nominal or ordinal data. Parametric statistics are

preferable to nonparametric statistics because the former will be more likely to reveal a significant outcome, if one exists.

11. Type I error is "accidentally" finding a significant effect when one does not truly exist. Type II error is failing to find a significant effect when one actually exists.

13. Effect size is reported when we find a significant result using our chosen p-value (usually .05). Effect size tells us how strong our results are and allows readers to decide if an outcome is meaningful. Depending on the statistical test, the numbers associated with weak, moderate, and strong effects differ.

CHAPTER 5

1. Expected frequency refers to how many people you expect to fall in a specific category in a study. Observed frequency is how many people *actually* fall in a specific category.

3. You must expect at least five people per category. It is ok if you *observe* fewer than five as long as you *expected* at least five per cell.

5. An effect size of .10 is small, .30 is medium, and .50 or beyond is a large effect.

7. a. Research hypothesis: *My sample of people who were put on a healthy diet and exercise program will show lower rates of heart disease than the overall U.S. population.* Null hypothesis: *My sample of people who were put on a healthy diet and exercise program will show the same rates of heart disease as the overall U.S. population.*

   b. Number of participants needed to find a medium effect size with 1 df: 88.

   c. Sample APA-style results:

Results

We used a one-way χ^2 to analyze the data. Observations differed significantly from expectations, $\chi^2(1, N = 116) = 9.97, p = .002, w = .29$. Although we expected 50.00% of participants to have signs of heart disease, only 35.34% did.

---

9. a. Research hypothesis: *The pattern of smoking cessation for women will differ for couples who live apart compared with couples living together.* Null hypothesis: *The pattern of smoking cessation for women will be the same for couples who live apart as for couples living together.*

   b. Number of participants needed to find a medium effect size with 2 df: 108.

c. Information needed for the results section:

$\chi^2(2, N = 120) = 15.96, p < .001, w = .36$

Expected frequencies: partner also quit = 67.00%, partner was a nonsmoker = 23.00%, partner kept smoking = 10.00%

Observed frequencies: partner also quit = 60.00%, partner was a nonsmoker = 36.67%, partner kept smoking = 3.33%

CHAPTER 6

1. A one-way χ^2 compares observed frequencies with what was expected in the normal population. A two-way χ^2 examines the potential relationship between two variables.

3. a. 2 (male versus female) × 2 (promoted or not promoted)

   b. Research hypothesis: *Among children exposed to lead, gender is related to whether children are promoted to first grade.* Null hypothesis: *Among children exposed to lead, gender is not related to whether children are promoted to first grade.*

   c. Number of participants needed to find a medium effect size with 1 *df*: 88.

   d. Sample results section:

Results

We analyzed these data using a 2 (boys, girls) X 2 (promoted, not promoted) χ^2. Gender of the children failed to relate with whether or not they moved to the first grade, $\chi^2(1, N = 137) = .01, p = .945$. Among girls, 90.7% were promoted. Among boys, 90.3% were promoted.

---

5. a. 3 (excited, anxious, or legendary) × 3 (terrible, okay, or wonderful)

   b. Research hypothesis: *Positive self-talk relates with singing performance.* Null hypothesis: *Positive self-talk does not relate with singing performance.*

   c. Number of participants needed to find a large effect size with 4 *df*: 48

   d. $\chi^2(4, N = 63) = 3.70, p = .448$

   - Percentages for excited: 20.8% terrible, 29.2% average, 50.0% wonderful
   - Percentages for anxious: 42.1% terrible, 31.6% average, 26.3% wonderful
   - Percentages for legendary: 25.0% terrible, 25.0% average, 50.0% wonderful

CHAPTER 7

1. A study design with two variables and simple frequency data is analyzed with the two-way χ^2. A study design with two interval or ratio variables is analyzed using Pearson's r.

3. a. Negative relationship

   b. Positive relationship

   c. No relationship

5. You subtract two from the total number of participants ($df = N - 2$).

7. For Pearson's r, the coefficient of determination indicates effect size. To calculate effect size, square the r-value.

9. a. Research hypothesis (two-tailed test): *Among people with high anxiety, amount of sleep relates to attention.* Null hypothesis: *Among people with high anxiety, amount of sleep and attention are not related.*

   b. No obvious problems exist in the data set.

   c. The number of participants needed to find a medium effect size is 85.

   d. Sample results write-up:

Results

We relied on a two-tailed Pearson's r to analyze the potential relationship between sleep and attention. In the overall sample, hours of sleep related with attention, $r(34) = .74$, $p < .001$, $r^2 = .55$. Students reported a mean of 7.76 sleep hours ($SD = 1.64$) and a mean of 75.08 ($SD = 15.58$) on the attention task.

---

11. a. Research hypothesis (one-tailed test): *Agreeableness is related to number of hours worked such that more agreeableness is related to more hours worked.* Null hypothesis: *Agreeableness is not related to number of hours worked.*

    b. An examination of the scatterplot of the data appears to show no clear relationship, though we will still run Pearson's r to make sure. The data set contains no obvious outliers.

    c. The number of participants needed to find a medium effect size is 85.

    d. $r(34) = .01$, $p = .479$, Hours ($M = 26.11$, $SD = 10.12$), Agreeableness ($M = 28.50$, $SD = 9.39$)

CHAPTER 8

1. Established measures are those that have been used by other researchers and shown to be both reliable (you get the same value each time you use it) and valid (measuring the construct of interest). Testing the psychometrics of a measure takes several steps. If you create your own measure, you cannot be sure that it is both reliable and valid.

3. a. **Test-Retest Reliability.** Two administrations of the same measure give researchers similar scores. A Pearson's r of at least .70 is acceptable, though higher is better.

   b. **Alternate-Forms Reliability.** Administrations of two different forms of the same test give researchers similar scores. A Pearson's r of at least .70 is acceptable, though higher is better.

   c. **Split-Half Reliability.** When you randomly select groups of items in the same test, they are highly correlated. A Pearson's r of at least .70 is acceptable, though higher is better.

   d. **Internal Consistency Reliability.** This type of reliability tells us whether items in a scale measure the same construct. Typically, we use Cronbach's alpha, which is based on all possible split-half estimates. A Cronbach's alpha of at least .70 is acceptable, though higher is better.

   e. **Interrater Reliability.** When two researchers measure the same subjective variable, they obtain similar scores. A Pearson's r of at least .70 is acceptable, though higher is better, and most researchers try to get at least a .90.

5. Lara's new measure of creativity shows good test-retest reliability ($r = .98$).

7. Chas's music test shows adequate split-half reliability ($r = .84$).

9. Pete and Gorbe have good inter-rater reliability ($r = .94$).

11. The PHAT does not show acceptable predictive validity for how many albums an artist will sell ($r = -.08$).

CHAPTER 9

1. A correlation analysis tells us if pairs of variables are related. If variables are not related, we have no reason to try to predict a variable.

3. Very rarely do we hypothesize a situation in which one variable is the only component that predicts another variable. More often, the picture is complex, with multiple predictor variables influencing an outcome.

5. a. Research hypothesis: *Scores on a pre-employment test of job skills will predict one-year job performance scores.* Null hypothesis: *Scores on a pre-employment test of job skills will not predict one-year job performance scores.*

   b. For adequate power, we need 55 participants.

   c. Sample results write-up:

Results

We correlated pre-employment job skills ($M = 83.00$, $SD = 11.60$) with job performance at 1 year of employment ($M = 40.92$, $SD = 6.59$). These two variables failed to relate, $r(22) = .27$, $p = .206$. Therefore we abandoned prediction of job performance from pre-employment job skills.

---

7. a. Research hypothesis: *We can predict happiness based on number of positive and negative text messages people receive.* Null hypothesis: *We cannot predict happiness based on number of positive and negative text messages people receive.*

   b. For adequate power, we need 68 participants.

   c. Data needed for results section:

   - Number of positive messages: $M = 4.94$, $SD = 3.18$
   - Number of negative messages: $M = 4.94$, $SD = 3.18$
   - Happiness: $M = 57.09$, $SD = 22.15$
   - Bivariate correlations:
     - Positive with negative messages, $r(32) = -.20$, $p = .269$
     - Positive messages with happiness, $r(32) = .13$, $p = .476$
     - Negative messages with happiness, $r(32) = -.12$, $p = .501$
     - None of the bivariate correlations were significant. With no meaningful overlap between pairs of variables, prediction is not logical. The predictors as a group fail to predict the outcome: $F(2, 31) = .40$, $p = .672$

CHAPTER 10

1. Gender, Hair Color, Age

3. When we have different people in the levels of our IV or quasi-IV, we call this an independent-samples design.

5. For the independent-samples t-test, df is calculated by subtracting 2 from the total sample size ($N - 2$).

7. To adjust for a one-tailed t-test, we divide the SPSS p-value provided by two.

9. Visual inspection of data usually indicates the existence of an outlier. Regardless of your approach to identify outliers, removing an outlier from a specific group requires it to be 3 SD from the mean for that group.

11. a. Research hypothesis (one-tailed test): *College students who do their own math homework will score higher on their final exams than those who have help.* Null hypothesis: *College students who do their own math homework will score the same on their final exams as those who have help.*

   b. For adequate power, we needed 128 participants.

   c. Sample results write-up:

Results

We used a one-tailed, independent-samples t-test to analyze these data. Whether students had help with the algebra homework failed to affect their score on the final exam, $t(40) = -.38$, $p = .353$. Those who completed their math homework at home scored similarly on the final ($M = 78.43$, $SD = 12.15$, $n = 21$) as those who completed their math homework at the tutoring center ($M = 79.81$, $SD = 11.34$, $n = 21$).

---

13. a. Research hypothesis (one-tailed test): *The use of Snapchat during a social outing will reduce memory of the event.* Null hypothesis: *The use of Snapchat during a social outing will not affect memory of the event.*

   b. For adequate power, we need 128 participants.

   c. Data needed for results section:

   - Picture: $M = 5.68$, $SD = 3.44$, $n = 22$

   - No picture: $M = 7.63$, $SD = 3.77$, $n = 24$

   - $t(44) = -1.82$, $p = .038$, CI $[-4.10, .21]$, Cohen's $d = -.54$

CHAPTER 11

1. Tukey's and Least Squares Difference (LSD) are both acceptable choices for the one-way, between-groups ANOVA. Tukey's is a slightly more conservative option than LSD, meaning that Tukey's post hoc comparisons will be slightly less likely to reveal a significant outcome, if one exists.

3. An η^2 of about .01 is considered small, .06 is moderate, and anything around or above .13 is considered a large effect.

5. Whether an IV is "true" or "quasi" makes no difference in how it is handled in SPSS. The way we interpret the data will vary depending on whether an IV is true or quasi.

7. SPSS provides 95% CIs for each difference between pairs of group means. The CIs provide the same information that the independent-samples t-test offers (see Chapter 10). In SPSS, ANOVA also allows a second set of CIs. We can choose Options and Descriptive statistics to obtain 95% CIs for each individual group mean. CIs surrounding individual group means are generally easier to understand than mean differences.

9. a. Research hypothesis: *People will differ in happiness after a commute based on different types of interactions with others.* Null hypothesis: *People will not differ in happiness after a commute based on different types of interactions with others.*

   b. For adequate power, we need 159 participants.

   c. Sample results write-up:

Results

We analyzed these data using a one-way, between-groups ANOVA. Tukey's post hoc group comparisons further analyzed a significant effect ($p < .05$). Whether a person spoke with a friend or stranger on a commute or sat in silence related to happiness, $F(2, 42) = 4.75$, $p = .014$, partial $\eta^2 = .18$. As shown in Figure 1, participants who spoke with a friend during their commute ($M = 3.63$, $SD = 2.09$, $n = 16$) and those who spoke with a stranger ($M = 3.57$, $SD = 2.14$, $n = 14$) reported more happiness than those who sat in silence ($M = 1.73$, $SD = 1.44$, $n = 15$). Happiness of those who spoke with a friend during their commute failed to differ from happiness of those who spoke with a stranger. The 95% CI for talking with a stranger, talking with a friend, and sitting in silence reflected limits of [2.54, 4.61], [2.66, 4.59], and [0.74, 2.73], respectively.

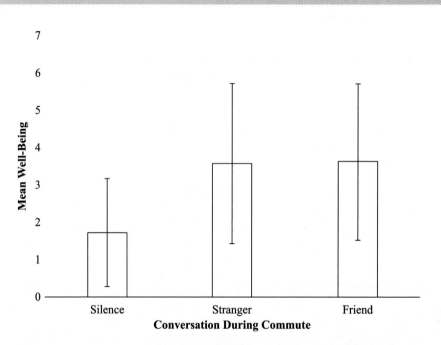

Figure 1. Conversation during a commute related to happiness. Participants who spoke with a friend reported more happiness than those who sat in silence. Error bars represent *SD*.

CHAPTER 12

1. An independent-samples design collects data from people in levels of the IV or quasi-IV that are in no way related. A related-samples design collects data from people related in some way prior to entering the study, such as siblings or people matched on an important variable, or the same people tested twice.

3. • An order effect happens when people are influenced during the study by levels of the IV they have already experienced.

   ○ Practice effect: Completing a DV the first time allows practice and may improve performance.

   ○ Fatigue effect: Participants get tired or bored across a repeated assessment, and their performance on the DV may suffer.

   • History effect: Participants change due to anything that occurs across the study.

   • Maturation: People age and change over time and may somehow respond differently to the DV based on factors other than the IV levels.

- As a way to work toward "solving" these problems, researchers can counterbalance the order of IV levels, meaning they randomly assign people to the order of exposure to levels of the IV whenever possible.

5. The effect size for the paired-samples *t*-test is Cohen's *d*. A Cohen's *d* of approximately .20 is considered a weak effect size, .50 is a moderate effect size, and .80 is a strong effect size.

7. a. Research hypothesis (one-tailed test): *Horseback riding reduces impairment among high-school-age teens with ASD*. Null hypothesis: *Horseback riding does not affect impairment among high-school-age teens with ASD*.

   b. For adequate power, we need 34 participants.

   c. Sample results write-up:

Results

We analyzed these data using a directional, paired-samples *t*-test. High-school teens with ASD rated their impairment lower after a 6-week horseback riding course, $t(15) = 2.26$, $p = .020$, 95% CI [0.06, 2.19], $d = .56$. Students reported lower preintervention impairment ($M = 4.06$, $SD = 1.81$) than at postintervention ($M = 2.94$, $SD = 1.53$).

CHAPTER 13

1. Several problems can occur if we do not vary the order of IV exposure in a repeated-measures design, including practice effects, fatigue, and history effects or maturation. Counterbalancing the order of IV levels helps change potential confounds to nuisance variables.

3. When an IV has more than two levels, Mauchly's test of sphericity tells us whether the variability in pair differences across two levels of a factor is similar to the variability in pair differences across the other levels of the factor. To use this test when interpreting SPSS output, check the *p*-value associated with Mauchly's test of sphericity. If $p > .05$, then we have not violated sphericity and we can move forward interpreting the first line of SPSS output on the Tests of Within-Subjects Effects table (sphericity assumed). If $p \leq .05$, then we have violated sphericity and have to use an alternative output line when reporting the data.

5. In *t*-tests, we are comparing only two groups, so if we find a difference, we already know it is between the two groups. In ANOVAs, we usually have more than two groups, and although the significant *F*-value tells us that at least two groups differ, we do yet not know specifically which groups differ. A significant *F*-value requires follow-up mean comparisons.

7. a. Research hypothesis: *Some types of bullying in high school are perceived as more harmful than others.* Null hypothesis: *Different types of bullying in high school are perceived as similar in harmfulness.*

    b. For adequate power, we need only 30 participants because they will be tested repeatedly.

    c. Sample results write-up:

Results

We analyzed these data using a one-way, repeated-measures ANOVA. We further analyzed a significant effect using LSD mean comparisons ($p < .05$). Type of bullying affected perceived ability to cause harm, $F(2, 18) = 6.04$, $p = .010$, partial $\eta^2 = .40$. As shown in Figure 1, students perceived covert bullying ($M = 7.30$, $SD = 2.26$) as more harmful than either physical bullying ($M = 5.70$, $SD = 2.36$) or verbal bullying ($M = 5.80$, $SD = 2.90$). Perceptions of physical bulling failed to differ from perceptions of verbal bullying. The 95% CI for physical, verbal, and covert bullying reflected limits of [4.01, 7.39], [3.73, 7.87], and [5.68, 8.92], respectively.

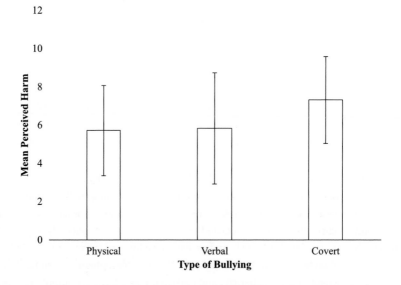

Figure 1. Type of bullying affected perceived ability to cause harm. Students perceived covert bullying as worse than either physical or verbal bullying. Error bars represent *SD*.

CHAPTER 14

1. A one-way design has one IV or quasi-IV. A two-way design has two IVs or quasi-IVs.

3. With a two-way ANOVA, we learn (a) whether differences exist between the levels of one factor, (b) whether differences exist between the levels of the second factor, and (c) whether the two factors interact to affect the DV (or relate to the DV if a variable is not manipulated).

5. A partial η^2 of .01 is considered small, .06 is moderate, and anything around or above .13 is considered a large effect.

7. a. A two-way design has three sets of hypotheses:

   - Research hypothesis (main effect for gender): *Gender relates to aggression after an insult.* Null hypothesis: *Gender does not relate to aggression after insult.*

   - Research hypothesis (main effect for region of birth): *Location of upbringing relates to aggression after insult.* Null hypothesis: *Location of upbringing does not relate to aggression after insult.*

   - Research hypothesis (interaction): *Gender and location of upbringing interact to relate to aggression after insult.* Null hypothesis: *Gender and location of upbringing do not interact to relate to aggression after insult.*

   b. For adequate power for the main effect of location of upbringing, we need 159 participants; for main effect of gender, we need 128 participants; and for the interaction, we need 211 participants.

   c. Sample results write-up:

Results

We analyzed these data using a 2 (male, female) X 3 (South, North, Midwest), between-groups ANOVA, and we relied on LSD comparisons for post hoc analysis of location ($p < .05$). Location of upbringing related to aggression, $F(2, 54) = 4.93$, $p = .011$, partial $\eta^2 = .15$. Gender failed to relate to aggression, $F(1, 54) = 1.98$, $p = .165$. Women ($M = 5.10$, $SD = 2.83$, $n = 30$) and men ($M = 6.00$, $SD = 2.56$, $n = 30$) showed similar levels of aggression. As seen in Figure 1, participants raised in the Midwest ($M = 4.15$, $SD = 2.62$, $n = 20$) evidenced lower aggression than those from the North ($M = 6.05$, $SD = 2.56$, $n = 20$) and the South ($M = 6.45$, $SD = 2.50$, $n = 20$). Participants from the North and South showed similar levels of aggression ($p > .05$). The 95% CI for participants raised in the North, South, and Midwest ranged between [4.94, 7.16], [5.34, 7.56], and [3.04, 5.26], respectively. Gender and location of upbringing failed to interact to relate to aggression $F(2, 54) = 2.58$, $p = .085$.

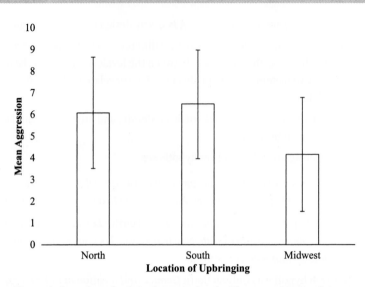

Figure 1. Location of upbringing associated with aggression. Participants from the Midwest exhibited less aggression than participants from the North or South. Error bars represent *SD*.

Appendix E

Glossary of Terms

Active Deception. Active deception refers to deliberately telling participants a lie during a study.

Alternate-Forms Reliability (Paralled-Forms Reliability). Alternate-forms reliability is established when two different versions of a measure result in similar numbers across two administrations.

Analysis of Variance (ANOVA). ANOVA is the statistical test used when a variable has two or more levels but usually is reserved for three or more levels of a variable. The outcome for ANOVA is an interval or ratio DV.

Anchors. On a rating scale, anchors are descriptions given to the numbers.

Anonymous. In research, participants are anonymous if the data do not reflect identity in any way.

Archival Data. Data collected and stored prior to the beginning of the study are called archival data.

Assent. Assent involves requesting permission for participation from someone in a special population. The person's caregiver must first provide consent.

Attrition. Attrition defines the loss of participants during a study. Studies with high attrition rates do not have strong external validity because those who drop out of the study might be different from those who remain in the study.

Between Groups. When we have different people in the levels of a factor, we have a between-groups design.

Between-Groups *t*-test. See *independent-samples* t-test.

Bias. When a study contains bias, results are inaccurate due to influences beyond the study variables.

Blind to Conditions (Scoring Blind). Whenever possible, researchers should collect or analyze data without knowing which level of the factor each participant experienced. This approach is called being blind to conditions. Scoring blind reduces the chance for researcher bias because the researcher has no idea which level of the factor is being assessed.

Block Random Assignment. Block random assignment is a procedure in which a participant is randomly assigned to one of the IV levels, and then the next participant is assigned to one of the remaining levels, and so forth, until all levels have been assigned once. Only after every level of the IV has been used do all IV levels become available again.

Carryover Effects. See *order effects*.

Cells. Cells are the boxes of data represented in a two-way design. For example, a 2×3 design contains six cells.

Chi Square (χ^2). Chi square is the statistic used to analyze simple frequency data, often defined by how many participants fall in a specific category.

Cluster Sampling. In cluster sampling, researchers find a way to put people into groups (or clusters) and randomly choose from the groups. This procedure is a way to randomly sample from the population more efficiently.

Coefficient of Determination. The coefficient of determination is the number that indicates the effect size of a significant *r*-value. To calculate the coefficient of determination, square the *r*-value.

Coercion. Coercion occurs when participants feel pressured to become involved in a study.

Cohen's *d*. When an independent-samples *t*-test is significant, we calculate effect size using Cohen's *d*.

Cohen's f^2. When variables significantly predict an outcome, effect size is quantified with Cohen's f^2.

Cohen's *w*. When a one-way χ^2 shows a significant relationship, Cohen's *w* provides a measure of effect size.

Cohort. A group of participants with something in common, such as attending the first grade together, is called a cohort.

Conditions. See *levels*.

Confederate. A confederate is a researcher who interacts with participants and pretends not to be a researcher.

Confidence Interval (CI). A confidence interval is a range of values that would contain the true population data a certain percentage of the time.

Confidence Limits. Confidence limits refer to the lower and upper values of a confidence interval.

Confidentiality. Confidentiality is achieved when participants' data remain a secret with the researcher(s).

Confound. See *confounding variable*.

Confounding Variable (Confound). An extraneous variable that changes along with levels of the IV is called a confounding variable. This type of variable causes studies to be flawed.

Construct. The concept you are interested in measuring is called a construct.

Content Validity. When evaluating content validity, researchers examine items to ensure that all aspects of the construct are represented. Content validity is based on logical thinking rather than a statistic.

Contingency Coefficient (C). When a two-way χ^2 shows a significant relationship, the contingency coefficient provides a measure of effect size for any design larger than a 2×2.

Control Group. A control group is an optional level of the IV in which participants are not manipulated but still complete the DV measure. A control group provides a comparison condition for the manipulated group(s).

Convenience Sampling. This sampling procedure is used most often in research and includes selecting a sample from the most available group that is part of the population of interest.

Convergent Construct Validity. When a measure of interest correlates with a similar or opposite measure of the construct, it is said to have good convergent validity. The correlation can be positive (with a similar measure) or negative (with an opposite measure), as long as the value is strong.

Correlation Coefficient. See *Pearson's* r.

Correlation Matrix. When more than two variables are in a correlational analysis, a correlation matrix provides data on all intercorrelations.

Correlational Design. See *correlational study*.

Correlational Study (Correlational Design). A type of study in which no variables are manipulated is called a correlational study. This type of research design explores relationships between existing variables.

Counterbalancing. Counterbalancing is accomplished by randomly assigning people to order of IV levels. This technique defends against order effects, history effects, and maturation.

Cramer's V. When a χ^2 design larger than a 2×2 reveals a significant outcome, Cramer's V provides a measure of effect size that is slightly less conservative than the contingency coefficient.

Criterion Variable. A criterion variable is an outcome predicted from another variable or variables.

Critical Region. In a graph of the normal population, the critical region is where values fall when they are considered truly different from normal.

Cronbach's alpha (α). Cronbach's alpha is a measure of a scale's reliability based on all possible split-half estimates.

Cross-Sectional Study. A cross-sectional study involves collecting data across several cohorts at one time. Researchers learn what might occur across a longer period of time for one cohort, but data collection is faster than it is with a longitudinal study.

Curvilinear Relationship. When the graph of a relationship is curved rather than a line, we call it a curvilinear relationship.

Debriefing. Debriefing entails telling participants about active deception at the end of a study.

Deception. Deception can be active or passive and occurs when the true nature or purpose of a study is concealed.

Degrees of Freedom (*df*). The number of values free to vary in a data set is termed the degrees of freedom. The *df* are needed when analyzing data using inferential statistics and reporting outcomes in APA style.

Dependent Variable (DV). A DV is the outcome variable in an experiment. The DV is free to vary across all levels of the IV.

Dependent-Samples Design. See *related-samples design*.

Differential Attrition. Differential attrition occurs when people in one level of a study drop out at a higher or lower rate than participants in the other level(s) of a study.

Directional Test (One-Tailed Test). If we have a specific idea (hypothesis) of whether the relationship will be positive or negative, we have a directional or one-tailed test.

Discriminant Construct Validity. When a measure of interest does not correlate with a measure of a logically unrelated construct, it is said to have discriminant validity.

Effect Size. Effect size refers to the strength of a significant effect.

Empirical. Empirical refers to observable or measureable behaviors.

Eta Squared (η^2). Eta squared is the effect size associated with ANOVA. SPSS offers partial η^2, which is not a problem because both measures of effect size yield the same value for a one-way ANOVA.

Ethics Training. Ethics training involves education on how to protect participants and conduct ethical research.

Expected Frequency. The number of people expected to fall in a category of a variable defines expected frequency.

Experiment (Experimental Design, Experimental Study). An experiment is a type of study in which at least one variable is manipulated (the IV), and one variable is measured as an outcome (DV).

Experimental Design. See *experiment*.

Experimental Study. See *experiment*.

External Validity. The extent to which study results can be generalized to other settings and groups is called external validity.

Extraneous Variable. Variables that introduce some type of variability in the data set that is not the focus of the study are called extraneous.

***F*-value**. *F* symbolizes the statistical outcome of ANOVA and is the symbol used to represent the statistic in an APA-style results section.

Face Validity. When items of a measure appear to assess the construct of interest, items have face validity. Face validity is based on logical thinking rather than a statistic.

Factor. In ANOVA, we refer to the IV or the quasi-IV as a factor.

Falsifiable. A hypothesis is falsifiable when it has been written in such a way that it can be tested and found either true or false.

Fatigue Effect. A specific type of order effect is fatigue. When participants get tired or bored across a repeated assessment, their performance on the DV may suffer, revealing a fatigue effect. After the first condition is experienced, and the DV is completed the first time, motivation and energy may decrease.

Fishing. When researchers "fish" in the data, they have no specific hypothesis or analysis in mind.

Generalizability. The extent to which results from a sample can be reasonably applied beyond the specific sample in the study indicates generalizability and reflects external validity.

Goodness-of-Fit Test. See *one-way* χ^2.

Groups. See *levels*.

History Effect. A history effect occurs when participants change due to anything that occurs across the study. A historical event between exposure to the two IV levels can alter outcomes on the second level.

Homogeneity of Variance. An approximately equal amount of variability in the DV across groups is termed homogeneity of variance.

Hypothesis. A specific testable question that addresses some part of a theory is called a hypothesis.

Independent Variable (IV). An IV is the manipulated variable in an experiment.

Independent-Samples Design. When we have different people in levels of our IV or quasi-IV (meaning that each person is exposed to only one level), we call the study an independent-samples design.

Independent-Samples *t*-test (Between-Groups *t*-test). The independent-samples *t*-test is a statistic used with two different groups of participants in two levels of an IV or quasi-IV with an interval or ratio DV.

Individual Differences. Variability across participants inherent to each person (e.g., personality) is called individual differences.

Inferential Statistics. Inferential statistics help researchers estimate what would happen in the population of interest based on sample outcomes.

Informed Consent. An informed-consent form is a document that describes the study and allows participants to freely choose whether they will participate. If the individual is a child or adult who is not capable of providing informed consent, then this document is signed by a parent, guardian, or other individual legally appointed to care for the participant.

Institutional Review Board (IRB). The IRB is a group of reviewers that evaluates research proposals. Members of the IRB conduct a cost-benefit analysis to determine if the study's benefits outweigh the risks.

Interaction. In a two-way ANOVA, the interaction indicates if the two IVs or quasi-IVs (i.e., factors) work together to influence the DV.

Internal Consistency. Internal consistency tells us the extent to which items within a scale measure the same construct.

Internal Validity. Internal validity is the extent to which an IV causes changes in the DV.

Interobserver Reliability. See *interrater reliability*.

Interrater Reliability (Interobserver Reliability). Given a subjective measure, the ability of two researchers to score the same construct in the same way is called inter-rater reliability.

Interval Variable. Interval data are characterized by equal intervals between numbers on the scale, but there is no true zero point.

Least Significant Difference (LSD). Least Significant Difference is a post hoc test for a significant ANOVA factor with more than two levels.

Level of Measurement. A variable's level of measurement defines its scale properties. Levels include nominal, ordinal, interval, and ratio.

Levels (Groups, Conditions, Treatments). Levels of a variable refer to groups or conditions (e.g., levels of academic classification include first year, sophomore, junior, and senior).

Levene's Test. Levene's test for equality of variances examines variability in the groups of a research design. If the test shows a significant difference in variability, researchers must report the *t*-test value from the SPSS output row marked "Equal variances not assumed."

Likert. A Likert item is one that contains a range of values and labels for at least some of the values. A Likert scale is usually composed of more than one Likert item.

Line of Prediction (Regression Line). The line of prediction or regression line allows prediction of a criterion variable from a predictor, as long as they are related in a linear way.

Linear Regression. When we want to predict one interval or ratio variable from another, we analyze data using linear regression.

Literature Review. A literature review is a summary of the available literature that discusses the theories and variables relevant to a study. The literature review builds a rationale for the study and hypotheses.

Longitudinal Study. A longitudinal study is a type of design that involves data collection from the same people across time.

Main Effect. In a two-way ANOVA, the main effect is the potential outcome of one factor associated with individual differences.

Matched-Pairs Design. See *related-samples design*.

Matching. Matching or pairing people based on a characteristic you believe will affect the DV, is a behind-the-scenes way to reduce variability, discover group differences if they exist.

Maturation. Maturation refers to the fact that people age and change across IV or quasi-IV levels when the levels occur far apart in time.

Mean (*M*). A mean is the mathematical middle of a data set.

Measure of Central Tendency. A measure of central tendency implies the value that best describes the data.

Median (*Mdn*). A median is the middle value in a data set.

Minimal Risk. When participants will encounter no more risk than would be expected in everyday life, a study is considered to have minimal risk.

Mode. A mode is the value that occurs most often in a sample.

Multiple Linear Regression. When we want to use more than one predictor to predict a criterion variable, we use multiple linear regression.

Multistage Sampling. Multistage sampling occurs when cluster sampling has more than two stages of sampling.

Mundane Realism. Mundane realism refers to the extent to which a study is similar to an activity a person might encounter in everyday life.

Naturalistic Setting. A naturalistic setting is an environment in which participants live their daily lives.

Nominal Variable. Nominal data represent categorical values with no meaningful order.

Nondirectional Test (Two-Tailed Test). If we have no educated guess about the direction of the relationship, we conduct a nondirectional or two-tailed test.

Nonparametric Statistics. Nonparametric statistics analyze nominal or ordinal data and are not as powerful as parametric statistics. That is, nonparametric statistics are not as likely as parametric statistics to reveal a significant outcome, if one exists.

Nonresponse Bias. Attrition that occurs when participants do not complete all parts of a study may lead to nonresponse bias.

Nuisance Variable. A variable that introduces random spread (variability) in your DV values is a nuisance variable. Nuisance variability occurs about equally across all levels of your IV and does not typically ruin an experiment.

Null Hypothesis. The null hypothesis reflects the idea that a sample will not differ from the normal population. Every inferential statistic in this book tests the null hypothesis, and researchers hope to reject it in favor of the research hypothesis.

Objective Measures. When a measure is objective, scores do not rely on interpretation by the researcher. Values on objective measures are usually reliable.

Observational Studies. Typically observational studies entail data collection through observation in a naturalistic setting.

Observed Frequency. The number of people in a sample who actually fall in each category of a variable defines observed frequency.

One-Tailed Test. See *directional test.*

One-Way Design. When we only have one IV (or quasi-IV), the design is called one-way.

One-Way χ^2 (Goodness-of-Fit Test). The one-way chi square is a statistic used to analyze frequency data from one variable of interest, regardless of the number of variable levels.

One-Way, Between-Groups ANOVA. A one-way, between-groups ANOVA is a statistic used to analyze responses from different people across levels of one factor. The factor and DV represents interval or ratio data.

One-Way, Repeated-Measures ANOVA. A one-way, repeated-measures ANOVA is a type of analysis used when we test the same people under every level of a single factor, and the DV represents interval or ratio data.

Operational Definition. Researchers use operational definitions to explain variables in enough detail to allow replication of the study.

Order Effects (Carryover Effects). Order effects occur when participants are influenced during the study by levels of the IV they already experienced. With a two-condition design, an order effect means the first condition influenced responses on the second condition.

Ordinal Variable. Ordinal data contain categories with a meaningful order but no equal intervals between levels.

Outlier. An outlier is an unusual value in a data set.

Outlier (for Grouped Data). An outlier is an unusual value in a data set. In a single sample of interval or ratio values, an outlier often is defined as a value three standard deviations from the mean.

Outlier (for Ungrouped Data). An outlier is a data point that is out of the ordinary. In other words, an outlier is a data point outside of the general relationship pattern.

Oversampling. Oversampling refers to selecting a larger number of participants from underrepresented groups during stratified random sampling.

p-value. The probability value used to indicate the likelihood of a result in the normal population is the *p*-value. Typically a *p*-value of .05 or less is considered significant.

Paired-Samples Design. See *related-samples design.*

Parallel-Forms Reliability. See *alternate-forms reliability.*

Parametric Statistics. Parametric statistics analyze interval or ratio data and are more powerful than nonparametric statistics. That is, parametric statistics are more likely than nonparametric statistics to reveal a significant outcome, if one exists.

Participants. People who participate in research studies are called participants.

Passive Deception. Passive deception is defined as allowing participants to draw their own conclusions, sometimes erroneously, about study components. For example, a confederate may act as a participant but not claim to be a participant, allowing participants to interpret the ambiguous situation.

Pearson's r (Correlation Coefficient). Pearson's r is the statistic used to analyze a potential relationship between two interval or ratio variables.

Phi Coefficient (φ). The phi coefficient quantifies effect size when a 2×2 χ^2 reveals a significant relationship.

Pilot Data. Pilot data can be collected prior to a study to help determine whether a specific methodology works well. We can also collect pilot data to see if means are in the expected direction before assessing a large sample.

Plagiarism. Plagiarism is defined as taking credit for the words or ideas of others.

Population. The group of people a researcher is interested in studying is called the population of interest.

Post Hoc. A post hoc test is conducted following an ANOVA that reveals a significant result. Post hoc mean comparisons reveal which group means differ from each other.

Power. Power is the ability to report a significant result when it is true.

Practice Effect. In some studies, completing a DV the first time allows practice and may improve performance when the DV is completed a second time, characterizing the practice effect.

Prediction Equation (Regression Equation). A prediction equation is a formula used to predict one variable from another. In linear regression, the prediction equation is the formula for a line.

Predictive Validity. The extent to which a measure correlates with a related behavior, attitude, or feeling at a later time is called predictive validity.

Predictor Variable. A predictor variable predicts a criterion variable if the two correlate.

Probability. In inferential statistics, probability is the likelihood that a result would happen in the normal population.

Psychometric Properties. Psychometric properties of a measure include reliability and validity.

Qualitative. Qualitative data have levels restricted to named categories, such as colors, ethnicity, and days of the week. Nominal and ordinal data represent qualitative data.

Quantitative. Levels of quantitative data are numbers with quantity, such as age, height, and weight. Interval and ratio data represent quantitative data.

Quasi-IV. When variables are not manipulated but still treated as IVs in an analysis, they are called quasi-IVs. Quasi-IVs yield correlational data and cannot establish cause and effect.

Quota Sampling. Quota sampling indicates the use of a larger number of participants from a specific group of interest while using a convenience sample. For example, a study of nurses might sample many male nurses to make sure both male and female nurses are in the sample.

Random Assignment (Simple Random Assignment). With random assignment to conditions, each participant in a sample has an equal chance of being put into each IV level.

Random Sampling (Simple Random Sampling). Random sampling occurs when everyone in the population of interest has an equal chance of being selected for a study.

Range. The lowest and highest values in a data set represent the range.

Rating Item. A rating item allows participants to rate their response on a single item with several response options. Options are discrete values with equal intervals between them.

Rating Scale. Rating scales are used when a researcher wants to collect interval data on a variable of interest, generally using more than one item.

Ratio Variable. Ratio data contain levels with equal intervals and a true zero. The presence of an absolute zero can be established if doubling values seems logical (e.g., 50 pounds is twice as heavy as 25 pounds).

Regression Equation. See *prediction equation.*

Regression Line. See *line of prediction.*

Related-Samples (Dependent-Samples Design, Paired-Samples Design, Matched-Pairs) Design. A related-samples design is defined by testing the same, similar, or matched participants across IV or quasi-IV levels.

Related-Samples *t*-test. The related-samples *t*-test is the statistical test used when a design has the same, similar, or matched participants in two levels of an IV or quasi-IV with one interval or ratio DV.

Reliability. A measure's ability to obtain similar values more than once is called reliability.

Repeated-Measures Design (Within-Participants Design). A research design with the same participants tested under every factor level is called a repeated-measures or within-participants design. Note that an older term for this design is *within-subjects*.

Representative Sample. When a sample has the same characteristics as the population of interest, we call it a representative sample.

Research Hypothesis. The research hypothesis represents what we expect to find in a study. It is the research question in the form of a statement.

Response Bias. Response bias refers to when participants respond to items in a systematic way while in a certain mindset. Bias potentially compromises the validity of a survey.

Restriction of Range. Restriction of range occurs when one variable in a data set has a narrow range of values. For example, if you are interested in sleep and grades, restriction of range would be indicated by a sample of participants who all sleep between seven and eight hours a night.

Sample. A sample is the group of people in a study. The participants compose a sample.

Sampling Error. Sampling error occurs when a sample statistic such as the mean does not equal the population value because some unusual people were selected by accident.

Sampling Selection Bias. See *selection bias*.

Scatterplot. A scatterplot is a graph that shows all data points in a data set, with one point for each participant.

Scientific Method. The scientific method is a step-by-step process of systematically addressing a research question through observation and critical thinking.

Scoring Blind. See *blind to conditions*.

Selection Bias (Sampling Selection Bias). Selection bias occurs when we choose participants in a way that alters our results.

Self-Selection Bias. When researchers accept any willing participants from a population, the study is in danger of self-selection bias, indicating that people who volunteer to participate may be different from the general population.

Semantic Differential. A semantic-differential scale contains terms with opposite meanings and a range of options between the terms. Participants choose from options on this continuum.

Significant (Significant Result). A result that is so unlikely that it would happen 5% of the time or less in the normal population is considered significant.

Significant Result. See *significant*.

Simple Frequency (*f*). Simple frequency represents the number of times a value occurs.

Simple Random Assignment. See *random assignment*.

Simple Random Sampling. See *random sampling*.

Slope. The value for slope tells us the slant of the regression line, including the angle and how much it slants. In the line formula, slope is symbolized by a *b*. In SPSS, *b* is represented by a capital *B* and has an associated *p*-value.

Social-Desirability Response Bias. Social-desirability response bias occurs when participants choose responses that make them appear more favorable.

Sphericity. Sphericity indicates that variability in pair differences across two levels of a factor is very similar to variability in pair differences across two other levels of the factor.

Split-Half Reliability. A measure of reliability based on correlating two randomly selected groups of items is called split-half reliability.

Standard Deviation (*SD*). Standard deviation represents an average variability around the mean.

Standard Error of the Estimate. In linear regression (prediction), the standard error of the estimate indicates about how far off predictions will be from actual outcomes, on average.

Stratified Random Sampling. Stratified random sampling occurs when we sample from specific groups (or strata) in the population.

Subjective Measures. When a measure is subjective, scoring is open to each researcher's interpretation.

***t*-test**. A *t*-test is the statistic used with two levels of an IV or quasi-IV and an interval or ratio DV.

Test-Retest Reliability. Test-retest reliability refers to the ability of a measure to result in similar numbers across two administrations of the same test.

Testable. A hypothesis is testable if it is written in such a way that empirical data can address the question of whether it is true.

Theory. A general way to explain a broad concept is called a theory. Within the structure of a theory, numerous testable hypotheses are possible.

Treatments. See *levels*.

Tukey's Comparisons. Tukey's post hoc comparisons offer a conservative post hoc test for a significant ANOVA.

Two-Tailed Test. See *nondirectional test*.

Two-Way Design. A two-way design uses two IVs or quasi-IVs, each of which has two or more levels.

Two-Way χ^2. A two-way χ^2 analyzes research designs with two variables of interest and an outcome of simple frequency.

Two-Way, Between-Groups ANOVA. A two-way, between-groups ANOVA is a statistic used to analyze two IVs or quasi-IVs with different people in each group and a single interval or ratio DV.

Type I Error. Type I error is defined by finding a significant result when the result actually does not exist.

Type II Error. Type II error refers to finding no significant result even though the result does, in fact, exist.

Validity. A measure's ability to assess the construct of interest is called validity.

Variability. Variability represents the spread of values on a variable.

Variable. A variable is anything that varies. In other words, variables have more than one possible value.

Visual Analogue. Visual analogue is a type of rating item not separated into categories. Instead, respondents make a mark on a continuous line to represent their response.

Within-Participants Design. See *repeated-measures design*.

Y-intercept. The value for the Y-intercept tells us the place at which the line would cross the Y-axis on a graph. In the line formula, the Y-intercept is symbolized by an *a*.

Index